COMMUNICATIVE SPEECH

Third Edition

COMMUNICATIVE SPEECH ·

ROBERT T. OLIVER

HAROLD P. ZELKO

PAUL D. HOLTZMAN

The Pennsylvania State University

HOLT, RINEHART AND WINSTON, NEW YORK

PICTURE CREDITS

Robert S. Beese, College of Agriculture, Pennsylvania State University: pp. 6, 23, 39, 64, 83, 145, 171, 179, 201, 234, 249, 254, 297, 336, 356, 360, 392
Goodyear Tire and Rubber Company: p. 261 (*top*)
Sarah Lawrence College: pp. 152, 199
The Pennsylvania State University: pp. 94, 105, 292, 382
N. P. C.: p. 385 (*bottom*)
Rebman Photo Service, Cleveland, Ohio: p. 165
Standard Oil Company, New Jersey: p. 14
Max Tharpe Photo Library, Statesville, North Carolina: pp. 139, 229
United Press International: (*frontispiece*)
United States Army: pp. 274, 385 (*top*)
United States Navy: p. 261 (*bottom*)

Preface

THERE IS BOTH CHALLENGE and opportunity in preparing a third edition. The wide and continuing use of the book in its first two editions suggests that in its general plan and philosophy it represents an approach many teachers of speech feel to be sound. The very extent of its use has provided an opportunity to profit in this revision from the experience and suggestions of many types of users. The challenge is to maintain the individuality—the personality—of the book while incorporating those added insights into the communicative process that are developing not only in the field of Speech but also in linguistics, anthropology, sociology, philosophy and psychology.

The authors want particularly to express their deep sense of sorrow and loss in the death of their late colleague, Dr. Dallas C. Dickey. His soundness of mind and sweetness of spirit contributed greatly to the initial developments of the book and to the warm comradeship his collaborators enjoyed in writing its first two editions; he also gave valued counsel and inspiration during the youthful days of the third author. At the same time, two of the authors wish to extend a cordial and appreciative welcome to their new collaborator, who has joined with sympathy and enthusiasm in plans to preserve the best of the old and to create a new approach that we believe represents realistically the needs of today and tomorrow.

This revision has gone far beyond the updating of the illustrative materials, clarifying obscure passages, filling in discovered gaps, eliminating prosy repetitions, tightening up of expository paragraphs, the search for more telling examples, the introduction of new pedagogical devices, and the reorganization of chapter sequence. In addition to these necessary chores, the whole concept of the book has been reexamined and in some basic respects reoriented.

This book, like every other, has perforce grown out of the particular characteristics of its writers. Each of them has had broad aca-

v

demic experience in teaching, research, and writing about both under-graduate and graduate areas of this broad profession. Each has also served variously in the professional organizations through which the aims and methods of the speech field are explored, questioned, and advanced through the cooperative endeavors of many scholars. And each of them has combined academic preparation with considerable immersion in the world of practical affairs: one as a professional clinician in speech and psychology and in private business, another as a lawyer and a consultant in training and communications in government and industry, the third in governmental policy formulation in consultative work at international conferences, and in public relations.

During the planning and extensive rewriting involved in this revision, two questions of principal concern have been: What do students really need to know and be helped to do in solving the specific oral-communication problems which they will surely encounter? What limitations in student experience and understanding, what misconceptions, what peculiarities of their classroom situation constitute barriers that must be overcome in helping them achieve the optimum realization of their own potentials? We have highlighted the fact that students' needs extend outward from and onward beyond the confines of the campus. And we have tried to offer guidance that leads from student perplexities and ambitions toward a fulfillment that will serve them and the needs of the tumultuous time in which we live.

Specifically, as an integrated study of the broad spectrum of the individual's oral-communicative needs, the leading characteristics of this new revision are:

1. It deals with the basic role of listening, or of evaluative response to communication, not only in a separate chapter (where the emphasis is upon listening to receive) but also throughout the book (where the emphasis is upon the speaker's interpretation of the behavior of listeners as a guide to creating the desired response). Far more than heretofore, the concern of this book (as it is surely the concern of students) is not only to help them prepare and present effective speeches, but also to adapt their insights and skills to actual conversation, discussion, conference, and interviews.

2. It makes what we trust is a meaningful, useful, and sharp distinction between *expression,* whereby the speaker attempts to manifest the integrity of his own self-evaluations, and *communication,* whereby he effectively seeks to direct the thought, feelings, and behavior of

those who hear him. Many of the problems encountered by students of speech and also by mature and experienced speakers derive from an uninterpreted confusion of purpose between their desire to express and their intent to communicate. We are hopeful that clarifying this distinction will accelerate the development both of ability in self-analysis and of skill in achieving the responses sought from others.

3. It maintains a sharp focus on the process of learning. What students are able to do at their current stage of development is often a chief handicap to the acquisition of insights and skills needed to transcend their present speaking abilities. To use a simple analogy, students who type by the hunt-and-peck system must be willing to undergo a considerable loss of typing capacity in order to shift to the vastly superior touch system. Similarly, students content to "do their best with what they have" in Speech class are handicapping their own growth by refusing to adopt more effective methods. Throughout, this book endeavors to keep in focus the *change* of habits based on new insights which lead to higher levels of achievement.

4. It aims to teach through understanding of problems and concepts, rather than through systems of rules. It is our belief that basic progress is possible only through seeing and understanding the problems to be solved and the goals to be attained. In this sense, this revision is more theoretical; but it is also more practical. The approach we are using has been tried out by a variety of teachers in many different classes with what seem to be gratifying results. Through the process of evaluation, we have sought to guide students to the formulation of basic governing principles and workable methods.

5. It attempts to integrate tightly the threefold approach recommended for every speaker in every type of speaking situation: (a) to analyze the subject to determine what is true and relevant, (b) to clarify his own purposes in utilizing the subject matter, and (c) to adapt his presentation to the response potentials of his listeners. This integration has led to some variations from traditional terminology that we believe are proving helpful to students in learning their way to more effective speech. For example, we discuss speech purposes in terms of desired listener responses. The specific purpose is shown to relate essentially to the central idea. Forms and methods of support are viewed as means of validating ideas, first for the speaker and secondly for his listeners. Proofs are treated as deriving from the

responses of listeners to validating ideas, rather than as being intrinsic in the materials themselves.

As in the two prior editions, the authors view speech education as a vital central factor in the preparation for fruitful living and effective citizenship. The speaker's ethical, intellectual, social, and personal responsibilities are stressed throughout the book. No chapter on ethics is needed, for at no point does the discussion deviate from insistence upon honesty in ascertaining the facts, integrity in maintaining convictions, and respect for the nature and the needs of listeners.

Rhetorical theory is supported by pertinent factual findings from social psychology and other relevant disciplines. The length of the book has again been increased, but not to the extent of making it a handicap to the laboratory experience which must always be the focal point of speech education. Exercises have been designed to serve two purposes: for review and class discussion of the chapter materials and for projects to be carried on in and out of class, through speaking and writing.

To assist instructors in guiding the interests of their students toward further work in Speech, Chapter 17 has been retained, with some improvements, from the preceding edition.

For specific suggestions and general cross-ventilation of ideas, the authors are particularly grateful to the entire staff of the Department of Speech of The Pennsylvania State University, as well as to their undergraduate and graduate students. As are all authors of textbooks, we are deeply indebted to many scholars who have published their own research findings, theories, and experiences in the national and regional journals of our own and other professions and in a wide variety of books. We are especially indebted to our wives and children, whose patient forebearance and enthusiastic support have gone far beyond normal limits. Nor can we neglect the opportunity to express cordial appreciation for the unusually considerate and helpful attitude of our publishers, who have done all they could to help make this revision less an onerous task than a challenging and rewarding opportunity.

R. T. O.

H. P. Z.

P. D. H.

Contents

Preface   v

Part I: THE BASES OF COMMUNICATIVE SPEECH

Chapter 1: Oral Communication   3

The Importance of Oral Communication   5
Expression and Communication   10
Speakers and Listeners: Bonds and Barriers   13
Language and Communicative Speech   20
Communicative Feedback   22
Conclusion   26
Exercises   26

Chapter 2: Standards of Effective Speech   29

Starting Where You Are   29
Bases for the Standards   31
Ethical Norm   34
Esthetic Norm   36
Effects Norm   38
Educational Norm   42
Your Potential for Meeting These Standards   44
Guiding Your Growth and Development   45
Conclusion   46
Exercises   46

Part II: DEVELOPING COMMUNICATIVE SPEECH

Chapter 3: You Prepare to Speak   51

Need for Preparation   52

Preparation: Mental Attitude 54
Preparation: The Specific Steps 58
Choosing the Speech Topic 59
Analyzing the Audience and Occasion 63
Conclusion 66
Exercises 67

Chapter 4: Purpose and Central Idea 69

General Responses 70
Specific Responses 76
A Listener Goal 81
The Central Idea 82
Testing Your Central Idea 85
Conclusion 88
Exercises 88

Chapter 5: Your Speech Materials 90

Starting the Search for Materials 91
Listening and Reading for Materials 96
How Do You Use Sources? 101
Integrity and Wisdom in Using Sources 103
Building the Speech File 106
Conclusion 109
Exercises 110

Chapter 6: Organizing 112

Benefits of Organizing 113
The Main Ideas 115
The Pattern of Organization 119
Outlining the Speech 128
Transition from Outline to Speech: Practice 138
Conclusion 140
Exercises 141

Chapter 7: Developing Ideas 143

Analytical Examination 144
Validation 153
Validation Forms 154
Validation Methods 160
Conclusion 167
Exercises 167

Chapter 8: Attention, Interest, and Style   169

Attention   170
Interest   177
Factors of Interest   178
Style   183
Conclusion   190
Exercises   190

Chapter 9: Delivering the Speech   192

Misconceptions About Speech Delivery   192
The Functions of Codes   194
The Visual Code   196
Empathy   198
Principles of Delivery   202
Summary   210
The Auditory Code   211
Voice   216
Articulation   218
Pronunciation   220
Conclusion   223
Exercises   224

Chapter 10: Listening   226

Responsibility for Listening   227
Values of Good Listening   230
Barriers to Listening   233
A Program for Better Listening   242
Conclusion   245
Exercises   245

Chapter 11: Using Visual Aids   248

Types of Visual Aids   253
Conclusion   266
Exercises   266

Part III: FORMS OF COMMUNICATIVE SPEECH

Chapter 12: Informative Speaking   271

Informative and Other Purposes Related   273

Clear to Whom?   277
Maintaining Objectivity   278
Organizing the Speech to Inform   280
Developing Informative Ideas   284
Application of Informative Speaking   286
Conclusion   287
Exercises   288

Chapter 13: Persuading   290

Learn by Listening   290
Persuasive Purposes   291
Persuasion and Other Speech Purposes   296
Listener Motives for Ideation   300
Persuasion and the Validating Forms and Methods   313
Persuasion and Language   314
Organizing and Developing for Persuasion   315
Outlining for Persuasion   323
Conclusion   326
Exercises   327

Chapter 14: Entertaining   329

Why Study Entertaining Speech?   330
Characteristics of Entertaining Speech   331
Delivery   335
Non-Humorous Speeches of Entertainment   339
After-Dinner Speaking   341
Organizing Entertaining Speeches   342
Conclusion   344
Exercises   345

Chapter 15: Discussion and Parliamentary Law   347

The Nature of Discussion   348
The Pattern of Discussion   349
Participation   355
Leadership   359
Parliamentary Procedure   362
Chart of Parliamentary Motions   370
Conclusion   371
Exercises   372

Chapter 16: Special Applications   374

The Job of the Chairman   374
Conversation   379
Interviews   381
Conferences   384
The Manuscript Speech   386
Speaking from Manuscript   390
Special Occasions   391
Conclusion   393
Exercises   393

Part IV: LOOKING AHEAD

Chapter 17: Responsibility for Further Growth   397

Social Responsibility   397
Personal Responsibility   400
Future Speech Demands   402
The Field of Speech   403
Your Plan for Further Growth   408
Conclusion   409
Exercises   409
      Index   411

For
MARY · SARAH · INGRID

PART I

The Bases of
COMMUNICATIVE
SPEECH

Oral Communication

THE BEGINNING STUDENT of speech often harbors either of two attitudes toward it: one is that it is too easy; the other is that it is too hard. Anyone who approaches the study of speech with a feeling that there can be little worth mastering in this area unwittingly reflects the sentiment expressed by Molière's principal character in his farce, *The Bourgeois Gentleman*: "I have been speaking prose for more than forty years without realizing it."

Of course, we all have been doing a great deal of speaking since infancy; and if it were only true that practice makes perfect, our speech should be highly effective, for talking and listening make up a very large portion of our lives. The real truth, however, is that practice makes permanent. Our bad habits, by constant repetition, become deeply ingrained. Ineffective oral communication is so commonplace that we take it for granted and even consider it normal. We try to explain something and are not understood; we ask, and are refused; we attempt to be witty or interesting, and we are disappointed with the result.

Let us think for a moment how heavy the demands for good speaking are: to have a purpose clearly in mind; to be able to recall instantly whatever it is we should know; to organize our ideas so that everything we say may lead directly toward accomplishment of our purpose; to illustrate our thoughts so as to make them clear, vivid and attractive; to apply instantly and appropriately the tests of logic, in order to avoid spurious reasoning; and to do all this in a mood and

3

manner which are effectively adapted to the circumstances and to our listeners. Even though we have been "talking prose all our lives," the evidence is overwhelming that neither we nor our associates speak very well. If we could communicate better, many problems would not arise and many others would be more easily solved.

But while the complexities of oral communication are not easy to master, neither is the course in speech difficult in the way many imagine it will be. The difficulties are actually greater than most beginning students realize; but they are quite different from what is commonly anticipated. Stage fright is the bugaboo most feared by beginners. The fear of forgetting, the fear of finding yourself on your feet before an audience without anything to say, the fear of sounding ridiculous—these are common elements of the view that the work in speech will be too difficult. Actually, problems of this sort are fairly easily solved. The real problem is how to communicate what you really want to say in a manner that will induce your audience to listen understandingly. The big task to be accomplished is to learn to think in a more orderly manner, to master the use of evidence, to be tactful when you must disagree, to explain complicated ideas clearly, and to illustrate what you have to say in ways that make the utmost sense and have the greatest appeal to your specific listeners.

The work in speech is neither a mere duplication of everyday experience in talking and listening, nor is it a series of exercises in good diction and graceful posture. True, you do have a wealth of experience on which to draw; and part of the work of this course is designed to help you to build upon what you already do well and to discard mannerisms that limit your present effectiveness. It is also true that you will experience emotional tensions in relatively formal speech situations, with the knowledge that the effectiveness of your presentation will be evaluated. But the factors toward which your attention will primarily be directed are:

1. Selection of topics that truly reflect your own knowledge, beliefs, and feelings, and that draw upon your whole background of experiences—in other words, becoming better acquainted with yourself

2. Analysis of these topics in order to limit and define them in forms suitable for a variety of types of speaking situations

3. Organization of your ideas to focus them upon a single theme and to develop a suitable conclusion from it

4. Development of each idea so as to make it clear, meaningful, and attractive

5. Testing of your ideas and of the evidence you plan to use to make sure that what you say adheres to sound principles of logical thinking

6. Presentation of your ideas in a suitable vocal and personal style

7. Inducing favorable attention and general acceptance by your listeners of what you tell them

The accomplishment of these aims is far from easy; it is in fact so difficult that no human being has ever achieved the ultimate of skill in any of them. On the other hand, the difficulties are of a nature that makes possible their systematic analysis and orderly progress in overcoming them. What you really will be learning is how to think more clearly, how to make your personality more effective in dealing with other people, and how to bring all your potential resources instantly to bear in social situations of a wide variety. The proper starting point is to clear your mind of misconceptions so that you can concentrate your efforts in the right way upon the real problems. To enter a speech course with the thought, "I always get stage fright when I stand up to talk," or with the wistful hope, "I want to learn how to be more poised while speaking," is to mislead yourself by misdirecting your attention. The question in your mind ought to be, "How can I learn to say what I ought to be saying in specific situations in a way that will achieve reasonably sound results?"

○ THE IMPORTANCE OF ORAL COMMUNICATION

The value of being able to talk communicatively[1]—i.e., to induce others to interpret an event, fact, opinion, or situation in the way the speaker intends it—has been recognized all through human history. Indeed, the oldest essay that has ever been discovered, a fragment of parchment addressed to Kagemni, eldest son of the Pharaoh Huni, written about 3,000 BC, consists of advice on how to speak effectively.

[1] Amid the vast literature on communication theory, students may well be advised to start with *The Communication of Ideas* (Lyman Bryson, editor). New York: Harper, 1948: "Communication and Social Action," *Annals* of the American Academy of Political and Social Science, March, 1947; and *The Process of Communication,* by David Berlo. New York: Holt, Rinehart and Winston, 1960.

In the classroom, on the job, even in the laboratory, and in all social living, human relations are largely verbal. Teaching and learning are continual processes. It is important to know how to question, how to listen, how to explain, and how to persuade. Effective speaking and evaluative listening depend on skills and insights worth acquiring.

The ancient Egyptian parchment reads: "Wide is the seat of the man
gentle of speech; but knives are prepared against one that forceth a
path, that he advance not. . . . If a man is lacking in good fellowship,
no speech hath any influence over him. He is sour of face toward the
glad-hearted that are kindly to him; he is a grief unto his mother and
his friends."

The earliest complete book that has been preserved, also composed in Egypt, about 2,675 BC, is likewise a treatise on effective
speech. It is the *Precepts* of a court councilor, Ptah-Hotep, written
for the guidance of the Pharaoh's son. The book opens with these
words: "Here begin the precepts of fair speech . . . instructing the
ignorant in the knowledge of exactness in fair speaking; the glory
of him that obeyeth, the shame of him that transgresseth them." The
purpose of the book, its author wrote, was to "instruct a man how
he shall speak, after he hath heard them; yea, he shall become as one
skillful in obeying, excellent in speaking, after he hath heard them.
Good fortune shall befall him, for he shall be of the highest rank." In
the conclusion, the book is summarized as follows: "Be cautious in
your speech when talking to an authority; seek to create favorable
opinion of those that listen to you. When you speak as an authority
yourself, speak with exact lips, that thy conduct may be seemly. . . .
Apply thine heart . . . to say such things that the nobles who listen
declare, 'How excellent is that which cometh out of his mouth.' "[2]

Two thousand five hundred years after these Egyptian instructions were written, the Greeks of ancient Athens organized an educational system, in which Isocrates, Aristotle, and Plato were the leading
teachers. Each of them gave special attention to speech. Isocrates
organized a school for the writing of speeches and the education of
speakers. Aristotle wrote one of his best books, *The Rhetoric*, on the
art of persuasive speaking. Plato, in "The Gorgias," posed a problem:
If a town wished to hire a public health officer, and if there were two
applicants for the position: a well-trained physician and a skillful
speaker, which would get the job? Plato decided that the job would be
won by the man who was skillful in presenting his own case—even

[2] *Cf.* Giles Wilkeson Gray, "The Precepts of Kagemni and Ptah-Hotep,"
in *The Quarterly Journal of Speech*, Vol. 32 (1946), pp. 446–454. The complete,
annotated text of these two valuable commentaries is printed in G. Gunn
Battiscombe, *The Instructions of Ptah-Hotep and the Instructions of Kagemni:
The Oldest Books in the World*, 1908.

though what the town needed was a good doctor. Then he added that the solution of this problem is to make sure that every physician, and every other man of skill, should also be educated in effective speech. Otherwise, virtue might be overwhelmed by evil, truth by error, and good men would be unable to achieve good results for themselves or to render proper service to others.

In Imperial Rome both the great orator, Cicero, and the great teacher, Quintilian, wrote books on speech which are still considered to be sound guides. Cicero praised effective speech as the art "which first bound men by the chains of right and law, formed the bonds of civil society, and made us quit a wild and savage life." Quintilian, in his monumental book, *Institutes of Oratory,*[3] wrote a description of the ideal speaker which has never been surpassed:

> The first essential for such a one is that he should be a good man, and consequently we demand of him not merely the possession of exceptional gifts of speech, but of all the excellencies of character as well. . . . The man who can really play his part as a citizen and is capable of meeting the demands both of public and private business, the man who can guide a state by his counsels, give it a firm basis by his legislation and purge its vices by his decisions as a judge, is assuredly no other than the orator of our quest. . . . I shall frequently be compelled to speak of such virtues as courage, justice, self-control. . . . As for the special uses and distinctions of words, they should be a subject of study common to all who give any thought to the meaning of language. . . . For eloquence depends in the main on the state of the mind, which must be moved, conceive images, and adapt itself to suit the nature of the subject which is the theme of the speech. Shall we marvel then, if oratory, the highest gift of providence to man, needs the assistance of many arts, which, although they do not reveal or intrude themselves in actual speaking, supply hidden forces and make their silent presence felt?

[3] The Loeb Classical Library edition of Quintilian's *Institutes of Oratory,* 1922, 4 vols., presents the Latin text with an English translation on facing pages. Harold Harding, "Quintilian's Witnesses," *Speech Monographs,* Vol. 1 (1934), pp. 1–20, traces the influence of Quintilian's ideas. For a general introduction to Greek and Roman rhetorical theory (and to the whole history of rhetoric in the West), *cf.* Lester Thonssen and A. Craig Baird, *Speech Criticism: The Development of Standards for Rhetorical Appraisal.* New York: Ronald, 1948. Note especially in the bibliography of that book the listing of articles by Bromley Smith on ancient rhetoricians (pp. 476–477), which appeared in *The Quarterly Journal of Speech* between 1918 and 1928.

When St. Augustine (354–430 AD)[4] confronted the problem of how to expand the influence of the fledgling Christian Church, his solution was to train the priests in the classical art of oratory. At the core of European education for the next one thousand years was the study of rhetoric, logic, and grammar: the effective mastery of words. Under the influence of the Renaissance, as it spread from Italy up through England, such books as Castiglione's *Art of the Courtier* and John Wilson's *Arte of Rhetoric* became popular guides to improvement in conversation and public speaking. During the seventeenth and eighteenth centuries, Aristotle's *Rhetoric* and Quintilian's *Institutes of Oratory* were among the basic textbooks used in the schools. In 1806–1809, John Quincy Adams, later to be the sixth President of the United States, served for three years as Lecturer in Speech at Harvard, helping to establish the tradition that every American college student should be educated to be an effective speaker. In 1830, Miss Frances Wright, the first American woman to speak from a public platform, organized classes in speech, declaring that, "public speaking ought to be the peculiar study of all Americans, even as public affairs ought to be their peculiar business."

Following this centuries-long tradition, speech in our own time is a subject widely taught in American colleges. For there is quiet agreement with the view expressed by Charles W. Eliot when he was president of Harvard: "I recognize but one mental acquisition as an essential part of the education of a lady or gentleman, namely, an accurate and refined use of the mother tongue." There is especially wide acceptance of the observation of Chauncey Depew (United States Senator, president of the New York Central Railroad, and popular after-dinner speaker) that: "There is no other accomplishment which any man can have that will so quickly make for him a career and secure recognition as the ability to speak acceptably."

The real purpose of education is to develop and expand the abilities of the individual. This aim was well stated by Eric W. Johnson, when in 1959 he wrote a book on education:

> The first value we should teach, I think, is the *value of an individual,* which is infinite and infinitely increasable. Someone has

---

[4] Augustine's principles of speech criticism are outlined in Charles Sears Baldwin, *Medieval Rhetoric and Poetic.* New York: Macmillan, 1928; a good brief reference for Augustine and all the other major rhetoricians is the article on Rhetoric in the *Encyclopaedia Britannica* by Richard Jebb.

pointed out that a pig of iron is worth $5.00; if it is made into horse-shoes, it is worth $10.50; if it has been refined and tempered and shaped into needles, it is worth $3,500; but if it has been fashioned into balance springs for watches, it is worth $25,000. How much more spectacularly does the value of an individual increase when he is given good surroundings, good training, and a challenge to his skills and spirit! The measure of success of a marriage or a family, of a nation or a society is the extent to which it makes possible the maximum of development of the potentialities of the individuals within it. And we as parents must remember this and teach this to our teen-agers, not so much by what we say as by treating them as infinitely worthy of our respect.[5]

Your course in speech, accordingly, will guide you to an analysis of yourself—helping you to understand your own qualities better, and to discover how to enhance them; to an appreciation of the nature of other people—helping you to understand better why and how differences exist; and the ways in which sound and constructive relationships may be established between you and your listeners. Your persistent aim should be to convey to your hearers your own conception of truth, for that is your primary reason for wanting to speak. But an essential secondary aim is to acquire sufficient understanding of others and of the communicative process to enable you to bridge the gulf that separates individuals from one another. The English novelist, George Eliot, once wrote: "We are all islands, shouting lies to one another across seas of misunderstandings." By *lies* Eliot meant that we do not ourselves understand what we mean; to cross the "seas of misunderstandings" we obviously need first to bridge the communicative gulf that separates us from our fellows.

○ EXPRESSION AND COMMUNICATION

One of our deepest desires is to be able to express what we honestly and actually know, believe, and feel. There is comparable satisfaction and also great practical utility in being able to communicate successfully, so that others will truly understand our knowledge, beliefs, and feelings. When, as often happens, we find ourselves saying, "No, I didn't mean *that*," the fault may lie in one or in both of two

[5] Eric W. Johnson, *How to Live through Junior High School*. Philadelphia: Lippincott, 1959.

causes: (1) we may have failed to formulate our own ideas accurately, or (2) we may have presented them faultily.[6] Often we place the blame upon the second cause when it really belongs on the first. The problems to be dealt with can be understood most readily by distinguishing clearly between the two processes of expression and communication.

Everyone has the experience very frequently, while alone, of "talking to himself," usually in the form of a silent and very lively conversation. One purpose of such talk is the clarification of our own thinking. But even when we are talking to others, we may be aware of a pleasure or perhaps of an uneasiness in listening to ourselves. Indeed, Wendell Johnson has written an intriguing book on the theme that you are yourself *Your Most Enchanted Listener.* "A man is never so serene as when he hears himself out," Johnson says. "Nor is he ever so gravely ill as when he stops his tongue with crying out 'Shame! Shame!' unto himself."[7] This self-renunciation, Johnson believes, is a principal cause of stuttering; it may also be a principal cause of much general ineffectiveness in everyday speech. *We must be able to express ourselves in ways satisfactory to ourselves before we can hope to communicate effectively to others.*

Expression means, fundamentally, the putting into symbols (words, vocal qualities, physical action, music, painting, etc.) what we consider to be reasonably accurate representations of our own inmost personal values, convictions, or reactions to a situation. Communication means, fundamentally, the stimulation in the minds of others of essentially your own awareness, understanding, and sense of importance of the event, feeling, fact, opinion, or situation you are attempting to depict. In expressionist art, the artist insists that his purpose is to present his own feelings and ideas: readers, listeners, or viewers are invited to find in his artistry any kind of message they may wish. In representational art, the artist strives to convey to his reader, listener, or viewer precisely the same interpretation of the object, or subject, that he has himself.

Expression and communication are as different from, and also as closely related to, one another as are the economic processes of pro-

[6] A third cause of misunderstanding—failure of the auditors to listen evaluatively—is discussed in Chapter 10.

[7] Wendell Johnson, *Your Most Enchanted Listener.* New York: Harper, 1956. Another good introduction to personality-speech relationships is Dominick A. Barbara, *Your Speech Reveals Your Personality.* Springfield, Ill.: Charles C Thomas, 1958.

duction and consumption. The key factor is that when we express we primarily are concerned with giving symbolic form to internal feelings or ideas; when we communicate we look inward to discover what we mean and we look outward (to the nature of the listeners and to the situation) to guide our efforts to achieve our desired effect.

The differences between expression and communication may be illustrated by what you might say and how you might say it if you hit your thumb with a hammer while hanging a picture. If you are alone, your expression of emotion will be designed simply to relieve explosive feelings. If guests are present, you will try to communicate in a way that will let you both relieve your feelings and sustain the attitude you wish them to hold toward you. If you are a man and some rather raucous classmates are watching, you might communicate your feelings even more violently than you would if alone, thinking this might enhance their attitude about your manliness and vigor. On the other hand, if the parents of your fiancée, or your college dean, or the wife of your prospective employer were present, you might curb your expression in order to communicate a sense of your calm self-control and mannerliness.

Great care is necessary to keep clearly in focus the differences between communication and expression. Sometimes you communicate to your listeners precisely what you mean, and nothing else, as when you say in answer to a question, "I am twenty-one years old." Sometimes you simultaneously (and unknowingly) express an additional meaning you do not intend to communicate, as when your tone of voice or facial expression or bodily stance suggests the additional idea, "which I consider a much better age than your seventeen years." Abraham Lincoln clearly understood this possible conflict between expression and communication when he refused to defend a client whom he considered to be guilty by telling him, "All the time I argued your innocence to the jury, they would understand what I really thought and would be saying to themselves, 'Lincoln, you're a liar.' " This is why a high premium is placed on sincerity. Your real attitude will somehow be expressed and therefore you should take care not to contradict the attitude you seek to communicate.

Both expression and communication should be accurate representations of your real understanding and purpose. Your expression is an account of the relationship you note between yourself and the subject matter you are discussing. Your communication is shaped to accord with a threefold relationship—linking the subject matter, your own understanding of or purpose in relation to it, and the nature of the listeners. Expression and communication tend most surely to assist and reinforce one another when you feel a genuine respect for yourself and also respect for your listeners. Then you want to satisfy both.

Communicative speech, then, adds a third dimension which is not present in expressive speech: the dimension of adaptation to an audience. The aim of this book is to help you to improve your mastery of all three of these aspects of it: (1) clarification of your own purposes; (2) sound understanding of the subject matter discussed; and (3) ability to understand and deal with the situation and the personalities that comprise your listeners. These factors are involved essentially in all communicative discourse: conversation, discussion, interviews, argumentative debate, and public speaking of all kinds.

○ SPEAKERS AND LISTENERS: BONDS AND BARRIERS

Sometimes we talk easily, our minds stimulated by enthusiasm for an idea or by the company we are in. At other times our minds seem frozen, our words falter, our very bearing seems stiff and awkward. The difference is one we all recognize. Situations, purposes, topics, and people are all part of the explanation for this difference. Sometimes they work together to tie speaker and listeners with communicative bonds that facilitate understanding and enhance rapport. Other combinations result in barriers of embarrassment, suspicion, or perhaps mere indifference. One basic problem in communication is to learn how to develop the potential bonds and how to penetrate the barriers.

One of the strongest bonds is the "one of us" feeling; one of the hardest barriers to cross is the suspicion that "he's against us." Social psychologists distinguish between in-group and out-group relationships; anthropologists assure us that in all societies there is a dislike for the unlike. In casual conversation, it is interesting to note how immediately a warmth of comradeship develops when those conversing accidentally discover that they may have an ancestor in common, or that they (or their grandparents) once lived in the same area. In public speaking it has become commonplace (because of its proven utility) to start by referring to experiences the speaker has had in common with his audience. This is known as establishment of common ground. Other significant aspects of speaker-listener relations that may emerge

An audience is not a shapeless mass; it consists of individuals and the skilled speaker reaches every member. Communication exists when each listener feels the speech is directed to his own personal needs and interests, whether he is one of an unseen audience or present in the front row.

either as bonds or barriers (depending on the way they are managed) relate to the status, the role, and the function of the speaker and the group with which he talks.

Common Ground

When you sit in the stands for the annual "Big Game," you feel a great surge of loyalty for "your team" and rivalry toward the traditional opponent. In an electoral campaign, you feel a bond with your own political party; in religious affairs your sympathies lie with your chosen church. In short, the groups and institutions to which we belong and the customs we share do make a difference in our feelings and affect our judgments. "Birds of a feather flock together." The wise speaker makes an effort to discover various ways in which he can stress his own identity with his audience. If there are obvious barriers to common ground, he seeks ways of overcoming them.

A speaker has an initial advantage in establishing rapport if he can use such in-group phrases as "we students," or "we engineering majors," or "we fraternity brothers." Sometimes a similar bond may be established through identification with common goals, as: "All of us are looking for jobs this spring"; or "All of us, students and faculty, will benefit if we can devise a better grading system." As the talk progresses, common ground may be developed by pointing out, "I can see you are doubtful about the conclusions I am reaching. Like you, I would be delighted if better solutions were available. But we all have to follow where the facts take us." Where manifest differences between the speaker and his listeners exist, it is better not to avoid them but to bridge them. If you happen to be a major in forestry and your listeners are mostly liberal arts students, you might say to them, "Just as I enjoy hearing you talk about literature and philosophy, as a means of broadening my own interests, so, I imagine, you will be interested in hearing from me about some of the trees you commonly see on your hikes"; or, "All of us have a common dislike for insects—you because you have to slap at them when you are on picnics and I because they are often injurious to trees and shrubs. Since my interest in them is vocational, I've had to learn more about them and I'll be glad to tell you about a new program for insect control."

The differences between a speaker and his audience may be of race, religion, education, social standing, wealth, amount of travel and experience, intelligence, or interests. Whenever these differences are permitted to stand out as differences, they tend to be barriers to effective communication. The differences that exist, however, are always open to interpretation as an advantage—a broadening of the experience of the group. For instance: "As a Unitarian I am especially happy to be able to talk about religion and education with you Catholics, for I am eager to come to a better understanding of your ideas and I hope you may be interested in mine." Or, "Most of you have grown up in large cities; I on a farm. In other words, my job has been to provide the eggs and milk and meat you have been eating. Now there is one need we all have in common—to work out a farm price-support program that will be fair to city taxpayers and to the farm food producers. I'm sure the problem is familiar to you, for the city industries have benefited for many years from tariff protection and fair trade laws. What we farmers want is to have our own needs met in much the same way yours have been." Or, "As a young college student, I am somewhat abashed to be talking to you businessmen. But the fact is, I am helping to spend part of the money you pay to support our schools. I'd like to tell you where this money is going and why we need still more of it."

Illustrations of how to establish common ground could be cited indefinitely. The point is, that wherever an obvious difference exists—in age, in race, in experience—the speaker should plan carefully to use that difference as a bridge; in other words he should convert the barrier into a bond. The examples are indicative of how it may be done. On the other hand, a factor that seems to unite a group may, if carelessly handled, turn into a barrier. For example, "I am a student and you are students. I'm sure we students all get tired of hearing one another talk about grades and examinations. After all, it is only the faculty who can do anything about them." The speaker who started his talk in this fashion was wise in identifying what appeared to be a common bond as being in reality a barrier. He might well go on, "This is why I have prepared my talk by discussing these questions with five of my professors. What I want to do now is tell you what they said and what I think about their attitudes." Or, "We are all Americans, and I am sure our awareness of this makes us a bit uneasy for fear we may fail to understand fully how other nations feel about international affairs. At least, let's start out by trying to determine whether there really is a typically American point of view."

Common ground, then, offers one sound and tested method by which bonds may be strengthened and barriers turned into bonds.

Status

Differing status levels as between speaker and listeners may also be either a bond or a barrier, depending on how they are treated. In the preceding section we have seen how the status differential of age was handled advantageously by a college student talking to businessmen. When we quoted earlier from the *Precepts* of Ptah-Hotep, we noted that from earliest times those of low status have been cautioned on how to speak to their superiors: with care, showing respect, yet making clear the contribution the speaker has to offer. High status normally carries with it enlarged duties and heavy responsibilities; in other words, people in positions of authority need all the help and advice they can get. Since the problems with which they deal are often complex, it is simply good judgment to offer them advice tentatively and in the form of information usable along with facts coming from other sources. For example, an employee called before a meeting of the Board of Directors to explain an idea for more efficient production in his department might well begin by saying his experience is limited and perhaps his plan has already been tried out somewhere . . . but for what it may be worth, here it is.

When a speaker of superior status talks to a group of inferiors (an adult talking to young people, for example) he must be especially careful not to sound condescending; similarly, a person of lower status talking to superiors should take care not to sound impertinent. When the speaker makes it clear that he is honestly trying to represent whatever he may be (boss or employee) and that he respects both the position and the person of his listeners, the barrier of status diminishes or disappears. But if the speaker assumes an arrogant air (whether to enhance his superiority or as a defense against an unwelcome inferiority) the barrier becomes much greater. Normally a genuine bond of fellowship can be established to bridge the differences that exist: "You who own the company and we who work in it all have the same interests— to make it successful for our mutual advantage"; or "The speaker I am to introduce has been elected by us as our Senator—which means that we like him; and since we are the ones who elected him, he no doubt likes us, too." Behind every status barrier there exists the bond of a larger unity. Effective communication is enhanced when the barrier is converted into a bond.

Role

Role-playing[8] has become a commonplace term in the social sciences because it dramatizes and clarifies the complexity of personality. We may ask about an individual, "What is he *really* like?" but we can scarcely get a meaningful answer; for he is certain to be different in different circumstances. As the psychologist Gordon Allport phrased it, "Personality is a factor of the situation as well as of the person." We behave one way in class, other ways within our own family, in our fraternity house, or in a conference with the dean. We exhibit one personality on the golf course, another at a concert, a third on the job, and a fourth on a date. *The role an individual plays in any situation is a presentation of himself in the way he wants to be viewed in that situation.*

The fact that we all play roles is beyond question. When you are about to be introduced for the first time to your fiancée's parents, you can feel yourself shifting into what you hope will be a favorable personality pattern. Similarly, as you walk into an office to apply for a job, or as you enter the dean's office for a discussion of your grades, or as you attend the meeting of a group you hope may invite you to membership, you probably ask yourself whether you are looking, doing, and saying what you should. In some ways you are always the same person; in other ways, you always adapt (appropriately, you hope) to the requirements of each specific situation. "Let's settle down now; the meeting is about to commence," is only one way of saying that we do consciously change our personality pattern to meet each change of circumstance. This fact of everyday life has special significance for those occasions on which we become the center of group attention through speaking.

The time to start establishing the most effective role for a speech situation is in the very first stages of preparation: when the purpose and topic are selected, as the materials for validation and illustration

[8] For a valuable account of how role-playing affects our whole manner of speaking, *cf.* Erving Goffman, *The Presentation of Self in Everyday Life.* New York: Doubleday, Anchor Book, 1959.

are being gathered, while the talk is being organized. The question the speaker should keep in mind as his guide is: "How do I want to be regarded by these people?" If you are satisfied to be considered frivolous and superficial, or awkward and disorganized, then it does little good to master the principles of effective communication. If you wish to be thought of as capable, thoughtful, and reasonably serious-minded, the role demands careful preparation. Most students in a beginning speech course think their major problem is to stand up and deliver what they have to say. Actually, the real problem is to prepare for the kind of talking which can be delivered with weight and influence. "I always forget while speaking" is another way of saying, "My preparation has been thoroughly incompetent."

Role-playing is especially important because the people with whom we talk always react more to the total personality of the speaker *as they understand it* than they do to what is said and the mechanisms of delivery. Quite possibly the audience might conclude after listening to a speech: "Henry is wrong about this, and he surely didn't speak very well; but he is a thoughtful and kindhearted person"; or, "Henry is right, of course, and he's awfully slick; but I just don't trust the guy." If you try to be thoughtful while speaking but reveal that you have prepared superficially, the audience will inevitably conclude that you really lack interest in both them and the topic. To enact a role well, it must be performed wholeheartedly and thoroughly, in all its stages.

Function

The function of a speaker is the purpose he wants to achieve with this particular group of listeners, at this immediate time, in relation to the topic he is discussing, or the relations he wants to maintain with the group. Sometimes the function is to explain something (the operation of a slide rule) so the audience will understand it; sometimes it is to persuade the group to do something (give blood to the Red Cross); sometimes it is to create the impression that the speaker is to be trusted with leadership responsibilities or that he is attractive as a potential friend or that he deserves a high grade. Many times, the speech may have one function for part of the audience and a different function for other parts. For example, if you happen to be a Republican speaking to a mixed political audience, you might be trying to convince the Democrats to shift their votes to your candidate and at the same time be trying to convince the Republicans that you should be given a chance to run as their nominee in the next election.

The *function* of a talk underlies all the other factors. Common ground may often be achieved by pointing out what you wish to accomplish that the group also wants done. Status differences often evaporate in teamwork when it becomes clear the purpose of the speaker is to serve the whole group. And the role the speaker is to enact is very often defined as that of a leader or instigator of an action that will be of use to all. "What are you trying to accomplish?" should be the principal guideline for every speaker at every stage of preparation and presentation. We should never be guilty of the muddle-mindedness of the woman who asked, "How can I tell what I think until I hear what I say?"

○ LANGUAGE AND COMMUNICATIVE SPEECH

The first thing to have in mind about language is that it is extremely important as by far the most useful way of sharing ideas, feelings, and attitudes; and the next thing to remember is that it is not all-important. For a very large part of every message we seek to communicate in words is always conveyed by the way we use our voice, by our appearance, and by how we act. What language does, what it can be made to do, and how it is and must be supplemented are vital considerations for every speaker.

The general desire to have a larger vocabulary is testimony to our realization of the values of language. So is our concern with grammar. "Give me the right word and the right accent with which to speak it," wrote Joseph Conrad, "and I will move the world." The French critic Buffon described style as "the right words in the right places." All of us have struggled with the tantalizing inability to say what we wish to say because the word we need won't come to mind. Since the English language is composed of some 700,000 words, while the average speaking vocabulary is only 30,000 or less, it is obvious that we fall far short of mastery of the major tool of communication.

The relationship of language to thought has also received considerable attention from linguists. Two of them, Edward Sapir and Benjamin Lee Whorf,[9] have formulated the concept that the language we use (vocabulary and grammar) limits and defines the way in which we perceive reality and think about it. As they point out, speakers whose language has no past tense and no plural form (such as the Hopi Indians) have difficulty in generalizing about the passage of time or about the behavior of large numbers of individuals. If in a given language hate and love are verbs but never nouns, the users of that language tend to think of love and hatred as transitory emotions rather than enduring states of mind. Similarly, if a student is able to use only a very simple vocabulary in very simple grammatical forms, he finds it difficult either to understand or communicate complex ideas. Moreover, with a limited command of the use of words, an individual is likely to become dogmatic and undiscriminating in his thinking, for qualifying phrases demand some skill in grammar and fine distinctions among ideas depend upon precision in terms.

Aside from command of vocabulary and grammar (which is to be sought not only in special English classes but in careful and attentive general reading, writing, speaking, and listening), effective communication depends upon the use of language typical of the group in which the talking is done. "He doesn't speak our language" is a judgment that identifies one of the major barriers to communication. Students use language differently when talking to students than when talking to professors; similarly, professors talking among themselves often use language far differently from the way they do in class. Language, then, must be geared to the purpose of the speaker; it should reflect his chosen role and be appropriate to the circumstances; and it is affected by the topic being discussed.

To emphasize the relationship between language and communicative effectiveness is one thing; how to acquire a wider vocabulary and a surer command of grammar is something else. Mastery of language ought to be a lifetime study, not confined to special courses nor pursued by study of word lists and grammatical rules. It consists of a

[9] *Cf.* Edward Sapir, "Communication," *Encyclopedia of the Social Sciences.* New York: Macmillan, 1933, and *Culture, Language, and Personality.* Berkeley, Cal.: University of California Press, 1956; Benjamin Lee Whorf, *Language, Thought and Reality.* New York: Wiley, 1956. For a discussion of the limitations of the Sapir-Whorf hypothesis, *cf.* Harry Hoijer, editor, *Language in Culture.* Chicago: University of Chicago Press, 1954.

sharply ingrained habit of listening and reading to note how ideas are best expressed and communicated and of practicing to improve one's skill in their expression and communication when writing and speaking.

But important as language is, the most basic elements in any communicative process are nonverbal. Listeners (and viewers) attain their surest and most dependable judgment concerning the moral thoughtfulness of the speaker, his attitudes toward the topic, toward the listeners, and toward himself, and his poise and self-mastery from watching his actions and listening to the tone of his voice. Bluff, uncertainty, pretense, arrogance, cynicism, indifference, and fear are revealed by such factors as unnaturally high pitch, a tremolo in the voice, a hardness of quality, a rate that is too rapid or too slow, a lack of inflectional variety (monotone), and other vocal aberrations. Just as surely, the voice also reflects calm assurance, eager interest, comradely affection, and genuine thoughtfulness. Similarly, untidy dress, a slouching posture, and either too much or too little muscular tension are signs of careless indifference to what others may be thinking. They may even be interpreted by the listeners as meaning the speaker lacks self-respect. They also seem to indicate a lack of conviction about or even interest in the subject being discussed. These cues may, of course, not be what they seem; but communicative effectiveness depends on how they are interpreted by the listeners.

◯ COMMUNICATIVE FEEDBACK

As we have just said, communicative effectiveness depends on listener-interpretation of what is said or seen. It also depends on whether and how the speaker interprets the continuous reactions of his listeners. For communication never is a one-way process: expression becomes communication when there is a continuing feedback of impressions from the listener to the speaker. As George Herbert Mead, author of the famous book, *Mind, Self, and Society*,[10] phrased it, the speaker "is affected just as the [listener] is. If the meaning of what he says affects the other, it affects himself in much the same way." In

[10] Mead is too difficult for any but advanced students. His contributions to communication theory are best presented in Anselm Strauss, editor, *The Social Psychology of George Herbert Mead*. Chicago: University of Chicago Press, Phoenix Books, 1956. For a sound and popularized version of the Meadian theories, *cf.* Walter Coutu, *Emergent Human Nature*. New York: Knopf, 1949.

With, not to ...

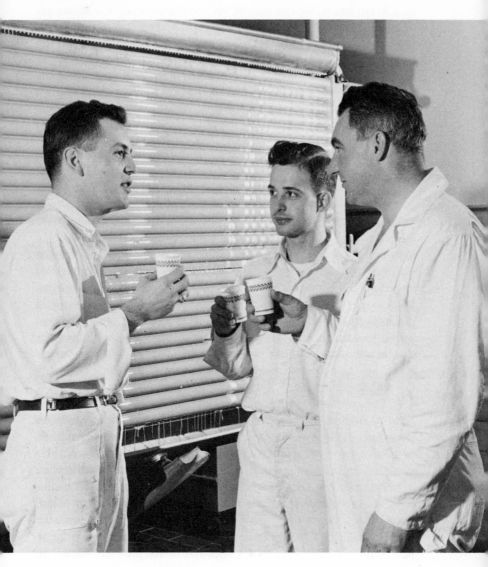

Circular response is constant stimulus: speaker to listener(s); listener(s) to speaker. Its catalyst is talking *with*, not *to* or *at*. Response is eye movement, facial expression, bodily posture, and the speaker should phrase his remarks as replies to these responses.

fact, Mead insists, we can only be sure of the meaning of what we say when we note how it affects our listeners. If you explain a complicated process, you can only be sure it is understood by observing the reactions of the listeners. If you urge acceptance of an opinion, you can only judge of your communicative effectiveness by noting accurately how it is received. This means that the speaker has to maintain a close alertness to pick up continually guiding clues from his listeners; and it means the listeners should aid the process by making their reactions clear and evident.

When one speaker is talking to one listener, the communicative process is somewhat like a game of catch: the ball (idea) is tossed, caught, returned, and tossed again—back and forth, so long as the game goes on. When one speaker talks to a group of listeners, his position is somewhat like that of a pitcher in a baseball game with the bases loaded; he cannot know what is happening and what is likely to happen unless he is aware of the actions and reactions of everyone on his own team and on base. Like all analogies, this one is somewhat imperfect. But perhaps it will help to clarify the great cardinal fact that speaking does not mean merely directing a stream of words out toward potential listeners. Much more truly, every speaking situation (even public speaking) is an enlarged conversation. The speaker has the dominant position and can put his ideas into words; but the listeners' minds are just as active as his: if they cannot actually talk back they can and do think back.

Skillful speakers often attain a very sensitive ability to detect and react to changes in the audience attitude—changes that are reflected in posture, in facial expressions, in movement or rigidity. Occasionally, of course, an audience reacts with laughter or applause—or with questions and comments—or with groans and hisses. But these are only dramatic extremes of a reaction pattern that is continuous. One possible reaction, of course, is boredom and indifference. When this occurs, the auditors stop listening and turn their attention elsewhere, perhaps inward, to deal with their own thoughts. When they do this—just as when they register strong approval or disapproval—their feelings are manifest in their appearance and behavior.

Adolf Hitler, in *Mein Kampf*, explained why "we relied chiefly on the spoken word" in building the Nazi party in pre-World War II Germany:

An orator receives continuous guidance from his audience, enabling him to correct his lecture, since he can measure all the time on the countenances of his hearers the extent to which they are successful in following his arguments intelligently and whether his words are producing the effect he desires. . . .

Suppose that an orator observes that his hearers do not understand him, he will make his explanation so elementary and clear that every single one must take it in; if he feels that they are incapable of following him, he will build up his ideas carefully and slowly until the weakest member has caught up; again, once he senses that they seem not to be convinced that he is correct in his arguments, he will repeat them over and over again with fresh illustrations and himself state their unspoken objections; he will continue thus until the last members of the opposition show him by their behavior and play of expression that they have capitulated to his demonstration of the case.[11]

The process by which the speaker guides himself by noting the reactions of his listeners is sometimes known as "circular response." The words of the speaker serve as a stimulus to the listeners and their reactions, in turn, serve as further stimuli to him. Talk thus is a very live process, with constant reaction flowing back and forth. This is a principal reason why genuine talk ought to be extemporaneous—that is, speech resulting from careful preparation, but taking its final form and being modified in its development while the speaker is actually addressing his listeners. Because of this fact, the distinction between public speaking and conversation is far less significant than its similarities. Good talk is that in which the speaker and his listeners jointly participate; it is, in fact, a creation of the listeners, just as it is of the speaker.

Feedback, then, consists of the stream of reactions which the speaker receives from his listeners and which he utilizes to affect the way in which he continues to speak to them. Feedback means that the speaker is receiving as well as giving out; it means that he is talking *with* and not *to* his listeners. It means that the listeners also have their right of self-expression, their own freedom of opinion, their own right to influence the decision being reached. Only when a speaker utilizes this principle is he engaged in genuinely communicative speech.

[11] Adolf Hitler, *Mein Kampf.* New York: Reynal and Hitchcock, 1941, pp. 704–706. Cf. Chapter VI, of Vol. II, "The Struggle of the Early Days; The Significance of the Spoken Word," *ibid.,* pp. 695–719.

○ **CONCLUSION**

The purpose of this chapter has been to explain the nature of the study of communicative speech. As was pointed out, it is not easy, even though we all have been speaking communicatively most of our lives. The difficulty, however, does not lie so much in the danger of stage fright as it does in the complexity of the process of deciding what to say, how to say it, and how to adapt what is said to the special circumstances of the listeners. The value of the study of speech, as well as a recognition of the nature of its problems, has been stressed by educators from the very earliest period of recorded history.

Basic to all improvement in communication is to note its relationship to and difference from expression. What the speaker believes and what he wishes to express are essential; but speech becomes communicative only when the message is adapted to the needs and the nature of the listeners. Between the speaker and his hearers there are many bonds which facilitate communication and many barriers that weaken or block it. By utilizing the principles underlying common ground, status relationships, role-playing, and function, a good speaker can convert the barriers into bonds, just as the ineffective speaker may change the bonds into barriers. In part the message is communicated through words, in part nonverbally. In either case, the speaker not only utters his message but also receives constant stimulation and guidance from the reactions of his audience. Thus even public speaking is, in a sense, enlarged conversation. For truly communicative speech, feedback is no less vital than utterance.

Another factor worthy of final emphasis is that the study of speech you will be engaged in is designed to help you in all kinds of speaking, including public speeches, conversation, discussion, and interviewing. And our aim is not merely to improve the speaking you will be doing in class but all your oral communication for the remainder of your life.

EXERCISES

Questions for Discussion

1. What is your own attitude concerning your work in speech? Has it been modified by what is said in this chapter? How will your attitude affect what you may do to improve your skills in speaking?

2. Why has work in speech been a central concern of education all through history? Restate the central ideas of Kagemni, Ptah-Hotep, Plato, Cicero, Quintilian, Augustine, Miss Wright, Eliot, Depew, and Eric and Wendell Johnson. What do you think speech education should do for you?

3. What are the basic differences between expression and communication? Do you need to cultivate skill in both? Why?

4. What do we mean by communicative barriers and communicative bonds? Give some examples of each that are not in this chapter. Using your own examples, illustrate how a barrier may be converted into a bond, and vice versa.

5. Discuss the meaning, in terms of communicative speech, of rapport, common ground, status, role, and function. Explain how each of these factors should enter into your preparation as well as into your classroom speaking. To what extent are they also important in conversation and group discussion?

6. How is language used in communication—and why and how must it be supplemented?

7. Explain "feedback" and "circular response." How are they related to communication? How are they related to the extemporaneous method of speaking? How does *extemporaneous* differ from *memorized* or *impromptu* speech? What are the similarities and differences between public speaking and conversation?

Projects for Speaking and Writing

1. Analyze your own personality in a brief essay which you will show to your instructor and keep for your own guidance during the remainder of your speech course. How does your image of yourself correlate with your role, or roles, and status in your group of chosen associates? What functions can you best perform in your speeches for the improvement of your status, the helpful revision of your role, and the growth of your personality? What convictions are you especially eager to communicate and fortify in your speeches to your classmates?

2. Prepare a three-minute speech that will illustrate some way in which speech is a necessity in a democratic society, in business, in the professions, or in your present activities as a student. In this speech, try to draw upon your own direct experience and observation. Make the speech *real* by building it around a concrete problem or situation and by citing people who are well known to your audience. Phrase for it a single, specific purpose that you want to accomplish, such as "I want my listeners to realize how skill in speech helps a teacher (or lawyer, or businessman, or citizen) to carry out his responsibilities better." Select one or several

specific examples or illustrations which might help you achieve this response. Conclude by summarizing your examples and restating your theme.

3. If speech is a required course in your curriculum, prepare a three-minute talk in which you present what appears to you to be the chief reasons why speech has been required. If you have chosen speech as an elective, give the audience in a three-minute speech your reasons for doing so.

4. If you disagree with any or several of the judgments regarding speech set forth in this chapter, present a three-minute speech setting forth as persuasively and clearly as you can your own point of view on the conclusions with which you disagree.

Chapter 2

Standards of Effective Speech

IN DEVELOPING ANY SKILL, the goal you set should be based on certain standards toward which you will always be working. It is therefore important to approach this matter of developing your ability to speak well both with a knowledge of the standards of effective speech and with a proper perspective on how these standards are related to your personal objectives. It is one thing to establish standards, which are usually based on the optimum achievement in a given field of endeavor; it is quite another thing to be realistic in applying these to yourself. In this connection, you must remember that there is probably no more personal and individual objective of self-development than the improvement of your speech. Always keep this in mind as you attempt to set up standards and, more especially, as you proceed to develop your speaking ability.

○ STARTING WHERE YOU ARE

You have already developed certain speaking habits—some good, some bad. Many of these are a part of you as a person. They explain to some extent why you are what you are and distinguish you from all others. Other habits are largely external mechanics that are not necessarily the essential you. These you can more readily change. Perhaps you do not look at others when you talk, sometimes you can-

29

not be heard, or you talk too fast. If we quickly say that good standards of effective speech call for looking at your listener, talking loud enough to be heard, and talking at a rate that can be easily understood, you can reach these standards relatively soon. On the other hand, if you have tended over the years to become self-centered, this characteristic may interfere with the communicative demand that you become more listener-centered, and it may take you a little longer than usual to reach these standards of effective speaking.

This is not to say that you should set your goals low and readily admit that you cannot reach high standards as a speaker. On the contrary; most of the evidence shows that the higher your goal the more surely will you work toward it. And if you have any notion that you are not gifted enough to become an effective speaker or that you do not have the basic abilities that it requires, remember that *most speakers are made, not born.* From the age of Demosthenes, who practiced with pebbles in his mouth to overcome a speech defect, to the age of Franklin Roosevelt, who studied and practiced for many years to become a better speaker, there are numerous examples of hard work and effort on the part of many speakers to achieve the standards you will want to reach.

We can go back through the ages and bring to mind famous rhetoricians and speakers who established standards or who illustrated them in their own writing or speaking. Aristotle's *Rhetoric* remains to this day one of the chief reference points for all speakers who wish to study thoroughly all the principles. Aristotle's standards are high, as are those of a later scholar, Quintilian, whom we have quoted in the first chapter as an exponent of the traditional ideal ethics and goodness as basic prerequisites for the good speaker. These men, although masters of the art of rhetoric, were not great speakers. Cicero, a rare combination of writer and speaker who wrote another sound rhetoric, *De Oratore,* is perhaps even better known for his outstanding oratory in the Roman classical era.

As we move through history and cite examples of men who exercised great influence through their speaking ability and as we observe the standards they set in achieving their own excellence, we have some difficulty deciding whether to imitate them in all respects. The forceful, impassioned speaking of Patrick Henry, who inspired the colonists toward revolution; the strong, reasoned logic of Daniel Webster; the energetic, crusading style of William Jennings Bryan; the dynamic sincerity of Theodore Roosevelt; and the eloquent common touch of Franklin Roosevelt all have contributed to our knowledge of the principles of effective speech. Each of these men was a great speaker; each in his own way applied standards of good speaking to his own habits and objectives; yet each one differed in many ways from all the others. The standards they sought to achieve, and the standards by which their effectiveness is judged are different in some degree for each of the speakers and for each of the periods in which they lived. There are also fundamental similarities among them. We need to identify the similarities—and also to note well that different speakers adapt the standards to their own personalities and circumstances. Each was great because his vital message was delivered in a crucial period and in a situation in which speaker, audience, and subject converged to produce the highest communicative opportunity. Each was great because he was aware that times were critical and applied the utmost sincerity and effort in the communication of his message. And each was great also because he never took lightly the obligation to use to the fullest the highest possible standards that he could apply to his speaking.

○ **BASES FOR THE STANDARDS**

Our problem is to determine the kinds of standards which we ought to apply to ourselves—here and now.[1] These standards should be determined by and for our own circumstances, just as the effectiveness of these men has to be measured in terms of their responsibilities and the situations confronting them. There are three governing factors which can serve as bases for establishing standards that will be helpful as we attempt to improve our own communicative speaking.

1. The goal we are seeking is improvement in all oral communication, not merely (and for most students not primarily) formal public speaking. The need we all have is for a wide variety of skills suited to a wide variety of uses: social conversation, interviews, dis-

---

[1] For three different and supplementary discussions of standards, *cf.* James H. McBurney and Ernest J. Wrage, *The Art of Good Speech.* Englewood Cliffs, N. J.: Prentice-Hall, 1953, Chapter II, "Standards of Good Speech"; Robert T. Oliver, *Effective Speech for Democratic Living.* Prentice-Hall, 1959, Chapter II, "Standards of Good Speech"; and Eugene E. White: *Practical Speech Fundamentals.* New York: Macmillan, 1960, Chapter II, "A Positive Approach to Speaking."

cussion, impromptu talks, and the informal, neighborly short speeches we will be making in community clubs and gatherings. Eventually, we shall also be called upon for oral reports in our business or profession, where we shall have to explain the work we are doing or try to persuade our superiors or associates to undertake projects we may recommend. Those who expect to rise to leadership in their communities may also be called upon from time to time for more formal speeches, such as addresses at commencement, and on national holidays. Others may enter professions, such as law, the ministry, or teaching, where a great deal of speaking is a daily necessity. Even foremen in factories have been found to spend more than half of their time talking with crew members and superiors. Everyone talks a great deal, and it is important to our work and our general welfare that we talk well. But, since the occasions are mostly informal and often require immediate and ready speech rather than a prepared talk, this circumstance, then, becomes a vital condition for the establishment of our standards of good speech.

2. The democratic character of our time has led to emphasis upon conversational talk with our listeners, rather than exhortations directed to them. In other words, our society values the exchange of ideas, the sharing of information, the cooperative solution of problems. We are developing a growing awareness of our social and ethical responsibilities toward one another and a greater respect for the thinking, judgment, and feelings of others. This spirit of mutual respect has led to a desire to "talk things over" with cooperative listeners rather than to "talk down" to them in the manner of an authoritarian orator. This does not mean that we underrate the value of enthusiasm, force, energy, and sincerity that have universally characterized great oratory; it does mean that we adapt these qualities to cultivation of a more intimate and conversational manner which will bring us closer to our listeners and to their reaction. This change in social circumstances has led to a change in style of speaking—and this also affects our standards for good talk.

3. In a beginning course in speech, our immediate problem is the improvement of ourselves as oral communicators. Our proper standards, then, must be related closely to the learning process. What should we do, and how should we do it, to achieve systematic progress in our own abilities? This focus demands that our standards involve ourselves as learners. They must guide us in determining our own

needs and our own capabilities in relation to the essential qualities of effective communication. Placing the emphasis upon learning rather than directly upon doing makes an essential difference in the attitude we must bring to the speaking assignments we shall have. Whether you fully understand and accept this difference will largely determine how much improvement you may hope to accomplish. It is an essential condition prerequisite to becoming a successful student of speech.

If you have ever played tennis, you may recall that in the beginning you learned to grasp the racket and to lob the ball back over the net. It may be that, playing against a similarly unskilled opponent, you gradually attained such skill that you could return a fair proportion of his strokes and win your share of games. Then, perhaps, a tennis coach may have taken you in hand. If so, he doubtless told you to hold the racket differently, and to balance your weight on the balls of your feet. Then he asked you to stop "patting" the ball and swing into it with all your weight. If you followed his instructions, you may have been dismayed, for the ball probably sailed high into the air, instead of over the net. If your object was to continue winning the little games you were accustomed to, you would rebel and return (when he wasn't watching) to your old "more successful" habits. But the coach would insist that you could never be really good unless you were willing to master the fundamentals, even though this meant an immediate loss of your puny and partial effectiveness.

The same experience is encountered by students who go out for track, or basketball, or any other sport. It is even more dramatically illustrated in the experience of the person who has learned to be fairly effective with the "hunt and peck" method of typing, and then tries to learn the touch system. First of all, there is a necessity for "unlearning" habits which have led to a low degree of success in order to replace them with habits that *at first* result in what appears to be failure. However, such a transformation of approach is necessary for progression into genuine skills.

Just so is it with your speaking. You will have to try using a tighter organization, a more purposive ordering of materials, an audience-centered rather than a self-centered view of methods, a variety of types of speaking, all of which may be unfamiliar. Gradually you will learn more and more skills that you will have to remember; the process of speaking will come to seem more and more complex. One result may be a loss of fluency, or an increased tension. Often you may feel that the methods insisted upon by your teacher are actually less effective than the ones you had picked up, hit-or-miss, through your random experience. Many students, for example, declare that outlining their talks does not help them—on the contrary, it interferes with their freedom of thought about the subject.

In other words, there is a natural tendency to resist giving up old, partially successful methods, for the sake of learning new ones that in the long run will be much better. This was true of the tennis player we referred to; it is true of many students of speech. But the unlearning, and the trying of tried and proven methods, are both essential if the course in speech is to have fundamental and lasting results.

As we think, then, of the standards which should govern the speaking of students in this course, we should view them according to these three factors: (1) that what is needed is improvement in a wide variety of forms of oral discourse; (2) that, in order to be effective, speech today must be addressed to listeners as co-participants in the communicative process; and (3) that the goal is not alone to speak well but to learn to speak better. With these factors in mind, we shall now consider the standards that apply to all of us under these stated circumstances. Four standards that merit consideration are the ethical norm, the esthetic norm, the effects norm, and the educational norm. Each of them suggests qualities you should seek to develop in your own speaking.

○ ETHICAL NORM

Ethics is concerned with moral values.[2] As we apply the ethical norm to the work you will be doing in your speech course, the following questions will need to be considered:

1. *Are you being truthful in what you say about your subject?* This test question suggests, first of all, that speakers should not deliberately lie to their listeners; facts should not be misrepresented, authorities should not be misquoted, and if illustrations or examples are "invented," the listeners should be told they are hypothetical, not

[2] The problem of ethics in speaking is discussed by many writers. *Cf.* Lionel Crocker, "Truth through Personality," *The Quarterly Journal of Speech,* Vol. 39 (April, 1953), pp. 1–5; Robert T. Oliver, *The Psychology of Persuasive Speech.* London: Longmans, 1957, Chapter II, "The Ethics of Persuasion"; and Karl Wallace, "An Ethical Basis of Communication," *The Speech Teacher,* Vol. 4 (January, 1955), pp. 1–9.

STANDARDS OF EFFECTIVE SPEECH · 35

real. Yet failure to represent a subject truthfully may result from the speaker's lack of understanding of it. Many subjects we commonly talk about (such as the prevalence of divorce, or labor-union leadership) are exceedingly complex. If you base your own understanding on just one magazine article (which may be prejudiced) you may mislead your listeners. Before you tell others what to think about a subject, you must be willing to take trouble enough to be sure you understand it yourself.

Ethical philosophers declare that there is an ethical responsibility to be "morally thoughtful," by which they mean that misrepresentation resulting from careless thinking or lack of information is in itself a form of deception. Since many subjects are so complex that you can scarcely hope to make certain your knowledge is complete and your understanding is wholly correct, you should make clear to your listeners that you are telling them only what you do know—and that much about the subject remains, in your mind, still in the realm of doubt. But when the real facts of the matter can be ascertained by thoughtful examination of sound reference sources, you have a genuine moral obligation to know what you are talking about.

2. *Are you satisfying reasonable requirements for both the facts and the opinions you present?* What is "true" about racial relations, for example, may be extremely difficult to determine; but you can at least make sure that when you state something regarding this (or any other topic) as a fact, you have taken the trouble to make sure the fact itself is true. Many people seem not to realize that there is a similar requirement for reasonable validation of their publicly stated opinions. You may have a "right to your own opinion," however foolish it may seem to others; but your listeners have an equal right to know on what your opinion is based—if you communicate that opinion to them. An opinion is no better than the facts and inferences on which it is based.

If an opinion is based on false information, superficial observation, or false reasoning, it is unethical to present it to listeners as something they should take seriously. Meanwhile, as listeners we need to be aware that intensity of conviction is not necessarily the equivalent of being right. A speaker may display the utmost emotional intensity in support of an idea that is factually unsound. It is common to make a clear-cut distinction between "facts" and "opinions"; this distinction has real value; but it does not mean that speakers have a free license to advocate opinions that belie the facts. There is no escape from the ethical obligation to be "morally thoughtful."

3. *Are you reasonably considerate of the feelings of the people to whom you are talking?* If your language or stories you may tell should be vulgar, this would be a clear violation of good taste which many would find offensive. If you make derogatory remarks about particular religious views, you may anger some listeners and hurt the feelings of others. If you disparage the qualities of women, or of Negroes, or of Jews, or of immigrants from southern Europe, or of Orientals, you risk offending your listeners. This is not to say that such subjects are always to be avoided. An honest discussion of the tenets of Protestantism as compared with Catholicism, or of Buddhism and Christianity, or of the comparative abilities of men and women, or of the characteristics of immigrants from various parts of the world are all sound subjects concerning which we feel a deep interest; for this reason they are perfectly suitable for discussion. What is important is that you demonstrate a respectful and responsible consideration for opposing points of view.

It is unfair, and therefore unethical, to use the opportunity accorded you as a speaker to attack a viewpoint which your listeners do not have adequate opportunity to defend. And it debases the value of oral communication to present a point of view with such vituperation and bitterness that it invites or perhaps compels replies in a similarly quarrelsome vein. The important consideration is to respect both your own views and those of the people to whom you talk.

○ ESTHETIC NORM

Speech, like music, or painting, or any other art, has one legitimate function in simply giving pleasure to speaker and listeners alike.[3] This is not true only of speeches that are intended to entertain. There is a true pleasure to be found in any performance artistically accomplished. We enjoy listening to a speech that is well constructed and well delivered. The pleasure derives from our appreciation of the artistry of the speaker.

1. *The structure of your talk should be suitable and well made.*

---

[3] For a detailed discussion of theories of speech style, *cf.* Lester Thonssen and A. Craig Baird, *Speech Criticism*. New York: Ronald, 1948, Chapter 15, "The Style of Public Address," pp. 405–433.

Sonnets, symphonies, plays, and short stories have "approved forms" of composition, and their writers or composers are evaluated in part by how well they can accomplish their individual goals within the limits of the prescribed forms. The same is true of speeches, discussions, and serious conversation. Rhetoricians from Aristotle to the present day have described a symmetry of design for good speaking, and it is a source of pleasure to observe a speaker conforming to these "patterns of expectation" while still rendering his talk vividly individual. For example, a speaker is expected to introduce a definite transition from one point to the next. If he fails to do so, the result is confusing, and creates a feeling of esthetic dissatisfaction in the listener, apart from an inability to understand clearly or fully what is said. In some instances, the transitions may be made clearly but inartistically. For instance, a speaker may introduce each point as "firstly," "secondly," etc. The result is clear but sounds artificial and mechanical. Artistic speaking demands that both clarity and artistry be combined. This is true not only for transitions but also for many larger aspects of speech construction, such as the form of the introduction and the conclusion, the relationship of the speaker's purpose to his central idea, the ways in which materials are used, the manner in which quotations are presented, and for all the other aspects of speech organization discussed in this book.

2. *The suitability of the language used is important.* One speaking situation might call for a very formal type of diction, another for a colloquial style. Artistry demands primarily that there be an appropriateness of style to the circumstances and that it be consistent throughout, or, if inconsistent, that there be a clearly evident reason. For example, in a technical discussion of a new medical discovery, the language might most suitably be technical; nevertheless, for humorous effect, a slang expression might be introduced. Both speaker and listeners should understand instantly why this shift is made and how it relates to the over-all design of the speech.

3. *Your manner as a speaker can often decide the outcome.* It is not always essential that the speaker be formal in his dress and general bearing; for some topics and for some situations, a very large measure of informality might be better. What is important, from the standpoint of artistry, is that the speaker should "suit his manner to the words, his words to the manner"; that he should adopt a definiteness of method

which is understood by his listeners, so that they can judge what he is doing in terms of what he is trying to do.

Frequently throughout this book you will be warned that speaking is not a performance, that you are to try to communicate your message rather than to try to impress your listeners with the skill with which you do it. In general this is very sound advice; much speaking fails of effectiveness because the speaker obviously is more concerned with whether he is doing it well than with what he is trying to get across to his listeners. Suffice it to say here that whenever the listeners think of your talk as a "performance" (good or bad) you are violating the esthetic norm. A speech conforms to the demands of this norm when the manner of composition and presentation are both so well managed that they are not even thought about separately from the message being presented. Style should not get in the way of content. But it is also true that the sheer fact of doing any act well (including speaking) is a source of genuine pleasure. Good craftsmanship is always appreciated, both by those exhibiting it and by those observing it.

○ EFFECTS NORM

There is a temptation to feel that our speaking should always and only be judged in terms of its effects—on the basis of whether or not the speaker did achieve what he set out to accomplish. "I tried to entertain them and they surely did enjoy it," is a defense a speaker might make of his presentation; or, "I wanted to get them to vote for my plan, and they did." The emphasis upon accomplishing the purpose is right and proper when suitable safeguards are taken into account.[4] There is much truth in the view that we can scarcely tell whether a particular speech was a good one until we know how the listeners responded to it. But consideration of the effects of the speaking should never be separated from the following factors:

1. *The end does not justify any means.* Entertainment achieved through vulgarisms or by ridicule of other people or by such self-debasement that it may weaken the respect of your listeners for your serious views is success purchased at too high a cost. Persuasion achieved by misrepresentation of facts or by attacks against the integ-

[4] For a valuable discussion of speakers who risked position and reputation to speak up for causes that could not succeed, *cf.* John F. Kennedy, *Profiles in Courage.* New York: Harper, 1956.

Understanding is the goal . . .

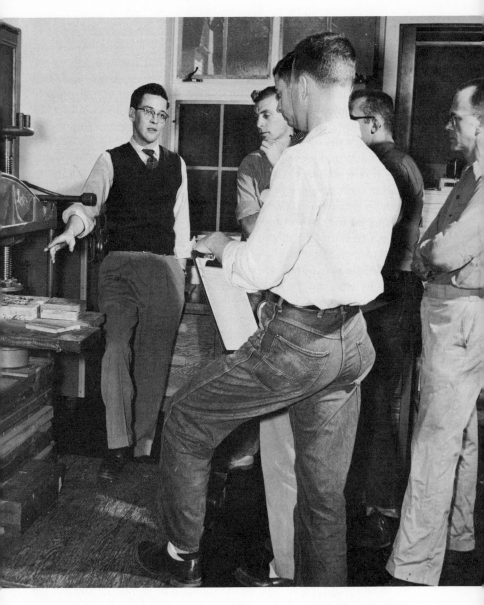

If a process is to be explained, a problem solved, or information conveyed, oral communication succeeds when listener needs are satisfied.

rity of honest people is in direct violation of the ethical norm. Clarity of understanding that is gained by oversimplification actually results in a misconception of the real truth of the matter discussed. When un-ethical means are used to accomplish even a just result, a part of the over-all effect is a weakening of the ethical principles involved. If a sound conclusion is supported by shoddy rationalization, the effect in part is to undermine respect for and ability in logical reasoning. We are never justified in pleading that audience reaction is the final test of the merit of the speaking unless the means used to secure a favorable reaction are thoroughly laudable.

2. *The listeners' reaction is secondary to your conviction as the speaker concerning the actual truth of the matter.* If you are interested solely in gaining a favorable response from your listeners, you might be tempted to tell them merely what they already believe, rather than attempt to shift their thinking from their basis of error to your more correct views. For example, if you are a confirmed Democrat, it would be a violation of your own fundamental political purposes, when speaking to Republicans, to seek a favorable effect by advocating election of their candidates. Whether the "effect achieved" by your speaking really means, then, that it is good speaking depends in part on whether the reaction you secure from your listeners conforms to the facts as you understand them and the principles in which you believe.

3. *The effect you achieve must be adjudged in terms of the nature of the problem with which you are dealing.* Success in gaining under-standing from your listeners on how to fill out the stub of a checkbook is really a failure resulting from too low a goal. Whether you can really *explain* effectively remains to be tested when you deal with a more complicated problem—such as how to estimate the relation of profits to costs in the operation of a diner. Demosthenes, often accounted the world's greatest orator, failed when he tried to persuade the Athenians to unite against the threat of conquest by Philip of Mace-donia. Similarly, Edmund Burke, England's greatest orator, failed to induce the Government of Great Britain to adopt policies that would have prevented the American Revolution. Sometimes duty impels a speaker to undertake tasks of such magnitude, or that meet so much opposition, that he cannot achieve a favorable audience response. If we should judge speech only by the standard of immediate success, we might well be tempted always to speak on popular sides of issues or to try to explain only very elementary ideas or processes. The effect

must always be evaluated in large part in terms of the nature of the speaker's goal.

Political analyst William V. Shannon, in the New York *Post,* August 6, 1961, discussed the relationships of this norm when he reported, "Stevenson's campaign ended in defeat, but the mere fact of victory or defeat is not always and at all times the most important fact, in politics or in anything else. . . . What matters is not whether a candidate wins or loses but whether he contributes anything to the dialogue by which our people gradually amass their common wisdom and, hopefully, go forward. Adlai Stevenson in defeat did more to contribute to our understanding of ourselves and the world in which we live than have many victors. That is justification enough."

4. *The effect toward which you aim should be reasonably adjusted to the reaction possibilities of the listeners.* If you were to speak on equality of races on two different occasions, once to a group in Augusta, Maine, and then to an audience in Augusta, Georgia, your basic point of view would be the same for both situations; but you might wisely try to accomplish something different in speaking to the Georgian audience from what you would try in Maine. This simply takes into account the fact that some things may easily be accomplished with a single speech (such as getting your roommate to go with you to the movies); whereas other objectives, such as improving the study habits of your younger brother, may require many talks, perhaps by several people. When we judge a speech by its effects, then, we need to inquire whether the effect sought was within the realm of reasonable attainment.

5. *Factors wholly outside the speech situation must not be overlooked.* Your attempt to "entertain" a particular listener might fail because he had just received a letter informing him of the death of his grandmother, or because he had a severe headache, or had just failed to be selected by a fraternity he wished to join. Similar disturbing factors (unobservable by the speaker) might interfere with the reception of skilled exposition or persuasion. On the other hand, relatively unskillful speaking (for instance, in explanation of the strange chemical complexities of water) might seem to succeed with your listeners—if they happened to have all heard a lecture on the subject given by their chemistry professor.

The importance of the "effects norm" should not be undervalued. All communicative speaking is presumably aimed to accomplish the speaker's precise purpose. It is entirely proper to estimate its success or failure in terms of how well it achieves its effect. These five reservations, however, should not be overlooked.

○ EDUCATIONAL NORM

The course in speech is a part—and should be an important part—of the entire educational program in which you are engaged.[5] Just as truly as in your other courses, it has educational values that derive from its own nature and functions. There are at least four educational values you should seek to gain, and to exemplify, in your speaking.

1. *Are your speeches helping you to learn and become habituated to disciplined methods of thinking and behaving that will help you to be a more dependable member of any vocational or social group?* In a speech class, it is important that every speaker be fully prepared at specific times, and in specific ways. You cannot fail to speak when your turn comes (even if you do have a cold, or oversleep, or find it convenient to be elsewhere). Moreover, you are given a stated period of time (perhaps five minutes) for your talk. If you use more time than this you steal that time away from other students, or from the opportunity your instructor has to teach the whole class through the medium of oral evaluations of the talks given that day. This same type of discipline, of course, is also taught in classes in English composition, mathematics, and laboratory sciences—in any class in which work is to be handed in on a regular schedule. The difference is that you cannot fail to meet your responsibilities in speech (including the responsibility to be an alert listener) without direct damage to other people. Reliability is a highly regarded asset. This is a good time and place to build it firmly into your habit structure.

2. *Does the speech serve a worthwhile function in broadening intellectual perspective, or in deepening understanding, of the speaker and of his listeners?* If the topic or its development is superficial, neither the speaker during his preparation nor the listeners during its presentation will learn much if anything of value. One attribute of

[5] The educational values of speech education are discussed in many places. For an introduction to the subject, *cf.* J. Samuel Bois, *Explorations in Awareness*. New York: Harper, 1957; Irving J. Lee, *How to Talk with People*, Harper, 1952; and Earl James McGrath, *Communication in General Education*. Dubuque, Iowa: Wm. C. Brown, 1949.

STANDARDS OF EFFECTIVE SPEECH · 43

positive value a speech may have is that it be intellectually challenging or stimulating. To learn a great deal while preparing the talk, or while listening to it, is a contribution to your education. Robert Browning's line, "A man's reach should exceed his grasp," may well be applied to your own selection of topics as well as to the work you do in developing them. It is educationally sound to be continually "reaching out" for greater understanding than we already possess. In parts of the following chapters you will find recommendations that you speak on matters drawn from your own experience and your own interests. This advice is sound; but in following it you should also seek to expand what you already know and what you are already interested in. If you have a vague notion that you ought to know something about Milton's use of symbolism in *Paradise Lost,* the fact that you actually do *not* know about it is a reason for choosing to speak on it, not a reason for avoiding the topic. What you learn as you study the subject will help you; and the very fact that it is not commonplace knowledge means that when you speak your listeners will also gain additional information. "Is what I am doing intellectually valuable?" is a sound guide to follow in your preparation for speaking.

3. *Does your talk function to increase your own skill in speaking?* If you are not very good at telling jokes, perhaps it is especially desirable for you to attain this skill; instead of accepting the limitation upon your communicative abilities, work at this particular weakness until you do improve. Similarly, you may have trouble in organizing your ideas clearly, or in making effective internal summaries as your talks progress from one point to another, or in using questions that genuinely arouse in your listeners a sense of active participation. Your first two or three talks presented to the class should serve a diagnostic purpose, as you and your instructor discover what kinds of problems you in particular need to solve. When this is determined, you should try successively in every speech or class discussion thereafter to make substantial progress in mastering those particular problems. What you can do well you naturally most enjoy doing; but what you do poorly is what you may most need to concentrate upon.

4. *Does your speaking contribute to the meaningful integration of your total learning, thinking, and feeling?* Your talk is a significant way of expressing your whole personality. If your work in college is helping you to attain a richer and truer understanding of social conditions, of economic problems, of political issues, of natural science, and

of human relations, this increased competence should be evidenced in all your talk. You may not always wish to talk seriously about vital problems, but surely you should progress in the direction of exemplifying the traits of an educated individual.

During your college experience, you are taking many different subjects, in different departments, with different professors. Meanwhile, you are also having a wide range of relatively new social experiences, including "bull sessions" on very serious topics. Somewhere, somehow, all these new experiences need to be brought together into a master integration. Your political ideas ought to be affected by what you learn in economics, sociology, and political science classes. How you think about personal and national problems ought to be influenced by your course in logic and perhaps by some of your work in natural science, as well as in the humanities and social sciences. Achieving a genuine integration of all you learn and of all you feel and believe ought to be one of your major concerns. There will be no better opportunity available to you than the one you have before you in your class in speech. Whatever topic you select for a particular talk, you should try to draw together in its preparation your wide range of new and old information—your new ideas and developing convictions, as well as your deep-seated ideals. Your speeches can and should be treated as laboratory exercises for the demonstration that your mind is enlarging and your sensitivities are becoming better defined.

○ YOUR POTENTIAL FOR MEETING THESE STANDARDS

Having set high standards in your effort to become a successful speaker, you must assess your potential for meeting these standards. In other words how close can you come to the goals you are setting up?

One way to answer this question is to appraise yourself as a speaker today. Make an inventory in which you list your assets and liabilities, and then try to ascertain what standards you think you can meet most readily, as well as those that might require the greatest amount of work. Then keep revising this inventory as you increase your skill.

We have already pointed out that *speakers are made*. There are no born orators nor born great actors, champion boxers, four-minute-milers. They all succeed through hard work and training; having set high goals, they are willing to exert the effort required to reach such goals. You must have a *will to win* if you want to get to the top; and there are few reasonable goals beyond your reach if you really want to try.

Few of us really want to be great orators or necessarily even the best speakers in our respective communities, clubs, or groups. We want to be good speakers, able to communicate with others when the occasion demands it, and we want to be able to meet the challenge of any communicative situation. So we set modest goals which are within reach.

Your potential to meet the standards of good speech is just what you make it. The chief determining question in accomplishing your objective is the attitude you take toward speech training and its potential importance to you. As long as your attitude is positive, enthusiastic, and sincere, you will do the things that are necessary to reach the standards you set for yourself. And, as you go along and find yourself reaching and then surpassing these standards, you will constantly revise them upward, for no one has yet reached the ultimate goal of perfect speaker.

○ GUIDING YOUR GROWTH AND DEVELOPMENT

Having set the standards and started on your development as a speaker, you will want to chart a systematic program for preparation and practice. The course in effective speaking will chart your program, but within this you will be able to do your own planning and to determine methods for best accomplishing your results. Keep these suggestions in mind at all times:

1. Keep in mind the scope of the *total process* of communication.
2. Recognize your *social* and *ethical responsibilities* as a speaker.
3. Set your *standards* soundly.
4. Measure your *present ability* in relation to your standards.
5. Set a *goal*, considering your *potential* to meet it.
6. Set aside enough *time* for work and practice.
7. *Prepare* every speech thoroughly; do your best when you converse.
8. *Practice* diligently.

9. Seize *every opportunity* to speak when you have something to say.
10. Use your speaking opportunities to exert your best *influence* as a person.

○ CONCLUSION

This chapter has aimed to bring into focus those standards for good speech which will serve as a foundation for your study and practice: for all the work you will do in this present course and during the rest of your life in your efforts to become an ever better oral communicator. We have examined the problem of how standards by which to evaluate your success may properly be selected, and we have analyzed four such standards. It is our hope that you will adopt these as guides by which to hasten your own individual improvement in the important art of communicative speaking. The standards that you, yourself, consider of greatest significance to yourself are the ones that will best motivate the nature and extent of your own progress.

You know that you will always be judged by others—in this course by your instructor and fellow students. You know, too, that how you talk will be a matter of interest and a source of judgment by all your associates, all through your life. In other words, it is wise to have in mind the standards other people will measure you by, and it is sensible to attempt to meet those standards. Even so, an individual is always most keenly aware of his own self-evaluation. In the long run, you will achieve not much more than you ask of yourself. You will best serve your own needs, as you take up this study of effective communicative speech, if you realize that your potential is high and set your own personal standards accordingly. The worst harm you can do to yourself is deliberately to aim toward goals lower than those you are capable of achieving.

EXERCISES

Questions for Discussion

1. What three factors should be taken into account in determining the standards of good speaking? Does each one apply personally to you? What is the significance of the emphasis upon *learning* rather than *doing*?

2. How do you interpret the conclusion that the standards of good speaking should be *adapted to* rather than *adopted by* each individual speaker—including yourself? Do you see any special adaptations of the suggested standards which you should make?

3. Under the four standards noted, fifteen subdivisions, or particular considerations, have been noted. Among these, pick out five which you feel are particularly pertinent for your own consideration at this stage of your development. In the class discussion of this question (or in "bull session" talk about it outside) why are there similarities and differences in the selection made by different students?

4. Are there any standards (or particular considerations arising from these standards) which apply with particular force only to public speaking? To discussion? To conversation?

5. In view of the statement that you will progress only insofar as you establish your own goals and then work systematically to achieve them, what specific standards will you establish for yourself for achievement during this course? If you should choose to adapt to your own needs all the suggested standards, which ones do you personally consider of most importance to yourself?

Projects for Speaking and Writing

1. Write down several reasons why it is difficult to establish a set of standards for evaluating the worth of conversation. Despite these difficulties, what standards would you suggest? Present these either in a brief talk to your class or in a short essay to be handed to your instructor.

2. Analyze your present level of ability in relation to the standards discussed in this chapter, indicating in what respects you feel you have greatest ability or weakness. Discuss this exercise outside of class with three or four of your classmates. Together with them, draw up in writing a brief list of requirements which you all feel should be applied in the judgment of talks to be given in your class during the next several weeks. As these reports are presented in class from each such "committee" of students, the class as a whole might decide on the standards by which they feel its first talks should be evaluated.

3. As you listen to the introductory talks given in your class, write a brief paper indicating which standards seem to be met most effectively and which ones are violated, and hence in need of special attention.

4. If there is some nationally or internationally famous speaker whom you particularly admire for his speaking ability (whether you like or dislike the nature of the influence he is exerting), evaluate his speaking in terms of the four standards we have discussed. See to what extent your

liking or disliking his views and personality may correspond with your judgments concerning his adherence to the standards. The results of this evaluation might be presented in a brief talk in class; and it may well be a subject of your conversation with your campus associates. Perhaps this exercise may become the basis of a letter to your parents, in which you demonstrate how "education" is affecting your opinions of outstanding leaders.

PART II

Developing
COMMUNICATIVE
SPEECH

Chapter 3

You Prepare to Speak

IN A VERY REAL SENSE, everything you do or have done is preparation for your speaking. Some students have traveled widely, some
have had interesting jobs, some have built up unusual backgrounds of
understanding in history or literature or science or philosophy. Everyone has had the experience of being a member of a family, of a community, of a circle of friends; all have gone through lower schools and
are now in college, taking a variety of courses. Most of you are on the
threshold of maturity, perhaps about to cast your first vote, preparing
for a vocation, getting ready to assume responsibilities of citizenship.
There is much in your experience to provide knowledge, ideas, feelings,
convictions, doubts, and questions.

Possibly you may be one who has not had unusual experiences;
and temperamentally you may not be drawn to strong advocacy of
social causes. You may incline to think of yourself as being "just
average," and this may lead you to fear that you are not very well
suited to being a public speaker. The fact is that your very normality
does insure that your opinions and attitudes are so much like those of
your fellows that you have a sound basis for the effective give-and-take
of ideas that provides the basis for communication.

Actually, our everyday conversation involves many of the principles of effective speech. When you converse, you introduce topics;
you analyze ideas; you have some purpose you want to achieve; you
try to create interest and hold attention; you organize your ideas into
some meaningful sequence; you use illustrations to make your meaning
clear. These factors are always present in all manner of speech, whether

51

you are addressing your roommate or standing on your feet addressing an audience of a hundred. In both situations the chief concern is whether the message you really do want to convey is received and interpreted as you wish it to be.

○ NEED FOR PREPARATION

Why, then, if what you have always been doing is the sum and substance of good speaking, do you need now to make a special study of the principles of effective speech? One reason is that in casual conversation you have not been accustomed to accomplishing the several processes just described with precision or completeness. You have known "something" about topics you talk about, but in ordinary conversation you have not felt impelled to know the subject matter thoroughly or to examine with care the implications of what you say. Your analysis of ideas has probably been hit-or-miss rather than systematic. You have perhaps never been aware of the wide range of available types of illustrative material. There remains a great deal to learn about how to develop interest, how to organize your thoughts, how to adapt them to the specific needs of your immediate listeners. There is much to learn about the methods of exposition, persuasion, and the use of humor. In other words, your introduction to the elements of good speech has been haphazard and now needs to be brought into sharper focus and more complete development.

Further, as you advance from adolescence into maturity, you will increasingly be expected to exercise more independence and more leadership. When you are on a job, your boss may ask you how the work is going and he will expect a systematic and well-organized report. You will have oral reports to give, both in your college classes and after graduation. You will be appointed to committees where you should contribute to the sound evolution of policies based on group thinking. On occasion you will be called upon for public speeches in which you will exercise leadership in guiding the thinking of others.

Perhaps you have been puzzled on occasion by what is meant by the term *maturity*. You know it is an important term and one you often encounter. When you have sought a summer job, perhaps you have been told you are not mature enough for it. Your parents may have told you that you were not mature enough to take the family car on a week-end trip, or to "go steady," or to get married, or to decide on your own vocational plans. When you have had a conference with your academic adviser, he may have said you do not show a sufficiently mature attitude in your studies.

Maturity obviously is a very desirable quality, yet it is something difficult to define. One aspect of maturity, perhaps its most important ingredient, is the ability to stand on your own feet, with full responsibility; to make decisions and to abide the consequences, whether good or ill, and to assume your share of the burden of making decisions and guiding the thinking of others. All these are qualities that are brought into prominence and are to some degree developed as you move from the casual and unsystematic talk of careless conversation into the realm of more deliberate speaking. In the latter situation you are marked as a leader-of-opinion, which is distinctly a mature responsibility. The purpose of this chapter is to help you set about your initial preparation for that role.

Through the ages, speakers have been looking for some substitute for hard work and preparation, some magic formula for success. Such pursuit is as vain as looking for the pot of gold at the end of the rainbow. There is no formula other than the careful and systematic application of all the steps that make up the process of preparing to speak. And, through the ages, all great speakers have found this to be true; they have accepted the fact that there is no substitute for preparation, no substitute for hard work. Nevertheless, many speech students still grope for a mysterious nostrum that will make them effective; or, failing this, they take refuge in the excuse that they are not born speakers.

No quest could be more futile and no excuse more unnecessary. The evidence is overwhelmingly in favor of hard work and preparation as the surest means to success as a speaker. The record is filled with examples from the lives of outstanding speakers that show diligence and perseverance in their efforts to develop their speaking ability. William Jennings Bryan is one such example. Although he was a poor speaker when he entered college, he grew to be one of America's outstanding speakers. He would go out to an open field and practice his speeches standing on an old tree stump in a cow pasture. After graduation he educated himself rigorously on the function of money in our economy and seized every opportunity to express his ideas to community audiences. After years of effort he finally developed the power that made him a truly great orator.

A speech is a significant event. It is an occasion on which your ideas, beliefs, attitudes, and personality are projected, emphasized, and brought into the central focus of attention of your listeners. While you are speaking, you cease to be simply a component part of the social scene and become, instead, the center around which it is organized. It is inevitable that, as a result of your position, opinions concerning your ability and general social qualities, as well as your ideas, will become more definitely formulated in the minds of all those who hear you speak. Obviously, such a position merits careful thought and preparation.

Although the presentation of a speech is important, there is no reason to think of it as a strange or mysterious kind of challenge. It calls merely for an organized, continuous, coherent, and public adaptation of the best kind of talking you have been accustomed to employ in private conversation. Your speech cannot be constructed of information, ideas, or convictions that you do not possess; it must be planned to utilize the resources you have or can acquire. You should not think of it as a performance, for which you must write a dramatic script and in which you enact the principal role. On the contrary, a speech calls for your best endeavor to represent *yourself,* as naturally as possible, to a larger number of auditors than you are accustomed to addressing in conversational talk.

There are two major aspects of preparation that apply to any job you have to do and any skill you want to develop. The first is the mental attitude and philosophy you need in approaching the objective. The second is the more specific series of steps, principles, and techniques required to accomplish the objective. Both are indispensable. The first requires that you prepare yourself, the second that you prepare your speech. The two processes are closely intertwined.

○ PREPARATION: MENTAL ATTITUDE

There is probably nothing that will contribute more to an attitude of confidence in one's ability to communicate a message than the feeling of being prepared. In our efforts to achieve assurance and confidence while making a speech, preparation may well play the most important part. As we have noted, it is entirely natural that you should approach your presentation of a speech with some concern for its success. You want to do a good job; you are going to be observed by others; the success of your speech means a lot to you. There is no speaker who does not wonder how his hearers are going to react to his remarks. In like manner, the actor approaches the first act of a play, the sprinter anticipates the crack of the starting gun, and the graduate seeks his first important job interview; all feel the same concern for the success of their ventures. This concern is usually manifested by a certain amount of nervous tension which can do us good or harm, depending, much of the time, on whether we feel that we are adequately prepared.

Preparation and Nervous Energy

It is quite generally agreed that the nervous energy an individual builds up in anticipating an event in which he will participate is one of his most important assets when it is directed into the proper channels. The chief factor in making it an asset is the feeling of proper preparation. The speaker who knows what he wants to say and how he wants to say it, the actor who knows his lines and cues, and the sprinter who feels that he is in top physical condition—all will approach the event in a confident manner. Their natural nervous energy will be directed toward an enthusiastic, animated, sincere effort to do their best. It is this feeling of being prepared, coupled with the natural "keyed up" reaction, that brings about the best prospect of success.

But if the speaker, actor, or sprinter sees the event draw near and realizes that he has not taken all the steps he can to meet it adequately, he begins to raise questions as to whether he can succeed: How shall I start? What do I really want to say? Will they like this point? Why didn't I start thinking about this a week or a month ago? It is inevitable that the nervous energy that is good for us when properly channelled then becomes a handicap and that worries develop. This worrying immediately affects our nervous system and our physical actions to such an extent that we begin to doubt our ability to make a speech. As in other matters, an ounce of prevention is worth a pound of cure, and, in this case, the prevention lies in preparation.

Preparation and Confidence

It behooves us, then, to consider some basic principles of preparation, which will serve to give us the feeling of confidence we want.

What is adequate preparation for speaking?[1] We shall soon see that there is a definite system of preparation we should follow and that it involves a specific series of steps. But before we do this, let us firmly fix these principles and suggestions in our minds:

1. *Start your preparation early.* As soon as you know you will have to make a speech, start to plan for it. Think about your speech in terms of the occasion, the audience, the subject, the general purpose of your speech, and the specific purpose. You do not necessarily have to sit down at a desk to do this. Think about your speech as you walk around, as you eat, as you talk with friends. The important thing to remember is that a speech grows slowly. It must gradually become a part of you and your thinking. You must become saturated with its ideas and its purpose. Speaking is your whole self communicating with others. It is not a mechanical presentation of words tacked on externally. The more gradual the process of building and developing your ideas, the more sincerely and effectively will you convey these ideas.

Remember, too, that a short speech does not necessarily require less time for preparation than a long one. Often the reverse is true. A program chairman once asked Woodrow Wilson to make a speech at a future meeting of his club. He asked Wilson how long in advance he would like to be informed of the precise date for the speech. Wilson replied, "If you want a ten-minute speech, I'd like two weeks' time to prepare; if you'll allow me thirty minutes for the speech, I can prepare it in about a week; and if you merely want me to come over and talk for an hour or two, just call me up five minutes before the luncheon." Consider, too, the incident of the preacher who told his congregation, "You'll have to excuse my long sermon this morning; I didn't have time to make it short."

It takes time to prepare a good short speech. Start your preparation *early.*

2. *Spread your preparation over the full time available.* Once you begin your preparation, be sure to spread it over as much time as you have available. You cannot anticipate the exact time required for each of the steps, for this will vary from one speech to another. But,

---

[1] Preparation of speeches is primarily self-education. If you have trouble with this problem we recommend David K. Berlo, *The Process of Communication.* New York: Holt, Rinehart, and Winston, 1960, Chapter 4, "Learning: Communication in a Personal Context."

if you ascertain the approximate total number of hours you have to spend, try to distribute this time over all the days from the time you start preparing until the speech is given. And keep in mind that after you have completed the formal preparation, you will need several days for the speech gradually to become a part of your natural speaking manner. Then think it over for a few minutes at a time as frequently as you can. This saturation process should be continuous.

3. *Work on* all *the steps in the preparation process.* One step in preparation may take only a few minutes, another several hours. If you are speaking on a subject with which you are familiar, which is a part of your background, you may need to spend little or no time in looking up material. But you must not overlook the gathering of material completely, for you will need to give some thought to just what part of your background material will be best suited for the speech. Even though you may feel that you have a clear idea of the arrangement and sequence, you will need some time to put an outline on paper. You may be so familiar with the subject and so confident of your background that you will not require much oral practice. But, in making decisions as to how much time you will spend on each step, you must consider all the steps. Do not skip any.

4. *Plan to spend enough total time.* Several factors will affect the total time needed to prepare a speech. The importance and general nature of the occasion may be the major considerations. We want to do a successful job every time we speak, but it would be unrealistic to say that all occasions are of equal importance. Other factors that will naturally affect your preparation time are: your background of knowledge and experience in relation to the subject; the nature of the subject, its complexity, and its scope; the specific purpose to be achieved; your own experience as a speaker; the nature of the audience; special considerations, for example, the presence in the audience of someone whose opinion you value especially.

There is no formula that prescribes the amount of time needed for the total preparation. You must feel your way, and gradually you will arrive at the method which best fits you as an individual and is flexible enough to be adapted to each situation. Remember that thorough preparation is probably the most important key to confidence. This means that you should start early, spread your preparation time, prepare all the steps in the process, and plan to spend enough total time. The observance of all these suggestions will give you a mental attitude of confidence and a desire to put your best foot forward in accomplishing your speech objectives.

○ PREPARATION: THE SPECIFIC STEPS

In presenting a specific series of steps which make up the whole process of preparing a speech, we are attempting to outline in sequence the things you will do from the time you first learn you are going to speak until you greet your audience. These are shown in a logical sequence which you would normally follow in order to be systematic and orderly. However, you would not necessarily have to follow this order rigidly, and some of the steps might be considered in groups. This would be particularly true of the first major steps of planning, when you address your thinking to the total situation, the objective to be accomplished in relation to your audience, and the nature and scope of your subject. But a word of caution might be indicated against skipping around too much.

One of the most common mistakes made in preparing to speak is that of "jumping the gun" and trying to solve all the problems and accomplish all the steps together. A typical mistake is to sit down with a sheet of paper and start outlining the speech, before the exact purpose is determined, the main points and sub-points known, and the organization and structure of the ideas established.

The best way to approach speech preparation is with the four major steps in mind: (1) you must first *plan* what you are going to talk about in relation to your listeners; (2) you then *organize* your ideas coherently; (3) you *develop* your ideas so that they are clear, acceptable, and interesting; and (4) you *present* them to accomplish your speech purpose with your particular listeners. All of us follow these steps in all our speaking, giving less thought to them in our informal and impromptu situations and more attention to them as our responsibility becomes greater to "make a speech."

We show the major steps and the specific steps under each in the table on page 59.

The first two of the specific steps are discussed in this chapter, the remainder in later chapters.

Steps in Preparing a Speech

Major Steps	Specific Steps
PLAN	1. Choose the topic 2. Analyze the audience 3. Arrive at the purpose 4. Research and gather materials
ORGANIZE	5. Determine the central idea and the main ideas 6. Make an organizational pattern 7. Construct the outline 8. Plan the Introduction and Conclusion
DEVELOP	9. Develop the ideas 10. Consider visual aids
PRESENT	11. Consider wording and style 12. Practice aloud

○ **CHOOSING THE SPEECH TOPIC**

What are you going to talk about? This question plagues many speakers, especially the inexperienced. The greatest mistake many of us make, however, is that of postponing the decision on a topic so long that it necessarily leaves less time than we should have for preparation. Keeping in mind the suggestions in the following paragraphs, try to develop a habit of *deciding on your topic as soon as possible after you know you are to speak.*

Frequently the occasion naturally gives rise to a certain topic; or you are asked to speak on a specific subject. Then this step in speech preparation is decided for you. But in your speech class you will probably be given the responsibility of choosing a topic. It is not uncommon to find individuals who insist that they cannot find a suitable subject. Usually they want to put off the job of planning and preparing the speech, hoping that some happy inspiration will come along and bring them the ideal topic.

If you find yourself in this situation, it may be because you are really trying to find a ready-made speech, which (if it is to be your own) is impossible. The belief that you just cannot find a topic—an unfounded belief for anyone—leads to a defeatist attitude. If you stop to analyze all your experiences, reading, education, attitudes, and feelings, you will realize that you have a dozen potential topics right at your fingertips: campus, local, and national political issues; the international situation; your hobby, or favorite pastime; unusual places you have visited; your belief in some of the finer things in life.

"But," you may retort, "I don't know enough about any of them to make a speech." There is the nub of the matter. The speaker who thinks that he is having trouble finding a speech topic is really pursuing the futile search for the ready-made speech. He wants to reach into his mind, as though it were a filing cabinet, and draw out a speech fully prepared. He tries one topic after another, only to discard each in turn because he does not know enough about it.

It is well to remember that the purpose of education is to expand the mind, not to teach it to feed on itself. The topics about which you know very little are often those that make the most absorbing speeches, because of all you've learned. Although the chief principle of topic selection is that you should talk on familiar subjects about which you have strong feelings and beliefs, nevertheless you must recognize that, even on familiar subjects, you will need to gather sound materials as a prerequisite for a good speech. Even if you ultimately find that all the material you need is in your own mind, you still need to probe deeply to make this decision, and this inevitably means hard work. Remember, then, when you are searching for a good speech topic, it is a *topic* you are looking for, not a prefabricated speech.

Some Suggestions for Choosing a Speech Topic

There is a disciplined and orderly process of deciding which one of possible subjects is most suitable for your speech. The problem is one of selection, not of discovery.[2] The following suggestions should prove helpful:

1. *Draw topics from your own interests, convictions, information, and experience.* The primary thing you have to offer to an audience is yourself. The basic approach to topic selection, then, is what *you* think and feel, not what someone else thinks. You are violating this principle if you rephrase the contents of an encyclopedia or magazine

[2] The role of creative imagination in finding and developing ideas is discussed by 38 writers and other creative thinkers in Brewster Ghiselin, *The Creative Process.* New York: Mentor, 1952.

article. You are representing someone else's ideas as your own rather than communicating what really means most to you or is best understood by you. Whether your experience has been broad or narrow, exciting or commonplace, it is yours, and you should insist upon it with Shakespeare's humble bravado, "A poor thing, but mine own." The significant topics for you to use are those that are most representative of yourself.

2. *The type of influence you wish to exert, what you wish to count for in the community, and the nature of your fundamental convictions will help to determine the subjects you talk about.* Basically this means: What do you want to accomplish by this speech? Perhaps your chief purpose is to further public understanding of preventive health measures; to sell real estate; to be elected to a public office; to share your convictions on world affairs; to improve the general standard of morality. Whatever your fundamental purposes may be, it is in them that you will find speech topics that most truly represent what you are and that therefore will be most meaningful to your listeners. For it is basic to your success in representing yourself that you give them your own most careful judgments. From your purposes in living you can most effectively derive your specific purposes and topics in speaking.

3. *The nature of your choice is almost always limited and directed in part by the nature of the audience.* Although the instructor in your speech class may give you complete freedom to select your own topic, your choice should be determined in part by the interests and attitudes of your classmates. In community situations, the nature of the audience often determines rather definitely the subject matter of the speech. A given organization may have as the basis of its existence the continuous study of local politics; another may be interested in growing flowers. To choose a *subject* that will *interest* your audience does not necessarily mean that you must adopt a *point of view* that will *please* your audience. On the contrary, you may often wish to tell them precisely what they do *not* want to hear: that, as taxpayers, they should pay higher taxes in order to provide better community recreation facilities; that, as students they should forego vacation periods so that they may better prepare for their professions; that, as responsible members of society, they should spend less on luxuries in order to have more to give to the Community Chest; that, as drivers, they should understand local traffic regulations. Your topic

should be selected in part according to the knowledge and interests of the audience and in part according to its lack of knowledge, its errors, and its shortcomings. After all, a chief purpose of speechmaking is to instruct or improve the listeners.

4. *The length of the speech will further help determine the nature of your topic.* A common error of speakers is to try to speak on a topic too broad to be covered adequately in the time allowed. Remember that after you pick a topic and know your general purpose, you will narrow it toward the formulation of your *specific purpose,* and your *central idea.* One of the factors determining the breadth and scope of the specific purpose is the length of the speech.

In a five-minute speech, you could not accomplish much on the broad topic of Russian-American relations. If this is your area of interest, start limiting it to a narrowed phase, such as the mistakes made at Yalta. The narrowing-down process is a basic part of topic selection, and you will do this progressively until you have arrived at perhaps one key aspect of the subject that you want to discuss. Or again, you may start with the topic, what is wrong with American politics? After some thought, you rephrase it as, we need more direct representation. That may still be too broad, so it becomes, a plan for the nomination of presidential candidates in direct primaries.

Similarly, your major interest in sports might be baseball, on which you have accumulated a great deal of information. So you decide to make an informative speech on it. Almost immediately your analysis of the subject leads you to realize how broad it is. You could talk on the "history of baseball," "how the major leagues are organized," "how to pitch (catch) (play the outfield)," and perhaps a dozen other areas. Which phase of the subject do you know most about? Which has the most readily available resource material for enlarging your knowledge? In which would your audience be most interested, or in which do they need more information?

You can cover only so much in the time available. Part of subject selection, then, is a narrowing process dealing with the phase, area, or scope to be covered. You are then ready to cast this into the phrasing of your specific purpose, which is discussed in the next chapter.

5. *Accept frankly and willingly the fact that you may have to do some research on the topic.* If you feel in a vague and general way that something is wrong with our American political system but you are not sure just what it is, your first step should consist of a plan for

finding out more about the subject. You may do considerable reading before making up your mind; you may discuss the subject with others, including experts, such as political science professors; and you may do other kinds of research. When you have done this, you will have made two notable advances: you will have added to your own knowledge and clarity of understanding, and you will have prepared yourself to make a real contribution to the knowledge and thinking of your listeners. You have had a great deal of instruction in gathering material in your English composition and other classes. What you have learned in other courses about assembling information will be of direct value in your speech.work. Additional suggestions for gathering material are found in Chapter 5.

The ideal speech topic, then, is one that is drawn from your own interests, knowledge, and convictions, all reconsidered in terms of the needs or interests of your listeners and fortified by enough special study to strengthen your confidence and your ability to achieve clear understanding and valid conclusions.

○ ANALYZING THE AUDIENCE AND OCCASION

Your audience is the specific group of listeners who hear your speech.[3] The occasion may be defined as the specific social context in which the speech is delivered, which includes the audience, the nature of the event, the setting and actual meeting place, other parts of the program, and any other factors giving it special significance. The nature of your audience and occasion will necessarily help shape the development of your projected speech, starting with the question of topic selection and following through other steps of speech preparation, including your specific purpose and theme, main ideas, speech organization, and materials to be used. The entire discussion in later chapters about these and other speech problems is considered in terms of the adaptation of the specific speech principle to the specific audience. We therefore see that audience analysis is a continuing problem.

When you are asked to make a speech in class, you of course know the nature of your audience, but you will still need to make an analysis of it in relation to the speech at hand. Normally you will be

---

[3] *Cf.* H. L. Hollingworth, *The Psychology of the Audience.* New York: American Book, 1935; and Alfred R. Lindesmith and Anselm Strauss, *Social Psychology,* Rev. New York: Holt, Rinehart, and Winston, 1956.

Surroundings make a difference . . .

The physical surroundings, the number and nature of the listeners, and the occasion are factors the speaker cannot change; but he must analyze and understand them in order to adapt his style accordingly. A formal lecture-hall treatment of the same topic would be inappropriate in style and manner in this setting.

told the length and the type of speech you are to make and perhaps will be given a specific speech plan to follow. When you are asked to speak to a community audience or club or organization, the procedure is quite similar. Such a speech is initiated by invitation, and you are usually told whether it is to be a special occasion, the approximate length of the speech, how it fits into the rest of the program, and other details. If the speech is part of a campaign for the community chest, or for Memorial Day, or for an alumni program, the topic may be suggested by the occasion or perhaps by the nature of the group.

The occasion may have special significance, such as Lincoln's Birthday, Mother's Day, a school commencement, a father-and-son banquet, a presentation of awards, or a sales convention. The audience may consist of the general public, parents, school classmates or friends, business associates, or members of a veterans' organization. The place of the meeting may have a decided influence, too—a church, a beautifully decorated banquet hall, the locker room of a gymnasium, the birthplace of a great man, or a noisy factory. Any special characteristics such as these should be considered in your speech preparation.

Thus, analysis of the audience and occasion is a preliminary planning step in the preparation for speaking that should never be ignored. Many inexperienced speakers prepare their remarks in a vacuum, as though the same thing could be said to any audience on any occasion. As you will find in reading later chapters, this assumption must not be made if one is to become a good speaker. Audiences are complex and audience analysis should be thorough. An audience is complex because people are complex, and it is extremely difficult to discover the composite interest, attitudes, and beliefs of a group of people in relation to your speech topic and purpose. However, this is precisely what audience analysis involves.

Although we usually look for the more obvious factors of age, educational level, occupation, sex, and other conditions in approaching the problem of audience analysis, actually there are more dynamic factors that may have greater importance in a given situation. Such factors may include religion, politics, or special prejudices or feelings that grow out of the given situation or event. These may have greater influence in gauging audience reaction to your message because they form the active background of the audience's thinking and feeling about the subject. For example, during a Presidential campaign, feelings about politics are so intensified that even friendship may be strained; whereas, in the period between elections, people are willing to discuss politics much more calmly and objectively. The conscientious speaker will give a great deal of thought to these dynamic and immediate factors.

Frequently the program chairman can supply you with valuable information about the occasion and the audience members. He will usually provide you with such details as who will introduce you, whether there will be a question-and-answer period, whether your general purpose should be to inform, persuade, or entertain, whether your talk should be formal or informal in style, and he may make other suggestions regarding the speech development. The chairman may also be able to supply you with special information or facts that you will want to use in the speech, such as statistical data at a meeting concerned with the Red Cross campaign.

It would be difficult to think of any speech situation so completely colorless and indeterminate as not to have some decisive influence upon the nature of the speeches to be presented. Whenever people meet together, it is for some purpose, which the speech should help to accomplish. Clearly it is the first duty of the speaker to find out precisely what the special requirements of the occasion will be, and his minimum aim should be to satisfy them as well as he can.

○ CONCLUSION

The preliminary stages of preparing to speak involve careful consideration of all the steps in the total process. In the broad area of planning, you must consider your audience and occasion, the purpose to be accomplished, and the subject or topic on which you will speak. These steps in speech preparation are usually accomplished together, as a unit; then you are ready to decide on the amount of preparing you will do in looking up material. Much depends on the attitude with which you approach the problem, the confidence you feel and can develop, the desire to do a good job, and the willingness to spend the necessary time and effort. As in any other skilled job, it is wise to have an over-all view of what needs to be done and to approach each of the steps systematically as part of one integrated process.

The nature and subject of a speech are determined, at least in part, by the occasion and the audience. In starting your speech plan, first make a careful analysis of these features while selecting your topic, then analyze just why you are making this speech and what it will accomplish for you and your listeners. Do not expect to find a ready-made speech in an imaginary filing cabinet, but be willing to look up material and to develop and support whatever topic you may select.

By laying a sound foundation of *planning,* you will be ready to proceed to the next steps of organizing and developing your ideas.

EXERCISES

Questions for Discussion

1. Preparation has been discussed in this chapter in relation to confidence and nervous energy. What are the principles of preparation that will ensure your building confidence and having proper control of nervous energy?

2. How much time do you think it should take to prepare a five-minute speech? How would you distribute this time over each of the major steps in the preparation process?

3. Which area of preparation do you think will cause you the most difficulty? The least?

4. In your experience in other activities or in developing other skills, how much of a part did preparation play? Is it logical to compare speech preparation to the training of an athlete? An actor?

5. The criteria for selecting topics show a variety of factors to consider before deciding on a topic for a speech. What is your reaction to these?

Projects for Speaking and Writing

1. Make a list of topics for potential speeches. What major area of interest do you have which might be the subject of several speeches?

2. Outline your key ideas about the value of nervous energy to a speaker and prepare to discuss them in class.

3. Describe an example of a speaking situation that you attended in

which the speaker showed inadequate or improper analysis of the audience or occasion in the selection of this topic, in his purpose, in the selection of his materials, or in his manner of speaking.

4. Discuss the pros and cons of using a different topic for every speech in class or of making several speeches from one general topic area.

5. Give at least three examples of narrowing a broad topic in order to arrive at a suitable subject for a brief speech.

Chapter 4

Purpose and Central Idea

WHEN YOU LEARNED TO BAT a baseball or to swing at a golf ball, you were repeatedly reminded that the most important consideration is to "keep your eye on the ball." You may have practiced different stances, backswings, grips, follow-throughs, and so on. What you were attempting to do was to make these techniques automatic, so that you could perform them without thinking. Then, when you stepped up to the batter's box or the first tee, you could concentrate on the *one* thing you were training yourself to do: *keep your eye on the ball.*

Similarly, in speaking to achieve a specific purpose, you must learn above all to keep your focus on the communicative ball. In the process of preparing to speak, you give considerable thought to the whole range of techniques of good speaking: to analysis of the audience, selection of a topic and supporting materials, organization, validating forms and methods, delivery, and style. These are all factors to be mastered. Many of them are accomplished before you approach the speaking situation; others must be learned so thoroughly that they become almost automatic.

If you find yourself struggling to remember techniques as you speak, you are dooming yourself to the embarrassment of the country-club duffer who approaches the driving tee with a mind concentrated on holding his left arm straight, keeping his head down and feet firmly planted, swinging his hips, holding his knees slightly bent, and so on and on. The result simply is a mounting and uncomfortable tension, and not better golf but worse. The real purpose is forgotten or subordinated; and even if the duffer is lucky enough to hit the ball, its flight is certain to be in some direction determined by chance.

Preparing yourself for speaking, as the preceding chapter indicates, consists of mastering a wide range of techniques, as well as gathering, organizing, and becoming familiar with a specific body of information concerning your chosen subject. All of this preparation will be fruitful only when and as it is brought into the one central focus indicated by your purpose in speaking. It is this purpose, rather than the general principles of effective speech, that should dominate your attention while you are talking with your listeners.

Even this early in the course you may have noted that one of your major problems is overcoming the emotional discomfort and tension which we call stage fright. You might feel quite sure that you could say the right things, and say them with proper effect, if only you weren't so nervous. But how can you not be nervous? Stage fright will be forgotten if you are prepared; and if you have just one main goal: to speak with your particular listeners in a way to make them understand, appreciate, or accept what you have to say.

Aside from worry about techniques, the chief problem that diverts the attention of a speaker from his purpose is trying to remember what he planned to say. Struggling to recall how you phrased ideas during practice sessions is akin to remembering to stand right and swing right while playing golf. You should have your subject matter so well in mind that you dare to trust yourself to take it for granted. What does require every iota of your attention is how to bring your ideas to bear upon these listeners—right now, while you are speaking—so that they will respond as you think they should. The real problem is your purpose; and this brings us to a consideration of what your purpose may be.

○ GENERAL RESPONSES

The purposes that may be accomplished through speech are best considered from the point of view of the desired listener response. The response you desire from your listener or listeners is, after all, your *goal* in speaking. Abraham Lincoln refused to let his advisers "dress up" his speeches by inserting into them impressive references that would suggest he had had a classical education. He admitted that his talk might not be very formal or dignified, but, he insisted, "The *people* will understand." He kept his eye on the communicative ball; his aim was not to "sound good" but to achieve a desired effect.[1]

A student whose aim is to "recite" fluently a prepared speech (or an essay) is aiming at a false goal and is resisting the opportunity to develop his personal effectiveness. Imagine what kind of golf you would play if your purpose was to impress spectators with your graceful stance! Yet precisely at this point the problem of stage fright emerges. The nervous tension results primarily from the fear of the speaker that he may not look good or sound good—that he may make a bad impression. For a great many students, learning to focus on the communicative goal demands a complete reversal of their past communicative behavior—at least, as it has been practiced in formal situations. In "bull sessions," on the other hand, stage fright is unknown; for on these occasions the aim of the speakers is to get their listeners to agree with them.

All kinds and types of communicative speaking have much in common. All of it seeks to gain attention and hold interest, to be reasonably entertaining or appealing, to give information, and to influence the thought and feeling of the listeners. Even so, we all realize that there are certain categories of general response which, on different occasions, we wish to arouse. We realize, too, that these differences in purpose dictate differences in the kinds of materials we use and in our manner of speaking. When these responses are stated as purposes, they are commonly listed as follows:

> To inform
> To persuade
> To entertain

If we rephrase these purposes in terms of the responses we wish to secure from our listeners, they appear as follows:

> To gain understanding
> To strengthen feeling or create belief
> To achieve interest, diversion, or enjoyment

These three responses may be considered as all-inclusive of the

---

[1] It is interesting to note that on occasions when Lincoln was instructing others to speak he discussed not what was to be said but what was to be accomplished—what responses were to be elicited. See, for instance, his instructions to General Grant in Carl Sandburg's *The War Years*. New York: Harcourt, 1937, Vol. II, pp. 543–544.

whole range of effects a speaker might have on the behavior of his listeners. But we know that some of the effects we seek are covert, or hidden, like getting listeners to change their minds or enabling them to understand an idea or a process. Other effects we sometimes seek are overt, or open—as when we want a listener to do something (such as raise his hand or answer a question). Because there are these two classes of response—covert and overt—it is helpful to restate once again the general responses we seek from our listeners, this time in six categories:

Covert responses	*Overt responses*
To gain understanding	To apply the information
To strengthen feeling or create belief	To *do* something based on feeling or belief
To achieve interest, diversion, or enjoyment	To express emotional reaction with laughter, tears, or applause.

Gaining Understanding

Everyone can improve his own personal effectiveness by improving his ability to get others to understand something. Every roommate, fraternity brother or sorority sister, parent, son, daughter, or teacher—as well as every lawyer, engineer, politician, dietician, businessman, or county agricultural agent—will help himself and his associates to better progress through stimulating others to attain a clear understanding of *an idea*: an idea concerning a process, a place, an event, a person, or a relationship.

In your speech class you will teach, and you will also learn, specific ideas about relationships of senatorial committee work to legislation, of laughter and psychological conflicts, time and space; about such processes as training Peace Corpsmen, timber cruising, and rocketing to the moon; about places like Xochimilco, Ceylon, and Washington, D. C.; about people like an outstanding teacher, Leonardo da Vinci, or the astronauts; things like the Mormon Tabernacle, the porpoise, and your college symbols.

Note that the emphasis was placed upon discussing an *idea* concerning your selected topic. A mere accumulation of information may itself confuse rather than clarify understanding. You could assemble a great many facts about the tariff, for example, which might serve to impress your listeners with the complexity of the subject and perhaps even with the extent of your knowledge of it. But clarity of understanding emerges only when you have a definite point of view around which to focus your facts and thereby bring them into a meaningful pattern.

Your idea may be that tariffs are differentiated by their purposes for gaining revenue and protecting home industries. Or it might be that certain tariff legislation has proved a block to international trade. Or it might be that political and economic consideration of a specific tariff bill are at cross purposes. Until you decide how you want your audience to respond to your discussion and what central idea, if grasped by your listeners, will serve to elicit that response, your factual data cannot be meaningfully selected and organized.

Further, you will need to decide whether the response you desire is covert or overt. Do you merely want your listeners to understand what you tell them; or do you wish to stimulate them to seek further information; or to act on it? Teaching (or informative speaking) is expository, insofar as the speaker tries to impart an accurate understanding of his subject. But there is also in most good teaching a further aim of arousing curiosity and interest that will challenge the students to pursue the subject independently. If your listeners respond to your talk by saying to themselves, "I understand," you have achieved a covert response; if they feel, however, that they do understand what you have said and are impelled to want to learn more about it, you have achieved an overt response. Similarly, if your listeners can now operate a machine or practice a skill, you have achieved an overt response. One vital question, as you prepare your talk, is whether your aim is to close the subject for your listeners or to open it for their own further examination.

Creating or Strengthening Belief

While there are some similarities between speaking to help your listeners understand the nature of issues in a campaign and speaking to induce them to support a particular program or to back a particular candidate, there is also a significant difference. The first kind of speaking is informative; the second is persuasive. In the latter type of speaking, the effort is to move the listeners to greater ardor in their present convictions or else induce them to adopt a new belief or new attitudes. In persuasive speaking you aim to impel your listeners to accept or to feel deeply their support of your views. Further, if you aim at an overt response, you will aim to move your listeners to take some appropriate action based on these strengthened or new views.

The very essence of our kind of democratic living is the encouragement of controversy, as contrasted with the suppression of controversy in areas of the world where that suppression has become symbolized by a "curtain" of censorship. In every walk of life and in every home, office, factory, or legislative group, decisions are made through open, acceptable controversy. Persuasion based on honest inquiry is one of the important means of arriving at decisions. This kind of persuasion— gaining acceptance of a belief—is often called speaking to convince. It results in the changing of opinions, a covert process. The aim of the speaker is to get his listeners to say, "I agree," or "That's right!"

Beyond this, in every home, office, factory, and legislative group, one of the essentials of leadership is a kind of speaking that renews, refocuses, and bolsters in the listeners a sense of family unity and love, or the importance of high quality on the job, or of sacrifice for cherished principles. This kind of talk is often called speaking to stimulate.

In your everyday conversation, or in your speech class, you will often persuade, or be persuaded, either covertly or overtly. For example, you may ask your listeners (or be asked) to:

Feel deeply a greater urgency for a particular cause
    (strengthen belief)
And possibly to contribute to that cause
    (gain action based on strengthened belief)
or
Doubt the effectiveness of some highly regarded organized charity
    (gain belief)
And possibly to contribute to some other agency
    (gain action based on new belief)
or
Feel a renewed conviction that the present, popular policy is best for
    insuring student honesty (strengthen belief)
And possibly to take specific action to insure honesty on your part
    and/or on the part of others (gain action based on strengthened
    belief)

or

Accept or find acceptable an unpopular policy for insuring student
honesty (gain belief)
And possibly to take some specific action to work for adoption of
that policy (gain action based on new belief)

In summary, persuasion is a constant ingredient of our everyday
communication; persuasion works both ways—upon you as a listener
as well as from you toward others; and persuasion sometimes asks
only for agreement, but sometimes for action as well.

Gaining Interest, Diversion, and Enjoyment

When you tell a joke, engage in generally whimsical talk, relate
an exciting experience, or describe unusual facts, the general response
you desire is often merely the enjoyment of your listener. There are
many occasions when relaxed enjoyment, fun, or diversion from the
cares of the day are much needed and desired by speaker and listeners
alike. Appropriate times for entertaining talk may be at the family
dinner table or at a banquet; in the preliminary period before a fraternity business meeting or at a session of the board of directors. At
home and on the job, when tempers are frayed or nerves are tense,
when problems accumulate and personal frustrations mount, there is
a positive therapeutic need for entertaining talk.

Entertaining discourse has its own rules and methods, which are
discussed (as are informing and persuading) in later chapters. What
we wish to do here is to emphasize two points. The first is that entertainment is one of the basic purposes of speech, not to be confused
with the other two; and that it does by itself and in itself represent a
positive value in human life. Our second point is that, however separate entertainment may be, it also has great value when lightly interwoven with either one of the other two general purposes.

If you seek to enlighten or to move your listeners to belief or
action, your fundamental intent is deeply serious. But you often can
reduce tensions, create a bond of good fellowship, and achieve a
willing desire to listen by interspersing relevant anecdotal material
through the serious facts or arguments. No talk can be effective unless
it holds the attention of the listeners, and humor is one of the relatively

easy means of doing this. For both these reasons, then—to contribute to the sheer enjoyment of the company, or to lighten the mood while you enlighten the minds of your listeners—you will want to improve your mastery of the principles and methods of entertaining speech.

As we conclude this section, the important thing for you to note is that talk is not "just talk." It always should be talk for a purpose. It always should be aimed to secure a particular type of response. If your talk fails to be clearly purposive (if your friends don't know, for example, whether you are "kidding" them or slyly attacking some pet beliefs) the effect is to confuse them and is likely to lead to ill will. Before you begin presenting your ideas about any subject to other people, you should decide clearly what kind of response you wish to secure: to have an idea understood, to strengthen or win agreement, or to create enjoyment. These are the general responses toward which all effective speech must be directed. But you do not talk "in general." You talk on specific topics to particular listeners under particular circumstances. Hence we shall carry our consideration now from the general to the specific.

○ SPECIFIC RESPONSES

Our discussion of the basic general responses was designed to help you to understand that what you do as a speaker varies in typical ways depending on the kind of reaction you want from your listeners: whether it is to be overt or covert, and whether it is to understand, to feel, to agree, to act, or to enjoy. We also pointed out at the start of this chapter that you approach every speech situation with your eye on the communicative ball. You do not try, at that time, to remember what words you have prepared, nor to remember a whole bevy of techniques. What you do have squarely in focus is a precise or specific response which you are trying to secure from your listeners. The way in which you prepare yourself should be aimed to free you from any inhibiting worry about forgetting what you wanted to say. It should also free you from uneasy worry that you may not say it properly. Your preparation should free you to be genuinely communicative, rather than restrict you to a mechanical and uninspiring recitation. Our concern now is to help you identify the specific *ball* upon which you should keep your mind's eye while you are preparing and as you are speaking.

The focus at the center of your attention should be an explicit, specific, desired listener response. The essence of meaning, any meaning, is the answer to the question, "What does it make the listener or viewer do?" This is the question which should guide you at every stage of your preparation, from your first choice of topic through the stages of organization and practice. It should occupy your mind as you sit waiting to be introduced; and it should continue to dominate your thinking while you are speaking: "What, specifically, do I want my listeners to do?" This is the question that guides you in defining and narrowing your general topic down to its central idea. It is your cardinal guide to analyzing the audience. It determines your choice of materials and of various methods for handling them. And it indicates (sometimes even dictates) the way you organize your remarks.

In considering a speech you will present to your classmates, you may decide you would like to talk about the United Nations. You recall that on an earlier occasion an architecture major had tried to arouse interest in the problems of designing buildings. You recall that a physics major has discussed the nature of acoustics. Your instructor may have commented on the desirability of speaking with sufficient projection so that every listener can hear you with ease. Your own interest in the United Nations may lie more with the mechanics of communication than with its political problems. This brief analysis of both your own interests and the nature of your audience may lead you to focus your talk on "Architectural Acoustics in the Assembly Hall of the United Nations." The topic now is narrowed and you can begin to assemble the factual information which you must have to develop it. But there still remains the essential question: develop it for what? What do you want your listeners to do about it?

Your first thought is that you don't want them to *do* anything—you just want them to understand the nature of the problem and how it is solved. Here, however, is at least the beginning of the answer you are seeking. You do want them to *understand*. You still have to be much more explicit regarding what you want them to know about the problem and about possible conclusions. Until this decision is made you do not have a specific communicative ball on which to focus.

Perhaps you want them to learn what principles are applied to optimize reflection and absorption of sound—with the United Nations Assembly Hall as your illustration, but with the principles applicable to any auditorium. Perhaps you want them to understand relationships of wave-lengths of sound to resonance in any building. You may want them to recognize the role of the acoustics engineer as a consultant to architects. Or perhaps you may have still a different "specific response" you want to achieve.

As you glance back over the preceding paragraphs, it becomes quite clear that you do not achieve focus by even what seems at first glance to be a quite precise topic: architectural acoustics in the United Nations General Assembly auditorium. It is clear also that of the specific topics listed in the immediately preceding paragraph, while they all deal with some phase of acoustics in the United Nations hall, each one requires quite a different speech: different in substance and also to some degree different in mood and style. Still, however, the focus remains incomplete, for you have not yet dealt with the question of what you want your listeners to do.

Let us say your topic becomes the consultative function of acoustic engineers for architects. As you analyze your classroom audience, you recall that you have in it one student of architecture and one physics major. Others may be majoring in art or agriculture or business administration. Your problem, then, is to decide what you want the various members of the audience to do. What, in short, can you do to speak in a way that genuinely and properly "fits" and will be of value to your listeners? One solution might be to change slightly but significantly the focus of your topic—to make the point that even widely separated vocations do overlap and supplement one another, making the point chiefly with the acoustics illustration, but broadening its application. Whatever your solution may be, at least you have clarified the nature of your communicative problem—how to adapt your own chosen topic with some precision to your listeners.

As we hope the illustration makes clear, the heart of this adaptation lies in the formulation of your specific purpose. And to assist you to keep this focus at the heart of your preparation and delivery, it will be wise for you to write at the top of your outline a clear and definitive sentence which begins, "I want my listeners to . . ." and which is completed with a statement of precisely what response you want to secure, such as, "I want my listeners to understand how acoustic engineers and architects supplement each other's work." Writing out the specific desired response is valuable both to insure that you do have a precise goal in mind and as a reminder to keep your thinking focused on it.

Criteria for Specific Response Statements

Our examples indicate something of the methodology of deciding upon a specific response, as well as the necessity to do so. However, you will need some guide lines or criteria to help you to determine whether or not the statement you arrive at actually is a satisfactory clarification of your focus point. There are several questions that should be applied as tests or criteria:

1. Is the statement really *specific?*

If you state your desired response as, "I want my listeners to understand something about permissiveness in child rearing," this is fairly vague—and not nearly as specific as, "I want my listeners to understand the difference between permissiveness and neglect in child rearing." If your statement reads, "I want my listeners to believe in the effectiveness of the United Nations," this lacks the specificity of: "I want my listeners to believe that the United Nations is the most effective available safeguard of world peace."

2. Is the stated response *achievable?*

In the classroom, and in any other speaking situation, there are factors which limit what can be accomplished by a speaker. You may be able to teach your classmates the meaning of "$E=MC^2$"—but can you do it in five minutes? Can you do it if your listeners are without a background in mathematics or physics? Can you do it on the Saturday morning before the big game? The amount of time you have available, the attitudes and knowledge of your listeners and of yourself, the occasion, and the availability of materials all may affect the practicality of your response-goal.

Moreover, unless you exercise care, you may be tempted to speak to a point that lies wholly beyond the capacity of your listeners. If you should speak for the specific response, "I want my listeners to join the Mayflower Society," you are likely to find it unachievable in the main; but you might succeed if your goal is the response, "I want my listeners to believe that members of the Mayflower Society are motivated primarily by patriotism." To argue that college football should be abolished may be impossible in your situation, but you may be able to achieve the purpose: "I want my listeners to believe that college football has become too professionalized."

3. Is the response *desirable?*

This question raises the problem of social ethics, which has been discussed in Chapter 2. Should your classmates believe in intermarriage of persons of different religions? Or would this lead them to unhappiness? Should you and your fellow students picket the administration or legislature to demand a change in admission standards or a lowering of tuition fees? Or would this act arouse resentment and make any needed reforms more difficult to achieve? Such questions remind us that a speaker must accept responsibility for the influence he attempts to exercise. It is one thing to demand that everyone must have the right to advocate whatever he believes. It is something else to consider soberly whether the speaker has earned the right to communicate an opinion unless or until he really has thought through the consequences of his communication.

4. Is your response-goal *consistent*?

That is to say, consistent with your general convictions. If you speak for admission of Red China to the United Nations on one day, and against it on another, the listeners may doubt your sincerity and your effectiveness will thereby be diminished. What the ancient rhetoricians called *ethos* is the persuasive effect of sound character and general trustworthiness. This is an ingredient of personal effectiveness far too precious to be lightly risked or carelessly dissipated.

Should you encourage others to diet when you obviously are overweight? Should a confirmed smoker ask his listeners to give up smoking? Ralph Waldo Emerson reminded us that, "For the most part, what you are stands over you and shouts so loud I cannot hear what you say to the contrary." Your words should accord with your acts.

5. Is your response-goal *significant* for your listeners?

Of what value is it to listeners who don't play or watch tennis to learn the forehand and backhand grips for a racket? One question you should always ask (before you use up 100 minutes of precious time by making a five-minute talk to twenty students) is whether what you would have them do is of genuine value to them.

The Specific Response as a Selective Process

By keeping your attention focused upon a specific desired response expected of your listeners, you can avoid many errors that are often made by unskillful speakers. As we have indicated, this focus will help relieve stage fright. It will eliminate a great deal of purposeless talk. It will save you from the mistake of commencing a speech about how to improve TV reception with the historical background on the origin of TV (or at least it will guide you toward selecting those parts of the history that may bear directly upon your purpose). It will help you to choose illustrative material that is strictly relevant in addition to being interesting. This focus will help you to select topics and to narrow them down to a useful and manageable form; it will help you to analyze your audience meaningfully; it will largely dictate the nature of your conclusion. For all these reasons, while you are preparing and while you are speaking you must have constantly and clearly in mind precisely how you hope to affect your listeners with what you have to say.

○ A LISTENER GOAL

We are all listeners. As a matter of fact, we each spend more time listening, and in situations where we might be listening, than in reading, speaking, or writing. As we have goals of response when we speak, we also have goals when we listen. Some of these listener goals are discussed in Chapter 11. However, one in particular is important here in order to alert you, as a preparing speaker, to a special requirement that listeners will place on your speaking.

Listening, like speaking, is a selecting process. Your listeners can choose to pay more or less attention to what is being said. You will want to understand listener behavior to find ways to make that attention more, rather than less. Further, listening does not just happen. Your audiences do not become listeners simply by being present—not even when they physically hear the sounds that are uttered. They will listen only as they are motivated to listen.

One of the most important listener goals for your consideration at this point is *listening to learn something.* People enjoy learning new facts, they want to understand, and they are disturbed if they fail to grasp what is brought to their attention. Further, they listen to know, "What's his idea?" or "What is he getting at?" In other words, your listeners will be wanting to know just exactly what they are expected to remember; and they will listen less if what you are saying isn't designed to help them remember.

Listener focus is on the central idea of your message.

○ **THE CENTRAL IDEA**

We have discussed the general and specific responses which you should aim to secure from your listeners. The question that is raised by our consideration of the listener's goal is, "On what central idea should the listener be focused in order to achieve the specific response desired?" The assumption is that you are speaking not because you have to say something, but because you have some *thing* to say. Your own chief motivating urge in speaking should be that you have an important idea which you feel ought to be understood, believed, or acted upon by these particular people; an idea you feel they should remember.

One of the fundamental necessities for meeting listener requirements, and hence for good speaking, is that you should analyze your own thinking to determine what idea it is that you most want your listeners to respond to. Granted that you have an important topic and only five minutes of time, what is it about that topic that you want to impress upon the minds of your audience? What, in other words, is the central idea you consider most valuable to develop?

The process of developing your central idea, and the specific response desired as well, leads you to self-examination. If your topic is socialized medicine, you examine your own convictions and you conclude that, what you really believe is that "No person who is ill should be left without medical assistance." This, then, may become your theme—the central idea that is so important both to you and your listeners that it is the principal impression you want to have carried away with them, because their agreement is the specific response you seek. Or, if you believe that your listeners should or would be interested in the hazards encountered by astronauts, you may decide that problems associated with protection against the multiplication of gravity forces would be most useful to develop. Thus, your specific purpose may be: "I want my listeners to understand how astronauts are protected from unendurable G-forces"; and your central idea becomes: "Astronauts are submerged in water to absorb the shock of blast-off."

The central idea and the desired listener response must be clearly related if your speaking is to be effective. As we have said, the one is the listener focus and the other the speaker focus. Let us say that you are focusing on the specific response, "I want my listeners to understand the basic principle of marriage annulments." Your central idea,

Speaking is preparation . . .

Use conversation as preparation for better speaking. Discussion of a topic tests whether the idea is significant, challenging to others, and communicable. It also alerts you to probable responses, stimulates additional ideas, and provides experience in presenting your viewpoint clearly, pointedly, interestingly, and economically.

on which you get your listeners to focus in order for you to achieve that response might be, "Only fraudulent statements or promises made before marriage are acceptable grounds for annulment." Or, if your aim is to secure a favorable listener response to a program of compulsory health insurance and you think that your listeners would be most moved by the prospect of saving money, your specific purpose may be, "I want my listeners to agree that a program of compulsory health insurance would be best for them"; and your central idea may be, "Compulsory health insurance is economically attractive."

Notice in these examples that each time both the specific response and the central idea are stated in complete sentences. This is essential, not for any stylistic reasons but because the English language and our thought processes operate in such a way that ambiguity is likely to derive from any "shorthand" statements. "G-forces," "marriage annulment," and "compulsory health insurance," are not ideas, they are topics. This can be seen immediately if you attempt to relate responses to them. To have listeners understand them would be too broad; the question is, *what* about them? To have listeners believe or feel anything about them is impossible until you know what about them is to be believed or felt; what is to be accepted and remembered.

It should be clear that the central idea for any speaking must be a single, significant idea. If you find yourself with several ideas about socialized medicine that you want to communicate, you make one of two choices: (1) select just one of them for this particular speech, saving the others for later discussion; or (2) look beyond or behind them for the single theme to which they are all related. Advertisers have long been keenly aware of the penetrative power of unitary ideas. LS/MFT may be right or wrong, but everyone knows what it means. "You can be *sure* if it's Westinghouse," is an idea that you remember. You may not remember all the examples you have been shown of dependability in support of this claim, but you remember it. Advertisers have learned that singleness of impression adds greatly to penetrative power. The same principle applies in speaking.

It should be kept in mind as you review this chapter (and all the others in this book as well) that the process of speaking is a whole process—occurring as a complex intermingling of unbreakable relationships. We are obliged to discuss the various stages of the process one by one, one after another. But your mind in thinking does not work this way, nor does the mind of anyone else. When you select a topic you are simultaneously thinking of what central idea you might develop and what response you wish from your listeners; quite likely, you are also thinking of some supporting ideas or illustrations you may use.

Nothing we say should lead to the idea that the preparation sequence will always follow in precisely the way that we have described. All of the steps must be taken, but each one has some effect on both those before and those after. Thus, you may write down the desired listener response, but sometime during your preparation you may find reasons to modify or alter it somewhat. You may even shift from one aspect of the topic to another that is quite different as you consider something else which may be more important to your listeners. In other words, the creative process in which you are engaged continues steadily—not just until your outline is finally completed and folded up, but actually until you come to the end of your talking. Speaking is a live relationship between yourself, your ideas and facts, and your listeners. If ever you find yourself with a "speech" which is "prepared" in a way that makes it a finished composition, to be delivered precisely as it has been planned, you know that somewhere, somehow you have forgotten the live and vital nature of the communicative process.

◯ TESTING YOUR CENTRAL IDEA

"True greatness lies in being, not in seeming," wrote Shakespeare, and the statement applies with particular pertinence to the central ideas you select and labor to develop in your speaking. How good are they, after all, when you reflect and take time to examine them in the light of calm analysis? Upon close inspection, some enthusiastically garnered ideas may be found to be invalid. Other ideas, which may have seemed commonplace or unpromising at first, grow in weight and value as they are developed and analyzed.

To the casual eye, a rhinestone looks like a diamond. Cheap merchandise is frequently given a polish which makes it more attractive at first glance than articles of substantial worth; and trained buyers, who can accurately appraise the value of an article, are less likely to be misled than are inexperienced purchasers. In making any examination, the first essential is to know what standards to apply. This is as true in evaluating ideas as it is in purchasing jewelry. One can be misled by shoddy thoughts as well as by shoddy goods.

Therefore, a central idea which you have tentatively selected as a basis upon which to prepare to speak should be subjected to the following three test questions:

1. *Is the idea of sufficient significance to merit expenditure of your own time in developing it and the time of others in considering your discussion of it?*

Is it of any practical consequence whether it is true? Are the facts on which it is based interesting, stimulating, or enlightening? Does anyone care about the answers to its questions or the solutions to its problems? Will the subject repay your trouble in analyzing it, investigating, interpreting, and integrating the facts that may support it? Will your work on the idea lead you into useful and stimulating reading and meditation?

If your problem is really vital, it is probable that its solution has already been sought by many, and others may have found solutions more satisfactory than yours. Perhaps your own solution will have little objective value. In that case, it is doubly important that your very search shall have value in itself, providing you with new information and stimulating your thinking along significant lines. Sometimes it is not only the goal we reach that is important, but also the satisfactions and learning achieved along the way. The first test, then, to which your central idea should be subjected is this: Does it have sufficient significance to you and your prospective audience to justify the time and trouble you will have to spend on it?

2. *Does your idea affect you with a feeling of uneasiness arising out of a need for answers to the questions, for solutions to the problems, it raises?*

It is necessary to have or to develop a real concern for your idea before you can make it of real concern to your audience, or before you yourself can work on it with genuine interest. But you may have to work for, and cultivate, this personal interest, as you have to work at other phases of ideational development. If an idea really contains a personal challenge and also has objective significance, you can be very certain that it contains the germ of personal concern and interest for your audience.

It is a familiar fact that the deeper we delve into a significant subject (whether a bidding problem in bridge or an idea for a speech) the more interesting it will become. Best for development are certainly those ideas that have been sown deep in the mind as the result of long experience. Old enthusiasms and long-continued interests yield the most abundant harvests. But your mind should not be allowed to become closed, ruling out all new interests. Our inquiring curiosity normally expands continuously in scope, and we develop interests tomorrow that today are beyond our remotest thought. This process of normal, healthy mental development should be encouraged. Our thinking should be cosmopolitan, not provincial.

You should discard the childish habit of clinging with homesick longing to old familiar thoughts. "I take all knowledge to be my province," wrote the young Francis Bacon to his uncle, Lord Burleigh, in 1592. "There is no information that I would not rather have than lack," Dr. Samuel Johnson told Boswell. Such generous receptivity of mind should be cultivated by all as providing one of the primary requisites of richness of thinking. The mind that simply feeds upon itself will show the effects of malnutrition.

3. *Is your speech idea specific and limited enough to permit it to be clearly and precisely communicated?*

When you are searching for a speech idea, your only legitimate concern is with those that you can pinpoint for communication. Ideas with vague outlines and incoherent implications must be clarified or discarded. To avoid fuzziness in thinking, to avoid talking around a subject without ever quite coming to the point, to avoid confusion as to just what the idea really is, you must pin down your idea as firmly as though it were a specimen on an entomologist's work table. In other words, it must be definitively phrased. Only as an idea is clearly stated does it become a satisfactory starting point for a speech. So long as it remains vague, it must remain in your sole possession, not to be aroused in others. Your job as a speaker is to find ideas that may, by your talking about them, be stimulated to arise in the thinking of your audience.

The three tests discussed above have been placed at the close of this chapter for the purpose of guiding you in the intricate task of finding and evaluating ideas for your speeches. They will have an important bearing, also, on your selection of materials for the analysis, treatment, and ultimate development of your ideas, which is discussed in the next chapter. As you anticipate your successive class speaking and the speaking you may do in your professional and social life, let the tests we have outlined serve to stimulate and guide you in channels that will enable you to formulate and state the best ideas of which you are capable. The application of the three tests must be practiced and learned if you are to develop communicable ideas.

○ CONCLUSION

With the listeners always in mind, the speaker prepares himself for the speaking situation by developing an explicit goal—a specific listener response—which becomes the focus for his thinking all during the stages of preparing and while he is speaking. Recognizing that listeners, too, must have a focus, the speaker formulates a statement of the central idea—the single, specific idea which the listeners are to remember. This is the cardinal message to which he desires a specific response.

EXERCISES

Questions for Discussion

1. Why is it important to think of *purposes* as *responses*?
2. What should the speaker be thinking about as he is speaking? Is this better than thinking about the words he had planned to say? Why?
3. Why might focus on listener response rather than speaker behavior help to alleviate stage fright?
4. Can you think of a single time that you have spoken with people in the past twenty-four hours when your purpose was not to achieve one of the general responses?
5. If you believe that a listener would benefit from understanding how important his college grades will be to him, and you speak accordingly, what general response would you be trying to arouse?
6. Distinguish between *covert* and *overt*. Can you think of some covert responses you may be trying to evoke in your classmates? Some overt responses?
7. Why are knowledge and skill in persuasion important for students today? Should controversy be avoided?
8. Is speaking to gain interest, diversion or enjoyment related to other general responses? How? Is it ever a *primary* purpose? When?
9. Why is it valuable to begin the statement of a specific desired response with the words, "I want my listeners to . . ."?
10. What are the criteria for specific response statements? For statements of central ideas? How are they related?

11. Why is the central idea called the "listener focus?" Why should it be "unitary?"

12. What is meant by the speaker preparing himself? How does this differ from preparing a speech?

Projects for Speaking and Writing

1. Write down several ideas which you might like to talk about. Be sure they are stated in complete sentences. Now consider what your specific desired response might be in each case if you were to talk with (1) the members of your speech class, (2) your roommate, (3) a certain professor or counselor, and (4) your parents.

2. Determine for each of the following situations what might be the general and specific responses you would seek and what central idea you might support to achieve those responses. Make certain in each case that the three answers are consistent.

a. You are stopped for speeding in an open area approaching a town. The policeman says that you were going 55 miles per hour in a 35 mph zone.

b. In a case of mistaken identity, your dean announces to you that you must be dropped from college for poor scholarship.

c. During a holiday visit at home, you meet a group of seniors from your high school who think they would like to come to your college.

d. You decide that it would be worthwhile to talk with your speech class about your home town.

e. You are to be interviewed for a job by a representative of some business or industry or professional institution of your choice.

3. Listen to a visiting lecturer and determine what general and specific responses he is trying to arouse in his listeners. See if you can see clearly his central idea. Estimate whether or not he achieved his specific purpose —the specific response desired—and see if you can analyze why he succeeded or failed.

Chapter 5

Your Speech Materials

STATING AN IDEA does not insure that it will be understood. George Williams, in his book, *Some of My Best Friends Are Professors,*[1] notes that even "at the kindergarten stage of simplicity" a statement, by itself, does not communicate:

> If I say to a small child, "Drink your milk," I am expecting him to interpret the command in a far more precise way than I may be justified in doing. The child may set his cup on the floor, and lap up the milk as he has seen his puppy doing; or he may dip it up with his cupped hand; or he may soak his napkin in it, and then suck the napkin. He is, in all these cases, following my command; he is drinking his milk. Not being a mind reader, how could he tell that when I said, "Drink your milk," I actually meant to say, "Raise the edge of your cup to your mouth, open your mouth slightly, insert the edge of your cup into the slightly opened mouth, tilt the cup just a little, pour a small quantity of milk into your mouth, swallow that milk, then tilt the cup a little more, and repeat the process until the cup is empty."

But it is not even this kind of detailed clarity that does the job. If you try this on a very young friend you are less apt to achieve the obvious desired response than you are to have him laugh in your crazy-sounding face. Parents find more successful means: "Isn't this a thirsty day?" "Superman gets his strength from milk." "Finish your milk before we have dessert."

[1] New York: Abelard-Schuman, 1958.

And when these fail, one parent says to the other, "*You* think of something." Translated, this means, "You research, you rack your brains for some materials that will help us get the desired response." It is the supporting materials (to be discussed in detail in Chapter 7) that do the communicating and increase the probability of gaining desired listener responses. And this is important to realize in a day when people and nations alike, if persuasion fails, turn to coercion as the next (and last) resort.

When listeners should learn, when they should feel or believe, when they should do something, there are ways to move them to do so. Crucial to effectiveness and artfulness in the process are the speaker's materials, for from them his *content* will be selected and adapted to listener knowledge, attitudes, and experiences.

As you prepare for classroom speaking, or any other, you will need to understand clearly the answers to these questions:

1. What sorts of materials?
2. How much material?
3. Where will I find materials?

○ STARTING THE SEARCH FOR MATERIALS

As in other kinds of work that you do, this search for materials needs to progress through several stages. First, you have to prepare yourself to begin by determining what you want to accomplish with your speech. From this as basis, you can decide how to set about the preliminary analysis of your own background related to the topic, of your listener's needs and interests, and of the availability of additional factual data. This preliminary stage, which we shall now describe for you, must precede the later systematic search for added materials and the building of a permanent speech file.

What Sorts of Materials?

A student's first thought might be, "I need to find out as much as possible about the subject." But this is only part of the process. If it were all, there would be no need to concern yourself with audience analysis, occasion, purpose. As a matter of fact you have probably missed some communicative goals when you said, "I had the subject down cold." The question for a speaker is not merely "How much do I know about the topic?" but "What do I know about anything that will make the central idea understandable or believable; that will serve to introduce that idea to my listeners; that will serve to make the conclusion memorable, so as to achieve my response-goal?"

You may know all there is to know about electrical circuits. But do you know enough to get your sister or a speech class to understand, really understand, concepts involving voltage, amperage, resistance, and the like? Part of what you need to know is related less to the nature of the subject than it is to the nature of the listeners. At least one basic text on electricity draws from materials on water systems in order to teach by analogy. Abraham Lincoln, to communicate ideas concerned with international diplomacy, frequently drew his stories (materials) from interpersonal relationships between farmers or lawyers.

Thus from all your experiences, all your research, all your browsing may be selected materials which can help you, through adaptation to subject, listeners, and the occasion, to succeed in your response-goal. What sorts of materials? Any examples, experiences, testimony, statistics, stories, comparisons that may have a special relevance to the central idea or the main ideas of your talks; that will get your particular listeners to see these ideas clearly, feel them strongly, believe them, or do what you think they should do about them.

How Much Material?

We have pointed out earlier that preparing yourself *and* speaking are both selection processes. And we have insisted that, rather than preparing speeches, you will be preparing yourself for the speaking situation. If all that you know is just what you say, any listeners will sense that you lack authority. And they will pay less attention. If all that you know is just what you say, one simple question can destroy clarity, or force of belief, or feeling in your listeners' minds. If all you know is just what you plan to say, you will be unprepared for questions, for listeners' puzzled frowns, for the news of the day which makes a difference in your proposition, or for a related speech which precedes yours.

How much material? The answer should be clear: *you can not have too much material.* If icebergs were only what they appear on the surface, they would have little effect upon shipping. And surface speaking will have little effect upon listeners. What gives icebergs authority in the shipping lanes is the seven-eighths of their bulk below the surface. Likewise, what gives a speaker authority in the minds of his listeners is the seven-eighths of his materials left unused because the one-eighth that was selected was deemed most likely to succeed in the moments of communication as speaker and listeners interact. This is what we mean by the "iceberg technique" in the gathering of materials.

Efficiency in Gathering Materials

It would be discouraging, of course, if this discussion were to leave you with the impression that you must seek out and digest all materials in any way relevant to your topic. This is far from the point. For if you have selected a narrowed topic, a clear, specific desired response and have in mind a central idea which must be understood, felt, believed or acted upon by your listeners, you have already saved yourself much waste effort and time. Imagine tracking down everything on education in preparation for a speaking situation! You would be forever falling behind an army of prolific writers. The same would be true if you limited the topic to, say, high school education. But if you are focusing on, for instance, programmed learning in the high school, you are somewhat, at least, saved. Further, if your purpose is persuasive, you are seeking, generally, for one set of materials; if your purpose is to gain understanding you will be after a somewhat different set.

The fact is, that every step of preparation to this point—choosing and narrowing the topic, analyzing the audience, determining the purpose and central idea—is designed to help you choose efficiently and not be hopelessly overburdened in the selection of speech materials.

Where Will I Find Materials?

Certainly one of the greatest marvels of the electronic age is the amazing computer, with its photoelectric scanners, its maze of internal interconnections, and its insatiable memory banks. But this great wonder pales into insignificance compared with another of man's instruments with multi-channeled scanners, with the possibility of more combinations of interconnections than there are atoms in the

Speech materials exist everywhere . . .

The alert speaker will find materials for speech preparation *everywhere*
—in social activities, in recreational reading, even in physical surroundings. The story heard during a coffee break may be precisely the illustration you need. The magazine article read to fill an idle ten minutes
may provide an idea for your next speech topic. A casual conversation
may be a proving ground for ideas, a stimulus to reshape your outline or
method of presentation. Preparation is a constant, continuing process; you
gain skill by perceiving and testing speech materials wherever you are.

universe, and with unfathomable memory storage facilities. This instrument is the human nervous system.

Each speech student, then, has the capacity for systematic scanning, interrelating, and remembering materials, both within himself and in other sources. The process of preparing yourself is one of processing data from many sources—your knowledge of the topic, of the audience, of the desired response, of speech principles—and adding and interrelating these data with others that you acquire in your research for materials. Once you have committed yourself to speak, as we have said earlier, you must begin your preparation immediately. Even though you will have to put off some preparatory steps because of the press of other work, take the time, as soon as you know the assignment, to feed into the marvelous human mechanism, your brain, the essential data (topic, purpose, central idea) so that the work will begin and will be carried on in part even as you do that other work. Or even as you sleep!

You will be surprised to find useful ideas everywhere. A story in your Russian reader, it may suddenly occur to you, illustrates clearly a point on education or carpentry; you may be struck by the similarity of an engineering principle and an idea on human relations which you want understood by others; you may hear a radio or television speech with materials that testify to the need or desirability of a proposal you plan to make; your roommate may make a chance remark which can be adapted to your communicative purpose. After all, this is what happens to you now in a more or less random manner, and therefore not very dependably, as you prepare to respond to questions every day.

Because materials are everywhere, you can now learn to be more methodical, comprehensive, and effective in preparing for speaking, the effects of which will be profoundly important in your life.

Begin with Yourself

The advice to begin early by "alerting" your nervous system is provided in recognition of the fact that your first source of materials is yourself. This is also the reason for admonishing you to select topics and purposes in which you have a genuine interest. The remarkably stubborn human mechanism *refuses* to process data in which it has no interest.

Remember, again, that in this self-inventory of ideas, you are seeking to find not merely "How much do I know about the topic," but "What do I know about anything that I can talk about to get the desired response?" So you are to survey your perceptions, your experiences, for related ideas; related because they contribute to clarity or force of feeling or belief. This becomes clearer if you remember that one idea leads to another. You know what happens if you begin thinking about some object. It reminds you of something and that reminds you of something else, and so on. Try to recall all your prior experiences, reading, and knowledge that is in *any* way related to the subject.

Continue Through Discussions with Others

If one idea leads your own mind to another, sources are multiplied by bringing in other people. Throughout the preparation process, at every opportunity, turn conversations to the subject of your scheduled speaking. Don't make it an artificial conversation. Don't begin by saying, "I'm giving a speech on the library." It will be more useful to begin with, "Don't you think we should have open stacks in the library?" or, "Do you know about the new reserve system in the library?"

There are at least four values to be gained from such discussions.

1. Other people are sources of ideas that you may use, adapt, or find elsewhere.

2. Conversations with others, as you try to get them to understand or feel or believe, will stimulate in you ideas, illustrations, analogies, things you have heard or read, that you hadn't thought of before and might not think of otherwise.

3. Discussions with others, as you try to get them to understand or feel or believe, will provide a test of some of the materials which you think might help you to your listener-response goal. On the basis of such testing, you may decide to use certain materials and reject others.

4. The best practice for speaking is speaking—speaking in situations where there is human interaction. Such conversations are excellent practice.

○ LISTENING AND READING FOR MATERIALS

Concurrently with talking out your ideas with others, as recommended for the preliminary stage of gathering materials, you should also commence a systematic search for the broader range of facts and more precise understanding which your speech will require. This second stage of preparation involves the utilization of various sources of materials that are readily available to you.

Draw upon Your College Courses

The engineering student who told his speech class how he first learned from a teacher that to achieve an understanding of a vacuum tube one can start with the simple principle of the water faucet illustrates how students can make use of their college courses for speech materials. All the courses you have and are taking are yours to draw upon for your materials. Speech classes are frequently filled with students from many areas of study. Hence, the history major will listen to the student of architecture as he discusses the use of the flying buttress in Gothic cathedrals. The student of forestry has much to tell his classmates about forest conservation, soil erosion, tree planting, identification of woods, and how the killing of helpful insects may be combated. The economics major can draw upon his courses to discuss such topics as the effect of reciprocal tariffs on national well-being and whether the unbalanced budget and deficit spending are really dangerous to the national economy. Science students should learn what people in the field of education are studying. The point to be emphasized is that you, as a college student enrolled in a variety of courses, should draw upon your courses for subjects and materials. In so doing you clarify your own understanding of what you are learning through having the opportunity to present it before receptive listeners.

Make Use of Radio and Television Broadcasts

An ever-present source of speech materials is the constant stream of radio and television programs available almost wherever you may be. Speeches of leading citizens in all walks of life, the broadcasts of news reporters and commentators, and the many forums on which discussions and debates are regularly featured, offer a great range of subjects and materials. *Meet the Press, Reporter's Round-up,* and *Face the Nation* are among those you may find of value.

Listen to Speeches and Lectures

College students are in an enviable position with regard to the accessibility of prominent lecturers. The varied backgrounds of many speakers who visit the campus may be drawn upon to meet the particular needs and interests of students. Likewise, on university faculties are distinguished scholars and authorities who in and outside their classrooms frequently deliver lectures containing valuable speech material. Also, the speech class itself is a forum for the exchange of ideas. Speaking by your classmates will provoke ideas in you and will cause you to want to answer or refute them or to approach certain of their subjects from your own point of view.

The free lecture on the campus, so often poorly attended by college students, is frequently the same lecture that people in isolated places pay good money to hear. These lectures provide another source of speech materials. A lecturer may discuss a topic that has long been of special interest to you. Or, if he is an authority on some national or international subject, you receive the benefit of his knowledge in one of these areas. Whatever the subject treated, you as a listener have the opportunity to acquire ideas which you can later incorporate into your speaking.

Do Systematic and Worthwhile Reading

The declaration of Ralph Waldo Emerson that "Books are the best of things well used; abused, among the worst" is worthy of mention in considering speech preparation. The ideas gained from reading should, of course, be tested and elaborated by your thought and in discussion. Too often we rush to the library and turn the pages of one magazine after another in hopes that some subject will present itself; if one is found, we may offer as our own what is rightly the research material of another person. The student who attempted to pass off as his own material printed in a prominent newspaper column (which his professor had also read) deserved the severe reprimand given him for doing an essentially dishonest thing.

But the uses of reading are infinitely greater than the abuses. Francis Bacon said, "Reading maketh a full man." The acquisition of the library habit is one of the greatest assets of the speaker. A good newspaper should be read every day. Books, periodicals, reports, summaries, digests, and reviews are among the great sources of materials for the speaker. When Senator Wayne Morse referred to his busy colleagues in the United States Senate as an increasingly unread group, he was expressing a tragic fact in the lives of our public leaders. Indeed, most people read too little, and this, although understandable, is inexcusable. Books and periodicals devoted to science, culture, current events, biography, drama, literature, interpretations of history and life, which come from the press in ever increasing numbers, should be read extensively by all speakers who wish to garner new information and thereby enlarge their horizons. Special interests which we have in life will naturally largely determine our selection of reading matter. One should, of course, read in his particular fields of vocational and cultural interests. Nevertheless, the speaker should avoid becoming so specialized that he fails to acquire the breadth of information and ideas which his speaking will require.

The habit of persistent, selective, and discriminating reading will stimulate your own growth as a speaker. Sometimes you may do nothing more than browse in the reading room of a library; again, you will find a book which you may read for days with delight and enthusiasm. As you read for speech materials as well as for interest and enjoyment, you will nearly always discover that your reading becomes increasingly profitable. Reading will make the fuller man and thereby enable you to become the readier man in your speaking.

Make Use of Library Reference Materials

Certain standard reference works are in every good college library, although a given book or periodical may not be readily available. These sources can be used for condensed factual information and for substantial material on almost every conceivable subject. A complete list would be too lengthy to provide here, but all of the following are sources with which you should be familiar.

Indexes

The card catalogue in your library. This index has a listing by author, title, and subject of all the books and periodicals in your library.
Readers' Guide to Periodical Literature, 1900 to date. These cumulative indexes list articles published in popular magazines by author, title, and subject.

New York Times Index, 1913 to date. This work lists alphabetically by subject the news stories published in the New York *Times.*

Cumulative Book Index, with supplements. These volumes list every book published in the United States and Great Britain according to author, title, and subject.

Basic Reference Works

Encyclopedia Americana
Encyclopædia Britannica
Who's Who in America
Who's Who in American Education
American Men of Science
The World Almanac and Book of Facts, 1868 to date
Yearbook of Agriculture, 1894 to date
Catholic Encyclopedia, 1914
Universal Jewish Encyclopedia, 1944
American Labor Year Book, 1916 to date
Familiar Quotations by John Bartlett, 13th ed., 1955
The Oxford Dictionary of Quotations, 2nd ed., 1953
Encyclopædia of the Social Sciences, 1930–1937
Dictionary of American Biography, 1928–1958
Commercial Atlas, 1870 to date
Encyclopedia of Religion and Ethics, new ed. 1928, 7 vols.
Who's Who. This volume consists principally of sketches of living Englishmen.
Dictionary of National Biography, 63 vols. These volumes provide information on prominent Englishmen who died prior to 1900.
Cambridge History of English Literature, 1941–1957
Cambridge History of American Literature, 1938
Oxford Companion to Classical Literature, 1951

Sources on Current Topics

Reference Shelf series
Public Affairs pamphlets
Headline Pamphlets
Intercollegiate Debates
Debaters' Annual
Current magazines and newspapers such as the New York *Times, Christian Science Monitor, Time, Newsweek, U. S. News and*

World Report, Vital Speeches of the Day, Look, Life, Holiday, Harper's Magazine, Atlantic Monthly, Annals of the American Society of Political and Social Sciences, *The Reporter, Atlas, Current*

In view of the availability of a vast number of facts provided in clearly organized and alphabetical order in such works as those listed above, there seems to be little excuse for the speaker who satisfies himself with a thin, superficial conglomeration or for the speaker who abandons a promising subject with the excuse "I don't know enough. . . ." Facts in abundance—specific, dependable, exact—are ready, waiting to be used.

○ HOW DO YOU USE SOURCES?

In Chapter 7 you will deal with specific forms of materials as supports in developing ideas for speaking. There are, however, some important general factors in the handling of materials which must be considered here, for they make a difference in how you may record and talk about these materials. The speaker has certain obligations to meet in his goal of developing speaking and listening effectiveness to serve throughout a lifetime.

"Where did you learn that President Kennedy favors Supreme Court reforms?" a student speaker was once asked. "I read it some place," was the response. Further questioning elicited the information that it came from "some magazine."

For want of the desire and the ability to use his sources properly, effectiveness was lost in this situation. But that is not all. The speaker lowered his standing as an authority for future speaking. And related to this loss was the inevitable reflection upon his honesty because of his willingness to present ideas or opinions from a source he could not verify.

Listeners should and will want to know the answers to these questions about your materials:

1. How do you know?
2. Is this an accurate report?
3. Does this agree with other sources?
4. What does this have to do with the subject?
5. What does this have to do with me?

How Do You Know?

It is first of all only honest to credit the exact sources of your materials. Further, it is dangerous to do otherwise at the risk of your present and future effectiveness in interpersonal relationships. Finally, in most cases, if the listener knows and respects your sources he is more likely to respond in the way you think he should.

Is This an Accurate Report?

Listeners will want to be assured that you quote accurately—and completely. "Eat, drink, and be merry," is hardly an appropriate admonition to attribute to the Bible, where the idea is followed by "But God said unto him, 'Thou fool.' "

Again, it is base dishonesty to attribute an opinion to a source—which that person, author, or group does not really hold—by quoting out of context or by other means of distortion. This, too, is a practice which can lead to both immediate and long-term *in*effectiveness. If a speaker reveals dishonesty even on an unimportant point, listener suspicion of dishonesty may be applied to anything else he has said. In addition, the speaker who uses materials inaccurately must be held responsible (sometimes with justified hostility) for the difficulties his listeners might get into in following through on the assumption that the speaker's report was accurate.

Does This Agree with Other Sources?

Human perception is determined in large part by what a person wants to perceive. You have experienced this when you have misconstrued a teacher's instruction, the radio report of the outcome of a game, or the attitude of a parent on a certain point. Scientists know this and insist on confirming results through repeated experiments and checking with the results of other scientists. Listeners, like the scientists, are wary of single, unconfirmed, results, reports or opinions. The effective speaker, then, must present confirming materials from a variety of sources rather than from just one or two.

What Does This Have to Do with the Subject?

Materials which have been selected for their support of an idea will seldom serve effectively in the same form in which you found them. The speaker must (1) adapt his materials to the ideas which they support, and (2) plan to talk about, or point out, the particular relationships of materials to ideas.

It is all too common to hear a speaker begin with a good story, unrelated to his subject, which gets the desired laughter and keeps the listeners chuckling about it instead of attending to the real message. On the other hand, the effective speaker selects materials, even the humorous ones, which are related to and lend support to his central idea or main ideas. This was done by the speaker who concluded a talk on the forces which are blocking progress in education, delivered to a group of educators, with the words of that comic strip possum, Pogo, "I have seen the enemy and he is us."

Or a speaker may see very clearly, as his listeners do not, the relationship of materials to idea. Then he must demonstrate that relationship. It is not enough to cite an authority who says that an airplane gains its lift not by being pushed up but by being pulled up. The listener will have to be told how the difference between the distances the air travels below and above the wing serves to create a vacuum above, which does the pulling.

What Does This Have to Do with Me?

Besides the relationships of materials to ideas which they support, any listener demands that both materials and ideas have some relationship, some importance, to him. Often, again, materials may be useless in the form in which you find them, yet be most effective if (1) you can adapt them for your listeners, (2) you talk about and point out how listener interests and experiences are involved. Death on the highway or on the battlefield is remote to listeners until they are forced to see and feel how it might affect them. Retiring a national debt of a quarter of a trillion dollars is meaningless until it is translated into what it would cost each of us.

○ INTEGRITY AND WISDOM IN USING SOURCES

Speakers are sometimes led, often innocently, into one of two traps which undermine or destroy their effectiveness. One is the snare of the single source of materials which limits any speaker's ability to serve both his and his listener's communicative needs. The other is the preferable risk of learning which may lead to the discovery that the speaker's idea or purpose, or both, are inappropriate or not true to the facts.

Predigested Sources

The student of speech, under pressure of his many courses, may be easily lured into a false goal in meeting speaking assignments. It must be remembered that the goal is not to make speeches but to learn, through speaking, how to engage in effective communication throughout a lifetime. Yet some will, as we mentioned earlier, be tempted to present speeches which *seem* ready-made in some sources: magazine articles or digests of magazine articles, newspaper stories, published speeches, or even speech outlines in a "fraternity file."

There is nothing wrong with any of these sources when properly and effectively used. They stimulate ideas, and they provide some materials for confirming others and for adapting to your speech purpose and your listeners. And they often suggest additional sources of materials. But there is nothing right, nothing educational, in paraphrasing or repeating from memory, or even extemporizing from a single predigested source.

It is easy for listeners to detect this kind of speaking and to feel cheated in consequence. The vocabulary and style are not the speaker's; the adaptation is clearly to some other (usually more general) audience. But, what is more important, there is little a speaker learns from a mere recital of someone else's ideas.

The essence of originality in speaking comes in the way in which the speaker selects materials and then integrates them with his own knowledge and experiences and the knowledge and experiences of his particular listeners in a particular situation.

A Worthwhile Risk in Seeking Materials

Gathering materials for speaking effectively is a process of inquiry. As an inquirer, sometimes you do not find what you want or expect to find. On the basis of your immersion in gathering available data on the needs of your listeners and on the facts of a topic, you should be able and willing to come sometimes to the conclusion that

Listen your way to effective speaking . . .

When you listen evaluatively to other's ideas you gain valuable help in testing your own thinking, thereby gaining a higher degree of dependability. Aim to be *right*, not merely forceful.

you are seeking an inappropriate goal. Maybe you can't find ways to get a particular group of listeners to understand the concept underlying the laws of thermodynamics. Or maybe you are led to the conclusion that the particular group of listeners has no need to understand it. In either case, the good speaker backtracks, re-examines his purpose and his listeners and comes up with another idea, perhaps closely related, that *is* communicable and potentially important to the intended listeners.

This warning is even more applicable in your persuasive speaking. Before you come fully to the conclusion that your listeners should condone capital punishment, you must make sure they understand the problem capital punishment is meant to solve. Chapter 15 is devoted to this kind of inquiry. So, as you gather materials, you should be fully prepared to discover that you no longer believe your proposition and that, therefore, neither your classmates nor anyone else should be led to believe it through your speaking. In this case, of course, you change the purpose you seek to accomplish.

○ BUILDING THE SPEECH FILE

By your industry and effort as well as by a sensitive awareness of all the subjects about which you think, talk, hear, and read, you will be supplied with materials for your speeches. Cultivate and enlarge these subjects and ideas so that you will have an ever-expanding fund of concepts, convictions, and points of view. All your materials will aid you in the choice of your subjects and purposes; from them you can select a topic that can be welded into a specific speech for a given occasion. The plight of many students who say they cannot find a subject for a speech or who disappoint their classmates and instructor by their shallow treatment of a substantial subject can be readily overcome by efforts expended in assembling in one place the materials which are needed for all of your student speaking.

Techniques of Recording

A notebook is standard equipment of the college student. In it are recorded the most important items from lectures you hear and the books you read. Many of these very items may be used as materials for many of your speeches. More specifically, a section of your notebook should be reserved for your course in speech and for the recording of speech materials drawn from other sources. Possibly you prefer some other recording method. One of the best is to develop a card index file. A few small cards of uniform size, which you carry with you at all times and upon which you record materials of many kinds, can be inserted into selected categories in your permanent file. Your memory, good as it may be, is not perfect enough to enable you to remember precisely what you heard or read two weeks or more ago. Perhaps the method of recording is relatively unimportant; what is important is that you should devise one suitable to yourself, so that you will have the materials you glean readily available for use in your speeches.[2]

Suggested Categories for Recording

We have just stressed that you should be certain that your recorded materials are organized for ready use. Thus, your recordings should not be a disorganized conglomeration of all the notes you have jotted down. Doubtless other categories will suggest themselves as you develop systematic recordings or note taking, but the following suggestions for classification, although not all-inclusive, may be of practical service to you, especially in the beginning:

1. *Make listings of topics or subjects which you might develop into speeches.* Often an event which you observe gives you an idea that you feel you would like to develop into a speech. Jot down your idea at once; you have thus begun your file of topics. Soon the three or four which you have accumulated will grow into twenty-five or more. Some topics will be discarded after thought and reflection as unsuitable, but others will be retained as you continue to add new ones. You will be surprised to find how your file of topics will grow. When you consult it from time to time in anticipation of successive speaking assignments, you will find it a valuable germinator of ideas.

2. *Make recordings of significant facts.* Items of information, valuable facts per se, are indispensable in speech making. You should make a selective recording of them, particularly when they have a bearing upon specific speech topics you are in the process of develop-

[2] These and other methods of recording materials are described and discussed in Jacques Barzun and Henry F. Graff, *The Modern Researcher*. New York: Harcourt, 1957, pp. 22–36.

ing. Sometimes they are of a statistical nature; again they may include or be associated with historic dates, events, incidents, or subjects of current interest. Facts are interesting in and of themselves, and they are especially interesting when they are highly relevant to the purpose and content of a given speech. You inevitably hear and read facts of one kind or another that you were never aware of before. You may be entirely justified in feeling that others, like yourself, do not know of them either. If a fact or item of information strikes you as important and as worth remembering, you should jot it down and file it for future use.

3. *Record striking and significant ideas.* Occasionally, you are struck with the power and force of an idea. It may be a different and unique expression of familiar thought, or it may be a powerful new concept that you have encountered for the first time. Obviously, either should be recorded in your files. The very act of recording it will plant the idea more firmly in your mind and will cause you to weigh and contemplate its worth. It may lose some of its significance after a time or may prove less vital than you first thought, but it may, on the other hand, grow in importance and in turn stimulate other ideas, which will become the essence of more than one good speech. New ideas are so infrequently encountered that when the speaker acquires one he should regard it as a precious possession, to be recorded and made accessible for use.

4. *Record examples, illustrations, and specific instances.* Incidents and examples often provide the highlights of a speech. You need to have a growing fund of them. They serve to make vital, concrete, and picturesque material that might otherwise be abstract and even uninteresting. Concrete comparisons and contrasts, an apt example, or a fresh analogy are needed for practically every good speech, especially for relatively long ones. Your file of examples will serve you well on many occasions. The best speakers have such a file, and one is needed especially by the beginning student of speaking.

5. *Record choice quotations and provocative sayings.* In spite of your best efforts at wording your ideas, you will sometimes find that another—an essayist, a poet, or another speaker—has said it better or has coined a truly fine literary gem which will epitomize what you wish to say. Shakespeare, the Bible, Ralph Waldo Emerson, and many other great writers and speakers have embodied ideas in language which you may want to quote in many a speech. Whether your quota-

tions are epigrams, aphorisms, figures of speech, or poetic phrasings, they make significant supplements to your own words and are, in the statement of Francis Bacon, like little "salt pits" which you may "extract salt out of, and sprinkle it where you will."

6. *Record jokes and humorous anecdotes.* In many speaking situations jokes and humorous anecdotes have a place. Read a speech by Adlai Stevenson if you doubt the helpful place of appropriate humor. You often read or hear good jokes—and generally forget them. If recorded, you will find them of value for many of your speeches.

7. *Record human interest stories.* Audiences welcome stories of extraordinary courage, sacrifice, and virtue. As a reader and observer, you will have many opportunities to acquire a store of them for your files. While they may serve a purpose in almost any kind of speech you deliver, they are especially fitting in speeches intended to stimulate or inspire.

○ CONCLUSION

It is important to realize that the mere statement of an idea does not communicate it and that the sources of new understanding, renewed feeling, new belief, or new action are the speaker's materials, developed and adapted to the communication situation. Adapted materials provide the content of speaking and listening. Discovering materials for effectiveness in speaking is a constant process, guided by formulation of speech ideas and desired listener responses. They are materials with a special relevance for those ideas and purposes: they give promise of supporting or making those ideas more understandable or more believable, thus leading to the listener-response goal. Speech materials are found everywhere that an alert speaker's perceptions are operating: in himself, in other people, in mass media, in bibliographic sources. They must be used honestly and wisely, with listener interests and requirements in mind. And when come upon they must be recorded and stored systematically.

Learning is a risky business. You never know when you will discover that you have been suffering from faulty perceptions and misconceptions. Still this is part of the fun of learning: risking error to make sure. Gathering materials for speaking should not be narrowly construed as merely a process of gathering support or proof. It is, rather, a process for learning the status of the subject, making sure you are right, and making sure your idea is right for your listeners. The materials which you find in the process will also serve to further your communicative purposes.

EXERCISES

Questions for Discussion

1. Why is the statement of an idea inadequate to *communicate* it?
2. How do you decide what kinds of materials you will need?
3. What is the "iceberg technique"? Why is it important?
4. How can you make easier your job of gathering materials for a speech? What can you learn from yourself? From discussions with others? From your other courses? From newspapers, magazines, radio and television? From general reading?
5. What library reference sources are available to you for your speaking? Which ones are you personally familiar with? Which among those listed have you never used? Which sources that have been unused by you in the past could be of most value?
6. What are the five cautions concerning your use of sources?
7. What is wrong with using a single source, or a predigested source? What proper use could you make from even a speech outline in a fraternity file?
8. What is the worthwhile risk you ought to take in searching for materials?
9. What are the seven categories suggested for a speech file? Which of these seem likely to be of most use to you? Are there other categories you would add? What kind of filing system do you find most helpful?

Projects for Speaking and Writing

1. Make a list of at least five topics on which you would like to talk. Jot down the central idea you would like to support about each one and note several main ideas by which you could support each central idea so as to gain some specific response from your classroom listeners. Note what areas of ignorance must be illuminated with fresh information before speaking on these topics.
2. Take one of these five topics and note, in writing, some ideas or facts seemingly unrelated to it that might serve you well in clarifying it for your listeners, or in making it more interesting for them, or in persuading them to believe, feel, or do something specific about it.

3. In your daily conversations, and also in the talks you present in class or elsewhere, make a habit of identifying the sources of the information you present, and of evaluating the dependability of those sources. Note the reactions of your listeners to try to determine whether you are not by this means acquiring more authority and arousing more confidence in your declared opinions.

4. Prepare a five-minute talk for delivery in class in which you reinforce the outline handed to your instructor with an appended note on the sources you have used, from all the kinds of sources discussed in this chapter. Be sure your preparation covers the subject so thoroughly that your own convictions will be supported by a much larger accumulation of data than you have time to present to your listeners. Be prepared to answer questions that may probe into the depth and breadth of your understanding of the topic.

Organizing

THE BETTER ORGANIZED a person's thoughts and activities are, the more he will usually accomplish in all walks of life. At least, he will surely get things done more easily and better than the person who is haphazard and unsystematic. Some of us find it easier than others do to stay well-organized, and have the ability to do this as part of the natural thinking process. Most of us have to work at it and, fortunately, there are some rather basic and specific principles to help us. This chapter will set forth those principles as they apply to speeches in particular, but they also apply to the kind of thinking we should do in all of our relations with people.

For the conversationalist who jumps from one point to another and cannot pursue an idea coherently in talking things over with a friend will find it extremely hard to make the other person understand him. In addition, there will be negative reactions from the listener which are bound to impede the communication between the two. The participant in a discussion, or in an interview, must strive to keep things orderly, developing a logical sequence of ideas, with sub-ideas in relation to them, and a weaving together of his complete remarks into a coherent whole. Justice Benjamin Cardozo once said of our legal system, "We do not pick our rules of law full-blossomed from the trees." The same is true of speech. The orderliness has to be systematically achieved. If it is not, the speaker is likely to find a confused group of listeners who walk away wondering what he had been trying to say.

○ BENEFITS OF ORGANIZING

Two men were overheard in such a situation as they were leaving the room after hearing a speech. One said to the other, "What was he driving at? What were his main ideas?" The other replied, "I'm really not sure, but I did count about seven or eight ideas." The first agreed, "Yes, he seemed to be going from one point to another so much that I found him hard to follow, and I don't know what they added up to."

In these remarks were couched at least two major criticisms of the speaker's organization: first, that seven or eight main points are too many for a speech, and these must have included a combination of main and sub-points; and, second, the speech was so lacking in organization that at least one listener did not comprehend any clear pattern or focus of meaning.

Speech organization is like the structure of a house. Most of us would not think of going ahead with construction without first having a blueprint. Rooms, general layout, closet, porches, exits, and entrances are all planned for orderly living. First we develop the total plan and the basic structure and elevations, then the room layout, and then the details and finishing work. This is like the speaker progressing in his organizing objective of determining his exact purpose, central idea, main ideas, sub-ideas, and their development. The blueprint is to the contractor what the outline is to the speaker.

It is essential to keep in mind that your speech is always for specific listeners. A fundamental principle here is that listeners do not like to have to work too hard to follow what you say.[1] Good organization benefits both listener and speaker.

The Benefit to the Listener

It is unfair to an audience for a speaker to discuss a subject in such a disorganized manner that he makes it difficult for his hearers to comprehend the main and subordinate ideas and to see the relationships between them and such supporting materials as specific examples, statistical data, anecdotes, or quotations. We all know the significance of the oft-quoted remark of being unable to see the forest for the trees.

[1] For a presentation of research studies on the effects upon listeners of varied kinds of speech organization, cf. Carl I. Hovland et al, *The Order of Presentation in Persuasion.* New Haven, Conn.: Yale University Press, 1957.

To present a speech in which the materials are disorganized, unrelated, merely a "crazy-quilt," so that any listener tends to lose connections—or worse still, fails to see any at all—is to impose an undue burden upon the listener. Understanding of a speech depends upon perceiving relationships among its various elements and is best achieved when the major and minor points that the speaker presents are synthesized and related for the best and most pleasant listening and comprehension. Chapter 4 stressed the importance of a specific purpose, by which the speaker directs the audience to the specific response he desires. For accomplishing the goal of his specific purpose, the speaker must depend upon the most careful ordering of his entire speech, from the first main point to the last subdivision.

The Benefit of the Speaker

The hazards of failure are too great for anyone to attempt the discussion of a problem without having drafted a plan (outline) for what he wants to do. We may think that we can arrange our thoughts as we go along or that the speech elements we know to be essential will be recalled and stated at the right time and place in the speech; but the risk is very great that, unless the speaker has planned carefully, such will not be the case. The remark that the best speeches are often made on the way home from the meeting is testimony that after many a speech is over the speaker finds himself recalling either some of his vital materials which he failed to present, or statements which might have been improved.

There is no greater contribution to the speaker's feeling of assurance than that provided by his knowledge that his materials have been so assembled and interrelated that he can move from the beginning to the end of his speech in a systematic and satisfying manner. When we recognize that the very process of organizing and arranging an outline on sheets of paper or cards helps to plant the arrangement in mind and thereby relates the materials directly to the speaker's thought processes, we perceive the primary purpose of this stage of his preparation. In short, the antidote to the rambling, incoherent speech is obvious: it rests with the speaker to organize for his speaking so as to ensure his own success.

The steps in organizing a speech are (1) to arrive at the main ideas needed to develop your central idea; (2) to support them with sub-ideas; (3) to work out a pattern of organization and to arrange your ideas in orderly sequence; (4) to make the outline, and (5) to plan and develop the Introduction and Conclusion.

○ THE MAIN IDEAS

The process of arriving at your main ideas is one of analysis and synthesis of your subject in relation to your central idea and your specific purpose. After you have decided upon what you believe and how to relate this to your listeners in a stated purpose, you should ask yourself: What main, chief, or basic points will support the central idea? These points will constitute the *Body* of your speech, and upon them will rest much of your success in accomplishing your specific purpose.

To determine what main points will support your central idea and thus help you achieve your purpose is not as simple as dividing up a pie. A speaker's mind is usually filled with many thoughts about his subject. At first they tend to be incoherent, possibly irrelevant, and probably too numerous. Ideas, facts, and random thoughts need to be analyzed for their support relationships with the essential main ideas that will best develop the theme and accomplish the purpose of the speech. This process requires a continuous and diligent concentration on the specific purpose and central idea in order to discover and select the main ideas that will best serve your presentation to the given audience.

This process of preliminary analysis, if ignored, often results in the speaker's talking around his subject without ever arriving at its real meaning. His ideas may lack clarity and meaningfulness. He may talk for some time and then have to say, "That isn't what I really meant." If an individual starts speaking before he knows what he wants the listener to grasp (and, unfortunately, this often happens), he finally is forced to retreat from positions he has assumed and lamely to admit that the conception his listeners are deriving from his talk is actually not what he intended to convey. "What I really meant . . ." is an expression that would be needed less often if more time were devoted to thought and analysis before the speaker began.

Arriving at the Main Ideas

Suppose we look at a subject you know something about and assume that you are going to make a short speech on "My Home Town." Your general purpose is to inform, and you decide that the specific purpose you want to accomplish is "I want my listeners to know and understand the kind of town in which I make my home." This is a rather broad and general purpose, and you probably may wish to narrow it, but let's keep it broad in applying some principles of analysis.

The first thing you are likely to do is to think and then put down on paper a list of things about the town that you want to talk about. Your list might be something like this:

KINDS OF PEOPLE

TRANSPORTATION FACILITIES

SCHOOLS

ADVANTAGES AND DISADVANTAGES

WORK OPPORTUNITIES

RECREATION FACILITIES

LAYOUT AND PLAN

SIZE

DESCRIPTION OF BUILDINGS

LOCATION AND GEOGRAPHY

CLIMATE

GOVERNMENT AND PEOPLE

HISTORY AND GROWTH

OUTSTANDING RESIDENTS

PARKS

A look at this list quickly reveals (a) that it is too long, (b) that obviously these are *not* all main ideas, (c) that there are main and sub-ideas mixed together. It will be necessary to group, regroup, and synthesize to arrive at the true *main ideas.* In so doing, decisions will be made as to which are sub-ideas and which may not belong at all, as not supporting the specific purpose. It may also be necessary to revise the specific purpose by limiting it and making it narrower, particularly for a shorter speech.

Now as you look at this random list of topics, you realize that you cannot select from (and add to), the list to organize a speech except in terms of two essentials: (1) what you believe about your home town—which we call your central idea; and (2) what you want your listeners to do, believe, or feel about it—which we call the specific response. Obviously, you may believe many different things about your community; and you may accordingly wish to secure a variety of listener-responses. This means that you could develop several different speeches, each based upon a different central idea and each leading toward a different specific purpose.

For example, you are not quite sure what central idea you wish to develop, nor for what purpose you wish to develop it. But you can look over your random listing of ideas and note several major groupings that seem significant. It will help you toward orderly analysis to make this new, more selective, listing:

1. Physical appearance of the town
2. History of the town
3. Business and industry
4. Social life
5. Educational facilities

These are, indeed, areas of interest or items of significance about your town. But what do they add up to? What feeling about your town emerges from their consideration? What response would you desire or expect from listeners? Thinking of these factors, you decide you might develop the point that your town is a good place in which to rear a family. In this case, your purpose may no longer be to gain understanding but to encourage people to move to it. Now you have a genuine basis for a meaningful selection of main ideas.

Once you see the indispensable necessity of fastening upon a central idea as *the* point of view you wish to develop and upon a specific purpose as *the* response you wish to evoke in your listeners, the problem of organizing a talk ceases to be mysterious or difficult and becomes systematic, not at all hit-or-miss. Just to demonstrate to yourself how easy it is, you now set about organizing not one but three separate talks, all drawn from your original random list of ideas. These take form in your notebook as follows (and if you wish to do the job for yourself, rather than have it done for you, it will not be difficult to make one, two, or three additional outlines along still other angles of the original topic):

Specific purpose: I want my listeners to understand how my home town started and has grown through the years.
Central idea: My home town has experienced a sudden spurt in growth.
1. It is located in a slow-growing area in central Pennsylvania.
2. Its early history showed slow growth.
3. It has grown rapidly during the past 30 years.

Specific purpose: I want my listeners to understand the nature of the business and industry of my home town.

Central idea: My home town is a typical American business community.

1. There are several large industries.
2. There are many small businesses.
3. Recent industrial growth and business prosperity have been reflections of post World War II American prosperity.

Specific purpose: I want my listeners to feel that my home town is a desirable community in which to live.

Central idea: My home town provides good social living.

1. Recreational facilities are varied.
2. Schools and libraries are excellent.
3. Civic leaders strive for steady improvement.

In these examples, the main ideas have been selected, first, to develop a point of view (central idea) about your subject which you feel to be true and significant; and, second, to suggest evidence which will lead your listeners to accept this point of view. The process you have followed was one of initial analysis, in which you thought of many individual aspects of your general topic, followed by a purposive synthesis, in which you selected particular phases of your topic in ways that would serve your specific purpose.

Our discussion thus far has related principally to an informative speech purpose. But, as in the last example, you may, of course, make a persuasive speech about your home town, such as might influence business men to locate a plant there, or other listeners to favor it as a place to raise a family. Or you might simply wish to be entertaining on the subject of the town's recreational facilities.

Principles Guiding Selection of Main Ideas

Here are ten suggestions and principles to keep in mind in selecting the main ideas for any speech.

In general, the main points or ideas should:

Accomplish the specific purpose and support the central idea
Be few in number (two to four)
Be selected in relation to the length and type of speech
Be arranged effectively

In relation to himself, the speaker should consider:
    His knowledge of the subject
    His degree of conviction and range of feelings
    His accumulated materials of support and evidence
In relation to the audience, the speaker should consider:
    Its knowledge of the subject
    Its interest in the subject
    Its attitude toward the purpose

As we have said, the most important factors influencing the selection of the main ideas are the *central idea* and the *specific purpose* of the speech, for everything you say or do should relate to them.

All your main ideas must combine to lead your audience to full understanding of your point of view and acceptance of your specific purpose. By this rule you can determine whether you have properly selected and worded the main ideas.

Main ideas should be few in number. This is true even for lengthy or extended addresses. A common error of inexperienced speakers is to include too many main ideas in a speech and to confuse main ideas with subordinate ideas and supporting evidence. The speaker should sift his thoughts and materials in order to group his ideas into the major points, which should not number more than two to four. There is no rigid rule regarding the number of major points, but a speech with more than four would probably be difficult for the audience to follow and remember and would indicate that the speaker had failed to group and synthesize his thoughts and materials.

○ THE PATTERN OF ORGANIZATION

All speeches must begin, must be developed in accordance with a plan, and must end. This is not to say that arbitrary and uniform rules of step-by-step development apply to all speeches. Variety has a place in speech making, as it does in most creative endeavors. There are certain patterns and principles, however, that can be generally applied. Traditionally, we have tended to refer to the parts of a speech as the Introduction, the Body (or discussion), and the Conclusion. To think of the parts of a speech only in these terms is to attach to them labels which may have little real significance to a given speech as it is actually developed and delivered. The real question is: What is this part of the speech doing to achieve the specific purpose or goal of the speaker with these specific listeners?

Purposive Patterning of Main Ideas

How, in view of the speaker's desire to accomplish his purpose, can he determine what the thought process of an audience is while listening to a speech? John Dewey, in his book *How We Think,*[2] made a significant contribution to an understanding of this question when he analyzed the normal human thought process in terms of the following sequence pattern: (1) Our *attention* is drawn or directed toward a situation or condition in society. (2) The situation or condition gradually appears to us as a *problem.* Whether this problem is large or small, dormant or active, our normal pattern of thinking leads us to investigate its origin, its causes, its present manifestations, and its importance. (3) We next weigh, consider, and apply to the problem a number of *possible solutions.* (4) We then hypothesize the most *satisfactory solution.* (5) This, in turn, must be translated into *action*—not necessarily physical action, but some kind of decision or future thinking in relation to the solution of the problem.

The problem need not be one that requires specific correction or even a solution. Sometimes it requires of us merely an awareness of our lack of knowledge on a specific subject, which is translated into a *desire* for information, which, in turn, may be satisfied by obtaining the information. Thus, the "solution" is really the satisfaction of knowing that we now have the information and can use it. Applying this sequence of problem solving in his book, *Principles and Types of Speech,*[3] Professor Alan H. Monroe has developed, with regard to any speech theme or purpose, a pattern which he calls the *motivated sequence.* The terms that label each step in the speech are intended to characterize audience reaction or motivation as the speech progresses. Closely related to the Dewey thought-process sequence, Monroe postulates the following steps: *attention, need, satisfaction, visualization,* and *action.*

Another writer, Richard C. Borden, has proposed in *Public*

[2] Rev. ed. Boston: Heath, 1933.
[3] Fourth ed. Chicago: Scott, Foresman, 1955.

Speaking as Listeners Like It[4] a formula for the divisions of a speech in terms of the changing attitudes of the listeners toward the speaker throughout the course of the speech. He applies to the parts of a speech these labels: *Ho-hum!*—indicating the indifference of the average listener toward the speech as it begins and the necessity for the speaker to capture audience attention. *Why bring that up?*—indicating the necessity for the speaker to make the listeners feel a need or desire for the subject and purpose. *For instance?*—indicating the listeners' feeling that the speaker should develop his points concretely and with specific materials. *So what?*—asking the speaker to relate the subject and purpose to the future thoughts and action of the listeners in order to answer the question *Well, what should we do about it?*

These formulations of the basic speech pattern in relation to listener reactions are all useful, and it is well to keep them in mind when preparing to speak and deciding upon organizational patterns. We may demonstrate the relationships among these various labels for the parts of a speech by the following table:

The Parts, or Divisions, of a Speech

Conventional Divisions	Dewey's Thought Pattern	Monroe's Motivated Sequence	Borden's Formula
Introduction	Attention	Attention	Ho-hum! Why bring that up?
Body	Problem Possible solutions Best solution	Need (may be in introduction) Satisfaction	For instance?
Conclusion	Action	Visualization Action	So what? Well, what should we do about it?

The Body. Within the broad pattern of organization your speech will follow, you must fit and arrange the main ideas which become the main points in the body of the speech. In considering the major speech divisions, the conventional terms *introduction, body,* and *conclusion*

[4] New York: Harper, 1935. For another "dynamic" organizational plan (i.e., one readily changed to adapt to listener reactions during the presentation), *cf.* Robert T. Oliver, *The Psychology of Persuasive Speech.* New York: Longmans, 1957, Chapter 15, "Organizing the Persuasive Speech."

are used; but you should keep in mind the other labels in the above table as a guide to the progressive development of your ideas in terms of listener-response.

Building the body of the speech involves arranging the main ideas in proper sequence and developing each to its maximum effectiveness. Later chapters which treat of speaking to inform, to persuade, and to entertain present more detailed information on procedure. In this section we consider the basic, most widely applicable, principles of arranging main ideas into a good speech organization.

THE SPEECH TO INFORM. After you have arrived at your specific purpose, central idea, and main ideas, your task of arranging them in the most effective sequence should be accomplished with relative ease, although even this task requires your care and good judgment. Four methods are well adapted to the development and arrangement of informative speeches. They are: *chronological* (time sequence); *causal* (cause to effect); *spatial* (space relations, which may be from north to south, east to west, front to back, or top to bottom); and *topical* (a listing of main ideas in which the order may be from least to greatest from impersonal to personal, from remote to urgent). Perhaps the best guide to procedure is your answer to this question: To what specific method does this topic lend itself?

As has been suggested, your subject for an informative speech may well indicate which method can best be adapted to accomplish your purpose. For example, the *chronological* method is ideal for such a topic as "The Rise of Hitler in Germany," or "The History of Our University." On the other hand, the *causal* method lends itself to such subjects as "Consequences of Health Neglect," or "Soil Erosion: Its Causes and Results." The *spatial* method proved to be best for the student who talked about "Yellowstone National Park." A student who discussed "Placing Furniture for Better Living" also found the spatial method to be most suitable. The *topical* arrangement was found most suitable for a student talk on "How to Play Second Base" and for another on "What to Look for in Judging a Dog Show." Naturally, everything depends on the best arrangement of all main ideas, regardless of the method finally chosen. Perhaps no better suggestion can be made than that all points should be organized to give the best climactic and interest-holding arrangement.

THE SPEECH TO PERSUADE. The patterns of organization of the speech to persuade are more complicated than those of the speech to inform, and many more factors will be involved in the ultimate wording and arrangement of the main ideas. A number of persuasive speeches lend themselves to the *problem-solution* pattern described by Dewey, since most persuasion involves the speaker's advocacy of a point of view, feeling, or action with respect to a difficulty or problem which exists in society. Very often, consequently, the first main point in the body of a persuasive speech is devoted to establishing or reinforcing the listener views that a serious problem exists, and the later ones are arranged to present an analysis of the problem, possible solutions, and the best solution or precise action that is desired.

In many persuasive speeches, because the problem is well known, the speaker will devote but little time to stating and defining it. Instead, he devotes the major part of his time to a thorough discussion of the recommended solution and advocacy of the action he believes should be taken. In such a procedure he is advocating *positive advantages* and *positive action* designed to meet and solve the problem. A genuine crisis in the financial affairs of a fraternity, church, or any other organization calls for remedies and solutions, not for a discussion of whether there is a problem.

In any variation of the problem-solution pattern of development, the main ideas of a persuasive speech typically pose and answer the most basic questions or inquiries that must naturally arise whenever people are facing controversial subjects or issues. These are often referred to as *stock issues* or *stock questions* and are employed in the argumentative or conviction speech rather than in those persuasive speeches in which the basic aim is to arouse feeling. The following are the stock issues in the form of questions:

Is there a need for a change?
Will the proposal satisfy the need?
Is the proposed solution practical?
Will the proposed solution bring new and greater evils?

Other special methods for organizing persuasive discourse will be discussed in Chapter 13.

THE SPEECH TO ENTERTAIN may vary in its organization from the very tight and carefully designed structure of a narrative to the comparatively loose succession of witticisms or humorous anecdotes. Everyone realizes that in relating any narrative (whether a dramatic story of a ghost invading your summer camp, or a simple joke) the effectiveness depends to a high degree on how well each point is established in its proper order and how successfully the transitions are made. Success in either exciting or humorous narration requires skill in building up by inevitable stages toward a climax—which is a precise matter of careful organization. Even in the kind of speaking we have described as "a loose succession of witticisms" or of jokes, the looseness is more apparent than real. If the speaking is to be truly entertaining, the stories must have a genuine relationship to one another—each one becoming a foundation or natural starting point for the one to follow. Moreover, if the speaking is to amount to more than merely a string of jokes, the stories should progress from one aspect of your central idea to another, so that (without noticeable effort or strain on your part or for the listeners) a point of view is gradually unfolded and illuminated. Along with the indispensable characteristics of apparent casualness and seeming ease (which humorous speaking must have), tightness of organization—achievable only by careful preplanning and practice—is essential. Similarly, to create the tense expectancy which marks exciting narrative entertainment, there must also be skill in leading the listeners from one incident or stage of action to the next, with every element making its own calculated contribution to the unity of the whole.

The Introduction

After the body of the speech has been prepared, the logical next step is to prepare an introduction that will be effective with its prospective listeners. In brief, the purpose of the introduction to a speech is to make the listeners receptive to what is to follow. Although an occasional introduction may be relatively lengthy, especially when the subject requires a careful groundwork, the introduction can normally be kept brief if the speaker plans it with care. No arbitrary rule applies. Perhaps the best suggestion is that it should be as long as necessary but as brief as possible. The danger is great, especially when the speaker is limited in time, that his introductory remarks will be too extended and hence will interfere with the development of his subject.

In preparing an introduction, the speaker should ask himself basically: *What should I do or say that will develop a genuine interest and desire on the part of listeners to hear what I have in mind to say?* The introduction is not the speech—it is those prefatory remarks the speaker makes which prepare the audience for the speech. Unless the listeners are well prepared, the remainder of the speaker's task will be extremely difficult. The arousing of attention, interest, curiosity, concern, and anticipation is the key purpose of the introduction.

Although good introductions may vary greatly in method and kind, the following principles will provide a good general guide to their preparation:

1. *You must establish acceptance of yourself as a person.* This involves both the speaker's conduct and the content of his opening remarks. To strive to be pleasant, modest, confident, and direct is a large undertaking, but it is such qualities as these that most readily win a favorable response. To greet the chairman and audience in a courteous manner shows that you are at ease and are approaching your subject with your listeners in mind.

2. *You must gain attention.* Remember that many people have no more than a perfunctory interest in your subject, or even in being present, and that the "Ho-hum" state of mind certainly prevails among some members of your audience. What, therefore, should the speaker do to capture attention and make the audience want to listen? The following have proved to be effective methods:

    a. Give an example to illustrate the significance of what you propose to develop in your topic.

    b. Tell an interesting story or anecdote which is related to your topic and which will lead your listeners to it. (Make sure the anecdote is in good taste.)

    c. Make use of one or more rhetorical questions which will stimulate the audience to think.

    d. Make a startling statement.

    e. Be ready to adapt your planned introduction to a preceding speech or other elements in the immediate situation.

3. *You must arouse a desire to accept your central idea.* In informative speaking you must create a desire for the information. In persuasive speaking you must arouse a feeling of need to recognize the problem or to find an acceptable solution for it. Because listeners vary so much in age and sex as well as in religious, social, cultural, economic, and political backgrounds, the problem of audience analysis is crucial to achieving listener acceptance of your point of view.

4. *You must find common ground.* Doubtless the most effective means of creating audience desire to accept your view or information is to demonstrate that the topic for discussion is one that you, as speaker, and your listeners have in common—a problem that immediately faces every one of us and that we must understand, think about, and solve. The common-ground method is normally employed at the very beginning of a speech, but as a principle it should be considered throughout the speech in order that your selection of supporting material may strengthen the relationship between you and your listeners.

5. *You may need to define some terms.* Consider carefully, in terms of your listeners and your subject, what terms it will be necessary for you to define. Some people understand the term *parity* with respect to the nation's agricultural problems, but others do not. Whatever your subject, decide whether specific terms or words require definition for clarity or for forcefulness.

6. *You may point up the timeliness of your subject or its relation to the occasion.* Every speech has a specific subject and is delivered to a specific public on a specific occasion. You may frequently find it appropriate to refer to the significance of the occasion and to tell why your subject is a vital one for the listeners assembled. Show how your speech bears on the welfare of the listeners at that specific time and thereby makes the occasion a significant one. If, for example, a particular event which has occurred recently or even in the presence of your listeners is relevant to your subject, you should incorporate a few remarks about it in your introduction.

7. *You must make a clear transition from your introduction to the body of your speech.* Many aspects of this principle must be considered, but the essential factor of clarity should be dominant. In the informative speech, it is often advisable to make a direct statement of purpose and a statement of the central idea to be taken up. In the persuasive speech, you may or may not want to do this, depending on the type of persuasion and the attitude of the listeners. Again, the general rule is to make the thinking of your hearers easy. Remember that they deserve to know when you start your main development and when you make a transition from one idea to another. Give careful consideration in your introduction to how you can lead your listeners into your first main point.

The introduction is discussed again in regard to factors of attention in Chapter 8.

The Conclusion

In concluding his speech, the speaker's concern is that his final words still leave a strong impact and advance his purpose. To achieve these aims, the conclusion must be prepared as carefully as the other parts of the speech. The conclusion should center around the question: What final impression do I wish my listeners to hold?

Good conclusions may vary in structure, especially as among different kinds of speeches. Your subject, central idea, and the particular audience you may be addressing are your guides. In later chapters which treat different kinds of speaking, more detailed instructions are given, but certain general precepts are in order now.

In many speeches the conclusion summarizes the main ideas and restates the central idea. This is especially true for the speech to inform, where clear understanding is the goal. Just as in the introduction the speaker motivates the hearers to want the information, so in the conclusion he suggests, besides simply summarizing them, the future use and application of the materials presented. In other words, the "So What?" question should be answered as the speaker visualizes with his listeners the present and future values of the materials he has discussed.

The conclusion of the persuasive speech is more complex and therefore demands a different consideration from that of the informative or the entertaining speech. Summarizing is often wise, even essential, particularly in a speech to convince, in which basic arguments and reasons need to be restated. For most persuasive speeches this summary is combined with appeals to thinking, feeling, or acting. Attention should be focused again on the essence of the speech, and the point of view of the speaker should be made to stand out favorably in contrast to any other. The values and benefits of this point of view should be visualized for future listener guidance and living. Moreover, just as stories, anecdotes, and quotations serve in introductions to focus attention on what will be said, they serve equally well in conclusions to impress and epitomize what has been said.

The conclusion of the speech to entertain is perhaps the simplest and least complicated of all, especially in humorous speaking. The conclusion of a speech of this kind—whose purpose has been to create a mood of relaxation, levity, and enjoyment—must leave the audience in a happy state of mind. One final choice story, a witty winding up, or a pleasant light turn of phrase suggestive of a moral to be drawn, will bring the speech to a quick and happy conclusion. An exciting narrative, of course, should end with the climax—related to the response you want from your listeners.

It was suggested above that the introduction should be as long as necessary but as brief as possible. This principle is equally applicable to the conclusion. Summary and appeal should be concise and pointed. Brevity will prevent you from being anticlimactic and therefore ineffective in the last words you say. Finally, regardless of the kind of conclusion or the kind of speech, always remember that you must "end strong."

○ OUTLINING THE SPEECH

We come now to a more detailed discussion of the subject of outlining—kinds, principles, and model forms—in order to prepare you to give better speeches. The importance of good outlining can scarcely be overstressed.

In brief, the outline is the recorded culmination of your prepared speech organization and development. When you have completed it, you have progressed to a point in your preparation where you can confidently proceed with oral practice. In other words, the outline is the final thought structure of the speech, which you actually put down on paper, and is the indispensable basis for good extemporaneous speaking. In general the principles of outlining that apply to speeches are the same as those you have already studied in your English composition classes.

Applying the aphorism that good writing is evidenced by a full wastepaper basket, you may find that more than one sheet of paper will be discarded before you are satisfied with your final outline for any given speech. There are times when a given subject, by its very nature and your approach to its treatment, will lend itself to rather ready outlining. More often, however, it will exact both time and effort in making several drafts, so that you will have to overcome the urge to hurry and hence do a poor job. Fortunately, outlining is a process which becomes easier with experience: it is almost automatic for an experienced speaker—and an outline that has been prepared according to sound principles offers many compensations for the work involved when you actually come to deliver your speech. The most important guiding principle is that you must think about your subject in terms of *your specific purpose, your central idea, main ideas which support your specific purpose, and subpoints and supporting materials for each main point,* all of which you must write down systematically, coherently, and logically. An analysis and inspection of your first drafts, followed by a reworking of them as many times as is necessary, will enable you to arrive at a final, satisfactory draft.

Keep in mind, however, the following cautions. Your outline is not a straitjacket which binds you rigidly in speaking. Rather, it is a *flexible* working guide to the communication that will take place. It must be adaptable to the live audience, to your individual style as a speaker, and to last-minute adaptations you need to make because of the new ideas and unexpected circumstances that may arise in the speaking situation. Your outline is not an end in itself; it is the *outlining experience* which helps you prepare for speaking. There is, of course, a sense of achievement to be derived from having made a good outline, but remember that you have made it only in order to prepare yourself more effectively.

Types of Outlines

The two basic types of outline are the *topical outline* and the *complete-sentence outline*. These are the types you will doubtless learn to make in your first course in speech.

The *topical outline*, as its name implies, states all the points in the outline as topics, words, or phrases. This type of outlining is adequate when the subject is not complex and the word or phrase readily makes clear the idea you are dealing with. If the subject is more complicated, or if you are advancing an opinion or point of view as in persuasion, it is much better to use complete sentences. In dealing with "My Home Town" earlier in this chapter, we started with the topical form of outline. But when we showed three different purposes and central ideas for three different speeches on this subject, we indicated the main ideas as brief sentences. It is well to get into the habit of using sentences even in a partial topical form, for it helps to keep the point clear in your own mind.

The *complete-sentence* outline[5] states all main points, major sub-

---

[5] The complete-sentence outline, often called a *brief,* is described in many books on debate, including the old classic, William T. Foster's *Argumentation and Debate*. Boston: Houghton Mifflin, 1917.

Outline of One Main Idea
(Complete sentence)

Technical Plot	*Outline (Body)*
NEED OR PROBLEM	I. There is a shocking problem of inadequate medical care in the United States today, *for*
APPEAL: *preservation of human race*	A. Many underprivileged are not getting adequate medical care, *for*
STATISTICAL DATA	1. There is considerably more illness among families on relief and earning less than $2000 a year than among higher income groups. 2. Infant mortality rate among such families is several times higher than that among families earning $4000 or more.
GENERAL EXAMPLE	3. There are many examples of appalling conditions of disease among low-income families, *for*
SPECIFIC EXAMPLES	a. In Altoona, Pennsylvania, slum sections produce many cases: (1). In the home of John Doe . . . (2). The case of the Smith family . . .
CUMULATION	b. In larger cities, such as Los Angeles and Washington, there are thousands of cases.
APPEAL: *preservation*	B. A lack of proper dental care is also apparent, *for*
STATISTICAL DATA	1. In examinations of men for the draft in World War II, the percentage of men with bad teeth was high: a. . . . b. . . .
TESTIMONY	2. Many leading dentists testify to this condition: a. . . . b. . . .

points, and sometimes subsidiary subpoints as complete sentences. It represents the best structure for many speeches as well as the best means for analyzing the support relationships between your ideas. It is valuable especially for subjects that are complex and that require precise phraseology in order to communicate accurately internal relationships. Most persuasive speeches need to be outlined in complete-sentence form. On the opposite page you will find an outline of the first point in the body of a speech for the specific response, "I want the listeners to support a plan for socialized medicine in the United States." This main point deals with the need or problem.

The example of the development of this point also demonstrates the use of the technical plot in the left margin—that is, the indication in the margin of the various devices, methods, and techniques being used, such as forms of support, appeals, forms of reasoning, common ground, definition, and other specialized techniques. The speaker can thus test his development to see whether he has included sufficient and varied materials and methods for a successful speech.

It is not always necessary to use complete sentences in stating subpoints of the level of a, b and (1), (2), which are usually the citation of supporting material to prove or develop the points, provided you understand fully the ideas represented. But it is not difficult to see that if the main and major subpoints were stated in the following topical form, instead of in sentence form, the topics would be entirely unclear to the speaker as the user of the outline:

I. Problem shocking today (*what problem?*)
   A. Underprivileged inadequate (*inadequate as to what?*)
   B. Dental care needed (*by whom?*)

In the complete-sentence outline you note the use of the term *for* or *for example* after each point. This is a useful practice which aids in following the logical continuity of the development from each main idea to its supporting material. Another way to check back to the main idea in order to test the adequacy of the development under it is to read all the subpoints on one level, such as 1, 2, and 3 under A, and then to see whether you can logically insert the word *therefore* before reading proposition A. This would read, "There is considerably more illness among families on relief and earning less than $2000 a year than among higher income groups, *and* infant mortality rate is several times higher than among families earning $4000 or more, *and* there are many examples of appalling conditions of disease among low-income families. *Therefore,* the underprivileged are not getting adequate care; *therefore,* there is a shocking problem of inadequate medical care in the United States today."

When statistical data, specific examples, and quotations are used in an outline, the question arises as to whether you should cite their sources. The logical brief always cites the source, but for practical purposes this need not always be shown in the usual speech outline. Your instructor, however, may ask you to include a bibliography.

Rules of Good Outlining

We should keep the following rules in mind in making an outline, both with regard to the form and appearance on paper and to the logic and coherence of the development of the speech itself:

1. *The title, general response, specific response, and central idea, should* precede *the outline.* These items may be set up on the page like this:

Title: Should labor be controlled?
General response: To persuade (create belief).
Specific response: I want my audience of local union members to believe that controls exercised by the U. S. Department of Labor are desirable.
Central idea: Labor Department regulations assure responsibility of leadership in our union.

2. *The outline should show the divisions of the speech as headings in the center of the page.* The main divisions of the speech should indicate the major speech areas:

Introduction
I. Introductory point
II. Introductory point

Body
I. Main point
II. Main point

Conclusion
I. Concluding point
II. Concluding point

3. *A uniform set of symbols should be used to designate main ideas and subpoints.* The symbols most generally used to designate the main ideas are the Roman numerals I, II, III, etc. Each subpoint is indented and designated by a symbol as follows:

I. Main idea
  A. Major subpoint. If this subpoint occupies more than one line, each succeeding line should start where the first line started,
it should not go back toward the margin like this or like this.
    1. Supporting subpoint
    2. Supporting subpoint
      a. Subpoint or supporting material
      b. Subpoint or supporting material
        (1) Subpoint or supporting material. This level of subdevelopment is generally used for the listing of supporting examples, statistics, testimony, illustration, or similar evidence.
        (2) Supporting material
  B. Major subpoint
  C. Major subpoint
II. Second main idea

In designating the main ideas with Roman numerals, you should start to number initially in each division of the outline. In other words, if the introduction has two Roman numerals, the first main idea in the body should be numbered I, not III, for this is really the first point in the main development.

4. *The main ideas and major subpoints in a complete-sentence outline should be complete sentences.* This has been indicated in our discussion of the difference between the topical and the complete-sentence forms of outline development.

5. *There should not be more than three or four main ideas in the body of the outline.* Hence, the outline of the body should not go beyond Roman numeral IV except in an unusual speech development.

6. *Each point in the outline, main and subpoints, should be proof, explanation, or support for the idea to which it is subordinate.* This is one of the most important rules of good outlining and of good speech development, particularly from the standpoint of the logical

sequence of ideas. Every point listed, at all levels, should be tested by this rule. The main ideas should prove, explain, or support the central idea and the major subpoints should in turn prove, explain, or support each main idea.

7. *There is no formula for the proper length of an outline.* The length naturally depends on the degree of sub-development of each point perhaps more than on any other factor. A good outline should break the sub-development down to the level of symbol 1, 2, and perhaps to a, b, etc. Remember, it is the *supporting material* which is most essential to communicative effectiveness.

8. *The outline should be neat, with a clear left margin.* Use a liberal margin and proper indentation at all levels for a neat outline. The left margin is used to record the technical plot if this device is employed to supplement the outline.

Your outline is a byproduct of your preparatory analysis and synthesis of your ideas and materials. It will provide you and your instructor with a clear picture of that process, from which may be drawn valuable suggestions for improving the effectiveness of your further preparation.

Sample Complete Sentence Outline*

TITLE: To Diet or Not to Diet.

GENERAL PURPOSE: To persuade (create a belief).

SPECIFIC PURPOSE: I want my listeners to believe that they should properly maintain their correct weight, especially during their youth and college years.

CENTRAL IDEA: Maintaining correct weight during college years will promote health and happiness.

OUTLINE

Technical Plot		Introduction
ATTENTION: *Rhetorical* *Questions*	I.	Girls, do you have trouble zipping up your gowns?
	II.	Men, are your shirt collars feeling a little tight lately?
COMMON GROUND	III.	Many of us have this difficulty. If we don't, we are concerned about it in others, or for ourselves in future years.

* Prepared by Marjorie E. Zelko in a speech class at The Pennsylvania State University.

	A.	We rationalize—clothes must have shrunk. I'm just growing.
INDICATE PROBLEM	B.	The problem may be much deeper—anxieties, overeating, wrong kind of food.
TIMELINESS	IV.	The advent of recent miracle products for reducing has focused interest on this problem, and today's style-conscious student is particularly concerned.
	V.	Here we are with excess pounds, maybe three or thirty, and we have the problem of losing them *correctly*.
TRANSITION: CENTRAL IDEA STATED		Let's see why it is important to maintain correct weight while we're young, and how we can do this in the safest manner. Correct weight now means better health and happiness today and tomorrow.

Body

PROBLEM	I.	Overweight college students may be affected at school mentally, physically, and socially.
	A.	The mental effect may be harmful in several ways.
CONCLUSIONS	1.	Others look critically at them.
	2.	They tend to be unwanted and withdraw to themselves.
SPECIFIC EXAMPLE	a.	A freshman girl in our dorm is a typical example.
	3.	They develop poor attitudes toward others.
AUTHORITY	a.	A leading psychologist said that weight consciousness contributes to negative attitudes toward normal social relations.
	B.	The physical effects may be more obvious.
BASIC DRIVE APPEAL DESCRIPTION	1.	It is difficult to keep up the rigorous pace of college life.
	a.	Class schedules are crowded.
	b.	We are under pressure in doing assignments.
	c.	Social and extra-curricular activities are a physical strain.

CONCLUSION	2. The fast pace of living is hard on the body and heart.
AUTHORITY	a. Obesity puts extra strain on the heart, according to Dr. John H. Light, leading local physician.
CONCLUSIONS	b. Extra weight may lead to other physical problems. (1) High blood pressure is a common result.
SPECIFIC EXAMPLE	(2) One student who recently had an appendectomy had to spend an extra week in the hospital recuperating because of the large incision due to his excess fat.
BASIC DRIVE APPEAL	C. Socially, overweight persons are under a handicap. 1. They are often excluded from organizations. 2. They may find it difficult to get dates.
EXAMPLE	a. Numerous examples show this, particularly in fraternities and sororities. 3. Feeling of rejection leads to compensatory eating.
AUTHORITY	a. According to leading psychologists, including Dr. Clifford Adams in the *Ladies Home Journal.*
PROBLEM FURTHER	II. When we recognize the problem, we are inclined to solve it in a number of harmful ways. A. Starvation diets are practiced. 1. It is fairly common to find college students going without breakfast on this campus.
EXAMPLES	2. Cigarette, coffee, and other non-nourishing liquid diets are practiced.
SPECIFIC EXAMPLE	3. Many food substitutes are a present fad.

AUTHORITY	B. Doctors are unanimous that all these are unsatisfactory methods and may be harmful.
SOLUTION	III. The safe and most effective way to diet is to have it prescribed by a physician or dietary expert for your own case.
	A. All of us are different, with different needs and bodily functions to be considered.
AUTHORITY	B. There is general agreement among the experts in setting down a set of principles, as suggested by a leading authority, Dr. Norman Jolliffe.
CLASSIFICATION	1. Body frame and present weight should be considered.
	2. Normal calorie needs are considered.
STATISTICS	a. We need more calories at our age than older persons.
	b. Men need 3000; women need 2000 daily.
	c. Reduce by 1000 to 1500 calories. Do not plan to lose more than two to three pounds a week.
	d. Calories are the basis of your weight control. Buy a calorie counter.
	3. Maintain proper balance of minerals and vitamins as listed in most calorie counters.
AUTHORITY	C. Our own College of Home Economics endorses these principles and has several experts on the staff who will give advice.
	1. Their records include many examples of persons who have dieted successfully.

Conclusion

RESTATEMENT	I. Proper weight control is very important to us as college students.
	A. Overweight affects us mentally, physically and socially.

SUMMARY

B. It is wrong to try to control weight by harmful means.

C. If overweight, diet correctly, with the advice of a physician or dietary expert.

CENTRAL IDEA
RESTATED

II. The habits we form now in this respect will stay with us in later life. We will all be happier and healthier today and when we're older by keeping physically fit in this way.

A. Let's look in the mirror and examine our needs.

ACTION APPEAL

B. Let's start today.

◯ TRANSITION FROM OUTLINE TO SPEECH: PRACTICE

With the analytical thought processes which led to the outlining now completed, the outline becomes the basis for your practice in the delivery of the speech. Your next step might be the preparation of a *key-word outline.* This is composed of key words or phrases selected from the original outline which will guide your memory and help you to achieve greater facility as you prepare for delivery of the speech.

An essential part of good preparation for extemporaneous speaking is practice. After the speech has been outlined, and all your developmental devices are determined, the next step is to practice it aloud—with an audience, if your roommate can be persuaded to listen, or with only an imagined audience if you have to go over it alone.

This practice should consist of going through the entire speech aloud, not once but many times at spaced intervals. And each time *practice using different words to talk about the ideas.* Sure, you will hesitate, pause, grope for words. But you will be extending your readiness to adapt to the listeners for whom you are preparing. Also you will be developing a clear notion of the time the speech will take or the changes you will need to make in order to conform to the amount of time you have been allotted.

The most careful thinking and preparation for speaking will not lead to successful presentation if all your preparation has been silent. You need the experience of going over your selected ideas (and not in the same words) time and again—and *aloud,* just as you will be speaking from ideas when listeners are there.

An opportunity . . .

When outlining is done early, there are many opportunities for improving effectiveness through practice. If your outline contains an "iceberg" of support, use these opportunities to test the success of your validation materials. Your own interest and your ability to elicit interest will increase during this stage of transition from outline to speech.

In all your practice, the key to effectiveness is to keep your listeners always in mind. If your roommate is listening to you, do not prevent him from interrupting you with questions, challenges or suggestions. Keep your speech so flexible in your mind that you are its master, not merely a channel through which it is poured out. Review the objectives of good delivery presented in Chapter 9.

○ CONCLUSION

This chapter has emphasized the importance of good organization to your general ability as a thinker, communicator, and speaker. Careful outlining is necessary for the benefit of both the audience and the speaker. After you have determined the specific purpose and central idea of a speech, the next step is the selection of your main ideas. These are then arranged as the main points in the body of the speech; all subpoints must also be arranged to support the main points.

It has been emphasized, also, that the parts of a speech are designed, in reality, to meet the reactions and needs of the listeners throughout the course of the speech. Different terms for the parts of a speech were presented in a chart to show their relationships. Although in this book we employ the traditional terms *Introduction, Body,* and *Conclusion,* you should understand the other names as designated by certain writers, and your instructor may ask you to outline one or more speeches by the other methods. Whatever the terms employed, all speeches should be outlined, and specific rules for outlining the three main types of speeches—informative, persuasive, and entertaining—have been discussed. In addition, guiding principles for the outlining of each part of the speech—introduction, body, and conclusion—have been presented.

These outlining rules and examples will assist you to accept and abide by the essential requirement that the ideas and materials in every part of the speech must be organized, and they will be the means for actually preparing your outlines. When the outlining is done, your practice of delivery can begin. For the final delivery of a speech, you may wish to reduce the more lengthy outline to one of a key-word or phrase type. By learning to outline well you will have mastered one essential prerequisite of successful speaking.

EXERCISES

Questions for Discussion

1. Do you agree that seven speech points are too many, or do you think the number of main ideas must depend on the subject?

2. What is meant by the statement that, "The best speeches are often made on the way home?"

3. How should an instructor respond when a student tells him: "I was doing all right in my speeches until you made me outline them. Now I'm all mixed up. May I speak without outlines in the future?"

4. What are a speaker's problems in formulating the specific purpose for a speech? How is this related to determining your central idea?

5. How do you suppose John Dewey arrived at his concept of the problem-solving formula?

6. How are Dewey's problem-solving formula and Monroe's motivated sequence comparable?

7. When should a given speech be prepared by means of complete-sentence outlining, and when may a topical outline serve as well? What are the advantages and disadvantages of each? At what point in your preparation should a key-word outline be used?

8. What is meant by common ground? In what part of a speech do you think special attention should be given to it?

9. What are good types of conclusions for the speech to inform? For the speech to persuade? For the speech to entertain?

Projects for Speaking and Writing

1. Select a broad subject and phrase five specific purposes and related central ideas for five different speeches on it. Under each central idea, list three main ideas.

2. Develop one of the foregoing main ideas in topical outline form.

3. Develop another main idea in complete-sentence outline form.

4. Develop a stock-issues sequence of main ideas on a problem which concerns you.

5. Using the same problem, outline a development with a solution by means of the Dewey problem-solving formula.

6. On a subject of importance to you and the audience, talk for two minutes, comparing two possible solutions to the problem involved.

7. With your classroom listeners in mind, develop a one-minute introduction for a speech, utilizing the common-ground approach.

8. As your classmates deliver their speeches, note down their main ideas. Determine which type of organization discussed in this chapter was used by each speaker.

9. Make a complete-sentence outline of a current speech for which you find the full text in your newspaper or in *Vital Speeches*.

10. Listen to a major speech on your campus and write a detailed criticism of the speaker's organization of his materials.

11. Make an outline of a lecture delivered by one of your professors.

12. Outline fully, by the complete-sentence method, the next speech which you are to deliver in your class.

Chapter 7

Developing Ideas

THUS FAR WE HAVE DISCUSSED the nature and purposes of communication, the standards determining the worth of a speech, the means of preparation for a specific talk, the kinds of purposes that motivate a speaker, the kinds of inquiry pursued in gathering needed speech materials, and ways of organizing ideas for oral communication. This chapter is concerned with the development of ideas. Stated another way, our present problem is to describe means by which ideas may be enriched—their significance clarified, their importance evaluated, their attractiveness heightened, their relevance indicated.

If you were to listen on different occasions to three individuals discussing "the values of education," one of them might say very little beyond the assertion that education is valuable; a second might pour out torrents of words that are all but devoid of specific meaning, and the third might make a series of crisp and cogent observations that instantly enlarge your understanding of the values (intellectual, esthetic, social, and financial) that education might have for you. The first speaker obviously needs to learn how to develop, not merely to state, his ideas. The second one also needs to learn how to develop what he means to say, and not merely shroud it in words. The third has learned a systematic method of analyzing, illustrating, evaluating and supporting his subject to serve his own purpose and the needs of the listener.

Some individuals sit silently in conversation and discussion groups, and have difficulty in presenting even a five-minute speech.

143

When questioned, they declare that they "say what they have to say," but that they aren't "wordy," like some of their friends. The glib and fluent ones, on the other hand, may easily command a quantity of words that are repetitive, vague, or largely irrelevant, so that listeners fail to detect any significant contribution to an enlarged understanding of the topic. Our purpose in this chapter is to teach methods of development that will help speakers to explore the genuine resources of meaning in their chosen subjects and to present those enrichments of meaning to their listeners both comprehensibly and helpfully.

The processes we shall recommend are: analytical examination and use of validation forms and validation methods. The following pages explain the functions and means of using each in developing ideas for speaking.

○ ANALYTICAL EXAMINATION

A number of analytical processes are involved in arriving at a sound development of your central idea.[1] These processes are limitation, definition, description, discrimination, qualification, classification, and redefinition or synthesis. As you study (and then put into practice) these processes, you will find them also equally valuable in conversation and discussion.

Preliminary Analysis

"What have we got here?" is a proper question to ask when encountering any new topic. "Race relations" might be a subject you are considering for a speech or for exploration in conversation or discussion. What is race? What particular races do you have in mind? What kinds of relationships are to be considered? What kinds may be taken for granted? What kinds are in dispute? What problems seem to exist? Why? What caused them? What has been done about them? Until such inquiries as these are pursued, the subject is incapable of development. The purpose of analysis is to discover such facts as: whether or why the topic is of importance; why it should be discussed; what aspects of it require consideration; what it really does mean, or what its implications may be for you and your listeners.

[1] For a detailed study of problems and methods of analysis, cf. John W. Keltner, *Group Discussion Processes*. New York: Longmans, Green, 1957, Section II, "Problem-Solving," pp. 26–99.

Use current information . . .

Preliminary analysis of the present situation must be made. Do not be guilty of talking in favor of initiating a program only to discover later that it has been in operation for some time. Use *all* the facilities at hand: library, professors in specialized fields, administration officials, current newspapers, and periodicals.

When the process of preliminary analysis has been ignored, a speaker often talks around his subject without ever coming to its real point. He may talk for some time before realizing that he is getting nowhere. To avoid such a painful dilemma, the following steps are recommended—after you have chosen a subject area and have done considerable thinking, observing, and reading to develop a background against which you can intelligently consider the topic.

Limitation toward a Central Idea

The less you know about any subject, the more broadly—and loosely—you tend to talk about it. For example, when newspapers devote considerable space to our concern over Communist penetration in some new area, you might adapt one of two generalized attitudes: "We have no business getting mixed up in these problems"; or, "We've got to stop Communist imperialism wherever it occurs." As you read more about the problem, you begin to direct your remarks along more specific lines: the differences among the major native factions, the nature of our aid program, the role of SEATO in the situation, or the choice of a possible mediator. An expert on the region might speak in specific detail of the influence of religion, or of the terrain, or of the social system, as each of these affects the people's defense of their independence.

For an example closer to your own experience, if you were allowed thirty minutes in which to prepare a five-minute talk on Civic Responsibility, you might decide to say a few words about what it means to be a good citizen, rewards of good citizenship, and causes and types of civic irresponsibility. If you had several days in which to consider the topic, you would doubtless be able to make a more meaningful talk on any *one* of these four aspects: characteristics of good citizenship, rewards of good citizenship, causes of civic irresponsibility, or types of civic irresponsibility. If you had had courses in sociology or political science, you could speak more specifically about suburban dispersion as a cause of civic irresponsibility, or the need for greater honesty in reporting taxable assets, or the quality of knowledge that lies behind voting on local issues.

Similarly, if you decide to stretch your mind (and the minds of your listeners) with a talk on Plato, you might direct your attention to how he differed from Aristotle, then to how his system of ethics differs from that of Aristotle, then more specifically to how Plato's ethical system emphasized the responsibility of the individual to the community. In each instance, limitation directs your inquiry more and more closely toward the formulation of a precise central idea.

Definition

You always need to know what you are talking about; so do your listeners. This may constitute more of a problem than you suspect. Let us suppose you are alarmed by the tremendous buildup of modern weapons and decide to appeal for immediate disarmament. The meanings you ascribe to these seemingly simple and familiar terms become a matter of immediate importance. By "disarmament" do you mean the complete elimination of all types of weapons and disbandment of all organized forces? Or would you retain sufficient force to exercise police functions? How much and what kinds of forces would you retain? By "immediate" do you mean a discontinuance of already authorized expenditures, a curtailment or abandonment of existing forces, or a prohibition on all or only some new appropriations for armament? Do you envisage unilateral disarmament or a planned reduction in orderly sequence by all (or some) nations?

It will be impossible to determine the facts and ideas you will need to support your point of view until after you decide what you mean by the key terms. Similarly, if you choose to talk about success, or happiness, or courage, or America's role in the United Nations, you can't even commence to think constructively about your topic, much less to talk about it, until you have pinned down its meaning.

Description

Definition points from the word you are defining to other words which are presumed to clarify its meaning. Description points from the word to the thing itself. Happiness might be *defined* by using "euphoria" as a synonym. But happiness could be *described* in terms of contentment in your work and social relations. Often speakers find description more valuable for their purposes than definition. "Asia" becomes "that great land mass of endless plains, sky-towering mountains, and river valleys bulging with peasants toiling and crowding together like ants in an ant hill."

A description of an idea, like a description of a landscape, depends upon seeing it from one point of view. Descriptions are focused around a central idea—such as "his general appearance suggested slyness," and a specific purpose—such as "I want my listeners to be wary of his persuasive charms." Descriptions become meaningful as they are unified around the central idea and point toward accomplishment of the specific purpose. "What I mean by dictatorship . . ." could introduce a general and incoherent listing of characteristics; or it could lead to a tight description of particular factors that make evident its suppression of personal liberties. What you need in all kinds of speaking situations is a clear description of your topic as it looks to you in relation to what you want your listeners to see in it or do about it.

Discrimination

In analysis, the discriminative ability is one that recognizes differences, and as such is of key importance. If your father, listening to a jukebox rendition of rock-and-roll, remarks, "This jazz is terrible," you realize that he has to be told some facts concerning differences in types of music. When a friend tells you he thinks the Un-American Activities Committee of the House of Representatives is unfair in charging a witness with contempt for refusing to answer questions, you might ask him to discriminate among the kinds of questions that are involved.

If you should undertake to prepare a speech on the influence of Taoism upon Existentialism, your first requirement would be to discriminate among the tenets of Taoism and the schools of Existentialism. Listening to a discussion of Riesman's book, *The Lonely Crowd,* you may mentally make a discriminatory analysis of your own personality, trying to decide in what ways you may be "tradition-directed," "inner-directed," "other-directed," or "autonomous." A great many errors of judgment—and speaking failures—result from the lazy habit of lumping together factors that are fundamentally different.

As a sheer matter of convenience, we depend a great deal upon labels and stereotypes, making such comments as, "Of course John isn't progressive; he's a Republican"; or, "He's one of those radical Democrats." The convenience of labeling does save an enormous amount of intellectual labor. But it results in adherence to half-truths and misleading conclusions. When you talk to others on this basis, it is no more satisfactory to them than is your father's indiscriminate labeling of all dance music as jazz.

Good thinking depends heavily upon the capacity to recognize a difference that makes a difference. For example, you might decide to discuss the hypothesis that "group thinking is superior to individual thinking." As you investigate published results of research on the subject, you find it makes a real difference what kind of problem is being thought about, what the size of the group is, and what degree of preparation and ability is represented by the participants. Instead of one arbitrary conclusion, you find that a series of carefully discriminated judgments constitute the right answer.

The same thing is true concerning almost any topic on which you may decide to speak. What is sometimes called the "fallacy of all-ness" should be avoided. When you hear someone saying that there is no good modern art, that all Japanese are imitative, all Agatha Christie detective novels are exciting, or all history proves that humanity is progressing, you know there has been a failure to exercise discrimination. The frequency with which such statements are heard should be a warning to remember the constant need for discriminatory analysis. Sound thinking depends on it.

Qualification

If we always knew the complete and precise truth about whatever subject we were discussing, we might be justified in making categorical statements about it. Generally, however, man's knowledge is surrounded and interspersed with areas of ignorance. Your judgment will deserve and receive higher confidence and respect from your listeners if you do not claim more understanding than you possess.

It is one thing to say, "The Kennedy Administration is popular." It is another thing to say, "The Kennedy Administration seems to be popular among the people I know, even though many complain about some of its policies." Qualified thinking results from realizing the vast difference between knowing and merely assuming. When someone asks you, "What kind of teacher is Professor George?" a qualified answer might be, "In the course I had with him, his lectures were helpful but his assignments were not always clear." Qualification depends upon discriminative judgment. A qualified statement indicates to your listeners that you try to limit your conclusions to the information you possess and are not guilty of rash statements.

Qualification not only is an essential attribute of good thinking; it also helps you in establishing friendly relations with others. If your talk is guarded by such phrases as, "So far as I know," and "To some extent, at least," your listeners feel that you are inviting them to complete or modify what you are saying in terms of their own experience. The habit of qualifying your statements indicates that you respect the opinions of your associates and are willing to reshape your conclusions to accord with new facts or insights which they may be able to offer. It is a sign of open-mindedness and of eagerness to learn more in order to understand better.

Classification

Just as qualification is one fruit of discriminatory analysis, classification is another. Discrimination emphasizes differences among seemingly similar items; classification is a regrouping of items in terms of their similarities. If you are discussing the writing of history, for example, you could classify historians as primarily descriptive, evaluative, or prophetic; you might further classify their subject matter as political, military, economic, or social; you could classify their interpretation of history as focused upon deterministic forces (economic needs, geography, climate, nationalistic sentiments), or upon the influence of powerful individuals. You might classify painting as impressionistic or representative, and wars as defensive or offensive. It is obvious that a large portion of our talk could not go on without classification.

It is also obvious that classification presents many difficulties. A war that may seem defensive from one point of view may appear offensive from another. Social history depends heavily upon economic and political factors. A prophetic history (such as Toynbee's) must be also descriptive and evaluative.

Dependable classification depends upon the definition of key characteristics which are invariable for all the items in the class being considered. Mathematicians can dependably catalog all numbers as either cardinal or ordinal. Anthropologists, on the other hand, have difficulty in categorizing implicit and explicit cultural traits. We may roughly classify some subjects (literature, philosophy, music, speech) as being liberal and others (engineering drawing, genetics, account-ing) as being vocational; yet it is obvious that the distinction is not definitive.

Classifications may be arbitrary or derivative. Arbitrary classifica-tions are based on legal or conventional definitions. In the army, for instance, all ranks below and including sergeants are non-commis-sioned; from the lieutenancy up, all ranks are commissioned. When using an arbitrary system of classification, you need only make clear to your listeners the agreed-upon basis for the groupings. Derivative classifications are presumably based on inherent characteristics of the objects being classified. Their validity depends on the quality of judg-ment on which the derivation is based. If derivative classifications are to be influential with listeners, they need a convincing explanation of their basis.

For example, a particular act may be "legal," but you may think it "immoral." The arbitrary classification determined by law may be easily identified; but the derivative classification required for moral distinction is much more a matter of personal judgment. What you need to do is to define morality, as you understand it, and to show that the act violates this definition. By such a method—but only when your system of derivative classification has been clearly explained—you might classify as "immoral" the failure of parents to discipline their children, or the failure of a nation to safeguard its basic natural resources.

Redefinition or Synthesis

Analysis that proceeds no further than breaking a subject apart does not go far enough. The central idea you hope to support emerges only when you put together your interpretation of the new meaning derived from your limitation, definition, description, discrimination, qualification, and classification. Here, for example, is an illustration of how analysis may be used to develop a central idea in your own speaking:

Language [you may say] is supposed to be a means of conveying ideas. For this reason we might condemn speech that is vague, con-fused, or lacking in precision. However, if you recall some of your own recent experiences, you will notice that you use language in a great many different ways, to accomplish very different purposes.

"Does it look this way to you?"

Analysis is the road to synthesis. Having examined the parts of the subject, put them back together to examine and redefine them in their total relationships. You perceive the subject in a new light and you *test* your perception—"Does it look this way to you?"

Suppose a close friend drops a hint that he feels hurt at not having been invited to a party you had the preceding evening. "Oh, it wasn't really a party," you might say. "I just had a few people in to go over some things we wanted to discuss." In order to avoid hurt feelings, you were really trying to be vague and noninformative. Clarity is one goal of language, but ambiguity is another. When saying what you mean would cause an unwelcome argument, it may be advisable to conceal your actual meaning behind a veil of vague or confused words. The social function of language is to unite people into friendly association, not to divide them by clarification and emphasis of their differences. One of the principal purposes of communication, then, may on occasion be served by deliberate obscurity.

The example is condensed. Even so, it contains two contrasting definitions of language: "a means of conveying ideas" and a device "to unite people into friendly association." You have tried to discriminate and qualify the ways in which words are used under differing circumstances. You have described the use of language by presenting an example, and you have classified language-usage into two principal categories. Finally, you synthesized your analysis by concluding that the use of language to avoid definite meaning can on occasion serve a communicative purpose. What you meant was communicated in part by taking the topic apart and was clarified by putting it together in a new way. This is the function of synthesis or redefinition.

○ VALIDATION

Analytical examination helps you to determine the nature of the subject with which you are dealing and provides you with materials you can use in stimulating listeners to see the subject in the same way.[2] Validation is another essential development step. You need to confirm, usually through research, the ideas you believe will be effective. Beyond this, validation processes enable you to make those ideas understood, felt, believed, or enjoyed by your listeners. Thus, validation is important, first, in guiding your own thinking to the best avail-

[2] The process of validating ideas is a type of research. For a helpful analysis of the processes most useful to speakers, *cf.* Clyde W. Dow, editor, *An Introduction to Graduate Study in Speech and Theatre.* Ann Arbor, Mich.: University of Michigan Press, 1961, especially Chapter 3, "The Library Survey," by William M. Sattler; Chapter 4, "The Historical Approach," by Gregg Phifer; and Chapter 5, "The Critical Approach," by Elton S. Carter and Iline Fife.

able conclusions, and second, in helping your listeners to understand and accept your interpretation of the subject. The problem, in both cases, is to make sure, insofar as you can, that the conclusions you recommend are *right*.

All education, in a sense, is directed toward this goal. Logic and scientific method are two approaches to it. You may not think of yourself as "research-minded," yet you do not want to come to wrong conclusions or be responsible for others' doing so. Since you want neither to think unsoundly nor to contribute to faulty thinking by your listeners, the validation of ideas is an everyday necessity. The means are rigorous, but they are reasonably clear and are available to anyone willing to take the trouble to think with precision.

The means of validation are of two kinds: forms of support, which include the kinds of materials that validate ideas; and methods of support, which are devices by which the forms are used. As you persevere in acquiring the qualities that will equip you to exert influence through communicative speaking, the single most important principle to keep in mind is that it is not your statement of ideas that gives them their power: it is your *validation* of them.

The following are most of the forms and methods of validation which you will need to study and put to effective use:

Validation Forms	Validation Methods
Historical perspective	Restating
Testimony of experts	Cumulating
Statistical data	Questioning
Examples	Comparing and contrasting
Narratives	Demonstrating visually

○ VALIDATION FORMS

In the discussions that follow, remember that what is said about your listeners must first be said of yourself. What your listeners question, you must first have questioned; what your listeners need to know, you will first have needed to know; what will move your listeners to feel, or believe, or do, will often be what has first moved you to feel, or believe, or to conclude must be done. This should be evident as you consider the means of validation of your ideas.

Historical Perspective

If your listeners wonder, as you speak to them, whether or not labor unions may have gained too much power, you will need to clarify their understanding by explaining the history of labor-union organization, to show why unions were organized, what goals they profess, what obstacles they have had to overcome, what they have accomplished, and why objections are now raised to some of their activities.

No matter what topic you select for a speech, conversation, or discussion, you often may need to explain when, where, why, and how it developed. Since this is a heavy demand to place upon yourself, you will be wise to choose subjects on which you already have a rather large amount of background information. Ignoring the historical perspective inevitably results in talking a great deal of nonsense. When you are ignorant, it is better to remain still. However, a sensible use of reference materials (encyclopedias, histories, biographies, textbooks) enables you to obtain at least the minimum of essential information on a wide range of topics.

Testimony of Experts

Precisely because it is difficult to learn a great deal about a topic that is relatively new to us, we often find ourselves in need of an opinion from those whose business it is to know about it. Our listeners feel this same need. An expert is a man who has earned the right to have a dependable opinion on a particular subject (1) by taking the trouble to learn its essentials; (2) by being fair-minded in his view of the subject; and (3) by reaching his conclusions on the basis of the facts rather than in accordance with his own prejudices. A representative of the American Management Association and a spokesman for the American Federation of Labor might both know a great deal about labor unions; but their professional commitments might lead them both to prejudiced conclusions. A professor of labor history ought to be impartial—though few people are wholly free of bias on any subject. Your first care, then, when using expert testimony, is to make sure that the person you are quoting is truly an objective and informed expert.

Beyond this, you need to observe several safeguards in your use of testimony. (1) Don't simply cite the expert's views or indicate vaguely that you "found this statement in a book"; but take the trouble to spell out for your listeners the nature of his expert qualifications. (2) If there is a reasonable doubt of his impartiality, cite facts which demonstrate his lack of prejudice. (3) Try to find some testimony that is offered by an expert who normally would take a point of view other than the one you are quoting from him; for instance, you might cite a successful author on the economic insecurity of the writing profession. (4) Make sure the testimony relates to present conditions, not to those that once existed but have now changed. (5) Make certain that your quotation is accepted by your listeners as accurate—perhaps by bringing with you the book or newspaper in which it appeared, and reading the passage to them. (6) Carefully select out of what the expert has said precisely and only the comments that apply directly to the point you wish to make—so that irrelevant materials will not divert attention from your central idea. (7) In selecting, be sure that what you take out of context does genuinely represent the expert's true opinion—and make sure your listeners understand this fact. (8) Finally, in view of the wide variety of even expert opinions on many subjects, it usually is wise, when using testimony as a form of support, to quote from several experts of different types or background.

Statistical Data

Statistics are numerical summaries of the frequency of occurrence of events or conditions.[3] Often the testimony of experts can and should be supported by statistical validation of their conclusions. Listeners may sometimes seem to be too easily impressed by assertions supported by statistics; yet all of us have properly learned to be suspicious of the sources from which such data come, the reliability of the compilers' methods, and the interpretations speakers may give of their significance. It has become a truism that, though figures may not lie, liars may figure. Carelessness, rather than deliberate deception, often results in misleading conclusions from either dependable or undependable statistics. Statistics, in any event, do not "speak for them-

[3] The use and abuse of statistics are presented nontechnically in Darrell Huff, *How to Lie with Statistics*. New York: Norton, 1954.

selves." When you use them, take care to interpret precisely what they mean and then to make that meaning vivid.

When the Department of Labor announces that the cost of living has risen by one-tenth of one per cent during the preceding month, listeners need to know that this statistic is based on a selected list of items priced in a particular set of communities. In your own town, the rise may have been greater, or there may have been a decline. A listener's own cost of living may be affected by the fact that he recently bought a car, or became engaged, or quit smoking. Thus, the statistic requires careful interpretation. Beyond this, it also must be made vivid or even its clarity of meaning may be lost.

One-tenth of one per cent seems almost nothing; actually, considering the whole population, it amounts to many millions of dollars. Monthly percentages of similarly miniscule size have cumulatively reduced the current value of the dollar to about 48 cents, measured in 1939 terms. A Republican Senator estimated the budgetary deficit of the Kennedy Administration in March, 1960, at one million dollars per hour, twenty-four hours a day, for every day since its inauguration. Making your statistical evidence vivid and meaningful to your own listeners is, then, one cardinal necessity if you want your validation to be effective.

Astute listeners furthermore, will very properly expect to learn the source of your statistics. They can then gauge how scientifically they were compiled, and what safeguards were taken to insure that the numerical summaries were truly representative and accurately tabulated. Moreover, if you cite accurate figures showing a rising curve of unemployment, listeners will want to know the significance of statistics showing a parallel rise in the curve of employment. More people are out of work—but more are also at work. The problem is not alone to find and cite dependable statistics but also to interpret them in their context.

The warning concerning limitations on the use of statistics is not intended to discourage their use. Obviously, without statistical data we could not know the size of the population of the United States, nor how it is shifting from East to West. Taxation depends on statistical data covering the extent and distribution of property and earnings. It is useful to have statistical confirmation of the steadily increasing life-span of human beings in many parts of the world; and plans for old-age security require statistical validation of the fact that in the United

States women live, on the average, six or seven years longer than men. What we need to remember is that statistics always deal with averages, norms, and other distributional data. There is point in the jibe that if a statistician had his head in an oven and his feet encased in ice he might conclude that "on the average" he felt fine.

Examples

Statistics represent an accumulation of data from many specific examples. But we often are led to conclusions by the specific examples themselves, regardless of their statistical grouping. Any number of experts might, let us say, testify that dictatorship is bad; but you may have a friend from Portugal who praises the dictator Salazar for the stability and prosperity achieved under his rule. The cost-of-living index is rising; but you notice happily that this month, for the first time all year, you were able to save some money. Historical records indicate that mankind is progressing toward improved individual welfare; but look at what is happening to individual freedom and welfare in many parts of the world.

As an aid to clear and effective thinking, examples are of value as evidence only when they are representative—exactly as the Department of Labor sample of commodities and communities must be representative if its cost-of-living index is to be dependable. Both you and your listeners would shun an example that is obviously exceptional—unless you want to validate the observation that there are exceptions to the general trend. Thus, what your friend sees in Portugal may be atypical of the over-all situation, and the fact that you saved money this month could also be due to exceptional circumstances.

In ordinary social discourse, it seldom is possible to subject examples cited to rigid tests of their representative quality; but we often do cite a contrary example that challenges the validity of the one presented. Just so will your listeners think of examples that may counter those you offer them. Thus, when you are speaking, it is wise to give careful attention to validating both the authenticity and the representativeness of examples you cite. There is, however, one special kind of example that is not authentic, but does have value in clarifying ideas, if not in proving them. This is known as the hypothetical example.

The hypothetical example, often employed in speeches, may be defined as an imaginary specific example. It is a concrete way for the speaker to show how his ideas would work if applied in a hypothetical situation. If a speaker were discussing the growing significance of space ships and were to ask his listeners to imagine the day when interplanetary flight will be as common as transoceanic flights are today, he might add, "That will be the time your son will take my son on a week-end flight to Mars." Again, a minister may request increased support for the church by asking his listeners to imagine what it would be like to live in a community where there were no churches.

The hypothetical case represents an attempt to demonstrate concretely ideas which cannot be developed by reference to actual experience. It should be used when a real example cannot be provided but when an imaginary example will enhance the listeners' understanding of the speaker's theme. Likewise, the probable consequences of a proposal may be put before the audience by hypothetical examples in a case in which no real example could make the point with equal force.

Narratives

Stories, anecdotes, and parables are useful forms of narrative in all kinds of speaking. As illustrations or examples, they contribute to validation by their specificity, and they also add considerably to the interest of listeners by helping to keep their minds centered closely upon the development of your theme. The frequent use of parables by Jesus and of anecdotes by Lincoln added considerably to their effectiveness as speakers. These narrative forms can be either quite extensive, or closely compressed. Jesus used parables in talking of the talents, the lilies of the field, the prodigal son, and the Good Samaritan. With an abbreviated anecdote, Lincoln summarized his criticism of a young lawyer who made lengthy courtroom speeches: "He is like a certain minister writing his sermon. He got to writing, and writing, and writing—and was too lazy to stop."

As an example of how and why an anecdote may be used, consider the difficult situation that confronted Charles W. Eliot, when he was President of Harvard and was asked to respond to a toast "To Harvard and Yale!" Here is how he began:

Harvard and Yale! Can any undergraduate of either institution, can any recent graduate of either institution, imagine a man responding to that toast? However, I must make the best of the position, and speak of some points upon which the two institutions are clearly agreed. And here I am reminded of a story of a certain New England farmer, who said that he and Squire Jones had more cows between them than all the rest of the village; and, his brag being disputed, he said he could prove it—for the Squire had forty-five cows and he had one, and the village altogether had not forty-six.

Story-telling for validation requires two elements. First, the anecdote must be told with sufficient interest—building toward an unexpected climax, and limited to the essential details—to hold the absorbed attention of the listeners. And, second, it must be selected because it reinforces the idea which it illustrates—and of this supporting function listeners cannot be left in any doubt. These are the two keys to both the success and the fame of the narratives told by Jesus and Lincoln. When either of the two factors is violated, a narrative may do more harm than good, either by destroying interest, or by diverting it away from the speaker's central theme.

Historical perspective, testimony by experts, statistical data, examples, and narratives are forms in which you may find validating materials. They should meet the tests cited here, and in Chapter 5, before you let your own thinking be influenced by them. Once you have determined their soundness, they become the principal *content* upon which to draw to influence your listeners toward acceptance of your purpose and central idea. The forms of validation and support are your research data. Now we turn to consideration of some ways of using these data to enhance their validating effectiveness.

○ VALIDATION METHODS

In your gathering of materials, you encountered communications that helped you to see ideas more clearly, more strikingly, or which gave those ideas more credibility. You may have noticed that the writers and speakers from whom you drew materials accomplished these results by restating important ideas and their supports, by cumulating examples, stories, statistics, or testimony, by questioning the reactions of readers and listeners, by comparing and contrasting data from various sources and in various forms, and by demonstrating visually through charts, maps, graphs, tables, objects, and pictures. Just as these methods helped you validate your ideas through research, so can they be used to validate your ideas in the minds of your listeners.

Restating

Broadly speaking, restating is precisely what you do when you apply any of the validating forms and methods. A good story restates the idea, as do examples, statistics, a historical review, and testimony. More narrowly, restatement refers to the deliberate recall to your listeners' attention of supports you have used previously, as when you say, "Remember the story I told you a while ago," or "Now think again of those statistics . . ."

Restatement serves primarily both clarity and emphasis. Its value in validation is in bringing back into listeners' minds the key ideas or facts which lead toward your conclusion. Often facts or ideas in isolation from one another have little significance; their real meaning emerges only as they are seen in their essential relationship. To make clear how idea number one or fact number one relates to facts or ideas two, three, and four, it often is necessary and almost always is helpful to restate the earlier ones. Research indicates that three or four repetitions of the central idea, interspersed among validating materials, appears to be the best way of assuring understanding and of having the message remembered. President Harry Truman, in presenting his famous "Point Four" program of technical assistance to underdeveloped countries, tried to indicate the breadth of support for his plan by restating the basic idea in five successive paragraphs, each with an introductory phrase linking it to large segments of his national audience: "I think people in this country will agree . . ."; "I think most farmers understand . . ."; "I think most workers understand . . ."; "I think our businessmen know . . ."; and "I think everyone knows . . ." Written messages, which may be studied again and again, may not depend so much on repetition; spoken messages, however, in which the words once heard may not be recalled, do emphasize the need for restatement.

Cumulating

The piling up of validating evidence in successive repetitions of the same form is a special kind of restatement called *cumulation*. If you can provide your listeners with a succession of examples, or of statistics from many sources, they will be impressed with the depth of your information.

Herbert Egerer, a student at the University of Omaha, used cumulation in a speech warning that America's leading position in the world might be lost. "Four thousand years ago," he said, "China was at the height of its culture; twenty-five hundred years ago Greece dominated the intellectual world; two thousand years ago the Roman Empire was in its highest glory; and one hundred-fifty years ago France reached the peak of its power. All these nations, and many others like them, had once risen to great heights; but all too quickly they slipped and sank back to cultural poverty." The use of several similar examples, together with the assertion, "and many more like them," is more convincing than merely a single instance. Similarly, reference to many experts is better validation than citation of just one. Whatever illustrative materials you may use, show your audience that your mind is richly stored with illustrations that support your point of view.

Questions

The chief value of using questions is that they draw your listeners actively into the discourse. They indicate that you care about what your listeners think and they invite active thought along with you as you unfold the subject. When you ask a question, pause to show that you value the answer, even though unspoken. Questions may take many forms; the ones you may find most useful are *direct, rhetorical, leading,* and *hypothetical.*

Direct questions call for an answer from the listeners. You must be prepared to adapt your subsequent remarks to the answers you receive. Thus, in discussing automobile accidents, you may ask: "How many of you have had an accident in the past year?" Perhaps the answer may be, "None of us." You might then continue, "Well, you are lucky. The fact is there have been seventeen deaths and several hundred personal injuries in our own county. Let's not let it happen to some of us next year." In much of your talking, whether in speeches or conversation, direct questions may be used with good effect to heighten the sense of listener-participation. But you must be prepared to proceed in your remarks with pertinent adaptation to the kinds of response your questions elicit.

Rhetorical questions are a means of emphasis, highlighting points of view held in common by speaker and listeners. "Who would admit he is dishonest?" a speaker might ask. "Yet we know cheating is prevalent in examinations."

Leading questions are a means of getting your audience to affirm a conclusion they might resist if it were stated as an assertion. "Haven't you seen a good many people on relief who ought to be working?" a speaker might ask. Or, "Don't you know some people who want prices lowered but *their* salaries raised?" And, "Aren't some of our taxes being used to construct jerry-built housing?"

Hypothetical questions are a device for introducing a new approach to your subject; in this sense, they are really transitional phrases. When you have concluded your point that relief is often misused, you might then proceed to your second point by asking a hypothetical question. "It might be agreed there is some small amount of abuse of the welfare system, but someone at this point may be wondering, 'Yes, but isn't it worth a small waste of funds in order to insure adequate care for those who are out of work through no fault of their own?' This is a question we shall now answer."

Comparing and Contrasting

Whenever an example is used, it may be helpful to compare it with other like examples and to contrast it with some that are dissimilar. Let us assume you are considering whether Africans are really ready for democratic self-government. An example of gross inefficiency might be placed in proper perspective by comparing it with a similar instance from American history; or it might be contrasted with a more successful example of how another African nation dealt with a similar problem. Comparison and contrast are both methods by which listeners are helped to see the representative character or application of particular validating materials. Your listeners might believe "cramming" for an examination is bad practice, for they know of instances in which it produced disastrous results. You might compare the examples they mention with others that will show small but important differences in methods of concentrated review; or you might contrast "cramming" with systematic study over a long period. No method of support presented singly can be quite as dependable as the analytical treatment of diverse materials through comparison and contrast.

Analogy, metaphor, and *simile* are useful devices in comparison and contrast. An analogy may be either literal or figurative, and both metaphor and simile are in reality compressed analogies. An example of a literal analogy is to liken the General Assembly of the United Nations to the Interfraternity Council, in which every fraternity is represented by one vote and in which common problems are discussed, although each fraternity maintains its independence. In contrast to the U. N., however, the IFC is required by university regulations to abide by stated regulations. A figurative analogy might liken the United Nations to a flight of sparrows: the birds fly together when it suits their convenience, but separate to go their individual ways whenever they wish.

A *metaphor* is an assertion that something is what it patently is not, the purpose being to stimulate the imagination of the listeners to appreciate the quality emphasized by the implied comparison. We are using a metaphor when we say, "He is a diamond in the rough." Walter Funk, a leading propagandist among the pre-World War II Nazis, explained the censorship of the German press by declaring the press was "no longer a barrel-organ out of which everybody is permitted to squeeze whatever melodies he likes, but a highly sensitive and far-sounding instrument or orchestra on which and with which only those shall play who know how, and in whose hands the Fuehrer himself has placed the conductor's baton."

A *simile* is a form of comparison which asserts an object resembles or "is like" something that in most respects is quite different from it. Adolf Hitler, using this method, once said: "I take my words and throw them like burning torches into the crowd—and they burn." In one of the *Arabian Nights* tales is found a descriptive series of similes that might be applied to Daniel Webster: "His head was like a dome, his hands like pitchforks, his mouth like a cavern, his teeth like rocks, his eyes like lamps, and he was stern and lowering of aspect."

Comparing and contrasting, discovering and pointing out similarities and differences, are fundamental methods of learning. Thus a child might ask, "What does a papaya taste like?" Or you say to a friend, "What is it like at Atlanta University?" or "What's the food like in your dining hall?" Listeners, of course, will exercise their own judgment as to how apt your comparisons and contrasts are.

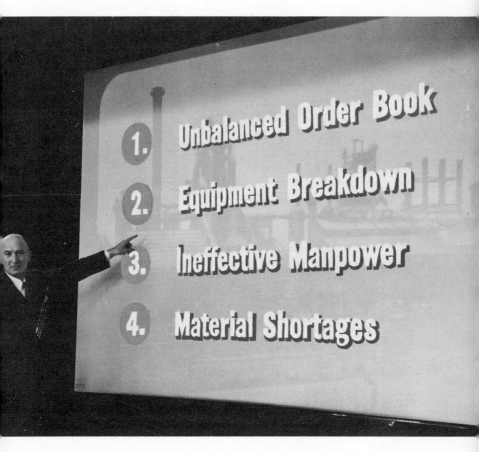

The first level of validation is selection of main ideas to support a clear central idea. By screen projection, this speaker is using a visual aid to clarify and dramatize four business hazards—four main ideas—and their interrelation instead of merely *talking* about them to his listeners.

Demonstrating Visually

Any of the analytical processes and validating forms or methods may frequently be made more effective if they are cast in some visual form.

Visual Aids have so much general usefulness in many kinds of speaking situations that they are discussed in detail in Chapter 11. In our everyday conversation we often have occasion to say, "Here, let me show you what I mean." Then we may demonstrate how to tie a bow tie, or work a problem in algebra, or use a slide rule. We may reach for a piece of paper to draw a simple map or diagram or chart. If we are talking about modern art, we find it much easier and more meaningful if we have some pictures to show. Whatever it may be that we wish to explain, or concerning which we wish to persuade, it is very often helpful to be able to display objects or to draw diagrams showing relationships. "Look at it for yourself" is an invitation helpful to both clarity and conviction. Similarly, in entertaining speeches, much enjoyment is shared by displaying ludicrous or unusual objects. For a talk on a hunting trip, for example, you would want to show pictures and, if possible, also your rifle and perhaps your camping equipment. These visual aids would do much to enhance the excitement of your narrative. There are few speeches in which visual aids might not be used to advantage and there are many that suffer greatly in effectiveness if the speaker fails to show while he is telling.

Illustration

The forms and methods of validation are sometimes grouped together under the term "illustration."[4] The term comes from the Latin, *illustrare,* "to shed light upon." Illustrations are concrete or specific instances of an abstraction or a generalization. Often we hear (or use) such statements as, "Let me illustrate this," followed by a story, an analogy, a quotation from an expert, or by statistics, or a brief review of the history of the question, or any one of the other forms or

---

[4] For practical guidance, consult Lionel Crocker, "Make the Illustration Linger," *Today's Speech,* Vol. 4 (January, 1956), pp. 3–5; and J. H. Baccus, "Building a Stock of Illustrations," *The Quarterly Journal of Speech,* Vol. 21 (June, 1935), pp. 373–375. How a popular evangelist made effective use of illustrations is presented vividly in William T. Ellis, *"Billy" Sunday: The Man and His Message.* Philadelphia: Universal Book and Bible House, 1914.

methods of validation we have described. "Let's get down to cases" is a familiar challenge, but the most celebrated is perhaps Gov. Alfred E. Smith's inimitable "Let's look at the record!" This is the process of validation: to illustrate, to specify, to render concrete, to turn away from mere assertions to look for the supports upon which they must rest. All good thinking depends on it. So does all good speaking.

○ **CONCLUSION**

As has been indicated in this chapter, the development of ideas rests upon three major types of support: (1) the use of analytic examination to help your listeners understand how and why you arrive at conclusions regarding your subject; (2) the use of forms of validation, which constitute the principal types of factual evidence your thinking requires, and (3) the use of methods of validation which cast your materials into meaningful patterns of support for your conclusions. Taken together, these three stages of development provide a checklist of sources and devices to guide you through the troubled periods when you think, "I don't know what I can do to develop the ideas for my talks any more fully." What you can do is easily summarized in this way:

ANALYTICAL EXAMINATION PROCESSES: limitation, definition, description, discrimination, qualification, classification, and redefinition or synthesis.

VALIDATION FORMS: historical perspective, testimony of experts, statistical data, examples, and narratives.

VALIDATION METHODS: restating, cumulating, questioning, comparing and contrasting, and demonstrating visually.

ILLUSTRATION: use singly or in combination of the validating forms and methods.

EXERCISES

Questions for Discussion

1. How do the various factors discussed in this chapter relate to the quality of your thinking? As you consider limitation, definition, discrimination, and qualification, for example, how are they used in your study of history, or chemistry, or engineering—or in your choice of friends, or of hobbies, or of a vocation? Does the speaking you hear reflect differing levels of intellectual ability, and if so, can you identify some of these

differences in terms of the factors presented in this chapter? Can you improve the quality of your own thinking by giving more precise attention to any or all of these factors?

2. What are the tests that should be applied to the testimony of experts? To statistics? Why are these tests important? Are there any noted in this chapter that you feel may be eliminated? If they are all essential, do you (and your classmates) always apply them in your use of testimony and statistics?

3. Why should a specific example be both authentic and representative? Do both these tests need to be met by a hypothetical example? Distinguish between the *uses* of the two kinds of examples.

4. What is the special value of the question? How may you impart at least a portion of this same value to the other factors used in developing ideas?

5. Distinguish between restating and cumulating, between defining and describing, between discriminating and qualifying, between a simile and a metaphor.

6. How do you illustrate an idea? Is there any one of the factors discussed in this chapter that may not be used for illustration? Are there any that you consider especially suitable for your own needs?

Projects for Speaking and Writing

1. Prepare a speech for your class in which you give particular and sequential attention to each of the processes of analytical examination. Then select from among the forms and methods of validation the factors which you *must* use to develop your ideas satisfactorily. After this is done, consider the remaining factors to decide whether there are others which you can use to advantage. Which ones do not apply, or are not needed, for this particular speech?

2. For a class discussion of conversation, prepare to illustrate some common faults and some exceptional merits of conversations in which you have participated. Use the factors described in this chapter as a guide in looking for both faults and merits. What recommendations would you make for improving the quality of the conversation of yourself and your associates?

3. Listen to a speech presented on the radio or television, or given on a public occasion on your campus, and evaluate the development of its ideas in terms of the factors we have presented. Take *one* of the main ideas of the speech and show how it could have better supported the central idea by a fuller utilization of one or several of these developmental factors.

Chapter 8

Attention, Interest, and Style

WHAT MAKES ONE MAN'S TALK INTERESTING, and another's dull, is a question that involves the whole range of content talked about, the manner of speaking, and the personality of the speakers. We describe some personalities as sparkling, exciting, engaging, appealing—representing the kinds of people we enjoy being with. We think of some subjects—like money, love, health, TV, fame—as being inherently interesting: the sort of thing we frequently enjoy discussing. We think of animated and vibrant voices, of unusually expressive gestures and facial variations, and of imaginative or vivid diction as being in themselves attractive.

On the other hand, we find some people generally unattractive (though we may add they are really quite nice when you come to know them well). We find some topics dull in themselves or worn threadbare by overmuch repetition. And we know that some people might describe a bull fight or a miracle with such drabness and lack of animation that they might as well be reading at random from the telephone directory. Attention, interest, and style, then, are not so much dependent upon methods as they are innate aspects of subject matter, speaker, and all the ways in which personality is revealed through voice, diction, and bodily expressiveness.

Nevertheless, our problem is to identify and describe some specific ways in which you, in your own speeches and everyday talk, can catch

169

the attention of listeners, develop their genuine interest, and present what you have to say in an attractive style. Every chapter of this book is designed in its own sphere of inquiry to help you accomplish this end. In the present chapter we shall group together suggestions particularly relevant to these three aspects of your speaking.

Attention, interest, and style are qualities with which you will need to be concerned in all your speaking. The function of attention is to bring what you have to say to the notice of listeners by signalling to them that you do have something worth their consideration. Interest develops and is maintained as you demonstrate that the attention paid to your talk is genuinely worth it: the ideas when examined prove equal to the expectation you have aroused. By style we mean a combination of agreeableness and appropriateness. What you have to say is attractive to your listeners and it fits their interpretation of your personality, their understanding (as you help them clarify it) of the subject matter, and their sense of the nature of the occasion. Attention is caught by a window display; your interest develops as you examine the merchandise (perhaps a suit) and find it is well-made, of good materials, and suitably priced; and you are content with the style if it is modish and adapted to the use you intend to make of it. What we need is to gain greater skill in utilizing attention-getting devices, in building and maintaining interests, and in heightening the appeal of our own individual style.

○ ATTENTION

We properly think of attention as something fleeting and momentary. Indeed, psychologists assure us that "absolute concentration of attention" can be maintained for at most a few seconds. Attention consists of a turning toward or an awareness of something that has come within the range of our perception. We are dimly aware of many items in our environment—colors, smells, shapes, sounds, textures, and memories. Psychologists, again, tell us the marvellous brain of man is capable of receiving as many as 1,000 impressions in a single perception unit, which they interpret as one-tenth of a second. We can be aware of a great deal, but we select only a very few items out of this potential range to receive our actual attention.

When we talk, our first task is to attract "full, fair, and favorable

"Full, fair, and favorable attention"

An effective speaker must not only attract or capture the attention of listeners, he must maintain attention while talking and must constantly be alert to individual responses.

attention"[1] to what we have to say; thereafter, when or if the attention of our hearers wanders, we need to recover it. The headline, as we have said, is an "attention-grasping" device; it is worth noting that in long news stories there are also subheads scattered through the columns, precisely to help hold attention to the end. Similarly, in our speeches we need special consideration of how to seize attention at the start, but we also need to utilize various attention-compelling factors as our talk continues. These functions may be achieved by means of a good title, an effective introduction, and a readiness to inject attention-holding items in the course of the talk, wherever and whenever they may be needed.

Titles

The title of a public speech is akin to an advertisement which attracts favorable attention to the merchandise offered and describes and illustrates it. The title may also be likened to the gift-wrapping which adds so much appeal to any gift. In another sense, a title may be like the surprise ending of a detective story. In other words, the title of a speech has at least four distinct functions to achieve: (1) to sound sufficiently appealing so that potential auditors will want to come to hear it; (2) to be sufficiently attractive so that in itself it may add pleasure to the listening; (3) to set or suggest the tone or mood of the speech; and (4) to contain a hidden but satisfying key to the central meaning. Not all titles can achieve all four of these diverse purposes, nor are all of them equally important for all speeches. But these are the principal guidelines you should have in mind in formulating your speech titles.

When you have a captive audience that is required to come hear what you will have to say, there is no positive need to attract them; even so, it obviously is an advantage to have your listeners waiting with anticipation. If a public lecture is scheduled and you have to decide whether or not you will go to hear it, the title may make the crucial difference. It should be definitive enough to indicate the subject and either elusive or challenging enough to intrigue the curiosity. "Why Communism is Winning in Asia" meets the qualifications better

[1] The phrase, often quoted, was used by James Albert Winans in his pioneer textbook, *Public Speaking*. New York: Appleton-Century-Crofts, 1915, which remains an excellent source for study of how to gain attention in speaking.

than "Foreign Policy Problems in the Far East." If you are told one of your classmates will speak on "Better Study Habits Are Needed," this would probably attract you less than the title, *"Gambling versus Investing* in Education." When you devise a title for your speech, one consideration should be: how can it be phrased so that people will want to come and listen to me?

Gone with the Wind and *Wayfaring through the Andes* are book titles that in themselves have imaginative appeal; even without reading the books, the mere savoring of the titles is pleasant. Good speech titles, similarly, create an impression that persists—helping to add interest to the speech and constituting a pleasant memory. "The Wheel Turns," "The Dharma Dervish of Delhi," "The Plato of the Cave," and "Witch-Doctors in Modern Dress" are titles that listeners are likely to remember and enjoy for their own suggestive implications.

A further function of the title is to suggest the mood in which the speech is to be developed. This may be helpful not only to the audience but also to the speaker. Some speakers, for this reason, find it just as important to select a title early in their preparation as they do to formulate their purpose. If you are going to discuss the social responsibilities of college graduates, an immediate question is whether you will adopt a tone of "preachy" exhortation, recognizing that your listeners are just as seriously concerned as you are yourself, or develop the theme in a playful or perhaps sharply challenging spirit.

What you say may not be greatly affected by which of these approaches you decide upon, but the mood or tone of the speech will be vastly influenced. As you think about how to handle this theme, you may help to render your decision concrete by finding a title that suggests the mood you wish to achieve. You can hardly make the same kind of speech under the title, "The Duties of Educated Citizenship," that you would if your title were, "Tit for Tat," or "You Got—Now Give," or "Dutiful Diplomas." Your choice of title can and should help you to develop a unified mood for the talk and it signals to the audience something of the quality they may expect. "Billions for Bombs," "The Cost of Defense," and "Pay or Perish" all suggest talks on a single theme; but they also indicate a considerable difference in the way in which the theme will be presented.

Another desirable attribute for a title is that it contain a hidden, rather than an obvious, key to the theme or purpose of the speech. "Plumed Antlers," for example, suggests a speech that will be light or humorous in tone (thereby fulfilling the preceding function of titles), for obviously antlers don't actually grow plumes. But in addition, when your speech is finished, your listeners may find lurking in the title the idea you wished to implant—namely, that much of the panoply of war is designed not alone to provide efficient weapons but also to enhance the love of glory. "Gory Glory" is another title that might fulfill the same purpose of hinting at the theme, but it surely suggests a more sober mood.

As all the foregoing examples indicate, a title should be short and should be a name for the speech, as well as an abbreviated statement of its theme. On your outline, the title should be centered at the top of the first sheet. Before the session starts you should give your title to the chairman, so that he may announce it in introducing you. It is not good practice for the speaker to commence by announcing his own title—though sometimes his introduction is contrived to lead toward a restatement of the title as a transition into the body of the talk. Sometimes, too, a speaker finds it useful to repeat his title at intervals through the speech—especially if it contains in capsule form the essence of his message: such as "Tit for Tat," or "Gory Glory." In sum, the title provides an important source of listener attention and deserves thoughtful consideration.

Introductions

It is the principal function of the introduction to seize audience attention and direct it favorably toward the speaker's theme. This function, along with others, has already been indicated in Chapter 6. Here we are concerned primarily with what the speaker may do to achieve the attention-compelling purpose. In general, there are two diverse methods: the sensational, and the unobtrusive.

SENSATIONAL INTRODUCTIONS. Henry Ward Beecher, the famous nineteenth-century minister of Brooklyn's Plymouth Church, is reputed to have commenced his sermon on a Sunday in July by stepping to the front of the platform, pulling from his pocket a large red bandana kerchief, wiping his forehead, and saying, "It's hotter than hell!" According to the story (which Beecher denied) he went on to say this was a comment he had heard on the sidewalk in front of the church and it had induced him to abandon his planned sermon in favor of an impromptu demonstration that hell is even hotter than New York in midsummer. On another occasion, when he was to deliver an anti-slavery sermon, Beecher remained in his study until time for the sermon to begin, then leaped through a back door onto the platform brandishing a chain over his head, after which he threw it to the floor, crying, "These are the bonds that bind your brethren in the South. I spit upon them; I spurn them!" Whereupon he did spit upon the chain and stamped upon it.

A student speaker once opened his talk by lighting a match and holding it till it burned out, without saying a word. Another removed his coat, turned it wrong side out, and put it on again. Another stepped to the window, opened it, then took a live sparrow from his pocket and liberated it. These are but a few of many ways in which speakers have used a sensational act to seize and center audience attention. To be effective, these devices must directly support the introductory point they are trying to make.

In similar vein, speakers sometimes commence with a striking or challenging statement, such as: "Half of you will be dead, mentally ill, invalided, imprisoned, or impoverished within thirty years"; or "Men are said to have descended from apes—and have not improved much on their heritage. Women are believed to have descended from angels—but if so it was a whale of a long descent"; or "In a democracy people may do as they wish; under a monarchy, they do what they must; but in such a mixture of democracy and aristocracy as we find on a college campus, they do what they can get away with." The purpose of the sensational statement is, first, to capture attention, and, second, to center that attention squarely upon the theme of the speech. In other words, it should be not merely sensational but also thematic.

A variant of the sensational openings is the method of starting a speech with one or more humorous stories, intended both to capture attention and to create a receptive attitude. When this is done, be sure that your stories have a point which is also the theme of your introduction or of your speech. Otherwise, the attention which you catch is actually directed away from, not toward, the purpose you wish to accomplish. Furthermore, the humorous beginning is scarcely ever effective unless the general tone of the speech is to be light and frolicsome. Many a speaker has undermined his ultimate purpose by using what he thinks is the easy means of getting attention with humor, and then attempting to shift quickly to a serious note. What he really has done is to deceive the expectation of his listeners; he has made it harder for himself to win them back to the mood he wishes to establish. If a sensational beginning is used, it must be presented with considerable dramatic skill. Unless the speaker is perfectly assured, confident, and in command of the situation, the contrast between the drama of his word or act and the indecisiveness of his manner is somewhat ludicrous, so that the effect is spoiled. Sensationalism is effective only when well managed. It is tempting but hazardous—better suited to skilled than inexperienced speakers.

UNOBTRUSIVE INTRODUCTIONS. When you seek to engage the attention of listeners, it is well to remember that people are more interested in themselves than in anything else. Generally it is wise to start your comments by speaking about your audience. "You have all been talking about . . . ," or "Most of you realize that . . ." are ways of starting a speech unobtrusively, indicating that you do not wish to startle your listeners but, rather, to pick up a thread of interest that already exists. For this same reason, it is often desirable to link your own talk directly with the one that has preceded it, by beginning with a reference to what others have said before you. "We have just heard a plea that capital punishment be abolished. This is an appeal to our better instincts. I would like you to continue thinking about what you have just heard while I discuss with you now some aspects of our free-enterprise capitalistic system."

The purpose of the unobtrusive introduction is to divert the attention of the audience from your speech as a performance in order to center it upon an idea. In effect, the very quietness and lack of sensationalism of your opening is a way of assuring your listeners that you are less interested in making a "good speech" than you are in considering with them a problem of genuine and mutual interest. It is an avoidance of "oratory" in favor of conversational naturalness. For most speakers, in most circumstances, the unobtrusive beginning—centered squarely upon where the thinking of your listeners is resting as you rise to speak—is the safest and most effective way to link your mind with theirs.

Attention Devices During the Talk

The attention of the audience may be diverted from your remarks during the course of your talk by some outside interference—such as a clap of thunder, a collapsing chair in the room, or a bird flying against the window. If it requires you to pause, instead of ignoring what has happened, you should try in some manner to weave it into your speech. When a passing truck back-fired loudly in the midst of a talk on the problems of democracy, the speaker instantly recalled the diverted attention of his listeners by exclaiming, "Perhaps the revolution has already started!" It is not always possible to rise to the unexpected with appropriate wit; but some reference to the interruption, relevant to your current remarks, is necessary if you are quickly to reclaim the attention that has been diverted.

If your talk is dull or seems to the listeners to have little to do with them, you are very likely to lose their attention completely. It is natural in such circumstances for the audience to turn their minds inward, to thoughts of their own, far removed from what you may be saying. This problem is best solved not by devices for recapturing attention but by maintaining throughout your talk the quality of genuine interest.

○ INTEREST

If Brigitte Bardot, or America's first astronaut, Alan B. Shepard, were to speak on your campus, you would probably want to attend from sheer interest in the personality of the speaker. If a talk were listed on "How to Make Money While in College," or "How to Get a Free Trip Abroad," you might want to hear it because of interest in the topic. If Bob Hope or Danny Kaye were to speak, you would probably attend with the expectation that their skill on the platform would assure a high degree of interest. In each instance, your interest is engaged because of what you expect to get from the talk for yourself; and the source of the interest is in the personality of the speaker, the nature of the subject, or in demonstrated platform skill. In your own speaking, you should aim to secure and maintain the interest of your own listeners from one and all of these sources.

Personality

Studies that have been made of attractive features of personality show that different people (or perhaps all of us in different moods) are attracted to a widely varying range of personality traits. We like thoughtfulness, quiet dependability, and considerateness for the feelings of others. In all such studies, however, there is a central core of approval for traits of social sympathy; apparently we all tend especially to like people who like us—who are friendly, helpful, good listeners, and responsive to our moods. Not many speakers can hope to attain the glamour attached to fame as an entertainer, explorer, politician, or athlete. But everyone can at least aim to be the dependable, friendly, and warmly responsive type of personality that most people like to be with. The communication of these personality traits as you are speaking is one way of attracting and maintaining interest.

Subject Matter

It has been said that no prospective beneficiary ever goes to sleep during the reading of a will. When what is said is sufficiently important or exciting, it will be listened to attentively. As we have indicated earlier, some subjects are inherently more interesting than others. But almost any subject may be developed in an interesting manner. It often happens that we wish to discuss a particular topic simply because it is *not* interesting to our listeners. If they are not interested in study, or international affairs, or social reform, or politics, this lack of interest may be precisely why you choose to bring such subjects to their attention.

○ FACTORS OF INTEREST

Various "factors of interest" have been identified as ways by which you can hope to arouse and hold interest that otherwise would be lacking. These factors are: *concreteness, specificity, vividness, familiarity, novelty, vitality, variety, suspense, conflict,* and *humor*.

CONCRETENESS. If you are discussing such abstract concepts as loyalty, or patriotism, or self-sacrifice for the sake of teamwork, it builds interest to support your abstractions with concrete examples, such as descriptions of the Marine training program at Paris Island base, or the work of the boys on the third and fourth string squads of the football team, or the contributions made under difficult conditions by members of the Peace Corps. Friendship is another abstract quality that is made real by citations of concrete instances of friendly acts and attitudes—perhaps sympathetic helpfulness communicated in particular ways by your roommate. "We were served a good meal" is less

Apply all *the factors of interest . . .*

The criterion for *selection* of speaker materials is validation of central idea; the criterion for *adaptation* of materials is maintenance of listener interest. Either one without the other fails to hold an audience.

concrete, and also less interesting, than "We were served roast duck with savory dressing, wild rice with curry sauce, and spicy, hot apple pie topped with vanilla ice cream." Try to make your listeners see, taste, hear, smell, and feel real instances that support your abstract point.

SPECIFICITY.   Similarly, if you offer a generalization, support it with specific examples. If you are discussing the migratory habits of birds, it is interesting to support your general conclusions with references to particular kinds of birds (such as robins or geese) and perhaps to cite specific experiences you have had with migratory flocks. A description of how migratory birds are banded and of how the individual records of their flights are maintained through the cooperation of local bird-watchers would be a way of rendering the topic specific. "The average life-expectancy is increasing" can be made more specific —and thereby more interesting—by tracing the history of life-expectancy statistics in a particular country, such as our own, or India.

VIVIDNESS.   Concrete and specific instances are more vivid than abstractions and generalizations. The vividness is enhanced through personalizing an incident by relating it directly to your listeners. Vividness is also enriched by the use of interesting details. The quality of vividness is excellently illustrated in a speech made in 1959 by Thomas W. Chumbley, of Loras College, in Dubuque, Iowa. Under the title, "Crawl Away From the Campfire," he discussed the theme that we waste human resources by retiring workers too early. "Among the most primitive tribes of Africa, the Amazon, or the Australian bush country, and down the reaches of time that stretch back to the caves of Switzerland, one ancient custom still marks the savage and his disregard for human life and feelings. When the hunter can no longer look forward to keeping up with the tribe on the next morning's trail, he is expected to crawl away from the campfire, to die unnoticed and unwanted as the younger men travel on."

FAMILIARITY.   As we have said, people are more interested in themselves than in anything else. It is often interesting to listeners to hear about lands or events far away and long ago; but to hold a depth of interest, they are best related to the here and the now, in ways that show the listeners how they themselves are affected. For example, in the same speech cited in the preceding paragraph, Mr. Chumbley went on to elaborate his point about old age by reference to the flood of advertising we all see every day. "Today's cosmetic peddler," he pointed out, "ties his sales pitch to the fear of 'old age.' Grey hair is to be shunned; a wrinkle is regarded in the same light as a livid scar. Likewise, myriad untested compounds are swallowed to give youthful sparkle. Diets of conflicting purposes, exercise machinery that is a complete fraud, and all the facial decorative arts learned since the Egyptians are called into play to 'stay young.' "

NOVELTY. William James observed that "It is an odd circumstance that neither the old nor the new, by itself, is interesting: the absolutely old is insipid; the absolutely new makes no appeal at all. The old *in* the new is what claims attention—the old with a slightly new turn." Politicians follow this principle when they speculate on what Abraham Lincoln or Thomas Jefferson would do if they were here to deal with today's problems. The same principle applies if you are speaking about something old and familiar—such as the reasons for the rise or decline of Napoleon Bonaparte. It will be more interesting to your listeners if you continuously compare what he did and the circumstances he confronted with present-day rulers and some events confronting them.

VITALITY. Vitality is a term used to signify factors of vital, or fundamental, concern to listeners. We laugh at jokes and are momentarily attracted by much that is merely frivolous or superficial; but our basic and lasting interest is reserved for matters of genuine importance. How to get a job, what kind of person to marry, whether—or where—to go to church, how to stay healthy, how to gain and keep friends: factors such as these have real vitality.

Psychologists and sociologists have drawn up lists of "vital urges" or basic drives which are common to all people. The various listings do not agree—because no one knows for sure what motivates people. We know that our "urges" differ depending on circumstances. Yet we also know that all of us value recognition, praise, friendly relations with others, health, independence, security, new experiences, and other values that are perhaps somewhat less "vital." Any speaking that appeals to one or several of these needs will tend to maintain interest simply because such urges are the basic factors from which interest flows.

VARIETY. It is proverbial that variety is the spice of life. Change in itself is interesting. Whatever interest-attracting methods a speaker may use, he should make a point of shifting from one to another. A series of statistics, or a string of quotations, or even a sequence of several examples of similar types, if presented dully, may all tend to induce listeners to feel they have had enough or perhaps too much. So simple a technique as alternating the types of supporting material results in variety, thereby heightening interest.

SUSPENSE. As we listen to a narrative or a good anecdote, we are held in suspense to the end. A joke loses its savor if we anticipate the "punch line." Similarly, when a speaker presents several possible solutions to a problem, he would normally do well to keep his listeners in suspense as they wait to find out which one is superior. The mode of indirect development, which will be discussed in Chapter 13, utilizes suspense; the listeners hear a succession of anecdotes or illustrations, but are left guessing for a time as to what conclusion emerges from them. Whenever a speaker causes his listeners to wonder what he is building up to or leads them to speculate on how he is going to solve the problem he is presenting, he is holding their interest through use of suspense. The conclusion of the speaker's remarks must, of course, satisfy the anticipations that have been aroused.

CONFLICT. Radio, television, and public discussions often deliberately build interest by heightening the conflict between opposing points of view. When there are several speakers, this conflict may take the form of debate. But even a single speaker can also depict conflict by making clear to his hearers that there are sharply differing views of the topic. Abraham Lincoln, in his 1858 debates with Stephen A. Douglas, utilized conflict effectively by his habit of giving a sympathetic summary in his opening remarks of the views expressed by his opponent. Interest would be heightened as his audience wondered how he would combat opinions that appeared to be so strongly supported.

A speaker who honestly confides to his listeners, "There is much to be said for both sides," and soundly presents the evidence for each point of view, is making effective use of the interest-generating principle of conflict. Another device is to depict for the audience the weight of opposition to the cause represented by the speaker. "The forces that make for war are as old as the human race, as basic as human nature, and as assertive as human selfishness and greed. But I think this enormous combination can be defeated or deflected—even by individuals as weak and unknown as we are right here in this group. Here is the way I propose by which you and I can fight back—can fight for peace."

HUMOR. The fact that humor is interesting is self-evident; we delight in jokes and in observing hilarious situations. When Henry Grady, from Atlanta, Georgia, undertook in 1886 to dispel the lingering bitterness left over from the Civil War, he made a speech called "The New South," to the New England Society of New York. He had a very serious theme, and a vital purpose over which he had meditated for many months; yet he found it advisable to present his plea in a light vein and to tell a number of humorous stories. The friendly and relaxed interest he was able to generate by this means put his listeners in a proper mood to hear his argument that the nation once more was united in spirit as well as in fact. The speech is well worth reading as a prime example of humor used in a persuasive speech to help hold the "full, fair, and favorable attention" the speaker needed to win acceptance for his purpose. Especially if the subject you have chosen to discuss seems to be rather heavy or dull, it is wise to use your ingenuity to devise means of injecting gleams of humor from time to time—taking care that they support your purpose rather than divert attention away from it.

As you reread these paragraphs on how to maintain a high level of interest, you will observe that they are not so much ornaments added to the speech as they are basic components out of which it is constructed. Interest is not a superficial overlay; it is or must be made part and parcel of what you have to say, as well as of how you say it. This same fact, we shall see, is also true of our next topic: style.

○ STYLE

Perhaps you may think that style is an aspect of speaking which is far too advanced for your present consideration. You may even discount it as representing an outmoded "oratorical" type of speech. When style is sought for its own sake, in order to make what we say seem impressive, we are likely to denounce it as "sophomoric." It may be true that a concern with style as an added gloss, or a surface sheen, or elaborate sentences ought to be regarded with suspicion. But surely it would not be wise to group all our objections to "bad style" and then to assume we are talking about style itself.

Actually, style is as much an integral part of your talk as personality is of your person. As you think of your friends, some have styles of speech that are habitually rather stolid, others lively; some like to speak in long, periodic sentences that abound in qualifications and reservations, others in short bursts of strong assertiveness; some represent a feeling for beauty, others are blunt and matter-of-fact. These are genuinely stylistic differences; but they are also differences in the personalities of the speakers. Style is innate in subject matter and in purpose; it changes as moods change; and it should be appropriate to the occasion and to the listeners. You would scarcely talk to a gathering of faculty members in the same manner as you would to a meeting of your fraternity; nor would you discuss a football game in the same style you would use in comparing Mozart and Beethoven.

It follows that your speaking style should be determined by your own temperament, by the situation in which you talk, and by the subject and theme you are speaking of. In this sense style is "built in" whatever speaking you do. But it is also true that we have to make choices concerning the proper style to employ for particular occasions. Questions to be determined include: what level of style will be appropriate? How does spoken style differ from written style? And what specific stylistic qualities merit consideration?

Levels of Style

Standards of style may be considered in successive levels. The minimum level should surely be mastered by anyone who is to speak at all. Higher levels should be approached and then surpassed as quickly as the speaker's abilities permit. Some types of speaking, such as the making of routine announcements, are properly marked by a very plain style in which little more is demanded than simple clarity and correctness. Other types, such as talks to businessmen, require additional elements of vividness, variety, and personalization. Still others —including many types of sermons or commemorative speeches—depend in part for their effectiveness upon qualities of solemnity, and beauty. Speeches that deserve to be considered orations are imbued with lofty emotion and may be akin to poetry in the evocation and stimulation of their phrasing. Finally, special types of talks, like humorous entertainment, require specific stylistic attributes suited to their purpose. These comments, however, should not suggest that there are objective stylistic factors that can be learned and applied as simple sets of rules, for style is so individualistic that the French rhetorician Buffon was led to conclude that "Style is the man himself."

Correctness of word usage, grammar, and taste is expected by listeners of all college students. Errors in grammar, vulgarisms, and slang should be sedulously avoided even in highly informal speeches. These are akin to mistakes of pronunciation, and even audiences that may accept such errors without overt objection will nevertheless form a lower opinion of the speaker for not avoiding them. Certainly in the college classroom, in the very midst of the process of acquiring an education, no student should permit himself to speak ungrammatically, to use profanity, or to substitute loose construction or slang for the precise statement of an idea. Bare acceptability demands correctness as the minimum standard.

Colloquialisms which are common in conversation should be used only when appropriate in public speaking. Informal conversational speech abounds in colloquial expressions, such as "hanging around," "digging into a subject," "boning up for an exam," and "arguing with the prof." This kind of colloquial speech is usually best reserved for "bull sessions." The informality of good platform talk can better be achieved by the use of contractions, such as, "don't" for "do not" and "I'm" for "I am"; idiomatic expressions, like "We're all in the same boat" and "Don't expect life to be a bowl of cherries"; and simple diction instead of formal locutions, such as "house" instead of "residence" and "job" instead of "vocation." The companionableness of genuine informality is far removed from crudities and mistakes in diction, which are acceptable in almost no type of conversation, unless for a special effect.

Formality should suit the occasion of the speech. When addressing an audience on a subject of some importance and on a somewhat formal occasion, as when speaking to a Rotary Club or a meeting of the PTA, it is advisable to adjust your stylistic level upward, just as you exchange your sport shirt and slacks for a business suit and a necktie. Not only should your speech be free of actual mistakes and colloquialisms, but your sentences should be formed with care and should make use of parallelisms, some imagery, rhetorical questions, and additional elements of vividness. A good example of such formal speech, which is neither cold nor severe, but warm, friendly, and direct, is the following paragraph from a speech delivered by Franklin D. Roosevelt on March 4, 1937:

> My great ambition on January 20, 1941, is to turn over the desk and chair in the White House—this desk and chair—to my succes-

sor, whoever he may be, with the assurance that I am at the same time turning over to him as President a nation intact, a nation at peace, a nation prosperous, a nation clear in what powers it has to serve its own citizens, a nation that is in a position to use those powers to the full in order to move forward steadily to meet the modern needs of humanity—a nation which has thus proved that the democratic forms and methods of national government can and will succeed.

Sublimity may sometimes be sought for and achieved. Few beginning speakers are in a position to strive for the highest levels of oratorical style, those that combine vividness of language, depth of feeling, intellectual insight, and a tone of moral uplift and mark the summit of speaking art. Yet the following example, from a speech by a college sophomore, illustrates a style of restrained grandeur which is worthy of emulation:

> History has lamented the horror of the Revolution, while admiring the genius of its promoters. Historians have decried the useless violence and slaughter of Napoleon, while praising his military and administrative genius. Mankind has leaned upon, but despised, the truer genius of a truer man, who had the courage, amid the madness of the age, to continue living his life. Had we stuff worthy of the project, we should carve from it a magnificent statue of this man who was not the greatest of the great nor the bravest of the brave, but, much better, the sanest of the sane, Gaston Lefarge, The Man Whom Nobody Praised.

Spoken Versus Written Style

Students who write out their speeches—thinking, perhaps, to attain a better style—are likely to make them stilted and to drain from them the direct communicativeness that should always link the speaker and his listeners. Generally, as compared with written style, spoken style uses shorter sentences, simpler language, more personal pronouns, more exclamatory expressions, and more personalized illustrations. The great aim of the speaker is to be direct in the communication of his thoughts to his audience. The writer normally does not know who will be reading what he writes, but the speaker is usually face to face with the people who are listening to him.

Even when speaking over the radio, speakers are advised to address their remarks to some particular group of people whom they can visualize as sitting before their home receivers. The aim of the speaker should be to have every listener say, "This is for me." Abraham Lincoln was praised for his ability to make public speeches that sounded as though he were seated in a buckboard talking to a man on the seat beside him as they drove together over the prairie. Directness and personalization are primary qualities of spoken speech.

Stylistic Qualities

Accuracy in the statement of facts and in the description of situations is the first consideration in discourse, oral or written. No effort to make your speech materials "interesting" or "effective" can be condoned if the result is to misrepresent your own best conception of what is true. This is not so much a matter of style as of simple honesty; it is brought again to your attention here, however, because, unless you have this requirement in mind, you may unconsciously be misled into misstating facts in order to give them more stylistic attractiveness.

Clarity is another absolute essential. There is little purpose in speaking unless what is said is readily understood. This means avoidance of technicalities (unless the material is technical, of course) and of undue complexities of language and logic. The hearer who does not immediately understand what is said has no means of "turning back" to listen again. Periodic summaries and transitions are especially important. The stylistic quality to master, then, is clarity, indispensable to instant comprehension.

Economy of style is another obligation the speaker owes his hearers. When a speech is verbose, unduly repetitive, rambling, or filled with qualifications, or when it wanders aimlessly from the central idea, the listeners wonder why the speaker does not come to the point and state concisely and directly what he has in mind. Speakers vary a great deal in the amount of information or the number of ideas that they can communicate in a five-minute speech. If you will think your speech through carefully until you know precisely what you want to say and then will practice it orally until you are able to whittle away all excess verbiage, you will find that you can considerably enlarge the content and enhance the worth of the message you are able to convey in any given period of time. Acquiring the ability to be concise is a goal worthy of your best endeavors.

Parallelisms are phrases or sentences used in a series, each with a similar grammatical form and with similarity of function or meaning. This method was used by President Kennedy in his speech in Canada in June, 1961, when he said: "Geography has made us neighbors. History has made us friends. Economics has made us partners; and necessity has made us allies." The effect is to narrow attention, thereby achieving emphasis, and also to create a vivid or memorable impression. Parallelism was used with good effect by a student of the University of South Dakota, Linda Yirak, in a speech on the hopelessness that overwhelmed an American soldier captured by the Communists in the Korean War, when she said: "He was cold, but not freezing, hungry but not starving, and yet he died." She used the same device again in her conclusion: "So there will be those who reject or scorn or ignore the facts from Korea. They will say that this was an isolated or exaggerated or unique situation. They will state that these things do not apply to Americans in the security of peacetime. And you, too, may choose—laugh, sneer, condemn, fear this story. Or take heed of it . . . and remember." Surely the weight of what Linda had to say was rendered all the greater by the stylistic device of parallelism she used.

Rhythm in speaking does not at all imply any such regularity of stress as is indicated by meter in poetry. Nevertheless, there is a natural swing or wavelike succession of sound patterns that marks speech and helps to distinguish it from writing. No matter how carefully you may write a speech, it is likely to sound like a prose composition. When we talk, our natural rhythms of feeling express themselves and add warmth and liveliness to our words. Cumbersome, complicated sentences seldom have a proper place in talk. The foregoing example by Miss Yirak illustrates good speech rhythm, as do those that follow from William Jennings Bryan and Charles de Gaulle. Rhythm is the quality Shakespeare probably had in mind when he had Hamlet advise the actors, "Speak the speech, I pray you, trippingly on the tongue." Our sense of rhythm is violated whenever we hear speech that sounds stilted or awkward or wooden.

Imagery, if well used, contributes to the vividness of speech. Good speakers are very much aware of the value of imagery in penetrating their listener's thoughts and feelings. Imagery is achieved through words that appeal to the senses, which are the avenues to the listener's mind. When you describe an event, a place, a happening, or a person to those listening to you, try to make them imagine they see, hear, feel, taste, and touch it, so that it appears real to them.

There are many examples of vivid language and imagery from famous speakers. As an example of William Jennings Bryan's use of imagery, we have his closing words uttered against the gold-standard bloc of Democrats in his famous "Cross of Gold" speech: "You shall not press down upon the brow of labor this crown of thorns, you shall not crucify mankind upon a cross of gold."

Another speaker who makes abundant use of imagery is Charles de Gaulle. This, for instance, is the way he described his feelings as he entered liberated Paris, in the fall of 1944:

> I went on, then, touched and yet tranquil, amid the inexpressible exultation of the crowd, beneath the storm of voices echoing my name, trying, as I advanced, to look at every person in that multitude in order that every eye might register my presence; this was one of those miracles of national consciousness, one of those gestures which sometimes, in the course of centuries, illuminate the history of France.

Force may be achieved by a variety of stylistic devices. Means of emphasis are frequently needed to overcome the natural apathy of listeners who cannot possibly be expected to have the same degree of interest in the speaker's subject as he himself has developed in working with it. Forcefulness can be given to ideas by the use of exclamatory sentences, challenging questions, startling statements of fact, successive short sentences, and pungent repetitions of the idea.

In all the speaking you may do, keep in mind that simple correctness of diction and grammar, and clarity of meaning, are three absolute basics. Colloquialisms are to be used sparingly and discreetly, though this is not meant to warn against informality of style. Good speech is marked by economy of statement, concrete imagery, and force. And always your speech should sound like talk, not like a forlorn essay trying to stand up and come to life from the pages of a manuscript. From such simple bases as these, you may perhaps go on to develop a style of grandeur, beauty, and even solemnity. But your aim should never fall below the minimum levels of correctness, accuracy, clarity, and interest.

○ **CONCLUSION**

Whatever a speaker may accomplish with his listeners depends upon attracting their attention and holding their interest. In large part this means talking with them realistically, about matters of concern to them, in terms that seem reasonable to them. The speaker's style should be clear, correct, and appropriate. In this chapter various means have been explored of dramatizing the interest inherent in the speaker's personality, in the subject, and in the audience expectations. Attention, interest, and style are not adornments added to the speech, but developed elements inherent in the speaker-subject-listener relationship.

EXERCISES

Questions for Discussion

1. What are the functions of attention, interest, and style—that is, what do they accomplish?

2. Discuss various titles used for speeches presented in your class, to determine how well they exemplify the four functions of a good title.

3. Turn back to Chapter 6 to review what is said there about the varied purposes of the Introduction. Discuss *sensational* and *unobtrusive* introductions, in terms of their attention-compelling function—using illustrations drawn from speeches you have heard in class and elsewhere. Which type of introduction do you yourself generally prefer? What factors help you decide which type to use?

4. What factors of interest derive from personality? Answer the question by citing a number of individuals whom you would be glad to listen to for quite different reasons. What factors of personality-interest do you possess? What additional ones might you develop?

5. Consider each of the factors of interest (as related to subject matter) in terms of topics that have been discussed in class. What factors of interest have been utilized? What additional ones might the speakers have developed?

6. Is style a matter for genuine concern by beginning students of speech? What differences of style do you note between your conversation and your classroom speaking? Between your writing and your talking? Is there a practical need to pay attention to levels of style? Which of the stylistic qualities are indispensable in all good talk? Which ones might you add to your own speaking with advantage? Do you find any of them artificial or awkward?

Projects for Speaking and Writing

1. Select a well-known speaker whom you have heard in person or on radio or television and present to your class a brief speech in which you analyze his methods of compelling attention, maintaining interest, and achieving a personalized style. Evaluate his speech in terms of the factors presented in this chapter.

2. Draw up for yourself a personalized guide-sheet on which you will list the factors of attention, interest, and style which you will make special effort to utilize in your own speaking. Make this an exercise in progressive learning by indicating which ones you will utilize in your next talk; which in the talk following; and which in the next after that. As you prepare and then deliver these talks, check back to this list to help you evaluate your success in adhering to your plan. This exercise will yield greater dividends in substantial improvement if you will join with a classmate in considering what each of you has set as a goal and evaluating for one another how well these goals are being achieved.

3. Draw upon your memory of two or three recent conversations in which you have engaged to try to estimate how successfully your day-by-day talk exemplifies the communicative use of factors of attention, interest, and style. Decide what specific improvements are within the range of your abilities and make a sustained effort to introduce these needed qualities into your conversation. If the results are not at first impressively successful, remember the analogy of the tennis game that was discussed under the "Educational Norm" in Chapter 2. When you are trying to do what will eventually yield optimum results, the systematic continuance of the effort is more desirable than immediate success. Once again, this learning experience will be more productive if you share evaluations of it with a fellow-student who is engaged in a similar program.

Chapter 9

Delivering the Speech

THE FEATURE OF THE SPEECH COURSE that distinguishes it most clearly from other courses of study is the requirement of standing and presenting yourself orally to a group. When that is done, your instructor and the class will discuss with you not only the content of your speech but also the skill and effectiveness of your presentation. Thus, you will learn to recognize the importance not only of what you know but also of your ability to communicate your knowledge, ideas, and convictions.[1]

○ MISCONCEPTIONS ABOUT SPEECH DELIVERY

The delivery of a speech should not be thought of as merely a mechanical process consisting of standing correctly, gesturing gracefully, and speaking with clear articulation and in well-modulated tones. Without question, your platform presence and your vocal qualities should be adequate; if they are not, you should welcome guidance that will lead to improvement. But the process is far from mechanical. Instead, it is at the heart of your basic relations with other people. What is required above all is that you accustom yourself to thinking of problems from the point of view of your listeners, trying to understand their needs and desires, and determining to do your best

---

[1] For an excellent discussion of the fact that we "communicate" with our total appearance and behavior, whether or not we intend to, *cf.* Edward T. Hall, *The Silent Language*. Greenwich, Conn.: Fawcett, Premier Book, 1959.

to make your own ideas and convictions meaningful and attractive to them.

Since false ideas about the delivery of a speech are often encountered, the following cautions are offered:

1. *The delivery of a speech is not a performance* such as dancing in a ballet which requires the learning of an intricate set of steps. Actually, to regard a speech as a set performance is an inducement to become artificial, and artificiality is one of the chief barriers to effectiveness. The platform performer directs his attention to his posture, gestures, and vocal qualities. To achieve his ends, he may memorize his speech and even memorize certain gestures to use while presenting it. The result is that what the audience sees is akin to a display of acting, the more so if the speech is eloquent. One of the first ideas to be discarded, however, is that a speech is some kind of artificial, dramatic production.

2. *Abundant practice is not the only means of achieving effective delivery.* Awkward, stilted, or self-conscious mannerisms will, if practiced steadily, become more, not less, permanently fixed. Practice acquires value when it is accompanied by a sound basic understanding of correct principles, by criticism from the listeners that points out what is effective and what is ineffective, and by continuous self-evaluation, resulting in a pattern of revision and improvement in successive speeches. Improvement in delivery will come as you follow these four steps: (1) study the reading assignments carefully to ensure that you know what you ought to be doing; (2) analyze closely the speeches by your classmates and other speakers to determine what is good and what is not so good in their presentation; (3) obtain meaningful criticisms of your own communicative characteristics; and (4) make a determined and intelligent application of all you learn in guiding your own progressive development. These steps should all be kept firmly in mind while you practice your speeches orally.

3. *There is no single pattern of good delivery* (including postural and vocal factors) that you must learn and adopt. Experience reveals that a great many people believe that there is a standard form of standing, gesturing, and vocalizing that is prescribed for platform speaking and that this form differs from the normal speech of animated conversation. Students who have a natural desire to pass their course in speech determine resignedly to master this set pattern for use in

their talks in speech class—but sensibly tell themselves that they certainly will not use it outside of class.

Of course, no such artificial standard exists. If it did, the aim should be to train all speakers to become alike—to become in effect automatons imitating a chosen model of the ideal good speaker. Actually, personalities vary widely, and the goal of every student of speech should be to develop his own most effective manner of speaking his own best ideas and convictions in a manner that gains in effectiveness by being so unobtrusive that the techniques of delivery are scarcely noticed.

○ THE FUNCTIONS OF CODES

Communicative speech involves three different channels: the visual, the auditory, and the linguistic. In other words, we convey meanings to one another in our normal oral discourse by what we say, by how we sound, and by how we look. Communication through our words is discussed throughout the book. It is a complex process, closely interwoven with how we think, what we think about, what we think of our listeners, and how we view our relations with them. All these things, and more, are revealed or hinted at by the words we use and the way in which we put them together. We all understand that the linguistic code is extremely intricate, that it serves a tremendous variety of functions, that it can both convey a vast amount of information and also cause a vast amount of confusion and misunderstanding. What is not so widely understood is that the visual and auditory codes are similarly complex, capable of conveying crucial information, and prone to errors in their use. In this chapter we shall consider ways by which you can make your visual communication and your voice, articulation, and diction more effective.

Code, as you know, means a system of symbols with agreed-upon or conventionalized meanings. The English language is a code—as are French, algebra, the cries of crows, and the secret cryptographs used to smuggle information through enemy territory. The examples used indicate some of the functions of codes.

First, they make sense to people who understand them—having at least roughly equivalent meanings for the user and the receiver; thus, both you and your listeners understand English and get the same rough and approximate meanings from English words spoken and heard. Second, French is a code also, but English users frequently do not understand French users, and vice versa. In other words, codes are systems of communication that have to be learned; different codes are learned by different groups of people; and a code that serves some people may not serve others. Third, algebra is a code that says some things that cannot be said in words; and many things that can be said in words cannot be conveyed by algebraic symbols. In other words, codes are of different types, serving different purposes, appealing to different senses, and usable only in specific ways. Fourth, the cries of crows are presumably adequate to serve the communicative needs of crows but for human beings they are less capable of conveying meanings than even the simplest of human languages. In other words, codes are devised to serve specialized needs and they are not necessarily comparable in regard to what they can do or what they are supposed to do. Finally, the distinguishing feature of secret cryptographs is that they are useful precisely because they can be understood by some people and not by others. A spy may carry a letter that says in English that the week he had just spent visiting with his Aunt Martha had been very pleasant; but the meaning concealed in the cryptographic code of those same sentences might be that unusual activity had been observed at the Cape Canaveral launching pad.

We have noted, then, five functions of codes: (1) to convey meaning; (2) to group people into different types of code-users; (3) to serve special and limited communication needs; (4) to serve needs of widely divergent levels of complexity; and (5) to convey meaning to selected receivers while simultaneously concealing it from others.

We may say then, that at its most comprehensive, the visual code covers all the ways in which these five functions may be achieved through the sense of sight. The visual code as used in speaking includes the use of visual aids—which will be discussed in Chapter 11: physical appearance, including dress; observable behavior, and all bodily action, including posture and gestures. The visual code has different functions from the auditory and linguistic codes, just as algebra and the cries of animals have different functions from human speech. The visual code conveys meaning just as truly as do words; and it has differences in style and manner as significant as the differences between French and English. Furthermore, there is the same possibility for secret communication through the visual as through the verbal code—for example, by the signals used in professional baseball.

○ THE VISUAL CODE

One of the strange things about the visual code is that we know a great deal about it without realizing how much we know. We started learning it very early in life, long before we were able to learn language; and we continue to study it closely and carefully all our lives. But most of our learning about the visual code is unconscious; hence we do not realize how much of it we understand or how broadly, intensively, and precisely we use it both to convey and to receive meaning. Through visual cues within the family, we learn to evaluate the moods of our parents and brothers and sisters—to tell whether they are happy or unhappy, confident or ill at ease, worried or content, nervous or calm, affectionate or irritated, gay or serious, alert or tired, eager or reluctant to communicate.

Similarly, we respond easily and naturally to visual attitudes of approval or disapproval, of enthusiasm or boredom, of assertiveness or submission, of interest or apathy. Moreover, we know that a great deal of meaning is conveyed merely through the sense of sight; by gestures, such as looking or motioning toward the salt when we want it; by inquiring glances, as when mother asks where you have been merely by looking at you with that look; by dress and manner, as when father appears in slippers and settles wearily into his chair—indicating, perhaps, that if the lawn is to be mowed he is not the one who is going to do it. The list of examples could be greatly expanded. As we all realize, a vast amount of what family members convey to one another is communicated wholly by appearance, manner, and behavior. Without any words being spoken, a vast amount of information is exchanged.

Outside the family, too, we communicate extensively with our friends purely through visual cues. One sign of friendship is the ability to understand one another, without explanation. Even when we are dealing with a broad range of acquaintances, and to a certain degree with complete strangers, we continue to receive and convey a great many meanings simply by the way we appear to one another. Attitudes of friendliness, indifference, or antagonism are easily communicated without a word being spoken. So are fear, anger, joy, enthusiasm, unhappiness, worry, and many more feelings.

If you have had the experience of traveling in a foreign country where you do not know the language, you have doubtless been pleased to find how readily your general needs (even the need for companionship) are satisfied through interchanges dependent upon bearing, mannerisms, and gestures. Smiles and frowns, gestures of acceptance or nonacceptance, cold stares versus friendly glances—these and many other visual cues determine a large portion of our relations with other people.

Some of the visual cues which we transmit or interpret are intentional, easily seen, and more or less conventionalized in meaning—such as a frown, a shrug of the shoulders, or a raised index finger. Others are produced unintentionally. Often these unintended signs are so minute that they are received and interpreted unconsciously. In this case they are called "subliminal"; that is, they do not sufficiently attract attention to be acknowledged. In psychological terms, they fall below the threshold of awareness. Nevertheless, cumulatively, even the tiny tightening of facial muscles, the minute straightening of the posture, the very slight forward motion of the body—none of which may be noted by itself—taken all together do give an impression of increased attentiveness. Many of the impressions by which we judge the reactions of others are based on this subliminal communicative pattern; still others are derived from obvious gestures consciously used and consciously interpreted.

Students of gesture have estimated that there are at least 600,000 different gestures (symbolic physical manifestations) that are capable of conveying fairly precise meanings: in effect, as many gestures as there are English words. It has also been ascertained that different cultural groups—races, nations, social classes—have their own fairly distinct types of gesture. A Frenchman is likely to be demonstrative, an Oriental decorously restrained. An aristocrat bears himself much differently from a beggar, so that if we happen to see a ragged individual whose posture and bearing suggest dignity and self-esteem we are likely to be startled by the thought that he bears himself like an aristocrat. In a democracy, it is said that "every man is a king," in part because he looks and acts as though he feels himself to be as good as anyone else. In short, much of what we think and feel is communicated and interpreted through the visual code.

○ EMPATHY

It has been indicated that we communicate far more than we realize through visual cues. In other words, we use the visual code for a great deal of our social communication, just as we use the oral and verbal codes. But whereas we are very conscious of our use of language, we seldom examine or think about our use of face or hands. Two principal reasons may be suggested for our failure to realize the richness and utility of our complex visual communicativeness. The first is that we hear our own words, but we usually do not see our own facial expressions or other bodily movements. And the second reason is that our words are interpreted mentally, whereas response to the visual cues supplied by others is more largely neuromuscular.

Empathy means the predominantly unconscious physical reaction which we have to observed meanings. Students of art tell us that harmony, or balance, in a painting seems beautiful or attractive to us in large part because it fits in with the harmonious balance of our own bodies. What we see we tend to imitate, much in the way it is said that "Monkey see, monkey do." Experience reminds us that when we watch a hard-fought football game, we come away tired, because our own muscles have strained in empathic response to the physical contest we have been observing.

How much of our learning is neuromuscular is indicated by the fact that we ride a bicycle well only when we cease to think about how we do it. Much the same is true of the way we drive a car, tie a necktie, and perform many other physical actions. Even in much of the work we think of as mental, our success depends at least partially upon our developing a "feel" for it; a writer, for example, may be more productive when seated at his own desk, in his own study, than when housecleaning relegates him for a time to typing in the breakfast nook. Similarly, we learn, or receive communication, from others in part through our muscular "feel" for the appearance and behavior of the speaker.

If the speaker's posture or gestures seem wrong to his listeners, it may be in part because they are unusual or unconventional, and thereby violate the audience's "pattern of expectation." It may also in part be because they are strained, or out of balance, thereby causing an imitative reaction in the listeners which is uncomfortable.

Empathy is a term deliberately coined to correspond to, while

Empathy is identification . . .

Mutual identification between speaker and listener creates a pattern of expectation which must be satisfied by visual communication. Empathy and sympathy are correlates—each reinforces and influences the other.

differing from, sympathy. We know that sympathy means an identification with the person being sympathetically viewed. People who are sympathetic in their relations are in rapport with one another; they share similar feelings; they react with similar emotions. In like manner, when we empathize with other people, we tend to take on their physical properties. We sympathize with a person who is obviously suffering pain; we tend to feel his pain ourselves, and we wish for its relief. But we also empathize with the sufferer; our own face reflects the strain and signs of suffering we note on his; our own muscles contract.

On other occasions, we respond to smiles with a smile and to frowns with a frown—partly from sympathetic feelings and partly from empathic imitativeness. In fact, the mere muscular empathizing that we do helps to create in ourselves a bodily pattern similar to another's, so that we are more prone to sympathize, or to recreate in ourselves his feelings. Empathy and sympathy are correlates; each one reinforces the other.

Reinforcement is recognized by psychologists as a major factor in influencing human behavior. When we reflect, or empathize, in response to certain elements in the behavior of another person, our own behavior strengthens those same tendencies in his. This is very evident when a mild argument between two persons develops into a violent quarrel; but it is equally relevant when we see one party to an argument diverted from quarreling by the "selective imitation" of a friend who seizes upon his silent indications of pleasantness and magnifies them in the response. Psychologists are prone to believe that we can actually change the mood and behavior of our associates significantly by giving them a pattern to which we want them to respond empathically. You yourself have no doubt done this on many occasions when you have "cheered up" a downcast friend largely by behaving toward him in a cheerful manner.

Empathy is a mode of communication, then, which operates more physically than mentally. Another way of saying it is that it operates largely unconsciously. Its effects are felt without becoming an object of focalized attention. You can say to your friend who is despondent, "Snap out of it; you have nothing to worry about!" But you may get a growl or an argument in response. Or you may greet him with a sympathetic reflection of part of his own mood, and then introduce a cheerful note in your whole manner. Many times the visible empathic influence is more effective than words would have been; more

Empathy is a mode of communication . . .

Empathy operates unconsciously. Its effects are *felt* without attracting focalized attention; *words* and *manner* work together toward the same goal.
If in speaking you are stiff, awkward, ill at ease, listeners will be distracted
from your ideas; if you are warm, friendly, and relaxed, listeners also
tend to be friendly and receptive.

often, probably, the words and the behavior or manner work together toward the same goal.

Whenever you are talking with people, the important consideration empathically is that they not only hear you but also see you. If you should droop wearily and gaze absently out the window while asserting that you are having a wonderful time, your companions are more likely to believe your manner than your words. What you have really done is to convey two contradictory messages through two separate codes. Your linguistic code will be interpreted by the brain, which through the visual organ, the eyes, will find reasons in your bearing to discount the words. Generally it appears to be true that "seeing is believing," and what we observe will outweigh what we hear.

Whether you are engaged in conversation, in discussion, or in giving a public speech, it is well to remember that you are simultaneously speaking with your whole person as well as with words from your mouth. Your companions will respond not alone to what they hear but also to what they see. If the two channels of communication work at cross purposes, the listener-observers will either be confused or will tend to trust their empathic responses. Sincerity is valued highly in human relations, primarily because it means that the message being delivered is all one: words and actions are unified, in harmony.

We tend to trust our empathic reactions to speakers precisely because we know it is more difficult to pretend with the whole body than it is with words alone. Communications delivered through the channel of empathy are likely to be believed. This is a major reason why bodily action—commonly known as *delivery*—is an important aspect of effective speaking. It is why Demosthenes, when asked to name the three cardinal attributes of good speech, said: "Action! Action! Action!" It is why Quintilian observed that sound ideas poorly presented are often less effective than ideas of less import that are delivered with active conviction.

○ PRINCIPLES OF DELIVERY

There is no single pattern of effective communicative speech. If there were, everyone should be trained to speak the same way; whereas on the contrary, we know that people vary greatly in their manner of speaking effectively. Each of us has to find and develop the kind of delivery that fits his own personality, his own purposes, his own conception of his relationship with his listeners. There are, nevertheless, some basic principles that in varied ways all of us should observe.

Be Natural

In a carefully restricted sense, the best advice for the delivery of a speech is, "Be natural." This means that you should talk to your listeners with the spontaneous, controlled enthusiasm that you would use in animated conversation. It does not mean that you should be tolerant of awkward mannerisms on the platform simply because they may have become habitual: twisting your hands together nervously, looking out of the window, and shifting your weight from one foot to the other with pendulum-like regularity. These mannerisms may serve to release nervous energy, but such escape mechanisms will arouse highly undesirable empathic responses in listeners and decrease the effectiveness of your speaking.

This nervous energy should be channeled into earnestness of voice and manner, directness of glance, and a natural vigor of bodily expressiveness, all designed to help convey your message to your hearers. To be "natural" in your speaking may require as much guidance as is needed by a sprinter who must learn the natural technique of leaping forward from the starting line at the instant he hears the crack of the starter's gun. Similarly, even natural posture, gestures, and directness on the platform may not be either natural to you or easy to achieve without careful observation of other speakers, much practice, and the mastery of self-consciousness.

Natural delivery, then, means that you walk confidently to the front of the room, encompass your listeners with a glance of genuine recognition and fellowship, and say what you have to say with the maximum communicativeness of words, voice, and bodily expressiveness.

Be Conversational

The two-way feature of good conversation is its chief characteristic. You speak and you also listen. You suit your comments to the perceived ideas of your associates. You respond directly and immediately to what is in their minds. The whole process is an *exchange* of feelings and ideas in which the understanding and convictions of each

204 · DEVELOPING COMMUNICATIVE SPEECH

member of the group are modified by the contributions of the others. A second important characteristic of good conversation is that it is an honest outpouring and interrelating of ideas and feelings and not at all a performance in which successive speakers seek to win admiration for their skill as speakers. Communication, rather than mere self-expression or personal display, is the goal.

Public speaking presents problems in communication that are less evident in conversation. It is more difficult for the public speaker than for the conversationalist to tailor what he is saying to the immediate reactions of his listeners. However, he should never forget that they have ideas and feelings, just as he has. They respond with doubt to some statements, with antagonism to others, and with willing acceptance to still others. Moreover, if the speaker is really talking *with* his listeners—and not *at* or *toward* them—he will be alert to detect and interpret their responses and will shift and adjust his modes of communication in accordance with the reactions of his audience. These reactions are not hard to detect, especially if the speaker invites responsiveness by making it clear that he is trying to think through a problem with his audience rather than simply unburdening himself to them for an allotted period of time. Talking to oneself in public is not good public speaking.

The conversational mode consists largely in seeking the circular response, through such techniques as asking rhetorical questions, referring to experiences shared by the speaker and his listeners, and making it clear that the speaker is trying to solve a problem or find a basis of understanding that is desired as much by the audience as by himself. The conversational mode abounds in personal pronouns, in questions, and in such linking phrases as "You yourselves have often observed . . ." and "Judge from your own experience."

Good conversation is a face-to-face relationship in which response follows and influences response. By gestures, facial expressions, and bodily activity—as well as by words—two or more people engaged in talking are obviously engrossed in the give and take of ideas being exchanged. These are qualities of conversation which should be retained, so far as possible, in the platform speech.

Develop the Urge to Communicate

Individuals vary a great deal in their desire to influence others, and not everyone possesses an instinct for leadership. It is obviously a waste of time for a speaker to address an audience unless he wants them to accept what he has to say. If your basic urge to communicate is not great, you will speak less often than another person who has a keen desire to move others to action. But it is axiomatic that when you do speak, you should devote yourself wholeheartedly and with intense earnestness to trying to win acceptance by your listeners of the facts and the convictions you have to present.

As a social being, you cannot and do not live alone. Your life is closely geared with the lives of those around you. The standards set by society govern and regulate your own behavior. You cannot avoid being interested in what these standards are, and, from a sheer desire for self-protection and self-development, you need to exert your own influence to help ensure that they are satisfactory. The fact that man is inescapably (and fortunately) a social creature demands that you be attentive to the kind of ideas presented in the talk to which you listen, and it similarly requires that from time to time you state your own convictions or contribute your own knowledge to the group. From the standpoint of effectiveness in speaking, it is important that, when you speak, you say what you mean and mean what you say. After preparing yourself for a speech that is worthy of being heard, pour yourself feelingly as well as intellectually into the task of communicating it so urgently and impellingly that your listeners will give it full consideration. ,

When you do speak, for at least that limited time and in that special circumstance, you are acting the role of a leader. You should exert all your energies to master yourself, your subject, and the audience situation so that, while you are speaking, you do in fact command. Even though you may question your own right or desire to control the reactions of an audience, you can at least prepare a body of facts and a pattern of convictions which are so true and so much needed by your listeners that you can imbue yourself with a zeal to win their acceptance. This is the spirit—the urge to communicate—which animates every speech and helps you give it effectiveness.

Speak Extempore

It should be evident that the conversational mode and the urge to communicate can be manifest only through extemporaneous speaking. Speeches that are read or memorized are usually stilted, indirect, dull, and artificial, although, as Chapter 16 indicates, they can and should be presented effectively. A high government official may read a manuscript setting forth the policies that the administration has adopted or that need to be presented for public consideration. Few speakers, however, ever have occasion to advertise to the listeners—by use of a prefabricated address—that their attitudes and their reactions are of no immediate concern to him. By all odds, the most useful, and most used, form of public speaking is the extemporaneous speech.

In using the extempore method the speaker knows, as a result of preliminary thinking and research, what he will say and the order in which he will say it; but the exact wording and sometimes even the choice among available examples or forms of proof are left until the moment of delivery. Such extempore speaking should never be confused with the *impromptu* method, which means to speak on the spur of the moment out of your general background experiences but with no specific preparation.

Actually, there is no limit to the amount of preparation for a speech that is delivered extemporaneously. For the extempore speech, the speaker prepares himself by selecting his *ideas,* gathering his *facts,* and carefully working out his *organization.* He knows what he wants to accomplish, the means by which he will support his assertions, and the order in which his ideas will be presented. His whole preparation is idea-centered and listener-centered. When he knows what purpose he wants to achieve and what audience he will address, he thinks through and plans for his speaking in detail. However, he will not permit it to become so thoroughly set that he becomes a prisoner of his own plans. Like a military patrol sent out to scout enemy territory, he prepares meticulously but leaves himself free to observe every obstacle, to detect every show of opposition, and to adapt his strategy so that he can bring his maximum strength to bear to accomplish his objective.

Use Approved Forms of Etiquette

Speech has its own rules of etiquette, most of which are comprised within the formula of demonstrating self-respect and respect for the others present. In conversation, this means sharing the opportunity to talk with others, not interrupting another, being ready to bear one's own share of responsibility for developing ideas, maintaining a sociable tone, showing a live interest in what others say, speaking briefly, and keeping alert to the desire of others to interject their own ideas. In public speaking, since the situation is more formalized, the rules of etiquette are more definite.

1. Whether, as a speaker, you are seated on the platform or in the audience while others are speaking, you should show a receptive interest in what is being said. Do not distract attention from the speaker by obviously scanning your own notes.

2. Your attire should be appropriate to the occasion. As a guiding principle, it is usually considered good taste for the speaker to be a little more formally dressed than his listeners, since he is the focus of attention. A good appearance helps create a good impression.

3. Take your position in front of the group calmly, confidently, and unhurriedly. It is natural, and therefore desirable, to acknowledge the introduction you have received with a "Thank you," or at least a smile and a nod addressed to the person who has introduced you. On formal occasions, it is ordinarily expected that the speaker should address the audience as "Ladies and gentlemen," or more explicitly— as, "Mr. President, members of the faculty, students, and friends." Speakers sometimes begin not with a salutation but with some such expression as, "I am glad to have this opportunity to talk with you today . . ." or, "Your chairman has aked me to talk with you tonight about . . ."

4. While you are speaking, concentrate your attention on your listeners, rather than on yourself. When you are first starting to speak, there is likely to be a nervous tendency to button and unbutton your coat, to shift about uneasily, or even to look out the window, at the ceiling or at the floor—anything to delay or avoid coming into direct relationship with the people with whom you are speaking. This, of course, is unnatural (even if it does occur often); and it gives an impression of awkwardness and lack of poise. It is advisable to develop a habit of planting yourself firmly, with your weight balanced evenly and without swaying either from side to side or forward and backward. Confidence and poise are valuable attributes in all social relations and perhaps more than ever when you are speaking.

5. Since everyone present is part of your audience, it is polite to distribute your remarks fairly evenly around the group. You will,

of course, want to be keenly aware of the responses of everyone present, as a guide to your continuous adaptation to their reactions.

6. When you conclude your talk, it is seldom advisable to end with a "Thank you." Better, plan your conclusion so that your final sentence is a definitive close—perhaps a question, or a challenge, or a summary—then turn the meeting back to the chairman with a nod or a smile in his direction, and resume your seat.

Bodily Bearing and Gestures

As we have said earlier in this chapter, your appearance (including dress, poise, and everything you do) is an important part of your means of communicating. If your muscles are overly tense and hence tend to twitch or quiver, such tension may communicate either timidity or excitement. You can convert this tension into an advantage by demonstrating through your words and the eagerness or urgency of your communicating manner that the excitement really is an indication of a desire to present your ideas. The total bodily action you manifest will either support your words or will contradict them. In either case, the reaction of the listeners will be determined by their interpretation of what you do as well as what you say.

Bodily bearing is a major cue to the meanings you are expressing. As we pointed out earlier, you may express one set of meanings while trying to communicate still another. If your elbows are tightly pressed against your sides and your body is bent into a kind of cringe, while your eyes shift uneasily away from your listeners, you are expressing a positive distaste for speaking with them. This expression will conflict seriously with your verbal assertion that you have something new to say which you can scarcely wait to impart to them. But if your posture is confidently and easily erect, if your arms and hands are free to signal your urge to reach out and get into contact with the people before you, and if your general appearance is that of a person who is speaking because he really does have an important message to communicate, then your expression and your communication combine to reinforce one another.

Gestures are the natural physical outlet of the speaker's desire to use all his resources to communicate. When a person nods his head, we know he is agreeing with us; if he shakes his head, he is disagreeing or questioning our point of view. Similarly, if the fist of the right hand is banged into the left palm, we recognize this as an emphatic declaration of strong feelings. If the right index finger is raised and pointed or moved decisively up and down, we all realize this is a way of asserting that what is said is of importance. In general, leaning or stepping forward, or raising the hands, palm upward, or raising the two fists (or one of them) in a gesture extending them toward the audience are all ways of urging acceptance of what is said. On the other hand, if you present an idea that you wish the audience to reject, you may physically renounce the notion by actually recoiling, or by sweeping your hands, palm down, away from your person. It is impractical and even impossible to catalog all the many gestures with which we continually enforce our real meanings. But we do recognize that one group is affirmative and inviting of acceptance, another group negative and rejective.

In normal conversation, since you do not feel a sense of strain, you naturally use a variety of gestures which tend to enforce your words simply because you mean what you say; hence you say it with your whole being. However, in a more formal situation, as, for instance, when you are making a speech, your gestures may betray your own state of inner conflict. In part you mean what your words are asserting; but perhaps in part you also mean that you feel this is a somewhat artificial or partially undesirable situation. In effect, your gestures are saying, "Don't take me seriously, because I don't really want to be here saying this." The best way to assure that your gestures will support your words is to prepare yourself as well as your speech. That is, don't just concentrate on having a message to deliver, but also talk yourself into an eagerness to gain listener response.

The number and kind of gestures you will (and should) use will depend on your own personality, on the subject, and on the nature of the situation. Individuals vary a great deal in personality structure. Some are exuberant, extroverted, and vitally expressive; others are quiet, introverted, and reserved in manner. Perhaps if your own personality is inadequately expressive of your genuine feelings, you may wish to develop habits of greater expressiveness. These habits can be developed by giving them thought and by consciously practicing the communicative art of speaking with your body as well as with your voice.

There is not, however, any single model of the effective speaker. Some generate an air of thoughtfulness by reserve in action, just as others generate an air of enthusiasm by more vigorous gesturing. Of course, the topic has its own influence. An appeal for students to attend a football rally would surely be ineffective if it were delivered in the manner of an appeal for blood donors; on the other hand, a eulogy of a departed friend would require a still different manner of presentation. Aside from the influence of the topic, the situation makes its own demands. With a half-alive audience (say, at eight in the morning) speakers need to be more vigorous in order to arouse interest. A large auditorium requires larger, more sweeping gestures than a small one—if only in order that they may be seen by listeners all over the house.

Facial Expressions

The face, especially the eyes and mouth, is wonderfully expressive. Tilts of the head, furrowing of the brow, smiles, frowns, puzzled expressions, pursing of the lips, firming the muscles of the jaw: these and literally hundreds of other small but significant variations of facial expression all convey a great deal of meaning. The "poker face" should be reserved for occasions in which you wish to conceal what you are thinking and feeling. When your aim is to communicate, you should bring into full play the naturally communicative faculties of quick and continuous variations of expression. As you know, when a friend makes a comment that seems odd or incomprehensible, you quickly look at his face, expecting to find there a clue to his real meaning. In like manner, you should help your audience to comprehend fully and easily what you wish to communicate to them by speaking with your facial expression as well as with your bodily bearing and your words.

○ SUMMARY

As we have seen, there are three parallel codes by which we all receive or impart meaning: by what we say, by how we sound, and by how we look. The third of these codes has been discussed in the preceding pages. We have noted the tremendous complexity of this code, resulting in part from the fact that there are some 600,000 separate gestures and in part from the fact that what we communicate visually is less amenable to our conscious mental control than is our words; hence it often happens that we say one thing verbally and transmit something contradictory to it through the use of our bodies. As we noted in discussing empathy, your hearers' neuromuscular reactions can be decisive. The awareness of meaning that comes through from this source is very real and influential, although one may not analyze it. The "feel" of what you say is projected more immediately than your words' meaning.

In using the complex visual code, including the principle of empathy, to help communicate your meanings, you should be natural, conversational, extemporaneous, and alert to your communicative etiquette—that is, appearance, bodily bearing, gestures, and facial expressions. All these may combine to help you accomplish the purpose of your talk, or (if neglected) they may counteract the meanings intended by your words. Speaking involves appealing to the eye as well as to the ear. This is a fact of life which becomes an important consideration in communicative speaking.

Since, nevertheless, speech is conventionally viewed as something to be heard, and presumably listened to, we shall turn now to a consideration of the ways in which we use our voices and articulate and pronounce the words we speak.

○ THE AUDITORY CODE

Many things seem important only when they are bad or derogatory. An ordinary man gains public attention by shooting his wife but not by bringing her flowers every week. Recently, a newspaperman in conversation praised a speech as timely, pertinent, a clear statement of a pressing problem. "But I can't send it in to my wire service," he added, "because the speaker wasn't mad at anybody."

When a man speaks with eloquence, when he meets the standards of good speech, you may note his moral fiber, you may praise the excellence of his communication, you may behave in the way that he purposes, you may note that you have learned something. But very likely you will *not* notice his voice, his articulation of speech sounds, or his pronunciation; you will probably pay little attention to how he sounds. On the other hand, if you do notice these aspects of his speaking, it is often unfavorably. If he lisps, you think him juvenile or effeminate; if he mispronounces a word or utters a Mortimer Snerd "duh," you think him stupid; if he makes the "r" sound a little like a "w," you say he is talking baby-talk; if his voice sounds rasping or shrill or bombastic, you find him irritating; if he speaks too softly or with muffled articulation, you decide he isn't worth listening to or that he doesn't really care about you.

You should know, however, that it is possible to err as grievously in overprecision of articulation and pronunciation as in carelessness and inaccuracy. Good utterance must not draw attention to itself any more than gesture, bodily movements, or any other aspects of our speaking. Whenever anyone is so overcareful in his articulation as to attract attention to it, he diverts the minds of his hearers to how something is being said rather than to what is being said, and he may be accused of affectation.

These are stereotyped responses in our culture. Though they may be wrong, they exist; they operate in listeners. Thus, the student of speaking and listening must learn to discount the effect on himself of such responses as a listener in order to come to grips with a speaker's ideas and communicative purposes. At the same time, he must examine his own vocal habits to make sure that, though he meets the other standards of good speech, he is not forcing on his own listeners the same kind of misconception of himself, the same kind of distractions.

This is one dilemma that cannot be avoided in the use of the auditory code: you are handicapped if you don't conform to what listeners expect—and you receive no praise if you do. But it should be clear that if you would be effective, you will not risk responses to how you are speaking instead of responses to what you are saying. So you will want to know how to bring voice, articulation, and pronunciation into line with inconspicuous norms.

This brings most speakers to a second dilemma. Robert Burns reminded us that we cannot see ourselves as others see us; so, too, might he have prayed that man be given the gift to *hear* himself as others hear him. If you have heard your speech recorded, as every student of speech should try to do, you have most likely insisted, "That doesn't sound like me!" You may have rejected the recorded speech patterns as your own on whatever grounds were available: "It's because I have a slight cold," or, "The recorder isn't hi-fi," or, "Somebody's trying to pull a fast one." And you forget the experience as soon as possible. But if that recording is played for anyone who knows you, that listener will immediately identify the voice as yours. Why?

First of all, you have simply learned to hear yourself in a particular way; in a way that you always expect to hear yourself and, therefore, automatically, your reactions conform to your expectations. Part (though not all) of the reason is that you hear yourself in different ways, through different channels, from those through which you hear others or your own recording. Secondly, whether your voice characteristics and articulation are all within acceptable, inconspicuous norms, or whether you have some few characteristics that are not, you have learned to hear yourself as within those norms. Thus, if you are saying "thithter," you are hearing it as identical with what you hear when someone else says "sister." If you are speaking too softly, you are hearing your voice volume as identically within the range of normal voices around you.

It should be clear, then, that it is important for voice and articulation to conform with those norms which you hear from the outside in order to keep acoustic properties from getting in the way of your communication. Also, it should be clear that your own ears are not to be trusted in determining whether you are in need of some adjustment in order to bring your vocal characteristics within those norms.

Diagnosing Voice and Articulation Differences

Most students whom we meet in college have thoroughly adequate voices and at least passably acceptable articulation. But if there is any question, it is wise to arrange for a voice and articulation check-up. That is, you may need to find out if there are characteristic differences that make a difference. You do and you should have some identifying characteristics of voice and articulation which make your voice recognizable to those who know you; but these will be within listener expectancies. You should not have the impression that the goal of any speech improvement program is to make you sound "just like everybody else." Far from it. The speech scientists and phoneticians tell us that no individual ever produces a speech sound in exactly the same way twice. There are myriad differences that do *not* make a difference in the communication process.

A speaker can get the necessary information about himself from several sources of varying dependability. A friend may or may not discern the differences that would be obvious to a stranger or a speech teacher or even to the speaker himself when listening to his voice recording. Parents, for instance, have been known to not hear severe speech pathologies in their children, even stuttering or extreme na- sality. There once was an advertising slogan that said, "Even your best friend won't tell you." This sometimes applies here. On the other hand, some friend or acquaintance might have developed an ear for the speech differences of yours that make a difference.

A recording of your speaking may provide a more dependable source—although its results may surprise you. Pretend it is somebody else, and listen for the characteristics that would distract you if it were someone else.

A third source for a voice and articulation inventory is your speech teacher or an expert in speech improvement or speech correc- tion in your college speech department or clinic. Here you can ar- range for a trained ear to make the necessary discriminations. But even in this case, you do not gain full understanding of the situation if your teacher says to you, "you have a slight frontal protrusion lisp," or "you have a harsh voice," or, "you distort the [aI] dipthong." The diagnosis is not complete until *you hear* the difference.

Learning to Recognize Voice and Sound Differences

The first and essential step in controlling voice and articulation characteristics that are "too different" is learning to recognize the difference between your utterances and those which fall in the incon- spicuous norm. Naturally, you would have no interest in improving errors which you cannot hear. Sometimes you can manage to hear them yourself. More dependably, you get needed help from a properly trained person.

But two suggestions may be made here. You might ask a friend or teacher, in the words of Marc Antony, to "lend me your ears." Then you can practice varying the characteristics of your voice, or the way in which you produce a particular sound or say words with that sound, as your helping listener makes judgments about the correctness of that characteristic or sound. Remember, you are trying to learn how that correct utterance sounds to *you* when you say it as compared to the way you have habitually said it. And be prepared for the proba- bility that the correct way may feel and sound wrong to you because of the listening dilemma referred to earlier.

Or, if a recorder is available, compare the way you sound using the troublesome speech characteristic with the way a friend who handles it acceptably sounds. Keep experimenting until you can, in recording, sound more like him. Again, remember that the important consideration is how the correct utterance sounds to you as you make it.

Correcting Differences that Make a Difference

We have said that the first step is recognition of the difference between a characteristic of voice or articulation which sounds normal to you but isn't, and a characteristic that may sound wrong to you but is within the range of acceptable norms. The next steps are not so simply stated. They will vary with the nature of the difficulty, with the causes of your more or less divergent sound productions, with the severity of or extent of deviation from the norm, and with the individual. There are limitations, therefore, to what you can accomplish alone, to what you can accomplish with the help of your speech teacher, and even, in some cases, to what can be accomplished with the help of trained, clinical personnel.

There are some difficulties, psychologically deep-seated in origin or directly related to physical irregularities, which will respond only to expert treatment. A qualified speech teacher should be able to outline a program of improvement for you, if that is what you need, or to refer you for more strictly clinical treatment, if that is what you need.

Remember, as we noted at the outset, practice makes permanent, not perfect. Inexpert, amateur help, or uninformed self-help can lead to mere reinforcement of a disturbing characteristic. You will need, at least, the help of one pair of ears physically separated from your speaking voice. Further, your speech instructor may suggest an appropriate textbook and specific sections or exercises in that book for your use.[2] Remember, too, that most college students have voices that are entirely adequate and articulation that is at least passably good.

There follows a brief description of auditory characteristics which

[2] Examples of popular textbooks on voice and articulation improvement are: Virgil A. Anderson, *Training the Speaking Voice.* New York: Oxford, 1942; Grant Fairbanks, *Voice and Articulation Drillbook,* New York: Harper 2nd ed., 1960; Elise Hahn, Charles W. Lomas, Donald E. Hargis, and Daniel Vandragen, *Basic Voice Training for Speech.* New York: McGraw-Hill, 1957.

should give you a general understanding of vocal processes and possibly help alert you to the differences that make a difference.

○ VOICE

Physically, voice is produced by a column of air that is forced from the lungs and sets up a vibration of the vocal folds in the larynx as it passes between them. Thus, sound waves are produced, and as they pass up the throat, mostly into the mouth, some are "screened" by a number of vocal cavities which are responsible primarily for the ultimate quality of the voice. The result is that the human voice has the same characteristics as any sound—namely, pitch (frequency), rate (time), quality (wave composition), and loudness (intensity and energy).

Pitch

Audiences are sensitive to the pitch of a speaker's voice, for pitch not only is correlated with sex (lower for men than for women) and with age (lower for adults than for children) but is also an index of the confidence and poise of the speaker. You may well recall how, in times of emotional stress, your pitch tends to rise, making your voice sound strained or even shrill. A further point to keep in mind is that in normal conversational speech there are continuous pitch variations known as inflections. Mono-pitch, or the fixation of the voice on one pitch level, is wearing upon listeners and should be avoided. The best means of obtaining good pitch variation is to follow the advice given earlier—to be conversational and communicative.

Loudness

The two principal faults of amplitude are speaking too loudly, thus blasting the ears of your listeners, and speaking too softly, thereby making it difficult for them to hear you. If you imagine you are talking to three or four individuals seated near the rear, and speak directly at (though, of course, not always to) them, you should achieve about the proper volume. Variations in loudness are of great value in achieving both over-all speech variety and emphasis. Remember that dropping the voice to a near whisper is often as effective for emphasis as raising it to a near shout, and in small groups may be far preferable. Some speakers tend not to vary the level of loudness, which prevents their using emphasis of this kind. And, like mono-pitch, the monotony of unvarying sound volume is wearing on listeners.

Rate

For most persons, normal speech tends to range from 125 to 160 words a minute; however, individuals vary considerably in this respect. There are two aspects of rate: the fundamental rate of speaking and the use of pauses between sentences and phrases to achieve good oral communication. Many individuals are warned by their families and friends that they "talk too fast" when their problem is more likely to be that they do not talk distinctly enough. Rate becomes a problem primarily when, because of nervousness, a speaker talks so rapidly that his words are jumbled together; or when he pours out his words at a uniform rate, without the natural pauses and variations that are required to lend their share of meaning to the ideas being communicated; or when interjections such as "uh" are interspersed through the speech; or when the sentences are broken up into relatively uniform breath-groups rather than into the naturally diversified groupings that relate to the meanings of the words.

Unduly slow speech drags, dissipating the listeners' interest. The rate should be energetic, varied, and suited to the needs of the occasion. When talking with a large group, or when speaking into a public address system, the rate normally should be somewhat slower than with a small group. Solemn or impressive subject matter also tends to require a slower pace. Scenes of excitement normally are described in rapid speech. As in other aspects of speaking, the standards of good conversation provide a generally safe guide.

Quality

The quality of a voice is one of its most individualized attributes. It is a leading cue to the personality of the speaker. When you recognize a voice over the telephone, it is probably the distinctive quality that provides the clue. This does not mean, however, that everyone should be satisfied with the quality of his voice simply because it is his. Speakers often develop a quality that is too thin. Another voice may be guttural or harsh or throaty. Confidence, friendliness, and a genuine interest in what you are saying and in your listeners have an immediate effect upon the quality of your voice, for it is peculiarly susceptible to psychological states and attitudes.

○ ARTICULATION

After voice is produced by vibration of the air in the vocal folds of the larynx and resonated in the cavities of the throat and head, we still do not have articulate human speech. There remains the final process in which such organs as the teeth, tongue, lips, and hard and soft palates are designed for the actual making of the specific and particular audible sounds that are the speech symbols. This process is called articulation. In a broad sense, we may define articulation as meaning the distinctness with which speech sounds are formed.

No speaker can afford to be careless of articulation. He inevitably pays too great a price for such inaccuracies and faults. Although important in everyday conversation, it becomes more so in the public situation. For one thing, public speech must be instantly intelligible so that the audience will not be distracted from what is being said.

Although a speech is more important for its ideas than for the articulation and pronunciation used to communicate the ideas, faulty articulation and pronunciation may become grave barriers to effective presentation, as we have noted earlier. Since faults in articulation and pronunciation are widespread, it is important to analyze those most frequently encountered.

One meaning of articulation is "jointed." The articulation of speech sounds, especially the consonants, is the function of the joint operation of two parts of the mechanism: tongue with hard palate, soft palate, or teeth; lip with teeth or the other lip; and, in the case of the sound [h], the vocal folds. This function is one of modifying the outgoing breath stream: squeezing it (as for [f] and [v]), and splitting it (as for [s] and [z]), stopping and exploding it (as for [p] and [b]). Another pair of articulators are the soft palate and back of the throat, which combine to keep the air stream from going through the nasal cavities. Among all English sounds, only those for the [n], [m], and the final sound in *ring* should have this "valve" open to permit nasal resonance.

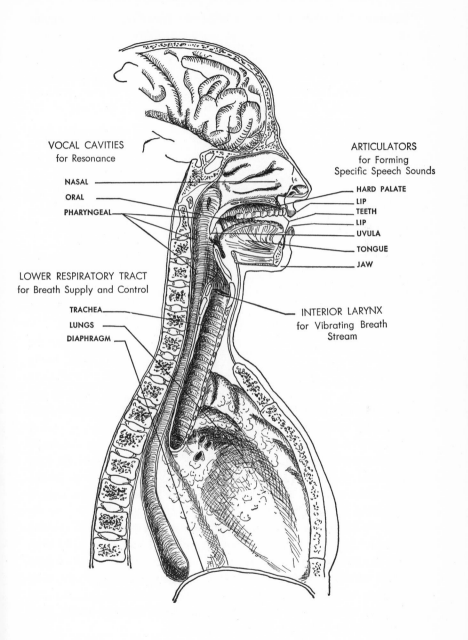

VOCAL CAVITIES
for Resonance

NASAL

ORAL

PHARYNGEAL

LOWER RESPIRATORY TRACT
for Breath Supply and Control

TRACHEA

LUNGS

DIAPHRAGM

ARTICULATORS
for Forming
Specific Speech Sounds

HARD PALATE

LIP

TEETH

LIP

UVULA

TONGUE

JAW

INTERIOR LARYNX
for Vibrating Breath
Stream

Errors of Articulation

There are many sources of error in articulation. The mechanism and the timing are so complex that it is truly amazing that we manage to stay within any norms at all. Physical and/or psychological effects in childhood, the emulation of an admired person, or even ordinary development of speech organs, can lead to articulation errors of distortion, substitution, or omission.

These and other characteristics of speech are not easily understood without the right kind of training. To the amateur ear, very often a slightly distorted sound, such as the [r] made through pursed lips, will seem to be a sound substitution, as, in this case, a [w]. Anyone can diagnose the voice quality that is heard when a person has a "code id his head" and the soft-palate-back-of-the-throat valve is closed, as "nasal," when the opposite is the case. What is being heard is *de*nasal quality, and the absence of normal nasal resonance.

As we have said, it is not important to learn all about voice and articulation, but it is important to know, as a listener, that voice and articulation errors may not indicate what they seem to about the speaker; and equally important for you to learn, as a speaker, is what faults, if any, you do have and how you can eliminate them.

○ **PRONUNCIATION**

Correct pronunciation refers to the utterance of words within listener norms or expectancies for sounds and stress or accent. If you habitually make an articulation error, a particular sound is always distorted or omitted wherever it may occur. Thus, if you habitually say something like "dis" for "dish," you are likely to say something like "sewer" for "sure." On the other hand, you may not make this kind of substitution, generally, but may have learned to mispronounce "issue" as "iss-you."

Pronunciation errors can be as damaging to the speaker's purpose as other speech deviations we have discussed. Listeners, usually without thinking, will respond to pronunciation errors as marks of ignorance, of lack of authority, of lack of common ground, and often very properly, as a sign of poor preparation. Just a small error in pronunciation can sometimes do irremediable damage to an initial communication in normal speaker-listener relationships.

Correct pronunciation is not governed by hard-and-fast rules. This is partly because some words are pronounced somewhat differently in different parts of the country. Although there are literally scores of dialect variants in the United States, it is commonly agreed that there are three major regional dialects—Eastern, General American, and Southern—and that pronunciation acceptable in these regions is considered correct.[3] Hence, your guide should be to use the best regional speech of the area in which you live. Unless you enter upon a career such as acting or radio announcing, you will normally find your regional speech satisfactory.

Dialect differences provide one reason why no firm rules can be set down. Another is that the language is always changing. *Canine* was once acceptably pronounced with the stress on the second syllable. Many people are still careful to pronounce the first "c" in Arctic, but this practice is disappearing over time. Many words are presently in transition so that they have more than one acceptable pronunciation, as *advertisement, interest,* and *protein.* And there are words of which you will frequently hear pronunciations that are not in your dictionary, but which may appear in it in the future. An example is the word *comparable,* whose only correct pronunciation, according to your dictionary, places the stress on the *first* syllable.

Kinds of Mispronunciations

There are four kinds of mispronunciations: misplaced stress, omission of a sound, addition of a sound, and substitution of a sound.

1. Because one of the important identifying characteristics of our language is its stress pattern (actually of *un*stress), the mere shift of stress, or accent, makes a striking difference. Compare *cómparable* with the common mispronunciation, *compárable,* or *mustáche* with *mústache.* If your ear expects one pronunciation, it sometimes has difficulty in even identifying the word when stressed the other way. This is partly because, you will notice, you automatically change the vowel sounds.

[3] Dialect regions are discussed in detail in Arthur J. Bronstein, *The Pronunciation of American English,* Appleton-Century-Crofts, 1960; and in Charles K. Thomas, *An Introduction to the Phonetics of American English,* 2nd ed. New York: Ronald, 1958. Regional differences in pronunciation of specific words are recorded in John S. Kenyon and Thomas A. Knott, *A Pronouncing Dictionary of American English.* Springfield, Mass.: Merriam, 1944.

2. Phoneticians identify many pronunciations marred by omission of a sound as typical of "less-educated" speech. Examples are: *guvment* for *government*, *ast* for *asked*, *blong* for *belong*, *recunize* for *recognize*, and *pitcher* for *picture*.

3. Similarly, certain pronunciations which have an extra sound added have been associated with "less-educated" speech. *Athelete* for *athlete*, *grievious* for *grievous*, *wunst* for *once*, and *filum* for *film*, are examples of such mispronunciations.

4. The fourth kind of mispronunciation is sound substitution: one sound made in place of another, as in the example of *issue* cited at the beginning of this section. Other examples include *git* for *get*, *imbred* for *inbred*, *strenth* for *strength*, and *goin'* for *going*.

Sources of Mispronunciation

Sources of these errors are many. Sometimes the mispronunciations are simply easier, sometimes they are left-over childhood errors, or sometimes we just hear a word mispronounced and accept it and use it as correct.

Two related sources are important for every student of speech to understand and to guard against. One is the spelling mispronunciation and the other is the stock of words in your reading, but not in your speaking, vocabulary. The *ch* in chasm is correctly pronounced *k*, the *sch* in schism is correctly pronounced *s*, the *b* in subtle and the *l* in calm and salmon are properly omitted. Yet, sometimes you will hear words pronounced as they are spelled. Similarly, the speaker risks unnecessarily distracting his listeners by allowing himself to pronounce unfamiliar words as they are spelled without making sure of the pronunciation that his listeners expect. Or, if he has not practiced orally, a word with which he is perfectly familiar in his reading seems unpronounceable in the speaking situation; it is not yet in his speaking vocabulary.

The solution is simple. *Do* practice orally. And if in doubt about a pronunciation, find out what is correct.

Finding the Correct Pronunciation

You would expect that finding correct pronunciations is a simple matter. And in most instances, it is. A recent dictionary, recent because the language is changing and any dictionary is starting to become obsolete as it leaves the presses, will be dependable in most instances of doubt.

Often, however, the editors of dictionaries recognize more than one pronunciation for certain words. What then? You need to learn which is preferred, as well as which, among your listeners, is the pronunciation that they are least likely to notice. The pronunciation expected by your particular listeners will depend largely upon geographical location in some cases, upon specialized vocabularies in others, or on the influence of a teacher or even the President of the United States. President Kennedy in 1961 probably influenced the expected pronunciation of *Laos*.

In some cases it may be a toss-up between two pronunciations. In such an instance, play it safe with the preferred one in the dictionary.

To assure correct pronunciation of both the familiar and unfamiliar words that you may use, determine how they are expected to be heard simply because it is the way they are usually heard and consult the dictionary freely when in doubt.

○ **CONCLUSION**

The *auditory code* has been discussed with particular concern for those acoustic aspects of speech delivery called voice, articulation, and pronunciation. Listeners associate certain faults in the use of these vocal processes with personality and communication traits that may or may not be appropriate to the speaker: ignorance, disinterest, lack of authority, incompetence. Further, any unusual characteristics of voice, articulation, and pronunciation are, at the least, distracting and, therefore, reduce the probability that a speaker will achieve his specific purposes. Before any improvement can be initiated, a speaker must learn to hear the differences that make a difference; it is not likely to help if he is merely told what is wrong. For voice and articulation faults, any improvement program is likely to require at least the guidance of a professional person in speech. The various kinds and sources of pronunciation errors are more easily identified and more easily remedied. In all cases, what you are aiming at is to bring or keep your voice and diction within inconspicuous norms.

For both the visual and the auditory codes, the factor of chief significance is that the "message" a speaker conveys to his listeners is comprised of many cues in addition to the words that are spoken. Unless standards of acceptability are maintained for bodily and vocal delivery, the speaker may often arouse reactions which are far different from those he desires. By attaining communicative skill in the visual and auditory codes, you can add new dimensions of influence to your speaking.

EXERCISES

Questions for Discussion

1. What do we mean by "code"? Discuss the five functions of codes which we have identified. What, specifically, is meant by visual code and auditory code?

2. What is meant by subliminal communicative cues? What effects do they have on speaker-listener relations?

3. Define empathy; illustrate your definition with examples. How may a speaker use empathy to help accomplish his aims? How may its effects counteract what he wishes to communicate?

4. How should the etiquette of speaking situations be adapted to your classroom? Have you noted instances on public occasions on which these rules of etiquette have been flouted? Were the results detrimental to effective communication?

5. What is meant by gesture? How many gestures have been identified? How many gestures do you use in your own speaking? How does your own use of gesture differ in varying circumstances?

6. To what extent and in what manner should gesturing be practiced? What dangers must be avoided in such practice? What is the fundamental source of effectiveness in use of gesture?

7. What is the importance of facial expressions in speaking? What is meant by the "poker face"? When is it helpful, and when detrimental?

8. Do you pronounce all of the words cited in the expected manner? If you found that you do have a pronunciation error, what would you say is its source?

9. Why do people hear themselves differently from the way others hear them? Is this a flaw in hearing? Is it *learned?*

10. What should you do if you find that some characteristic of your voice or articulation does not come within the inconspicuous norm?

Projects for Speaking and Writing

1. The class may be divided into pairs and each student asked to give a brief speech analyzing the total delivery characteristics of his paired classmate. Each pair should talk over the project to ensure full understanding and to try to have each speech present suggestions and evaluations that will be truly helpful to the student whose delivery is being analyzed. The speeches should present constructive suggestions and avoid fault-finding. The purpose of this assignment is twofold: (1) to help you become a better critic of delivery and (2) to give to each member of the class an objective and constructive analysis of his speaking manner by a classmate.

2. Select a well-known public speaker whom you have heard in person or on radio or television, and present to the class a brief speech in which you evaluate and characterize in some detail his qualities of delivery.

3. Analyze your own delivery in the speeches that you have thus far delivered, noting your elements of strength and the ways in which you need to improve. If a recording machine is available to you, record a two- or three-minute speech, and evaluate your own vocal qualities by means of a playback. Discuss your delivery in a conference with your instructor and determine to profit from the suggestions he makes to you.

4. Make recordings of each member of the class in which you each say exactly the same thing for the first four or five sentences. Play them back in a different order and see how easily each speaker will be identified by everyone but himself. Discuss with each other and your instructor the significance of this phenomenon.

Chapter 10

Listening

THROUGHOUT OUR DISCUSSION of the principles of effective communicative speech, we have emphasized that they apply to the relationship between speakers and their listeners. Communication exists only in the interest of this relationship. You can speak communicatively only as you inter-relate your thinking with that of your listeners. You can affect what goes on in their minds only as your own mental processes are continuously being affected by theirs. The good speaker must necessarily be a good observer-and-listener. This point of view is implicit throughout the book. Here, however, we turn more explicitly to the emphasis upon listening itself. What is it; why is it important; what prevents us from listening better than we do; what can we do to improve? For as you improve the quality of your listening, you will be helped to become a more effective speaker. But good listening is of great value for its own sake.

Our need is not so much to learn as it is to *re*learn how to listen. Just as children pepper adults with questions, so do they listen acutely to what is said around them. It is proverbial that "little pitchers have big ears." As we grow older we become more self-centered, more sure about what we already know and believe, less impressed by wonder at the great unknown lying about us, less curious, less receptive. In short, growing up is, unfortunately, in part a process of growing away from the good listening practice of our childhood. What we need at this stage is a reopening of this partially blocked channel of communication.

Too few of us realize the importance of listening as a com-

226

municative tool. We either take it for granted or assume that listening is "natural," rather than a skill that needs to be developed. The amount of time we spend listening is indeed impressive. Some studies indicate that we spend about 9 per cent of our communicative time writing, 16 per cent reading, 30 per cent speaking, and 45 per cent listening. You might find the proportion of your listening time even higher if you were to check the frequency and duration of your listening to someone else's words in a wide variety of situations—conversation, groups, meetings, interviews, and speeches; then add the radio, television, movies, and the telephone, and you will find that it is a staggering amount of time.[1]

During speech training, you will listen to twenty or so more speeches in class than you will deliver. As you go through life, you will probably spend about the same proportion of your time as a listener, unless you are especially active as a speaker. The point is that on any realistic balancing of values, listening deserves much more attention than it normally receives. And the rewards of good listening are far too great to be ignored. Furthermore, effective listening is too complex and difficult to be taken for granted. To analyze your own listening habits, to learn the requirements for good listening, and to master them through practice are goals that deserve your consistent effort.

Good listening starts with an attitude of wanting to participate fully in the communicative situation. It encompasses a desire to listen and get as much as possible out of what is being said; a positive rather than a negative frame of mind; and an understanding approach to things and to people, that is, an approach in which there is a complete willingness to put yourself in the position of the speaker and try to understand his message. We spoke of the importance of the listener-oriented attitude which you must have as a speaker. Listeners, too, must not be self-centered, for good listening demands an active interest in others and in their ideas, feelings, and points of view.

○ RESPONSIBILITY FOR LISTENING

As a listener you have at least three kinds of responsibility: to the *speaker,* to the *other listeners,* and to *yourself.* Although these can

[1] See Paul T. Rankin, "Listening Ability," *Chicago Schools Journal,* XII, June, 1930; and other studies reported in Ralph G. Nichols and Leonard A. Stevens, *Are You Listening?* New York: McGraw-Hill, 1957.

be considered separately, a speaking situation must be regarded as an indissoluble whole wherein speaker, listener, and occasion form a complete social event. A speaking situation does not consist of an abstract throwing of words into space by one individual and a passive attempt by another to decide whether he should really become a part of the event and "tune in" on the speaker. It is not, however, uncommon for members of an audience to sit with chips on their shoulders and chins sticking out, wearing an air of "Try and get to me if you can, Mr. Speaker. This is your show and your responsibility to interest me." To place the full responsibility on the speaker in this way not only makes unrealistic demands on his skill and ability but certainly denies the listener the full benefit that he might receive from the speaker's message. Neither listener nor speaker can avoid responsibility by shifting it wholly to the other.

It is a curious perversion of judgment to believe that the full responsibility for communication rests wholly on the communicator. We do not make this error in regard to reading. When we study from books, most of us are accustomed to concentrate, to underline key passages, and to look up difficult words in a dictionary so that we can understand the writer's meaning and intent. But the same careful readers may be observed sitting apathetically in an audience, refusing to make any effort to follow the speaker and excusing themselves with the plea that he was dull or the topic was difficult. When Boswell made a similar complaint to Dr. Samuel Johnson about a book, he was sternly admonished, "Sir, read it again." Since it is usually impossible to hear most speeches again, the obvious course is to listen so carefully to what is being said that it will be understood while it is being spoken.

The responsibility to other listeners becomes obvious when we examine what happens as a result of bad listening. The listening function is being completely denied when a member of the audience reads, writes, exchanges notes with a neighbor, thinks about subjects far removed, or slumps into vacant daydreaming. To be thus physically present but to make it patently evident that you are actively avoiding even the appearance of listening is the worst offense you can commit against a speaker. It is more than grossly impolite; it is an assault on the fundamentals of the communicative situation. The obviously inattentive listener is advertising his indifference and even suggesting contempt for the speaker. Furthermore, he affects the members of

Penalty for poor listening . . .

Ineligible receiver downfield? A fifteen-yard penalty for poor listening. You are responsible for accurate listening. Lack of alertness causes "I thought this exam was to be next week," or "I was sure the appointment was for today instead of yesterday," or "But I thought you said the order should be canceled, not expedited."

the audience around him so that their attention also is drawn from the speaker to the inattentive listener. Any such action may be so infectious that it affects the whole group, destroying completely the mutual respect that speaker and listeners should have for each other.

Some listeners are conscious of this social responsibility to the group and therefore pretend to listen. This can be done by giving every physical appearance of close attention when in reality the mind may be occupied with problems or pleasures wholly apart from the speaker or his message. Such conduct causes no disappointment in the group. The real loss is to the one who does not listen, for he has failed to derive any value from the speaking situation and might better have spent his time elsewhere.

○ **VALUES OF GOOD LISTENING**

Several paratroopers were seated in a room awaiting the arrival of the instructor. He walked into the room carrying a packed parachute. "This," he said, "is a new parachute we have just developed. It has never been used in the field before. You men were selected to try it out tomorrow morning at six. You will jump from a plane at two thousand feet. I'd now like to show you how it works."

There is no doubt about why these men should listen. They either understand clearly every word of the instructor or they court the risk of jumping out of an airplane with a parachute that fails to work. If you find yourself in an equally crucial situation *vis-à-vis* a speaker, you too will listen well. But there are much broader values. One who cultivates good listening habits accumulates all sorts of knowledge and useful information. He is also better liked by his associates, as a good listener stimulates the speaker and induces him to share confidences.

It is interesting to note the quality of listening of outstanding business and public figures. Executives, and management leaders at all levels, have learned the value of listening as a management tool. They draw on and consult with the people who work for them for advice, counsel, and information which must be tapped in order to make better decisions and plans. In the world of business, many stories are written about Charles Schwab, the great steel executive, and his ability to listen. Merle Crowell wrote, "Without saying a word, Mr. Schwab can flatter more than any man I ever met. Listening, to him, is an instinct as well as a rare charm. Whoever talks to him, be he day laborer or financier, faces a man who hearkens gravely, attentively, eye to eye, until the speaker is quite done."

Among leaders in public life, Generals George C. Marshall and Dwight Eisenhower were known for their listening ability when calling on their staffs for advice and judgment. Mr. Eisenhower carried this ability to the White House when he was President, as did his successor, John F. Kennedy, another great believer in the value of listening to his staff of experts. In being good listeners, they not only benefit from the thinking of their staffs, but they also win their loyalty by respecting their judgment. To listen well is, in effect, to mobilize for one's own use the accumulated knowledge and experience of others.

Calvin Coolidge, a comparatively poor speaker, was said to be "Northampton, Massachusetts' champion listener. He listened his way into all the offices the town would give him, and then into the White House," according to his biographers. Theodore Roosevelt, known more as a rough-and-tumble speaker, was also an extremely sensitive listener. A contemporary wrote this about him:

> Though a brilliant, humorous, high-powered talker, he was more ear than mouth. On the slightest indication that one of his guests had anything to contribute, he would jam on all the verbal brakes, stop dead in the middle of a sentence and, seizing the other's arm— if accessible—in a powerful grip, urgently demand: 'Yes, yes, what are you going to say?' . . . He was perhaps the most creative listener I have ever encountered. If we all had such audiences, we would continually excel ourselves.

In many ways, from many sources, the values of good listening are stressed. *The Living Talmud,* by Judah Goldin, quotes this admonition from the Old Testament, "Note the difference between your ears and your mouth. For the Holy One, blessed be He, created for you two ears and one mouth, so that you might listen twice as much as you speak." In *From Many Lands,* Louis Adamic gives a description of a good listener—an immigrant laborer who has learned to appreciate people. It is a most perceptive description of the physical and mental attitude and enthusiasm of the good listener:

> Everything interests him. As one talks to him he has a listening look about him, as though his ears were standing up. He is one of the best listeners I know—a rare quality in people who are also good talkers. His body is poised to catch every word and sound. Now and

then his entire body seems concentrated in the pupils of his eyes. He listens with his head slightly tilted down, his eyes lifted wide, waiting, evoking and absorbing your words and meaning. And when he talks all of him appears to be thinking, speaking, responding. Yet his manner is not compulsive, it is inviting. While not egoless, the man is humble. He conveys to you his vitality, draws you to his quest.

It is interesting to note that this description emphasizes the active participation of the listener, and the writer even says that he is "thinking, speaking, responding." This is of course the essence of listening, that although still silent vocally, the listener represents an actual speaking response, letting the person talking know his thoughts and reactions.

Specific Rewards of Good Listening

1. *Understanding and increase of information and knowledge.* This is of course a fundamental objective, and you have but to think over the way this applies to your college education and your need for knowledge in life to realize its importance.

2. *Evaluation and formation of judgments.* We do not observe, receive, and interpret what we hear just for the sake of knowledge alone. The thinking person is constantly drawing inferences, making judgments, forming attitudes. He must develop this ability to its fullest. In listening to others, he is concerned that what he hears is true and accurate. Then he evaluates its usefulness to him or to society.

3. *Better speaking technique.* Part of the evaluative process is to sharpen your perception of the speaker's use of and application of good speech principles and methods. As you make judgments of him, you are yourself applying these principles and will make more careful use of them in your future speaking. In your speech class, the more you participate as a critic and evaluator, both silently and when called upon, the better speaker you become.

4. *Stimulation of better speaking from the speaker.* An appreciative listener draws the maximum of animation and effectiveness from the speaker. You have but to recall situations where someone, or an audience, indicated to you as a speaker that he fully appreciated what you were saying, wanted you to continue, hung on to your every word. Going back to the circular nature of the communicative process, the more dynamic the listener, the more empathy he stimulates in his

responses, the more the total process becomes enthusiastic and alive.

5. *Appreciation and enjoyment.* This is naturally a prime objective of good listening. It would apply to good music, a good play, and other types of entertainment situations. We are said to develop an ear for good music by developing our hearing and appreciation of it. In the same manner, one should enjoy a good speaker. And if the speaker is at first disappointing, you can stimulate him to be better, as we have just pointed out, for he may have a vital message nevertheless.

6. *Stimulation of better group response.* A good listener is contagious and tends to encourage others to want to listen better.

○ **BARRIERS TO LISTENING**

The act of listening does not appear to be complex.[2] But it is complex, and fantastically so, with interplay of basic and situational attitudes, of perceptual expectancies and value systems and of speaker and listener needs. The actual act of listening involves the stages of hearing, understanding, and interpreting what is heard, and recalling and applying it in the future.

Most of what is wrong with our listening is attitudinal. We either put the whole responsibility for the communication on the speaker, or we are indifferent to his ideas, or we smugly feel that we know what he is talking about (or more), or we take it for granted that we will listen. Any or all of these attitudes leads to failure to concentrate and to ignoring the other requirements of good listening which we discuss later in this chapter.

Barriers to effective listening confront us to such a degree that, singly or in combination, they can impede the process. Let's analyze these and say at the outset that the major thing wrong with our listening is the failure to break through these barriers:

The seemingly passive nature of listening
Jumping to conclusions about speaker and subject
Rate of ability to listen
Status or position of speaker and listener
Prestige levels of speaker and listener

[2] The complexity of the physical and psychological factors in listening is described in Dominick A. Barbara, *The Art of Listening.* Springfield, Ill.: Charles C Thomas, 1958.

Which of these listeners is you?

Barriers to listening exist here. They may be overcome by the listeners and by the speakers. How often do you conclude that there is little to be gained from listening, or daydream, or simply think of other things, and thus miss the opportunities at hand?

Background and environment
Attitude: prejudices and beliefs
Preoccupation with self
Language
Physical conditions
Lack of perspective
Daydreaming

The Seemingly Passive Nature of Listening

It is interesting to observe that the act of listening requires little physical movement and is usually engaged in while seated. This appears to be conducive to a relaxed manner rather than an animated one. In speaking, the speaker uses his voice and body actively. The listener is less active physically, using chiefly the mind. But it is very important that the mental processes be active, alert, animated, and constantly working in the direction of the speaker's thoughts. The listener must therefore make a conscious effort to keep the listening process active, to have his body, facial expression, eyes, and mind alert and directed toward the speaker at all times.

Jumping to Conclusions

We have all formed judgments, conclusions, and generalizations about people and subjects. Frequently these judgments are wrong and based on insufficient or biased observation or evidence. We just don't like certain things about people. The speaker's appearance may strike you negatively in one or many ways. You don't like the way he combs his hair, wears his tie, or fails to press his trousers. When he starts to speak, his voice is thin and a little higher-pitched than voices you prefer. The tendency to form first impressions is very strong. We expect to receive certain ideas from certain people, or from people with certain characteristics. This becomes a barrier when our conception of a speaker acts to deafen us to what he has to say. Some of our other barriers deal with faulty or twisted thinking in relation to conclusions about the speaker's points.

Rate of Ability to Listen

The average person speaks at a rate of about 125 to 160 words a minute. It takes far less time to think than it does to speak. It has been estimated that we can think about four times as fast as we can speak, or at the rate of about 500 words a minute. For listeners, then, there is a margin over speakers of about 350 words of extra thinking time each minute. This excess time forms one of the major barriers to effective listening. What do we do with this time? If we use it for better listening, it can be a tremendous asset; otherwise, the very existence of excess time permits us to wander away from the speaker. If we are listening attentively when he starts to speak, we find that there is time for other thoughts to creep in. Then we shut them off and focus on the speaker, but we soon find again that we can follow him all right and still use the time on other thoughts. Each time we wander away and come back to the speaker, we find it more difficult to tune in and to understand him. We must, therefore, use this time constructively to watch the speaker, observe his manner and expression, and constantly analyze what he is saying. This barrier can thus be turned into an asset for the listener.

Status of Speaker and Listener

Frequently we are told that the good speaker will adapt his remarks to his listeners and talk on the level of the audience. It was said that Lincoln was always able to achieve this as a speaker, even after he became president and occupied a position high above that of his listeners. This is a rare quality among speakers that always makes listening easier and more pleasant. But all too frequently the speaker occupies a position either above or so far different from that of the listener that the very relationship forms a barrier. This is more often true of interpersonal communication, perhaps, than of public speaking situations.

When a supervisor talks to a worker, a vice-president to a staff official, a teacher to a student, an older person to a younger, and in countless other relationships, speaker and listener are in widely different positions. In these situations, the responsibility for adaptation rests more upon the speaker than upon the listener. But the listener wants to understand what is said. He should therefore try to bridge the gap between the speaker and himself by trying to interpret what is said in the light of the speaker's position in relation to his own. Frequently the position of the speaker will induce greater respect from the listener and therefore better listening. However, the occasional tendency among listeners to resent or misunderstand the speaker's position should be guarded against, lest this barrier seriously interfere with good listening.

Prestige Levels of Speaker and Listener

Frequently the position of the speaker will determine your regard for him. In addition to position, other factors or characteristics may cause you to respect his prestige. Manner, bearing, and appearance, for example, are some of the personal attributes that contribute to an individual's prestige. When we respect a person, we tend to listen more attentively. But occasionally we allow ourselves to think too much of the speaker as a person, and thus we think too little about what he is saying.

On the other hand, if a listener develops a feeling of personal superiority over the speaker, such an unfortunate condition may lead to a belief that everything the speaker says is unimportant or wrong. This can occur, for example, when a listener feels so strongly about his political or religious beliefs that he is contemptuous of anything said by a person of opposite, or different, beliefs. Sometimes such a condition results from a subjective concentration on one's own ideas and feelings to the complete exclusion of other points of view. Such a listener may exhibit a habitual contentiousness which meets every attempt to communicate by another individual as something to be attacked and destroyed.

This kind of listening may be attentive, but it is not listening for understanding. Rather, the listener's attentiveness is that of a hawk poised for attack. Although this type of listening may stimulate some speakers, it presents an unpleasant situation in which the barrier is obvious and the speech occasion is a field of combat rather than social communication. The good listener cannot allow concern for his own prestige level or for that of the speaker to prevent maximum understanding of what is being said.

Background and Environment of Speaker and Listener

Speaker and listener may be far apart in their respective backgrounds or their current environments. We know that both background and environment affect our thinking and our points of view. Each person, however, should show regard for the person on the other end of the communication situation. This means the listener must put himself in the speaker's position, try to evaluate what he is saying in terms of *his* background, and then relate it to his own. Our listening barrier in this respect is the tendency to understand and evaluate everything we hear in terms of our own background and experience. The executive who can forget his own background in listening to the grievance of a worker will be much more effective for having overcome this listening barrier. The worker should listen as attentively and understandingly to a superior who gained his position through attendance at Groton and Harvard as he does to one who rose through the ranks.

Attitude: Prejudices and Beliefs

Attitude is probably the chief factor that can be an aid or a barrier to effective listening. Probably all the other things we are concerned about add up to the attitude with which we approach a situation, a person, or his point of view. The attitude may be open-minded, unprejudiced, objective, cooperative, and understanding; or it may be biased, subjective, contentious, or contemptuous of the speaker. There is no doubt that we are all entitled to our own beliefs, although the world would be better if they were never based on prejudice. By the same token, if we assume that we have a right to our own beliefs, the democratic code decrees that we must grant the same right to others. In listening, this means being open-minded and considerate.

It is not always easy to maintain an attitude of open-mindedness, for open-mindedness is more a way of life than a development of specific skills. Adherence to democratic principles is a very deep-seated belief in America. But does this mean that our attitude toward a speaker who, for example, is explaining socialism should be one of closing our minds or of listening only carefully enough to be able to argue with him? We should listen to this speaker as carefully as to any other because it is advantageous to understand socialism. Again, one's religion is often a deep-seated belief. Does this mean that a Protestant's attitude toward a Catholic speaker should be antagonistic because the speaker is a Catholic or because he is speaking on a subject that shows a difference of belief? We all have a great deal of self-control to exercise lest our prejudices and beliefs induce an attitude barrier to effective listening.

Preoccupation with Self

The natural tendency of most of us to think more about ourselves than about anything else is a barrier to listening in that it does not allow us to concentrate fully on the speaker and his ideas. We have discussed self-preoccupation on the part of the speaker and the way in which it contributes to lack of poise and confidence. In the listener, self-preoccupation usually takes the form of trying to solve personal problems while listening to a speaker. The excess time we have as listeners is applied to matters far removed from the speaker and his message. The completely self-centered listener is probably present only in body, and he could as well not be there. In this respect, a person's listening habits may parallel somewhat his habits as an individual. Or it may be that a specific situation causes one to concentrate his thoughts inwardly rather than on the speaker. Illness or an emotional disturbance can quickly bring about a degree of preoccupation that precludes good communication. Actually, if a listener makes an active effort to listen and to direct his thoughts to the speaker, he may become so absorbed that he quickly forgets his own problems. We should not allow our self-concern to stand in the way of good listening.[3]

Language

Occasionally we find someone who refuses to listen to a speaker because he's not "talking my language." Such criticism may mean that the speaker's ideas and over-all point of view are not in agreement with the listener's; or it may mean simply that the listener finds it difficult to understand the language used. This misunderstanding may apply in individual words, to terms, to the way that sentences are put together, and to concepts. If a speaker makes no attempt to use language adapted to the listener, fails to define his terms, or perhaps talks in technical jargon, it may be impossible for the listener to understand, no matter how attentive he may be. In such a situation, the best the listener can

---

[3] *Cf.* Paul D. Holtzman, "Communication Versus Expression in Speaking and Listening," in Dominick A. Barbara, editor, *Psychological and Psychiatric Aspects of Speech and Hearing.* Springfield, Ill.: Charles C Thomas, 1960.

do is to try to piece together the meaning by rephrasing the speaker's points and relating what is obscure to what he can understand.

Another language difficulty occurs when the listener perceives one meaning of a word and the speaker intends another. The word *cheap,* for example, can mean both low in price and petty, vulgar, or otherwise unattractive. As listeners, we must be careful to distinguish the speaker's intended meaning and not permit a different meaning to create a barrier to understanding. Vague words such as *liberty* and *fairness* may be used in a context so general that the listener has to try to penetrate the more precise meaning of the word in order to understand fully just what the speaker has said. By becoming better students of language, we shall be better equipped to understand and discern the meaning the speaker intends to convey.

Physical Conditions

Of all the barriers to listening, those due to physical conditions are perhaps easiest to remedy. Usually this means that the listener should do whatever is necessary to compensate for physical distractions. The distraction may not be easily removed, but generally it can be overcome. Outside noises can be reduced by closing a door or window; the listener can move closer to a speaker who is not speaking loud enough; or the listener can sit up alertly and focus his attention to the fullest. Concentration is the essence of good listening, especially when poor conditions exist.

The listener himself sometimes contributes to the physical situation by equipping himself with materials for note taking, which may distract both him and the speaker. It may sometimes be necessary, for certain reasons, to take notes, but it is a mistake to assume that constant note taking is good listening. We become so absorbed in the mechanics of taking notes that the dominant objective is to concentrate on the notes rather than on the speaker and his message. Usually you will take away more from the speaking situation if you listen for main ideas and make notes only about them—perhaps jotting down fuller details after the talk is over.

Lack of Perspective

A listener's lack of perspective, a common perceptual barrier to effective listening, might be characterized by the popular aphorism,

"He cannot see the forest for the trees." From time to time our preoccupation with details becomes so dominant that we lose sight of the whole. In listening, this error may take several forms. It occurs when we listen for minor points of evidence solely for the purpose of refuting what is said. It occurs, too, when our attention is focused on the speaker as a person, or on the chairman, or on other physical conditions, so that appearance, clothes, or manner becomes the dominant consideration as we pretend to listen. In such a listening mood, we may not know it, but we have lost perspective completely.

Perhaps the greatest barrier to perspective is caused by concentrating on facts and supporting details to the exclusion from our attention of the speaker's main points and basic purpose. Usually, facts are presented in the form of examples, cases, stories, figures, and comparisons in order to make a point clear or persuasive. True, good listeners always want to hear the facts in order to try to understand or accept the main idea; but they apply their attention to the details not because of an interest in the details per se but in order to aid their understanding of the main idea.

Daydreaming

The barrier of daydreaming is involved in many of the other typical habits of bad listening that we have already discussed. For this very reason it deserves special mention. For example, we go to a speech just to be present, knowing that we can use the time to think about other things; we give overt attention while our thoughts are elsewhere. Or we think we are paying attention but we are using the extra time we have as listeners for reverie and retrospection. Again, in informal situations, such as conversations, group discussions, meetings, or conferences, we let the others talk it out while we think about more pleasant things. Instead of listening to instructions from a superior, we feel that we already know enough about the subject so that we can think about a coming fishing trip or a social event. In the end we have to go back to him to hear the instructions again. To strengthen our determination not to daydream we must recognize that we are hurting primarily ourselves by not getting as much from the speaker as we might.

○ **A PROGRAM FOR BETTER LISTENING**

It is frequently estimated that your listening ability can be improved by at least 25 per cent, and usually much more, by observing some of the suggestions made above for eliminating the barriers to effective listening.[4] *Attitude* is probably the primary requisite. If you have a real desire to listen, you will probably observe all the cautions noted in this chapter with very little conscious attention to them. But it may be well to make some of the cautions more concrete by listing a series of specific steps leading to better listening.

Before the Occasion

Anticipate the occasion, whether it be a speech, interview, or conference, and have a clear understanding of why you are present. Then give some thought to the speaker, his position, his prestige value, and his background; and try to relate these to his message. Anticipate broadly—and tentatively—what his position regarding the message may be. Review your own experience and background in relation to the message, and try to determine how it will fit into your own thinking and values. Maybe you'll want to do some reading on the subject. The point is that you will go into the listening situation conditioned to get the most out of it.

During the Speech

Physically, seat yourself close enough to the speaker so that you can hear him without strain; concentrate on him and his message, not on yourself and your own personal problems and prejudices; try to avoid distractions and daydreaming. Look at him. Keep your body and mind alert.

Listen for a statement of purpose or main theme. It is essential that you know what the speaker is trying to accomplish. A good speaker will usually help you grasp and understand the key idea around which his speech is built. If he does not, your job as a listener is more difficult. In a well-organized speech, the central idea will often be made clear in the introduction or in the opening of the main de-

[4] For a discussion of barriers to effective listening, *cf.* Wendell Johnson, *Your Most Enchanted Listener*. New York: Harper, 1956.

velopment of the speech. And the main ideas will usually be used to enforce or clarify the central idea. The art of listening begins with an appraisal of the speaker's purpose and ideas, which should be kept in mind and possibly amended as the speech progresses.

Determine the significance of the purpose in relation to your own knowledge and beliefs. If the speaker is explaining or presenting new information, how does this compare with what you already know? How useful is it to you? If it is a controversial point of view, how does it fit into your own convictions and beliefs? Whatever he is saying is useful only as it is related to you. If his subject is one of which you are totally ignorant, you will want to take in the real knowledge for your future needs and possible use.

Listen for main ideas. If the speaker is clear and direct, he will usually first state his main points, then develop them. But he may choose to present facts and supporting material from which he expects you to infer his main ideas, so that you as a listener will help formulate them with him. In either case, good listening demands that you understand what these main ideas are and how they fit into the pattern of his total theme or purpose. While doing this, you will of course be concerned with the facts and evidence which prove or clarify his ideas. You will discern whether such facts really prove the speaker's point, whether he makes unsupported assertions, or whether the point is obviously prejudiced or charged with emotional feeling. You will also weigh his points in relation to your own thinking on the subject, trying, however, to control your own prejudices and feelings.

Supplement the speaker's materials with your own. We have pointed out that you have some extra time as a listener which you can use to review your thoughts and experiences on the point the speaker is making. You may recall something you have read or an experience you have had, all of which will enrich your ability to appreciate and to understand the speaker's point. Such contributory thinking is quite the opposite of daydreaming.

Actually you should find yourself delivering a supplementary address to yourself along parallel lines with the speech. How elaborately you do this will depend, of course, upon your general intellectual quickness and the amount of information you already have on the subject. But whether you do this well or poorly for a specific speech, you should habituate yourself to this practice as a means of entering fully, actively, and personally into the speaker-listener relationship.

Ask Questions

You will of course ask many questions of yourself as you listen. If the occasion is an interview or conference, you will ask them of the person speaking, as the discussion proceeds. If a question-forum period is held, ask the speaker to clarify any doubtful points, or to supplement the information in more detail or with new facts.

Evaluate what you hear. As you develop more critical judgment through closer listening, you will want to place values on the speaker's purpose, his main ideas, his reasoning, and his facts and evidence. Do they all add up to a sound point of view? Is his a logical conclusion? Will it affect your future thinking on the subject? Is the information or instruction clear and useful to you? This does not mean that we want to develop an attitude of doubt and skepticism about all that we hear. It does mean that we constantly want to apply what we know about good speaking when we listen to a speaker.

After the Speech

Summarize and review what you have heard. The speech ought to leave some permanent residue in your mind. Every new idea, fact, or attitude that you assimilate requires a certain amount of readjustment of what you previously believed. The process of education consists largely of the intelligent adaptation of new information and points of view.

Acquiring the habit of reviewing the ideas a speaker has presented offers a sound standard for evaluating the real worth of the speech. Sometimes the charm of the speaker's personality may persuade you to attach more significance to his ideas than they really deserve. The need for distinguishing between the immediate and the lasting effects of a speaker's words led Senator William E. Borah to refuse to listen to the "Fireside Chats" of President Franklin D. Roosevelt. Borah insisted that the charm of the President's delivery tended to mislead the listener. He preferred to read the speeches in newspapers so that he could concentrate purely on the actual merit of the ideas. This, of course, was an extreme case of avoiding personal influence. Yet each of us can benefit from a few moments of reflection after a speech or a discussion with others who have heard it.

Ten Basic Rules of Good Listening

From these considerations we may derive the following rules of good listening:

1. Prepare for listening by anticipating the objective.
2. Develop a positive attitude toward speaker and objective.
3. Be physically alert; sit up; look at the speaker.
4. Be objective; don't let your prejudices interfere.
5. Listen for the speaker's purpose and central idea.
6. Follow the main ideas, noting transitions and summaries.
7. Compare the speaker's purpose and ideas with your own.
8. Evaluate facts and opinions.
9. Evaluate the speaker's total effectiveness.
10. Relate what you have heard to your future thinking and action.

○ CONCLUSION

We have said a great deal in this chapter about listening, which appears to be a comparatively simple process but is in reality, as we have seen, extremely complex, involving all the factors of human behavior and relationships that make the whole process of communication anything but simple. We have tried to point out the values to be gained from improving your listening—values of better enjoyment, better understanding, and a better individual contribution to the group situation. In order to set about to improve your listening, you must understand the barriers and attempt to eliminate them as you develop a proper attitude, avoid prejudices, listen objectively, take advantage of the discrepancy between listening rate and speaking rate, and understand the speaker's language. Then put to work all the basic principles, which add up largely to the total effort you make to project yourself as fully as possible toward an appreciation and understanding of the speaker and his message.

EXERCISES

Questions for Discussion

1. To what extent should an audience feel compelled to give a speaker an attentive hearing? Is it almost entirely the speaker's responsibility to interest the audience?

2. What is your reaction to the listening barrier created by your ability to listen four times faster than a person can speak? What do you do with this extra time when you listen?

3. We all hear speeches occasionally that are not worth the time we spend listening to them. What kind of listening should you manifest in this situation? Why?

4. What are the values of each of the following in making you want to listen to a speaker?

> Direct eye contact
> Attitude of sincerity
> Clear organization of main points
> Use of concrete supporting material
> Use of other factors of attention
> Good voice
> Good bodily activity and gestures
> Use of variety in voice
> Thoughtful consideration of topic
> Use of common-ground approach
> Consideration for audience point of view

5. Prepare to participate in a debate in class on whether it is primarily the speaker's or the listener's responsibility to ensure good listening.

Projects for Speaking and Writing

1. Attend some speaking occasion for the purpose of observing the listening habits of those in attendance. Make a report on your observations, including such items as: (a) the degree to which the audience in general gave the speaker close attention; (b) the extent to which people appeared to listen for a time and then failed to do so; (c) your classification of the listeners as effective or ineffective.

2. Write a few paragraphs analyzing and evaluating yourself as a listener. Point out in what way you think you are a good listener, listing your assets; then list your liabilities as a listener. Which barrier seems most to affect your listening?

3. While listening to a speaker, try to remember the main ideas of his speech as he progresses. After you go home, write down the central idea and the specific purpose, and construct a brief outline of his speech. To what extent did transitions, summaries, and the use of the direct and indirect methods of development influence the speaker's clarity?

4. Write a brief analysis of the question of the speaker's responsibility versus the listener's responsibility for bringing about good listening.

5. What is your reaction to this statement in this chapter: "Actually you should find yourself delivering a supplementary address to yourself along parallel lines with the speech"? Write a few paragraphs about how you might utilize this concept, including such considerations as: (a) the extent to which you would give greater emphasis to the speaker's central idea; (b) how you might supplement his supporting material; and (c) the degree to which you accept, reject, or understand his main ideas.

6. Select some outstanding and successful person. Analyze the factors contributing to his success and plan to present them briefly to the class, emphasizing his qualities as a listener.

7. Prepare a two-minute speech for the class on the value that listening offers in the management of people.

8. Discuss the subject of listening barriers with the class, singling out one barrier in particular for comment and examples.

9. In a recent speech you have heard, at what point did the speaker seem to have best audience attention? When did the audience display emotional tension or laughter? Comment on what the speaker was doing at these times from the standpoint of both his content and his delivery.

Chapter 11

Using Visual Aids

ONE OF THE SKILLS needed for effective speech is the ability to make appropriate use of visual aids. In the preceding chapters attention has naturally been directed to problems of *oral* communication, since speaking and listening are our central concerns. Nevertheless, the eyes of the audience are of great importance and no speaker should ignore the visual channel of communication. The value of visual aids for training purposes has been demonstrated by the armed forces and industry. They also have come to play a significant role in all kinds of oral communication and in academic education. Perhaps a public-relations counselor did not overstate the importance of visual aids when he said, "I would never think of advising a business executive to leave out charts and other visual aids when he makes a speech."

Visual Learning

Psychologists agree that most people are more eye-minded than ear-minded. If you want to be certain that you will remember a name, the chances are that you will write it down and look at it, instead of trying to remember the sounds alone. In learning a foreign language, you may hear the words spoken as if they were a stream of unfamiliar vocables, but when the words are written down, you can trace out their meaning. Mental arithmetic is far more difficult than working out a problem on paper. Similarly, if you ask for directions on how to reach a given destination, you usually are relieved to have them cast

"Oh, I see. . . ."

Proper visual demonstration saves time, improves validating processes, and strengthens understanding, feeling, or belief. Visual aids must be selected, prepared, and handled *primarily* to validate ideas; they must, therefore, be fine examples of *communicative* art, not necessarily of *expressive* art.

in the form of a diagram or map. Many examples might be offered to demonstrate that the eye is our most valuable instrument in the learning process.

This conclusion is reinforced by the findings of the United States Army and Navy World War II training programs that up to 85 percent of learning is gained through the eyes. Their experiments also indicate that people normally learn one-third faster through visual instruction than through aural instruction alone and that material that is seen is remembered 55 percent better than material that is only heard. H. E. Nelson and A. W. VanderMeer, studying the teaching effectiveness of film instructions presented both with and without verbal exposition to accompany the pictures, found that, "The proportion of learning that is attributable solely to listening to the commentary is significantly smaller than that which is attributable to viewing the film with both picture and sound."[1] In other words, we learn best when the eyes and ears work together.

The great increase in the sale of television sets (so that in 1961 there were more television sets than refrigerators or bathtubs in use in the United States) and the continued popularity of motion pictures are further evidence of our widespread use of visual media, as are the wide appeal of the comic strips and comic books and the use of cartoons to point up editorial opinions and the messages of advertisers. Modern man has found no reason to disagree with the old Chinese adage, "One picture is worth a thousand words."

Values of Visual Aids

As was pointed out in Chapter 7, visual aids are a method of validation. They can be made to serve well the speaker's efforts to make clear to his listeners what he means—to enhance their *understanding* of his subject. Their clarifying function makes them valuable as a means of persuasion; and when used as "props" they contribute to entertaining speech, whether humorous or adventurous. The method by which they are used may be either direct or analogous, depending on what the speaker is trying to accomplish with them. Meanwhile, they also have the added values of helping the speaker to hold attention, to reduce his own nervous tension, and to remember his main

[1] *Speech Monographs,* XX (November 1953), p. 7.

ideas. Each of these values should be cultivated by you in your own speaking, where you will find visual aids a source of added effectiveness.

UNDERSTANDING. On some subjects, an audience will understand the speaker's message much faster and more fully if he uses a chart, model, design, or sample, instead of depending upon words alone. Words are *discursive;* that is, they have to be presented and received one by one, with the full meaning obscured until the entire sentence, or paragraph, or composition has been transmitted. Visual symbols, on the other hand, are *presentational,* their full meaning being presented all at once.[2] This is why a political cartoon often has more effect than a complicated, detailed editorial. Similarly, a graph showing by two lines the relationship between average income and the cost-of-living index will carry a clear message instantaneously to the minds of an audience, whereas an exclusively verbal explanation could be comprehended only slowly and might even prove confusing. On the other hand, the graph or the chart may oversimplify the data, and often accurate understanding will be attained only if a qualifying verbal explanation is presented along with the visual aid.

GENERAL SPEECH EFFECTIVENESS. Visual aids may be used to enhance the effectiveness of all kinds of speaking: entertaining as well as informative and persuasive. As has already been indicated, when your purpose is to inform, there is great advantage in presenting data to the eyes as well as to the ears of listeners. In persuasive speech, it is an established axiom that "Seeing is believing." In the area of sheer entertainment, humorists on the platform, in the movies, and on television make considerable use of props, such as odd clothing, false mustaches, and cigars that explode. In inspirational speaking, flags, religious symbols, and appropriate enlarged photographs are often used.

DIRECT AND ANALOGICAL USES. The direct use consists of the display of a visual aid (for example, a cut-out model of the vocal apparatus) that directly exemplifies what the speaker is discussing. As examples of analogical use, the speaker may use a rolling pin and a pile of dough to show how steel is flattened into sheets; or he may use a fountain pen and both cube and loose sugar to demonstrate differences

---

[2] For a full treatment of this interesting difference, see Susanne Langer, *Philosophy in a New Key.* Cambridge, Mass.: Harvard University Press, 1942, Chap. 3, "Discursive and Presentational Forms."

in absorption of moisture by firm and loose surfaces—thus illustrating how proper cultivation can reduce loss of soil through erosion. An imaginative speaker can develop a wide range of analogical uses of visual aids, thereby adding considerably to the interest of his speaking.

ATTENTION. Visual aids are of value in holding the attention and interest of an audience. In listening to detailed explanations, such as an analysis of a budget, the minds of the auditors may become so wearied by lists of figures that they refuse to try to keep them in mind and simply relieve themselves of labor by ignoring the speech and thinking about something else. For other topics, such as the bodily structure of a snake, the showing of an actual specimen adds a dramatic aspect to a talk that otherwise might be dull.

REDUCTION OF TENSION. Visual aids help a speaker by reducing nervous tension. If nervousness is one of your problems while speaking, you can control it by having something to show your listeners and thereby focusing their attention (and your own) on the visual aid instead of upon yourself. In addition, the motion involved in showing the visual aid helps the speaker by utilizing his bodily tension and thus tending to make him feel relaxed. You should be careful, however, not to "escape" from the audience by concentrating your own attention on your visual aid. If you stand staring at the blackboard it may reduce your tension; but it surely will constitute a barrier (not an aid) to your communicative effectiveness.

MEMORY AIDS. Visual aids can also be utilized as effective notes. Since the chart you may place on the blackboard or the model or object you may hold in your hand represents essential points you wish to convey to your listeners, these and other visual aids constitute effective notes to aid your memory. They have a decided advantage over notes written on sheets of paper or cards, for the audience recognizes that the visual aid is offered primarily for its benefit and will not even realize that the speaker is also using the chart or object to reinforce his own memory.

Visual Impact of the Speaker

Your own appearance inevitably makes a visual impact upon your audience. The listeners, who are also observers, form positive and sometimes determining impressions of the speaker from his appearance, regardless of what he says.

For example, if a speaker slouches onto the platform, dressed in dirty or messy clothes, with uncombed hair, a smudge on his chin, and a pencil stuck behind his ear, the audience immediately forms an unfavorable impression which it will be extremely difficult for him to overcome. If the speaker then proceeds to twist and contort his body into awkward postures, to look at the floor or out the window, and to wring his hands or wipe them across his face, there is little chance that anything he says will have a favorable effect on his observant listeners. If the eyes of the audience tell them that the speaker is awkward and insecure, they will not easily be convinced by their ears that he actually has something worthwhile to say.

We all know that first impressions are often definitive—and that an audience sees a speaker before it hears him. Naturally, then, a speaker will want to achieve the best possible effects from the visual impact made by his person upon his listeners. He should be appropriately dressed, neat, confident in bearing, and direct and well poised in posture. Since many different meanings are transmissible by gesture, we should do our best to make our movements and posture convey an impression that supports the message of our words.

○ TYPES OF VISUAL AIDS

Visual aids consist of any of the speaker's materials that the audience can see. The following types are most widely used:

1. Writing or printing on the blackboard or an easel pad.
2. Simple picturizations of data: photographs, charts, graphs, maps, line drawings, cartoons.
3. Complex or coordinate picturizations: filmstrips, slides, motion pictures.
4. Actual objects: samples, models, cut-out models.
5. Live models: people, insects, birds, animals.
6. Handouts: leaflets, pamphlets, mimeographed sheets.
7. Guided tours in which the audience is taken to the scene to be described, such as a battlefield, cave, or factory.

The Blackboard

Probably the easiest and most useful visual medium for supplementing the speech message is the blackboard. Far too often, however,

But can you see . . . ?

Visual aids must be selected and *designed* for the particular situation, listeners, and the idea to be validated. The camera did not pick up the data on this three-piece chart; neither could the listeners a few rows back. In addition, listeners will empathize with and be distracted by awkward handling of visual aids even when legible.

it is used ineffectively. A speaker may suddenly realize, as the speech progresses, that there is a blackboard behind him and that he might as well write something on it. The result is often haphazard and disorganized—the speaker mumbles as he writes illegible words or figures on the board or conceals the material with his own body.

The use of the blackboard should be planned in advance. Many different kinds of material can be advantageously displayed on the blackboard: important speech points which are being stressed; the basic outline of the speech; definitions; summaries of points presented; statistical data in table or graph form; and diagrams or figures. A few simple rules apply to all blackboard material.

PRESENTATION AND COORDINATION. Blackboard material should be coordinated with the spoken word. Most blackboard material is written or drawn on the board as you speak. There is a knack of doing this while you are speaking so that you give the impression of not breaking eye contact with the audience and so that your voice projection continues to be aimed at them. It is best to continue to speak while you are writing or drawing on the board. Under unusual circumstances, silence may be appropriate, but you should bear in mind that a prolonged silent period is distracting.

As you are making your point orally, turn toward the board and start your writing or drawing. Write only a little at a time, and frequently re-establish eye contact with the audience. Keep your voice projection up. As much as possible, keep your right arm and shoulder from concealing your writing. Step away frequently, to the side of the material. Remember that what you are doing is helping to make a point for your listeners—you are not entertaining yourself by writing on the board.

ORGANIZATION AND PLANNING. Material should be well organized and planned in advance. There is seldom an excuse for a sudden decision to go to the blackboard and put something on it. If you consider the importance of the visual medium in attracting the attention of the audience, you will want to do the best job you can of writing, printing, or drawing. While you are preparing the speech, think over what points can be best presented with the aid of the board. In handling complicated material, you should practice putting it on the board, or, if a board is not at hand, see how it looks on a sheet of paper. Make the main headings stand out. Be certain that the material shows coherent organization and that your diagram is a clear picture of what you wish to portray.

Diagrams sometimes need to be put on the blackboard in advance of the speech. A complicated drawing of a machine, for example, cannot be made while you are speaking to the audience. A major difficulty in this connection, however, is that the diagram will distract attention from you and your speech until you come to the point at which you explain and make use of it. This factor should be considered carefully before you make a decision to put material on the board in advance. If you do so, try to cover it in some way so that it can be revealed at the appropriate point in the speech. You may be able to cover it with a drapery or place it on a part of the board removed from the speaker's position so that it will not be noticed until you move over to it to bring it into your talk. You may decide that it would be more effective to put the drawing on a large chart, which can be kept out of sight until you are ready to display it.

A CLEAN BOARD.   See that the board is clean before your speech starts. This is especially important when you follow other speakers. Remove charts, pictures, or other distracting displays that may have been left hanging, and erase all material which has been left on the board.

POSITIONED AND ATTRACTIVE MATERIAL.   The material should be written, printed, or drawn so that it will best attract and hold attention. This means that it should be placed on the center of the board if possible. If you are using a small portable blackboard, place it in the center of the platform and at an angle that ensures optimum visibility. Writing or printing should be large enough to be seen clearly; consideration must be given to the size of the group. Lines should be heavy, and this usually requires bearing down on the chalk. Faint lines or words that cannot be seen might better not have been put on the board; diagrams too small for clarity or visibility are worse than no diagrams at all. Remember that you are using the blackboard for the benefit of your listeners.

When the board is small, it is necessary to plan the visual material in sequence—to erase one visual aid before presenting the next one. This possible handicap should be kept in mind when making plans for blackboard work and may constitute a reason for using large white charts instead of the board.

STANCE OF THE SPEAKER.   Most people are right-handed and

cover part of the material with the right arm and shoulder while working at the board. This is unavoidable, at least for part of the time. But you can avoid concealing the material, after it has been written, while you are pointing to it. Stand facing the audience, using your left hand to point to the material, and, if possible, use a pointer for this. You should know the material so well that it is not necessary for you to look at it as you explain it. You should be looking at your listeners in order to hold attention, to maintain eye contact, and to determine whether everyone is following what you are saying.

GRAPHS AND DIAGRAMS. In many speeches, the most effective method for displaying figures, statistics, and trends is by means of a graph. In some cases, you can best use this medium by preparing the graph in advance of the speech on a chart or on the blackboard, to be uncovered later. But often it is more practical and even more effective to make the graph as you are speaking. A speaker skilled in using the blackboard while speaking can masterfully hold the attention of his hearers through the optimum combined appeal to the auditory and visual senses. The graph must be neat, clear, and large enough to be seen and understood.

There are four basic types of graphs: the line or curve graph, the bar graph, the circle or pie graph, and the picture graph. (These are shown on the following pages.)

Charts

Large white charts, which may be used instead of the blackboard, have the values discussed above. This medium is not used so frequently as the blackboard, probably because the charts are more difficult to

Easel pad

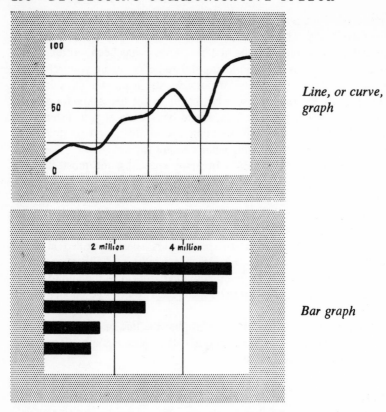

Line, or curve, graph

Bar graph

obtain and the physical arrangement for their use may require more planning. A pad of large white heavy paper or light cardboard should be securely fastened to the top of a rigid easel. The most effective and convenient size is about 30 by 40 inches. The speaker, using heavy black crayon, writes, prints, or draws on the charts just as he would on a blackboard.

The chief value of this medium is that it provides a more lasting record of the visual material. Whereas blackboard work must be erased to make room for more material, the speaker can draw several successive charts without destroying the early ones. This method is exceedingly effective in an informational or training conference in which the speaker is a conference leader drawing information from the group. As the group contributes major points, the leader inserts them on the chart, thus building up a permanent record of development of the sub-

Circle, or pie, graph

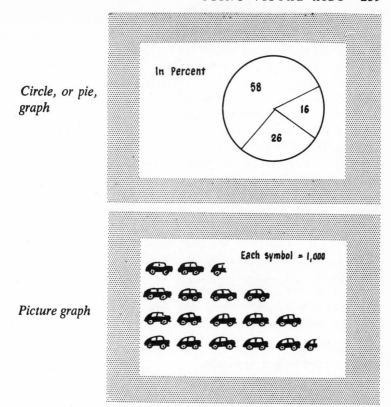

Picture graph

ject and the points brought out in the meeting. As a chart is completed, the leader may remove it from the easel and hang it on the wall in sight of the group. This can be done quickly with cellulose tape or thumbtacks. As the meeting progresses and draws to a conclusion, the charts can be referred to for review or discussion. If review is not desired, completed charts can be folded back out of sight over the easel as the leader proceeds to work on another chart.

The prepared chart may also be used in conferences. Many speakers use this medium to stimulate discussion and elicit the ideas of the group. It is also effective as a supplement. Some carefully planned training programs incorporate a series of charts to be shown at strategic points in the presentation. These may be drawn on large sheets and placed on an easel, as is the pad of blank chart paper described above. As the speaker finishes his explanation and discussion of a chart, he turns it back and proceeds to the next one. Such charts should obviously be carefully prepared and should be displayed so as to be clearly visible to the group. The timing of presentation should be coordinated with the speech discussion.

The average speaker will perhaps more often use a smaller chart which he has prepared in advance and which he will display at the appropriate time. A common mistake is to make such a chart too small. Another is to fail to display it to good advantage; if the speaker is more concerned with looking at the chart himself than with showing it to his listeners, he may hold it perpendicular, half facing himself and half facing them. Visual aids held by the speaker should be held facing the audience and high enough and close enough to the listeners so that nothing obstructs any part of the material from the listener's view.

Another variation of the chart method is to combine prepared charts with charts drawn during the course of the speech. In this way, the speaker may supplement prepared visual material with graphic demonstration of new points that he himself develops or that are contributed by the group. This method serves to dramatize the speech material and to encourage audience participation.

Objects, Models, and Apparatus

Use of a flannel or magnetic board is a method of presenting prepared visual materials. Items may be picked up while you are speaking and affixed to the board's adhesive or magnetic surface, and then removed and rearranged. A wide variety of separate objects may be used to supplement the oral presentation. These may include a model of or the actual object about which you are speaking—such as a baseball in a speech on how to pitch; a model of a gasoline station in a speech on the importance of safety while working in a gas station; or a piece of apparatus in a speech on how a machine works. Apparatus as a visual aid may be the actual object about which you are speaking, a miniature, a sectional part, or a specially prepared transparent model.

The principle of display is the same for all of these. They should be held up or placed in clear view of the audience. They should be pointed to and explained. Until they are used, they should be kept out of sight, if possible, in order to avoid distraction. In demonstrating how

The materials used as visual aids are as varied as the interests of the audience for whom they are intended. To the salesmen above, the display of tires is as vitally interesting as the diagram is to the naval officers below. Both these visual aids will stimulate questions and help to answer them.

But neither would be appropriate for a nonprofessional group.

to use something, such as a baseball bat, for example, keep your activity in the center of the platform and in sight of your listeners at all times. *Face them* as much as possible during the demonstration; *look at them; show them* what you are doing.

Handout Materials

Outlines, summaries, bibliographies, and pamphlets may be used as a supplement so that the listener will have a permanent record of the message or can add to his knowledge of the subject by reading additional literature after the speech. The chief caution in using these is that they must not distract attention from you as a speaker. Most such supplementary material should be passed out after you have finished speaking. Any object placed in the hands of a listener will attract his attention. He will invariably want to read it or thumb through it while you are speaking, despite the fact that you may expressly request him not to. Many speakers, however, make the mistake of passing out material without a word of explanation about how it should be used or in what way it is related to the speech. Always explain the material as you are passing it out.

There is one use of supplementary printed material which may form an exception to the rule that it should not be passed out until the speech is over. This is the handout consisting of data or, perhaps, a sample case which the speaker wants to make use of in promoting discussion or procuring contributions from his audience. In the training conference, where the speaker is a leader who wants to draw some of the information from his audience, this is an established device. The sheet is passed out during a pause in the presentation. The speaker reads it or has someone in the group read it. While everyone focuses attention on the material on the sheet, the speaker guides the group into a discussion of it, being very careful to retain control of the discussion.

Slides

Words or pictures projected on a screen through the medium of slides are well-recognized visual supports for a speaker. Slides are projected with an ordinary slide projector or with the opaque projector (Balopticon). The latter will project other materials in addition to slides. Materials for projection may be prepared by the speaker or purchased commercially. One who has visited a foreign country and taken pictures may easily have them made into slides so that he may give an illustrated lecture about his trip. Diagrams and drawings of apparatus can also be clearly reproduced through a slide.

The use of slides requires that especially careful planning and preparation of the speech and of the physical arrangement of the room be made in connection with the projected display material. Modern slide projectors have a remote control button which the speaker may operate from the front of the room while he is speaking. If a separate operator is needed, coordination with the operator of the machine is also essential. A signal must be arranged so that he will know when to change to the next slide. This medium must be used in a darkened room. The speaker should stand beside the screen, preferably with a pointer, and speak clearly, firmly, and with variety, so that he will command attention even though he is not seen. The method has an advantage over the motion picture or sound strip film in that the speaker can talk for as long as he wishes, or even conduct a group discussion, before he goes on to the next slide.

The Overhead Projector

There are several overhead projectors, such as the Visualcast, Visualizer, Vu-Graph, and Keystone Overhead Projector, which will project words, diagrams, graphs, and other material on a screen in back of the speaker in a lighted room. The instrument has advantages over the Balopticon projector, in that it is operated by the speaker as he faces and talks to his audience and that it operates in daylight or in a well-lighted room. The Visualcast, for example, has a lighted glass surface which is in front or at the side of the speaker and on which he can write, print, or draw as he speaks, just as he would at the board except that he faces his audience while the material appears on the screen behind him.

There are two basic uses for this type of instrument: (1) as a substitute for the conventional blackboard or paper charts drawn during the course of the speech; and (2) as a substitute for prepared charts demonstrated by various methods, including a multiple method of showing parts of a chart at a time and adding to this by successive charts.

Audio-Visual Aids[3]

Two major types of audio-visual aids are the sound motion picture, chiefly in the form of the 16-mm. training film, and the filmstrip, usually 35-mm., accompanied by sound record. The filmstrip is sometimes shown without accompanying sound record, and in such use it is similar to slides, but it is more valuable when used with sound which is integrated and coordinated with the visual projected material.

As a rule these aids are not used during the course of a speech, and, when the film message is the main objective of the gathering, its use may be an end in itself. The mechanics and physical arrangement for showing films are, of course, the same whether the film is to be the chief reason for the meeting or whether it is to be used as a supplement to the speech. Probably the chief use of the film as a medium for supplementing or supporting the message of the speaker is in the instructional talk. The growth in the preparation and use of training films has been tremendous during and since World War II, and films will continue to be a growing medium for instruction. There are also some persuasive speaking situations in which a documentary or inspirational film can help accomplish the purpose of the speaker. And the use of films for entertainment is well known.

In planning to use a film you should observe the following rules.

FILM SELECTION. The film should further the message of the speaker if it is used to supplement the speech. Often a poorly selected film does more harm than good. It may detract from the speech presentation if it is not closely related; it may be tiresome if it is too long; and it may be a poor film. Do not plan to show a film just because you heard somewhere that films constitute a good visual medium to convey a message.

PREVIEWING. Do not plan to see the film for the first time when your audience does. See it during your preparation of the speech, and plan how you will use the points it brings out. Make a concise statement of the purpose of the film, note the main ideas, and determine

---

[3] The chief sources of films and filmstrips are college and university film libraries, commercial distributors and producers, and governmental agencies. Some major compilations listing educational films and sources of rental and purchase are *Educational Film Guide.* New York: H. W. Wilson, which is published yearly with periodic supplements; *1000 and 1.* Educational Screen Magazine, Chicago; and *Educators' Guide to Free Films,* Educators' Progress Service, Randolph, Wis.

how they relate to the points you want the audience to derive from the meeting.

PLANNED QUESTIONS. If the film is supplementing a speech, perhaps you will first present the major part of your speech and conclude by laying a foundation for the film. Or you may show it in the middle of your planned speech and then discuss it after it has been shown. Whatever time for showing you choose, make a brief introduction in which you point up the purpose of the film, what it emphasizes, what main ideas to look for, and other aspects your listeners can keep in mind as they see and hear it. Ask some pointed questions which will be a basis for discussion after the film has been shown.

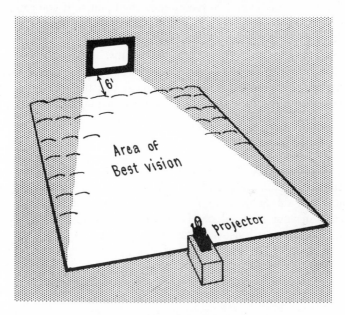

VIEWING CONDITIONS. The physical arrangement of the room is important. Usually a small portable screen is used, and this should be set at the proper distance from the projector, so as to get the largest and clearest image. The viewers can be seated fairly close to the screen, but not closer than six feet. It is best not to seat anyone too close to the projector, for the 16-mm. sound projector makes some noise and throws light, both of which may be distracting. Darken the room as much as possible. Pay especial attention to the position of the sound speaker and the volume. The speaker should be placed off the floor, in the front of the room, and near the screen.

In showing 35-mm. strip film with sound record, be sure that the sound is properly coordinated with the picture, that the first frame appears properly in relation to the narration, and that the succeeding frames are turned at the right time.

FOLLOW-UP. If part of your speech is to follow the showing, integrate the message of the film with your remarks; or conduct a discussion which has reference to the film. When the film has been used as an instruction medium and is short, it is sometimes worthwhile to show it a second time. You may want to write on the blackboard while conducting the discussion, to record important points. If you can place the screen in the center of a large blackboard, the purpose of the film may be written at the left and the main points to look for at the right.

CAUTION: DO NOT OVERUSE VISUAL AIDS. Their purpose is to supplement not to supplant the spoken word. They are rarely ends in themselves and should not be so prominent that the speech becomes secondary to them. You *show* as a means of helping to *tell*.

○ **CONCLUSION**

This chapter has discussed the importance of the visual medium in validating the speaker's ideas, and the wide variety of visual and audio-visual aids at his disposal. Consider whether you might use some of these in your next speech. Develop your use of the blackboard, charts, and prepared visual materials so that you can integrate them with the speech. The effective use of visual aids requires careful planning, preparation, practice, and perhaps some originality. But visual aids well used will enhance the effectiveness of your speaking.

EXERCISES

Questions for Discussion

1. What is the visual code? Why is it important?
2. What are six values of visual aids? How is the speaker helped by their use? How are the listeners helped? Are there subjects for which visual aids would not be helpful to either speaker or listener?
3. In what respects is the speaker his own chief "visual aid"?

4. What types of visual aids are available for use in your classroom speaking? What precautions should you observe in employing them?

5. Name the types of graphs, and indicate ways in which each might be used to advantage.

6. What cautions should be observed in handing out materials to your audience?

7. Describe in detail the best methods of using the blackboard. What errors should be guarded against?

Projects for Speaking or Writing

1. In your next speech to be delivered in class, plan to use the blackboard to record the main points you wish the audience to remember. Along with your speech outline, hand in to the instructor a sheet showing how the blackboard will look when you have inscribed your points on it.

2. Plan a three-minute speech in which you explain a process, such as a play in a football game. As part of your preparation, plan how you will chart the play on the backboard. Hand in a sheet showing how this will look on the board.

3. For a short speech in which you will explain how a machine operates or a tool is used, plan a blackboard drawing of the machine or tool and prepare a sheet showing this drawing as it will appear on the board.

4. For any of the above exercises, prepare a chart containing the material you wish to show while you are speaking. Plan how you will use the chart in the speech presentation.

5. Bring an object to class, such as a football, golf club, model airplane, or similar item, and plan to explain and demonstrate the use or construction of this object to the audience in a short talk.

6. From magazines, newspapers, or other sources, clip several outstanding advertisements which make unusual use of the visual sense either to attract attention or to explain something. Which is the primary use in each case?

7. Bring to class an example of each major type of graph. Go to the front of the class and present information which will be supplemented by your drawing a suitable graph on the blackboard as you speak.

8. Prepare a brief summary or outline on a sheet which you will pass out to the audience to supplement your speech. Plan in advance just when you will pass it out and how you will ask the audience to make use of it.

9. Recall a speech you have heard which was accompanied by slides, filmstrips, or motion pictures, and write a brief criticism of the use of these by the speaker.

PART III

Forms of
COMMUNICATIVE
SPEECH

Chapter 12

Informative Speaking

OUR MOST CONSISTENT COMMUNICATION need is to achieve understanding with other people, both in the messages we wish to convey and in those we receive. To be clearly understood is the great challenge of almost all speaking, whether our major objective is to inform, or whether it also includes a persuasive or entertaining purpose. The problem of being clear is one we can never lose sight of, regardless of the objective.[1]

This chapter, like the others on types of speaking, deals with the application of all the principles of effective speaking to particular speech purposes and objectives. Here we shall be concerned primarily with the *informative speaking* process.

The first general principle is that all the concepts, principles, methods, and techniques that make up the total process of good communication apply in some measure to any particular speaking objective. The mature and resourceful speaker will learn to make the necessary adaptation and revision of a form of effectiveness so as to best meet the specific communication requirements. He will have learned that good speaking is not materially different as he moves from one situation to another, one listener to another, or one objective to another.

---

[1] Despite the categorical statement of the need for absolute clarity, there is a case to be made for ambiguity when the speaker understands fully what he is doing and what purpose obscurity is to serve. For a discussion of ambiguity in diplomatic speaking, *cf.* Ambassador Ben C. Limb, "Speech: The Life of a Diplomat," *The Quarterly Journal of Speech,* Vol. 43 (February, 1957), pp. 55–61.

Therefore much of what we take up in this chapter has already been discussed in earlier chapters, and we will be making constant reference to how you may draw on them and integrate your total knowledge in applying the principles you have already learned.

All you have to do to realize the use you make of the informative speaking process is to make a list of the situations in which you find yourself in any one day. You awaken to the radio just as the news is being broadcast, so you apply your best analytical listening habits to understand clearly what is being said. Now your roommate is awake and wants you to tell him what you heard. So you have the job of conveying clear factual information that is accurate, specific, concise, uncolored by inference or opinion, and well understood by your listener.

While dressing, you are also asked to explain a theory of economics to this same roommate who did not understand the assigned chapter. You try to formulate a brief statement defining the theory, you show that it has several parts which you neatly divide, you explain each part, and you use an example in the immediate community to make the theory concrete and better understood. At breakfast, you discuss this same theory with other students, and you ask one another questions in order to clarify doubtful points. When you go to class, the instructor elects to teach this theory by having the class discuss it and gradually develop its meaning by the discussion process of the group.

On returning to your room after lunch, your long-awaited long distance call comes through from your parents who have just returned from Europe. They try in a few moments to give you their chief impressions fresh from the trip. Afterwards, you must prepare a very important presentation you will make to a student government group, as chairman of a committee which reports that night. You try to make a clear exposition of the facts you were asked to ascertain, and you explain a proposed plan your committee recommends. Informative speaking? These are only a few of the needs that confront you on a typical day. Add to them the need to explain (and demonstrate) to your kid brother how to solve a problem in geometry, attempt to make clear to a motorist the location of a certain building in your community when you are both two miles away from it, or the problem of giving a report to your professor on the progress of your term research project.

○ INFORMATIVE AND OTHER PURPOSES RELATED

We have established that the three major purposes in speaking are to *inform, persuade,* and *entertain.* By far the greater part of our speaking is to inform and persuade. With regard to the objective of entertaining, let it suffice to say that all speaking should be interesting and pleasing to the listener. But even when we have no objective but pure entertainment, we are basically presenting information of some sort, with the need to choose our material for qualities of human interest or humor that will accomplish this end. So we can conclude that all good speeches should please the listener and hold his attention and interest, whether or not he may agree with our persuasive purpose; and that all speaking for entertainment makes use of the informative process.

The relationship between informative and persuasive speaking purposes is a vital one to understand, and it is exceedingly important to recognize that they are not mutually exclusive. The first important thing for the speaker to determine is his basic and essential purpose. If this is informative, he will endeavor in the best way possible to make his ideas clear, factual if necessary, specific and concrete, interesting, and adapted to the listener.

Let us assume his purpose is to inform his listeners about a specific problem in international affairs. If he does this well, he will first arouse their interest and *motivate* them (a type of persuasion) to realize the importance of this information to them and to create a positive attitude of wanting to listen.[2] As he proceeds to present the information, he may bring in reference sources to which those interested can go for additional information, and he may suggest in his conclusion the future use and application of his subject. As a result, his listeners are persuaded to read more and to discuss the subject further. The speaker's basic intent was to gain understanding of the problem he presented, yet he achieves a motivational and even an action result. In this sense, a good informative speech may also be persuasive.

The relations among the three types of speeches and the difficulty of sharply differentiating one from another may be clarified by use of

---

[2] The relationships between informative and persuasive speaking are interestingly illustrated in the *good will talks* presented by public relations representatives of business organizations. Typically, such speeches *inform* about some phase of the work of the companies, the principal purpose being to persuade—that is, to create good will.

Understanding is basic . . .

For all speech purposes, understanding is basic and an ability to gain understanding in listeners is essential. Watch your listener. Does he *really* understand? Does he understand incompletely? Or is he just being polite? Don't "hope" he understands, *make sure*.

an extended example. As a student of international relations, you may decide to give a series of speeches on Nationalist China. In your first speech you may decide to be *informative,* in your second *persuasive,* and in your third *entertaining.* Although the subject is the same, the three speeches will differ very greatly from one another because the audience response you are seeking differs basically in each instance. Nevertheless, it is probable that all three talks will contain informative, persuasive, and entertaining materials.

Having the general purpose to inform and the specific purpose to make the audience understand the degree to which the government of Chiang Kai-shek instituted a series of democratic reforms in Formosa, you might select such a title as "Island Laboratory in Democracy," with the central idea: Formosa is showing signs of democratic growth.

While preparing your speech, you recall that your audience has doubtless heard and read a great deal of criticism of the Chinese Nationalists, which has had the effect of creating a generally unfavorable attitude toward them. Thus, you may develop a persuasive introduction, designed to induce your listeners to guard against the effects of propaganda and to fortify their conviction that they ought to make up their own minds on the basis of solid factual information. This phase of the speech is the process of clearing away barriers of misunderstanding; thus, it is persuasion used for purposes of exposition. After this has been accomplished, the body of the speech should consist of an informative presentation of reform measures, each stated as a main idea, such as:

1. Freedom of speech has been extended, if not fully achieved.
2. The land-tenure system has been revised and improved.
3. A two-party political system is being considered.

In your conclusion you may again ask your listeners to base their thinking upon facts rather than upon propagandistic distortions, and you may then present an expository summary leading to a clear understanding of what has been explained. Since your general purpose is to inform, you will take care in the development of your ideas to balance the achievements with the failures, so that your audience will understand both the achievements and the inadequacies of the democratic experiment in Formosa. To ensure that their interest does not lag, your illustrative material will be chosen for its interest potential as well as for clarity.

In your next speech, in which your general purpose is to persuade, your specific purpose might be to induce your listeners to support the continued membership of Nationalist China in the United Nations. Your central idea or theme might be that the Government on Formosa represents the traditional civilization of China. Selecting such a title as "Representing the Real China," you might phrase such main ideas as:

1. The Chinese people have long preferred the United States to Russia.
2. The Nationalist Government represents the fundamental interests of China far better than does the Communist Government.
3. The maintenance of the Nationalist Government provides for the people of China their best hope of realizing their own national needs.

In developing these main ideas, you will need to present a sound body of representative factual information, and again your illustrative materials should be selected in part for their interest value; but your general purpose is to lead your audience to agree that international recognition of the Nationalist Government of China should be continued. You have used information and entertainment specifically for persuasive effect.

In a speech to entertain, your specific purpose might be to give your listeners a vivid picture of the life of a typical Chinese family which has fled from the mainland to Formosa. Your central idea might be that private living becomes ludicrously distorted under the demands of political revolutionary conditions.

With a title such as "A Home away from Home," you could develop such main ideas as:

1. Chinese family life centers around the graves and traditions of its ancestors.
2. Fleeing from an old established home to seek a new one on an overcrowded island involves many adventures.
3. Living on an island while maintaining one's spiritual ties to a mainland ancestral home causes some manifestations of a split personality.

In developing these ideas, you give the audience a great deal of factual information about the plight of the Chinese refugees, and you exercise a persuasive effect of creating sympathy for their desire to regain their homeland. But these effects are incidental. Your principal endeavor is to entertain them with a mingling of humor and pathos, created through the relating of a series of anecdotes and examples.

The foregoing illustration does not imply that the three types of speeches are always so closely interrelated; it does demonstrate that, even when the interrelationship is close and extensive, the type of speech is determined by the general purpose.

○ CLEAR TO WHOM?

The goal that should be achieved, after you have finished your speech, is that what you set out to do is *clear to your listener*. Unless it is, you have not communicated. If he found it interesting but could not really understand the connection between your points, your purpose was not achieved. Only if he understands your central idea can you hope to attain your major goal. This is not to say that informative speeches should be dull and uninteresting. Quite the contrary, every consideration should be given to the use of the kind of material and presentation that will best hold the attention and interest of your particular listeners. Unfortunately, too many lecturers do not take this vital principle into consideration.

You must realize that listeners represent all degrees of prior knowledge and understanding of your subject before you even begin the speech. They may be largely uninformed, as when you set out to explain the operation of a new device. They may have general but inaccurate information on a subject like the prediction of weather. Their knowledge may be distorted by prejudices, as when, for example, you speak on the relative intelligence of cats and dogs. They may have false information, as when you talk on the comparative size of the armed forces of Soviet Russia and the United States.

Listeners may also differ considerably in their capacity to understand and follow your speech development. If they have little prior knowledge, you will have to start on a more elementary level. If their capacity to understand is high, as in a group of physics majors on the subject of a new nuclear device, you can proceed to more complex aspects of the subject more rapidly than if you were giving the same talk to high school seniors or housewives.

The egocentric tendency of all of us is a major barrier to sufficient analysis and adaptation to the listener. Too much of the time we consider the topic in terms of whether it is clear to us as speakers rather than clear to our listeners, thus disregarding the immediate goal of achieving clarity and understanding for them. Although the primary consideration in accomplishing speech goals should be directed toward the listener, the obvious prior consideration in preparation is whether you as speaker understand the subject clearly yourself. And even if you do, you will have to extend your knowledge far beyond the material you put in the speech, so that you can make constant adaptations to the listeners, answer their questions (unspoken or spoken), and show that you know what you are talking about. The "iceberg" technique referred to earlier would apply here. Strive to relate informative purposes and material to:

1. *Listener interest,* by motivating a desire to accept this information through appeal to listener wants and needs in the introduction and by continuous adaptation throughout the speech.

2. *Listener experiences,* by using examples and other supports that are known to him or are within his background of experience.

3. *Listener language level,* by using words that he understands.

4. *Listener application,* by pointing out the uses for this information and the way it may be applied, particularly in the introduction and the conclusion, but also throughout the speech.

A constant concern with motivation of the listener in these ways will help you adapt your talk to your auditors.

○ **MAINTAINING OBJECTIVITY**

The tendency to inject inferences, opinions, and value judgments, frequently based on prejudice, should be avoided in informative speaking. These usually reflect the personal bias of the speaker and will tend to color the information. The objective is to be factual, impartial, and clear. Make it a practice to avoid these pitfalls:

1. *One-sided inferences, opinions, and value judgments.* In presenting facts, figures, dimensions, and other material to convey information, it is very easy to draw conclusions which are other than

factual. For example, in describing the features of a particular car, such as the French Peugeot, let's assume that you have just described and explained the engine. You add, "This type of engine is superior to most American engines . . . ," or "You can obviously see the greater efficiency of this engine over the American. . . ." Observe that you are shifting from exposition to opinion—opinion which may be based on your own prejudice because you own a Peugeot.

In describing life at a coeducational college and comparing it with a man's college, one is inclined to point up that which he likes better and conclude by saying, "I'm sure all of you can see that the coed college is far preferable." It's all right to state and try to prove such an opinion (or argument when the point is controversial), but usually not in an informative speech. If this is what you want to convince your listeners to believe, your speech is persuasive and should be developed with that end in mind.

2. *Prejudiced attitudes.* Your attitude and bias on a subject may be much stronger than just having knowledge of it. You should try to avoid all displays of prejudice and should strive to see the subject as it is, not as you wish it were. Avoid strong adjectives and adverbs. Avoid self-projection and develop your points in a nonpersonal manner, with objectivity and an analytical rather than a subjective attitude.

3. *Undue emphasis.* It is best to keep emphasis properly balanced, so that the listener does not conclude that you are pushing one point as against another because of personal feeling. This does not mean that some points should not have fuller development than others, or that some are not more important than others in understanding the subject. But if this is not the case, points should be handled with more equal emphasis.

4. *Inconsistent standards.* Going back to the subject of cars, you might give an informative speech in which your purpose is to analyze and compare the Peugeot with the Ford. In discussing the features of each engine, if your standard is economy, you can present certain data from which the audience may infer their own conclusions against the standards you set. Make your standards clear, too, so that the listener has no doubt that they remain the same as you discuss one car and then the other.

5. *Too much generality.* Generalized or abstract statements and explanations are apt to be understood and interpreted differently by

different listeners. The more concreteness you include in the form of data, specific examples, and accurate description, the less likelihood there is of inaccurate and vague perceptions by the listener.

Just as in all speech objectives, there are at least three crucial points in an informative speech where it will be found necessary to give specific consideration to principles for achieving maximum clarity of understanding. These are (1) in *organizing* your ideas (assuming you have already arrived at the clearest possible specific purpose), (2) in *developing* your ideas, and (3) in *presenting* them to your listeners.

○ ORGANIZING THE SPEECH TO INFORM

All the methods of planning and organizing discussed generally in Chapters 3, 4, and 6—the necessity for selecting a good subject and specific purpose, the careful choice of main and subordinate points, the building of an outline, and the making of careful transitions from one main point to the next—are applicable to the organization of the informative speech. We need to consider, however, the special modifications of these principles in relation to each kind of speaking. In the following pages special attention is given to organizing the informative speech. The introduction and conclusion of an informative speech have special expository functions to fulfill. The body of the informative speech may follow any one of several types of organization, depending upon the nature of the subject.

The Introduction

The purpose of the introduction to any speech is to prepare the audience for the main part which is developed in the body. This statement applies also to the informative speech. But more specifically in the informative speech, the function of the introduction is to prepare the listeners to understand the material that is to be presented in the body of the speech. The following suggestions should help you to prepare for the complete task of exposition.

Your opening remarks should be designed to gain the interest and attention of the audience through personalized references and demonstration of common ground.

You should give clear definitions or explanations of any difficult

or confusing concepts or terms which you want your listeners to understand exactly.

You should make clear the significance of the subject you have
chosen and the need for everyone to appreciate the importance of what
is to be treated. Remember how frequently listeners are apathetic or
indifferent to subjects which are chosen by speakers—responding with
attitudes of "Ho-hum" or "Why bring that up?" Hence, you must not
delay the process of motivating and arousing a desire for the information to be given.

You should indicate the direction the speech as a whole will take
by eliminating certain materials which are irrelevant and beyond the
scope of the given topic, thus narrowing it to the point where you can
state and support your central idea.

You should, by a brief initial summary, provide a preview of the
main points to be taken up in the body of the speech.

The Body

In the body of the speech the task of the speaker is to take up
one after another the main points, all of which must help to fulfill or
support the specific purpose. In the outline which you prepare, the
subpoints under each main point must be evident, and all the methods
of exposition to be employed—statistics, examples, illustrations, and
authoritative quotations—must be placed where they are to be used.
Still other problems will confront you. In making the outline for the
body you must decide on the best over-all design for your topic.
Certain subjects can best be treated in one way, whereas others should
be handled otherwise. More specifically, your task is to decide which
one of the following general methods you will want to follow. This
decision depends upon the nature of your specific purpose, subject
matter, and audience.

CHRONOLOGICAL ORDER.   Many expository topics lend themselves
to treatment in chronological order. If you are describing the history
of a movement or the development of an institution, time order may
be the one you will wish to follow. By this method you can in one main
point describe its earliest stages of development, in another main point
the story of its subsequent progress, and in still another its present
growth, size, and characteristics.

Let us assume you are giving a speech on the subject "The History of Our University." Your central idea could be: the university has steadily improved in quality while it has grown larger. Obviously, the chronological method can be used to describe the early history of the institution, its later growth, and finally its present status.

SPATIAL ORDER. Treatment in spatial order is especially effective in describing a scenic area or a physical plant, such as a group of buildings. You can describe from "top to bottom" or from "north to south, and east to west." Let us assume your subject is "Our University Campus" and your central idea is: the focal point of the campus is the library. You might describe the campus as a whole from east to west, or you might select certain buildings which you would describe from the basement to the top floor, or you might describe the buildings as they have been planned as units in the over-all campus design.

CAUSAL ORDER. In using the causal order, you will be treating as your central idea the forces and circumstances which have operated to bring into existence and perpetuate the institution you are talking about. It is an explanation of the causes and effects which will provide the main features of your outline. For example, in the topic "The Growth of Our University," you might have as main points the vision and influence of the founders, the money made available for its growth and development, and the increased enrollment which has necessitated the enlarging of the buildings and the erection of new ones. In this order you are very obviously talking about causes and effects which have operated to make the institution what it is.

TOPICAL ORDER. There are some subjects in which the speaker will find an inherent logical classification or arrangement of materials, and the listeners will expect him to observe this order in his treatment. If he is talking on how some institution is organized—for example, with the central idea that growth is always organic, with functions developing out of needs and purposes—he will very likely follow in his speech the organization as he finds it to be. Thus, if you are talking on "Our University—Its Financial Structure," you might very logically divide your speech into such main topics as its assets, its liabilities, and its expenditures. If you should be treating its over-all organization, you might plan the outline to discuss its administrative structure, its division into various colleges, and the colleges' individual departments and staffs.

SPECIAL ORDERS. On occasion speakers will choose to present

their main ideas in the order of the simplest to the most complex, the most familiar to the least familiar, the least important to the most important, or the most acceptable to the least acceptable.

Transitions are a key tool for keeping the organization of your ideas clear, and they should be used frequently throughout your speech. The first major transition is the point where you go from the introduction to the start of the main development in the body. In an informative speech, this is usually best accomplished by indicating clearly the specific purpose, central idea, and main points. The latter are indicated by an initial summary, as we have already pointed out. This summary should be in the same order as that in which the points will be developed. After making it, restate your first main point again as you start to take it up.

It is then important to show clearly where you leave a point and go to the next. To avoid artificiality and monotony, you should develop a variety of transition and connective words and phrases, such as "next in order," "now to turn to another phase . . . ," "in addition . . . ," "finally. . . ."

As you move from point to point, internal summaries are helpful to keep the continuity clear. Summarize the two points taken up in relation to your central idea as you make your transition to your third point. Remember the basic principle that your listeners do not want to work too hard to be able to follow you. There is no excuse for a speaker to be well into the development of a new point while his audience still thinks he is on the preceding one. Everything you say should be designed to help your listeners keep your central idea and main points in sharp focus.

The Conclusion

It must be remembered that the purpose of the speech to inform is clear understanding. Thus, the conclusion, like the other parts of the speech, should contribute to this objective. Suggestions for the conclusion, therefore, may be stated very simply.

You should give a summary of what has been said in order to review clearly the chief points which you have stressed and explained.

You may tell the audience where additional information can be secured on the subject you have discussed. This may be a plea that your listeners do additional reading or investigation, or simply a suggestion for those who have been stimulated to want additional information. You may name books or periodicals, tell who may be interviewed, or explain where the object, invention, or institution may be found.

You may suggest future application and use by the audience of the information given.

You may end with a specific illustration or example in which the main points and central idea you have discussed are briefly reviewed by means of a story.

○ DEVELOPING INFORMATIVE IDEAS

Chapter 7, "Developing Ideas," should be reviewed at this point, to bring once again clearly into focus the various means you may use for the development of full clarity of understanding by your listeners. As you turn back to it, you will find discussed under the heading, *Analytic Examination,* the essential processes of limiting your subject matter around a definite central idea which is sufficiently restricted in scope to permit adequate explanation of all its relevant phases. You will note what may and should be accomplished by way of defining and describing your key concepts. You will refresh your memory on how to discriminate and qualify the judgments and conclusions which are necessary in explaining your chosen theme. You will also recall the values and methods (as well as the possible dangers) of classifying your material into meaningful categories. And you will be reminded of the essential requirement of bringing your diverse threads of explanation into a final redefinition or synthesis as a part of your conclusion.

The *Validation Forms* discussed in Chapter 7 show the need for and value of presenting the historical perspective on many kinds of questions. In informative speaking this will often be of special value in helping your listeners to understand a complex situation—for example, the nature of Southeastern Asian reactions to Communism. However, the historical review should not be introduced unless it is needed. If you are to explain the strategy of playing "double-dummy" in bridge, it would be useless and distracting to introduce your explanation with a history of the game. Validation forms which are useful for most informative talks, and which, therefore, should be carefully reviewed, are examples (sometimes in detail), narratives and other illustrations, testimony of experts, and statistical data.

Among the *Validating Methods* explained in Chapter 7, there is none that does not have a very direct usefulness in informative speaking. Various forms of restatement are especially helpful if you are explaining a complicated process, in which the understanding of one stage depends upon a clear recollection of those that have preceeded it. Cumulative piling up of examples is often of value, particularly when you are trying to explain an abstraction, such as beauty, or a generalization such as, "establishing habits depends upon consistency of practice." The use of questions has special merit in informative speaking, for it is particularly necessary that you not proceed further or faster than the understanding of your listeners. "Do you understand this?" is a question you have probably often heard from a professor in the midst of a lecture. "If this is true, what would you expect would naturally follow?" is a kind of question that both serves as a transition and also helps bring your listeners' thinking directly to bear upon the problem being discussed.

Comparison and contrast are so essentially a part of informative speaking that it is difficult to explain anything new to your listeners without using these devices. Many a time you will find it helpful to say to them that what you are describing now is in such-and-such a way like something they already understand well. For example, "Kant's principle of the categorical imperative is like the Golden Rule," following which you can explain why. Then, using contrast as well as comparison, you might add, "But it differs from it in being largely negative—by warning us of what we should not do, instead of stating what should be done." Finally, the validating method of demonstrating visually what you are trying to explain is of such widespread usefulness that an entire chapter, Chapter 11, is devoted to it.

Once again it is worth recalling that informative speaking depends upon principles described in all the other chapters, with perhaps special attention to Chapters 5, 6, 7, and 8.

Presenting Ideas for Maximum Clarity

Although there is little we need add to the discussion of speech presentation in Chapter 9, it is well to remember certain principles that are particularly important for achieving clarity.

1. *Words and sentences* should be short, simple, and used with a minimum of complexity. Language should be vivid and meaningful,

with particular stress on clear meaning of words. When in doubt, pause and define.

2. *Oral punctuation,* particularly at ends of sentences and thoughts, should be obvious, with more stress on pauses.

3. *Repetition and restatement* should be used abundantly.

4. *Transitions* are especially important.

5. *Clear and distinct voice* projection and articulation may make the difference between clear understanding and misunderstanding.

6. *Reliance on the visual* should be maximum, with every effort made to use visual aids that will best supplement the clarity of the message.

7. *Notice your listeners* for signs of understanding or perplexity. You can frequently tell whether your audience understands and is following you by the expression on their faces, their degree of alertness, and the presence or absence of fidgeting and restless movement.

○ APPLICATION OF INFORMATIVE SPEAKING

As we pointed out at the beginning of this chapter, there are countless situations that daily demand of you the ability to communicate clearly and achieve understanding with others.[3] These might be summarized under three major types of communication objectives: speeches to groups in the form of prepared talks, oral reports, book reports, and similar messages; informal two-person situations taking the form of conversation or interview; and group discussion and conferences. On the other side of the communicative process, we might of course add the objective of listening to gain understanding from the messages of other speakers. This is discussed in Chapter 10.

Talking to groups in prepared speech situations would make use of all the principles of this chapter. Similarly, when you are in a situation which requires that you get up on your feet and talk to a group impromptu or without formal preparation, you should try to apply systematically as many principles as you can. Determine what your purpose is, and keep it narrow. Select one or two main ideas and quickly decide the best order of their presentation. Make these ideas

[3] In a survey by Franklin H. Knower, published in *Speech Education in Ohio.* Columbus: The Ohio State University, 1950, the company managers who were questioned listed the ability to present clear explanations as the most valuable speaking ability required for businessmen.

clear by explanation, definition, and then concrete example or statistics. Summarize and restate.

In conversation and interviewing, which we discuss more fully along with the treatment of informal conferences in Chapter 16, you should do all you can to make your own ideas clear whenever you are speaking. As a listener, you should encourage the person who is speaking to follow principles and methods that will improve his clarity. You should ask him to restate, to define, to explain by example or to offer more concrete facts, to show how his thought applies to you, and to help you to understand him better.

In discussion and conferences, where you are equally responsible with others to develop informational material, concepts, facts, principles, or instruction, you should use the principles of this chapter in adapting to the points of others and in making original contributions yourself. This requires careful listening and knowledge of what has been said by the members of the group and relating it to your own knowledge and information. Then, when you do speak, you should be as clear as possible while watching for signs of understanding in others.

○ **CONCLUSION**

This chapter has attempted to integrate a number of principles and methods of effective communication discussed throughout the book and apply them to the objective of attaining clear understanding. This is usually called *informative speaking,* and the most vital message of this chapter is to emphasize that clarity is the basis of all communication. It should be understood that informative and persuasive speaking are distinct from each other in intent; but each one contains supporting elements of the other. The principles applicable to an informative speech are equally applicable in the more informal communication situations of conversation, interview, and discussion. The primary consideration is that your message be clear to your listener, which demands that it be clear to you first and then that you should make every possible adaptation to the listener in achieving clarity in your organization, your development, and your presentation. The methods and processes of exposition should be used fully, developed by appropriate use of supporting tools for concreteness and for greater listener motivation and understanding.

If you master the ability to speak clearly, from your listener's standpoint, you will probably be on the road to success in all your speaking objectives.

EXERCISES

Questions for Discussion

1. Review the distinctions that are made in defining the general purposes, in Chapter 6. Discuss the "relations among the three types of speeches" with those earlier distinctions clearly in mind. (Note the chief point that must be kept in mind: the ultimate intent of the speaker to inform, to persuade, or to entertain his audience *must not be in doubt*.) Similarly, it is also important to make effective use of all three types of materials (informative, persuasive, and entertaining) wherever and whenever they may assist you, regardless of the nature of your general purpose.)

2. Taking as a model the text's treatment of the topic "Nationalist China," utilize another general topic, selected by your instructor or yourself (such as "labor unions" or "grades" or "liberal education"), to work out parallel methods of development which will show both the differentiation and the intermingling of the three general speech purposes.

3. Illustrate in class discussion the characteristics of the speech to inform, by reference to talks that have been given in your class or that you have recently heard or read.

4. Redefine each of the five types of organization discussed in this chapter. In your course in English composition, or elsewhere, have you encountered any other classification of the types? If so, present this other listing to the class, with your explanation of it.

5. Repeat exercise 4, basing it this time on the validating forms and methods.

6. Discuss the materials of this chapter in relation to the substance of Chapter 9.

7. Note the special problems of the introduction, body, and conclusion that must be taken into account in preparing and delivering speeches to inform.

Projects for Speaking and Writing

1. Prepare a brief informative speech, noting in the technical plot of your outline the forms of support and the types of exposition utilized and the order in which your ideas are organized.

2. Each member of the class may select one of the types of exposition (with guidance from the instructor to ensure that each type is repre-

sented) and deliver a brief speech to the class based directly on that mode of exposition. Note that each of the different types is suited, to a degree, to a different kind of subject matter.

3. After you have selected a subject for an expository speech, write a brief essay answering the question "What inadequate or mistaken ideas are probably held by members of my classroom audience about this particular subject?"

4. After your selection of a subject for an expository speech to your classroom audience, prepare and deliver a one-minute talk explaining why you selected the particular "order of organization" which you have decided to use.

5. Select one of the speeches given by a classmate and write a critique in which you state clearly (1) what you learned from it and (2) how the speech changed your previous understanding of its subject. Conclude by suggesting ways in which the speaker could have made his ideas clearer, made a greater contribution to your understanding, or helped to resolve your own perplexities concerning the subject.

6. Write a one-page account of a recent informal conversation or discussion with friends in which your endeavor was to explain or clarify a principle or concept.

Chapter 13

Persuading

IN DAYS OF CRISIS, when your lives and ours might have hung in
the balance, a recent American president declared: "What we need
is action, not mere rhetoric!" If you heard him, you probably were
aroused by that particular piece of "rhetoric." Yet we live in the
stronghold of democratic government and living, built upon controversy and persuasion as the prime means of arriving at final decisions.
We depend upon persuasion in our legislative committees, in our business meetings and conferences, in our election campaigns, and even in
our homes. We take pride in our freedom to choose, on the basis of
competitive persuasion, who shall be our leaders. And we insist upon
this freedom as a right. Yet even you, perhaps, shun persuasion or
view it with suspicion as vaguely threatening and "hidden."

You now have an opportunity to learn to persuade more effectively and, in the process, to learn to respond to persuasion intelligently
and analytically in order to make better decisions.

○ LEARN BY LISTENING

The late George V. Denny, for many years moderator of
America's Town Meeting of the Air, repeatedly declared that while
we in the United States have by statute the freedom of speech for
which our forefathers fought, we don't practice it. He was not com-
plaining about the occasional banning of speakers from college cam-
puses and certain other places, but about something far more serious.

He meant that we don't listen to the other side; we don't go to hear or tune in a speaker for the other political party. When this happens, said Denny, we lose every advantage that freedom of speech is designed to provide. Does it apply to you? If so, you may be like the group of college professors who served on a special review board to consider student petitions for reinstatement, waiving of requirements, and the like. One member proposed that more appropriate decisions could be made if there were more information about each petitioning student. But another member insisted, "Oh, no! If we know more about the student it will be harder to come to a decision."

True, it is harder to decide if we admit to mind all sides of a controversy. But what else is freedom of speech (and the press and religion) for but to assure valid decisions by an informed public?

The student of speech—or, for that matter, any thoughtful citizen —will learn about issues and learn about persuasion if he begins *practicing* freedom of speech by developing a freedom to listen to all sides—to all of the persuasion—when a decision must be made either by himself or by others with whom he may speak.

○ PERSUASIVE PURPOSES

Persuasion is any effort to influence the attitudes, feelings, or beliefs of others, or to influence action based on those attitudes, feelings, or beliefs. Thus, in Chapter 4, we described the persuasive purposes as:

Covert	1.	to stimulate or strengthen feeling or belief
	2.	to create or change belief
Overt	3.	to gain action based on strengthened feeling or belief
	4.	to gain action based on a new belief

It should be clear that these are everyday occurrences, and that they will continue increasingly to confront you throughout your lives. Many times in the past twenty-four hours you have probably tried to persuade some other person and probably someone has tried to persuade you. Generally, you will be able to classify each attempt at persuasion as having one of these four purposes.

Fundamentally, what is special about those characteristics is the listener-central-idea relationship.

From within . . .

Effective persuasion comes from within. The various devices for strength-ening feelings, creating belief, and moving to action—in your speech class and elsewhere—are of little avail unless the speaker *knows* he is right and *feels urgently* that it is important to his listeners that he ac-complish his speech purpose.

Strengthening Listener Feeling

What is often called, in a special sense, the speech to stimulate, is designed to arouse or re-arouse listeners' beliefs, attitudes, or feelings which have become dormant; to inspire the apathetic; to uplift. For you to understand this kind of speaking, you must first understand the nature of the listeners for whom such speaking may be designed.

1. *Listeners* who make up an audience which requires your speaking to strengthen feeling or existing belief, have first of all, no real quarrel with the speaker or his idea. They believe that they should respect an honored guest or admire a political idea or be fearful of an atomic attack or appreciate the advantages of a college education. But they are, like everyone else, busy with their daily problems. These listeners are depending on the speaker to intensify those feelings and attitudes.

Who are these listeners? They are those who gather at a political rally or a retirement banquet; they are also you at a pep rally, you at a kick-off dinner for a fund-raising or other campaign, frequently you at a chapel or church service. They are also a discouraged roommate or members of a fraternity or sorority renewing allegiance to their organization's goals. They are anyone with whom we share goals, enthusiasms, values, beliefs, attitudes or feelings, and who, we are sure, need to have bolstered their goal-seeking, enthusiasms, values, beliefs, attitudes, or feeling.

2. *Speakers* who would strengthen these feelings—who are they? They are the commencement speaker, the minister, the candidate, the campaign director, the football coach. And they are the roommate, fraternity brother, the parent, or a doting aunt. All are seeking to arouse feelings; all are wanting to inspire; all would move their listeners to higher things. Their ideas are lofty, noble; their appeal is to emotional motives for there is little they must prove to their listeners.

Speaking to strengthen attitudes is essential and appropriate whenever men need to have ambitions re-aroused and when they need to be challenged anew. Our allegiance too often becomes merely a matter of lip service: hence the need for the minister, educator, reformer—in the final analysis, for all leaders—to speak with their respective groups on themes that stir and revive the ideals and aspirations of men and women to their noblest and best.

Creating Listener Belief

Talking to convince goes on all about us. It takes place whenever a speaker is himself convinced that it is important for another to change a belief. Creating a belief in others means inducing others to see solutions or facts differently; and it should mean inducing them to see solutions and facts more in accordance with their own needs and benefits, and in accordance with perceivable truth.

1. *Listeners* who are amenable to conviction on the score of a belief are generally concerned with the same *problem* as the speaker. They believe that justice is essential in a court of law; they believe that good relations with Latin America are essential; they believe that American education should be the best in the world; or they believe that a government farm program should provide fair treatment and fair returns to farmers. Or such listeners may be you, concerned with the problems of race relations, of getting the most out of college courses and college activities, or of understanding the value of the requirements and restrictions that are imposed upon curriculum, dormitory living, or driving on campus.

These listeners share with the speaker a concern, or can be brought to a concern, for problems, goals, values, or the truth. Further, they are likely to be in disagreement with that speaker, to some extent at least, regarding the best solution to a problem, the best means to a goal, relative values of an idea, or just what are "the facts of the matter."

2. *Speakers* who would create belief in listeners—who are they? They are attorneys addressing a jury, an undersecretary of state for Latin America on "Meet the Press," a spokesman for the Kennedy Farm Program, a dean of education challenging other educators. Or they are a friend evoking your approval of an unpopular plan for racial integration, or arguing the value of a college course, or a dean eliciting acceptance of inconvenient campus regulations.

These speakers, if they carry conviction, share listener problems, goals, values, and concern for what is right. But more than this, they have inquired into these questions, analyzed them, learned what and who are involved, considered many solutions. And on the basis of these considerations they have become, themselves, convinced or strengthened in their belief that both they and their listeners should hold a certain belief, because it is best for all concerned.

Eliciting Action

It is well known that belief and action are two different things, that "you can lead a horse to water but you can't make him drink," also that you are convinced that you must study and yet you go to a movie. Motivational researchers discovered that when questioned, people *say* they prefer one kind of magazine but they read another. Therefore it is necessary for speakers to be concerned with the motives people have for engaging in action based on strengthened feelings or new beliefs.

Yet speakers commonly make the error of assuming that belief will automatically lead to appropriate action. They are not explicit on what, specifically, should be done. They make no plans for making the action itself attractive, perhaps easier. Compare the student speaker who strengthened the favorable attitudes of his classmates toward Red Cross blood donation and concluded, weakly, "Be sure to do your part when the Red Cross Bloodmobile comes next time," with the student who also stimulated and reinforced the same attitude and concluded by providing a sign-up sheet on which his listeners could immediately commit themselves to specific times to appear at the Bloodmobile. The point is that to induce others to engage in needed action, it takes special, specific preparation and planning, in addition to that designed to strengthen or create belief.

1. *Listeners,* when speaking is designed to actuate, are much the same as they are for the other persuasive purposes: strengthening feeling, or creating belief. But in addition, they have now become more enthusiastic, even inspired; or they have now come to the new belief. And, if that feeling or belief requires some specific action, they need to be moved to act. They now believe that supporting the building of a new church or hospital requires some sacrifice on their part, but it takes more to make them sign a pledge, dig into their pockets, or translate "sacrifice" into a sizable sum on a check. They may now believe that a certain college course, though difficult and demanding, would be most valuable, but it takes more to make them register for it. Listeners who have been attracted to an idea must, in addition, if action is needed, be persuaded to the action.

2. *Speakers* with the conviction that a specific action by their listeners is essential to the well-being or progress of those listeners or of society in general are, similarly, the same speakers who intend to

strengthen feeling or create belief. They are the candidate or campaign managers who must move their listeners to do more than vote: ring doorbells, contribute money, or distribute posters or handbills. Or they are the county agricultural agents moving farmers to produce, or to restrain themselves from producing, certain foods.

These speakers carry conviction. That is, they are themselves persuaded that the action is necessary both for themselves and for their listeners, and they have, further, communicated this persuasively. Further, they plan specifically to make it both easy and attractive for the listeners to engage in the desired action.

The persuasive purposes may be summarized in this manner:

Persuasion

Stimulation	*Conviction*
meaning: arousing, or strengthening of a listener attitude, feeling, or belief	meaning: to create a new listener belief based upon a strengthened, common, speaker-listener attitude, feeling or belief
which: *may* be specifically designed to evoke a specific action based upon a strengthened listener attitude, feeling, or belief.	which: *may* be specifically designed to evoke a specific action based upon a new listener belief.

⭕ PERSUASION AND OTHER SPEECH PURPOSES

Persuasive speaking is closely related to other speech purposes. It will be helpful, both to your understanding of persuasion and your understanding of the others, to examine those relationships.

Persuasion and Gaining Understanding

Because of the relationship between persuasion and gaining understanding, students sometimes become unsure or confused as to

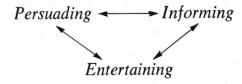

Persuading ◄————► *Informing*

Entertaining

All speech principles operate in persuasion. A momentary diversion contributes to general good will, which becomes the will to reach agreement. Decision-making based upon persuasion must first be based on inquiry and the communication of information; these create premises from which listeners form new views, new inspirations, new purposeful activities.

whether their purpose is one or the other. So, too, do listeners. In Chapter 12, where these relationships were discussed, we noted that all speaking contains information. Speech materials, analytic data, validating forms, all provide information. The essential question is: What communicative motivation led to the speaker's selection of the materials or ideas; or how does the speaker expect the listener to respond to the information? Thus, if you would have your classmates understand the arguments against United States participation in the UN, whether you believe in such participation or not, you will select, almost automatically, one set of materials, data, validating forms, and validating methods. If, however, you want your listeners to accept or believe the arguments, you will select differently and you will talk differently.

Differentiating between persuasive and informative purposes is not so much a matter of what is said as it is a matter of what moves you to say it; nor is it judged by a statement in an outline but by what, fundamentally, you really want to happen to your listeners on the inside. There is a line to be drawn between the two purposes. And it is not necessarily a fine one. The haziness comes only when the speaker himself does not understand his own purpose.

However, while the two general motivations for speaking can be clearly different, much of what you learn about one needs to be applied to the other. We might think of these applications as persuasion that leads to understanding and understanding that leads to persuasion.

1. *Persuasion that leads to understanding* is what takes place in the introduction to an effective talk whose purpose is to gain understanding. You motivate the listener to want to learn and remember your central idea. Thus, you strengthen or create a belief that what you are to talk about is worth knowing. If you would have listeners understand that the use of fluorescent paint is cutting down on mid-air collisions, you first make it an attractive idea to learn by relating it to the fears that some listeners might have, to the curiosity of others, and to the concern of others for proper air safety. If you are persuasive enough, even though you may not be informative enough, you may still be effective because your listeners will take it upon themselves to learn what you have not been successful in communicating. You know that when you have been powerfully motivated to learn, you have done so even if burdened with an uncommunicative teacher.

Similarly, you may be persuasive to gain understanding in the conclusion of a speech, in which you urge listeners to learn more about the subject by consulting other sources.

2. *Understanding that leads to persuasion* becomes the goal of a speaker whose fundamental purpose is to persuade, when he knows that his listeners may oppose an idea simply because they do not understand it. Most often, in this situation, applying the principles in Chapter 12 of achieving clarity and understanding will bring about the desired effect. Part of what makes this true is that listeners are more receptive to persuasion which does not appear to be persuasion. To understand this, consider the reverse situation in which you immediately build your own defenses against an obvious sales appeal.

If your listeners do not believe that the Citroen automobile represents advanced engineering design simply because they do not know about or do not understand its hydraulic system, adjustable chassis height, and automatic jack; if you are convinced that understanding is all that is needed for acceptance, then it can be effective to proceed *as if* endeavoring to gain listener understanding, in order to achieve the purpose of persuasion. On the other hand, if your listeners cannot accept the idea of a foreign car representing possible advances over American engineering design, then your persuasion will be differently designed and you will need to depend upon suggestions contained in this chapter.

Keep in mind, however, that throughout any persuasive speaking the ability to "achieve clarity and understanding" will contribute to the effectiveness of the ideas you use to make your central idea believable or more strongly felt.

Persuasion and Enjoyment

The next chapter deals with talking to entertain. This is described for you as a communicative process which keeps the listener interested and diverted. And we have said earlier that all speaking must accomplish this, not as a goal but as a minimum essential. Speaking which does not hold your attention cannot be expected to have much of any other kind of effect. This, then, is the essential relationship of persuasive speaking and entertaining speaking: both depend upon the maintenance of listener attention and interest for their effectiveness. Adhering to this principle provides the first listener motive for forming ideas in response to the speaker and his speech. We turn now to those listener motives which are of special and added importance in the persuasion processes.

○ LISTENER MOTIVES FOR IDEATION

While the factors of attention and interest operate to provide a general basis for listening to all speaking, there are some specific listener processes which, beyond just listening, make the speaker's ideas attractive and thus more strongly felt, or believed, or acted upon. These processes have been variously named since the early days of rhetoric: Aristotle's classification was proof by argument, pathos, and ethos. Another is logical proof, emotional proof, and ethical proof. Still another is logical appeal, emotional appeal, and personal appeal. One more is reasoning, disposing, and accrediting. In brief, each of these labels refers, in order, to the processes by which listeners may move from speaker materials or the premises they support to conclusions: by response to the logic of the speaker's ideas, by response to the appeal of the speaker's ideas, and by response to the "image" of the speaker himself.

We hesitate to adopt any of the traditional sets of labels for several reasons. It is necessary for you to understand that often what are called "proofs" do not prove. Further, what may be an inescapable logical conclusion may have no "appeal"—as in the choice of "the lesser of two evils." Finally, it is important to keep in mind that these are listener processes: that the nature of the material or idea does not determine which process may be operating; it is the nature of the listener-response that does so.

Response to the Logic of the Speaker's Ideas

An underlying requirement of any persuasive speaking is that it makes sense. That is, it must enable the listener to arrive at the speaker's conclusion through his own processes of reasoning from the speaker's validating materials. This is the nature of reasoning: moving or thinking logically from an accepted premise or body of facts to a probable conclusion, whether that conclusion is desirable or not.

The beginning of the process, then, is the validating material of the speaker. And for the process to begin to take place, there are two essentials: listener acceptance of the premise and listener acceptance of the logic.

1. *Listener acceptance of the premise.* In previous chapters, especially Chapters 5 and 7, you have been warned that for testimony to be effective, the source must be deemed an authority by the listeners; that sources of statistics must be credible to the listener; that examples be true or hypothetically believable, and so on. This is primarily in recognition of the fact that no listening process in the desired direction can take place if the validating material is rejected by the listener. It is this material which provides the springboard for reasoning or feeling processes.

There may be a clear, logical step from the premise, "It is the lack of rigorous discipline in our schools which is leading to mounting juvenile delinquency," to belief in a program of rigid requirements for behavior and severe punishment for violators. But no reasonable listener will take that step if he does not know the source of that premise; nor will he if he knows the source to be biased; nor will he if he knows the speaker only as a famous naval architect. He may be willing to—the probabilities are increased that he will be willing to— take that logical step if he learns that the source is a well-known psychologist who has been studying the problems of discipline in American schools for many years. In short: the process of reasoning will proceed in the direction of the speaker's point only if the listener accepts the authority of the source and the idea.

It should be clear, then, that materials selected as premises for listener reasoning processes must be selected for their credibility and they must be presented by whatever means will enhance that credibility. Such a statement as "I read it in a magazine" impedes credibility; whereas another, "Secretary Ribicoff stated it in summary of the results of three independent long-range studies," enhances credibility.

One other factor contributes to the usefulness of a premise and thus to listener readiness to begin a reasoning process. That is confirmation of the premise from more than one source and in more than one validating form. Thus, we earlier urged you to use the "iceberg technique," to use more than one item of support, to use the validating method of cumulating. In short: the way to have enough evidence is to "over-support."

Only when the speaker is confident that his premise will be

accepted can he have confidence in the probability that his listeners will want to reason from that premise.

2. *Listener acceptance of the logic.* Every listener tests for himself whether an idea makes sense. Sometimes those tests may be inaccurate simply because the idea appeals to him; he moves from premise to conclusion for psychological rather than logical reasons, or he may accept an idea on both grounds. Nevertheless, it is important for both speaker and listener to know how to test the logical processes from fact to conclusion, for the psychological appeals may be transitory, while the logical relationships remain more constant.

We would not presume to provide in these few pages all that is needed by way of understanding logical processes.[1] However, there are certain principles of response to the logic of speakers' ideas which should be noted. These are principles of deduction, induction, causality, and analogy.

DEDUCTION. If the generalization is accepted that any copper wire is a conductor of electricity, you may reason, by deduction, that a particular piece of copper wire will conduct electrical current. Similarly, if it is accepted that all birds with a certain shape of beak are seed eaters, you may reason that a particular bird with a beak shaped in that particular way will welcome seeds in your birdfeeder. *Deduction,* then, is that logical process of reasoning which asserts that any member of a class will have all the characteristics of that class; it is reasoning from the general to the specific.

Listeners may be asked to deduce in a way that is perfectly acceptable from the point of view of listener acceptance of the logic but the reasoning will not take place if it is not acceptable from the point of view of listener acceptance of the premise. You may reason clearly enough from the premise that movie stars' family living is unstable to the conclusion that a particular star will be headed, sooner or later, to the divorce court. You can be wrong, of course, but not because of poor reasoning; it will be because of an error in acceptance of the generalization, or the premise. You will find it difficult to make many generalizations serve as premises. All students in this college are . . . ?

[1] For more detailed discussions of reasoning processes in persuasion, see any textbooks on debate (or discussion and debate) such as Alan Nichols, *Discussion and Debate.* New York: Harcourt, 1941; and H. L. Ewbank and Jeffrey Auer, *Discussion and Debate,* Rev. ed. New York: Appleton-Century-Crofts, 1951.

All Speech majors are . . . ? If you can complete these sentences acceptably, you may be able to reason from them to a conclusion about one student. Your listeners, however, will probably desert you at this point.

Here are some tests of the dependability of conclusions drawn deductively:

1. Is the generalization (premise) universally true?
2. Does the specific item really belong in the general class?
3. Or does the specific item represent an exception to the cited general class?
4. Is the conclusion confirmed through other reasoning processes?

INDUCTION. More frequently, as a speaker, you will be asking listeners to engage in inductive reasoning from your validating materials to an idea or conclusion. You will ask listeners to agree that statistics which you have made acceptable as a premise lead to the conclusion that the soil bank program did not achieve its goal; that the testimony of many experts leads, logically, to the conclusion that our high schools need to expand their curricula in certain areas, or that examples of many accidents, all caused by speeding, indicate speed as a major cause of highway accidents.

It is important to keep in mind that induction is a means of predicting the probability that a conclusion is right. A single example in support of the idea that your college produces leaders in business, industry, the professions, and government does not lend high probability. Even the example of an outstanding graduate in each field does not raise the probability of the accuracy of your statement very much. But the more that are added, the more probable is the conclusion, in the minds of your listeners, that the school does make a notable contribution to leadership. Leading the listener to think inductively is enhanced by an abundance of similar, representative validating materials.

It is true, of course, that some people are willing to reason from even a single instance, such as, "My brother has a friend who had that make of automobile and he had nothing but trouble with it." But this is easily upset by a counter example, "Yes, but my family had one for years which needed no repairs at all." This stops progress, cancels out reasoning, accomplishes little or nothing. Here, again, is why it is important to gather an "iceberg" of support to insure listener willingness to engage in inductive reasoning.

We have said earlier that an example must be representative of the people or events or behavior from which it is drawn. This increases the possibility that reasoning will take place. If more similar examples are used, both the probability that listeners will reason and the probability that they will reason to the desired conclusion are enhanced. Similarly, statistics must be representative or they will mislead both speaker and listener. The reasoning of week-end hitch-hikers among you will not follow inductively from the statistic once cited in our classroom: "Three out of every five hitch-hikers have a prison record." Hostility, not reasoning, motivated the response.

So it is with the use of any of the validating forms of support: inductive reasoning can be expected to follow in the desired direction if the tests of representativeness and adequate support for the premise are met.

But the direction of the reasoning may not always be clear-cut. Unless a speaker has, himself, examined the possible logical conclusions that may be drawn, his efforts to gain this kind of response may backfire. British debaters in this country have made a reputation for themselves in building tightly logical cases from the evidence presented by their American collegiate opposition. You may reason from figures on the Gross National Product that production must be stimulated; but from your chosen facts a listener may reason to the conclusion that there is danger of a depression from overproduction. Or you might cite statistics on the number of student-owned automobiles as a premise for the conclusion that more parking facilities are needed on your campus; but others may see this leading logically, desirable or not, to the conclusion that more restrictions are needed. The speaker must test for flaws in reasoning.[2]

Tests for the dependability of conclusions derived inductively are:

1. Are the validating materials true?
2. Are enough cases cited?
3. Are instances representative of the whole being considered?

[2] Flaws in reasoning, or *fallacies*, are discussed in most debate textbooks. See also W. Ward Fearnside and William B. Holther, *Fallacy: The Counterfeit of Argument*. Englewood Cliffs, N. J.: Prentice-Hall, 1959.

4. Are there exceptions which do not lead to the expected conclusion?
5. Are all instances drawn from comparable situations?
6. Is the conclusion confirmed through other reasoning processes?

CAUSALITY.   Another kind of reasoning which is asked of listeners is causal. We are frequently observed inferring causes for phenomena. If a tire goes flat, we reason that a sharp object on the road somewhere has punctured it. Usually our inference is confirmed by the discovery of a nail or piece of glass. Sometimes we have found that it was a tire flaw or even a prank. Or, when we speak with others about war, we infer from validating materials a variety of causes, from armament races to personal greed. Historian Ari Hoogenboom has playfully cited as the cause of the American Civil War the aggressiveness caused by the wearing of beards. Some experts ask us to reason from certain incidents to the conclusion that comic books or television dramas contribute to, or cause, juvenile acts of violence and crime; from the coincidence of cigarette smoking and lung cancer to cigarette smoking as the cause; from the incident of Sputnik I's ascent into orbit as a cause for nationwide concern about American education.

Two special warnings about the use of reasoning from causal relations are pertinent for the student of speech; one has to do with *plural causes* and the other with *assumed causes*.

Human affairs are, as you know, complex in nature. It is seldom possible, through reasoning or any other processes, to determine *the* cause of an accident, a war, happiness, the winning of a game, or the failure of a course. This is usually because there is not a single cause; there are causes. Thus, it is safest, more accurate, and probably more effective to acknowledge that you want a listener to view armament races as *a* cause of wars, constant conflict in the home as *a* cause of juvenile delinquency, or the blocking by your All-American tackle as *a* cause of victory. Do not claim more validity for causal relationships than you can demonstrate.

Another violation of the logic of causality lies in *assuming* causal relations in a sequence of events. It is more or less true that effects follow causes; but so do coincident events. You may no longer attribute an accident on the way home to the black cat which crossed your path on the road. But you may be willing to ask listeners to blame bad weather in New York on previous nuclear bomb tests in Nevada; or you may be willing to infer that a cold was caused by a draft. Inferring that what follows an event is necessarily caused by it is a temptation that not all listeners will yield to, especially if you are relying upon their logical processes. If the imputation of cause appeals to them, that may be another matter.

Causal reasoning occurs in two directions: we are sometimes trying to prove that a given cause will produce a certain result in the future (*a priori*) or that a given result (present condition) was derived from a certain cause (*a posteriori*).

Tests for the dependability of conclusions drawn from inferences of causality are:

1. Is the cause really capable of producing the effect?
2. Was the cause really operating?
3. Are there possibly other intervening causes?
4. Is the conclusion confirmed through other reasoning processes?

ANALOGY. The validating method of analogy, discussed in Chapter 7, also depends upon inference or reasoning. In persuasion, the literal analogy is particularly effective but also is a frequent source of error. Much learning consists of reasoning by analogy. If you look at any field guide to birds, for instance, you will be struck by the use of similarities with and differences from other birds when a particular bird is being described. Similarly, in persuasion, examination of comparable problems or solutions can lead listeners effectively to appropriate conclusions. Thus, you may speak of needed improvements on your campus by analogy with comparable institutions which are already benefiting from such improvements; or you may ask listeners to believe in a program of state medicine by describing the results of such a program in a comparable country.

The key to both effectiveness and error lies in the term *comparable*. The other campus situations which you cite need not be and, of course, can not be identical with your own. Still, the desired reasoning response will take place to the extent that the two situations are identical in the characteristics being considered, such as: size of student body, how supported, whether essentially urban or rural in setting; or presence in the two countries of identical medical problems, medical traditions, tax structures. If the two things or events or people compared are not comparable in the essential aspects, the reasoning by analogy is not sound and you should not expect it to be accepted by your listeners.

Tests for the dependability of conclusions drawn by analogy are:

1. Are the things compared related in essential details?
2. Does the comparison overlook fundamental differences?
3. Are the statements of similarity true?
4. Is the analogous situation representative?
5. Is the conclusion confirmed through other reasoning processes?

Speakers and listeners, especially in a democracy, must be alert to the processes of reasoning that are available for persuasion and for critical listening to persuasion. We have dealt here in a limited way with four kinds of listening processes: deduction, induction, causality, and analogy.

The Appeal of the Speaker's Ideas

We have discussed logical processes as a way by which listeners may be led from the speaker's premise to the speaker's conclusion. However, we all know that another complex set of motivations called "emotional" may often be even more influential than logical thought. Sometimes the distinction is made that logic focuses and centralizes thought upon strictly relevant and significant factors; whereas an emotional response is disorganized and diffused. Thus, when you learn of the death of a loved one, or win a National Science Foundation scholarship, your reaction is one of general upset or excitement. In speaking, we use the motivating process of emotional appeal carefully, with the aim of securing an organizing, concerting, focusing effect. By logic we point the thinking of the listeners toward the right conclusion; by emotion we inject the driving force of powerful feelings to impel more rapid or stronger reactions of support for the indicated conclusion.

Motives are powerful driving forces in all human existence and in all human decisions. They may be ignoble, or they may bring out the best in man. They foster his ambitions, lead him to make choices, aid in cultivating his tastes and sentiments, and help to elevate him to the highest pinnacles of esthetic appreciation. In spite of all rational developments in man, his natural wants or needs are basic, and he lives by the dictates of what appeals to him as surely as he does by reason. We prize the logic and the thought processes of man; but we must know, too, that his love of nature, music, and art and his attributes of love, affection, kindness, sympathy, pride, benevolence, courtesy, honor, and curiosity are significant sources of his motivations.

You may consider emotional appeals as not being worthy of the best kind of speaking; but we know this is a mistaken concept. We recognize that many great speeches by leaders in religion, education, reform, and statecraft are in the class of superior and sublime utterance because they are charged with appeal to human emotions. Further, it is well known that we do not arrive at belief and action through the reasoning processes alone. We must, in addition, be moved to such belief and action. Do not hesitate, therefore, to draw on materials which will motivate your own listeners to move to the ideas you would have them accept because those ideas appeal to them.

SPECIAL APPEALS. Each of your listeners, in speech class or anywhere else, has special likes, hostilities, blind spots, ambitions, fears, attitudes, feelings, and values. The more you learn about these individual sources of special appeals, the more surely you can motivate your listeners as you wish and avoid setting up counter-motivations. A careless remark indicating lack of respect for mathematicians, or artists, or chiropractors, or Italians might, by itself, convert one or more listeners into resentful resistance to your central idea—even though this remark has no particular relevance to your theme. On the contrary, analysis of the special attitudes and interests of members of the listening group may enable you to use illustrations that heighten the motivational appeals you are using.

In advocating a new student co-op bookstore, it is important to know whether some of your listeners are deeply interested simply in such small savings as may accrue, and whether others may have a generalized misconception of co-operative free enterprise as a form of "socialism." In appealing for added members for the Outing Club, if you know listeners who are afraid of snakes, you can inject reassurance that few such disagreeable creatures will be encountered.

It encourages favorable reception of your ideas to say, "Three of you are Business Administration majors and two of you are in Industrial Management. I feel sure all five of you will agree with me that . . . Moreover, six of you are Liberal Arts majors who naturally will want to know the social effects of this program I am proposing." Or, "Before our meeting I discussed this question with three members of our group who raised some questions I think all of you might want to have considered." In other words, personalization of your appeal will heighten audience interest. The mere fact that you take the trouble to learn about, and to take notice of, special attributes of your listeners will enhance their image of you as a speaker. The fact that you show you are interested in your listeners will help make them interested in what you have to say.

VITAL APPEALS. People generally act, feel, and believe from what seems a vast variety of motives. Social psychologists, in identifying these wants, needs, drives, and urges, have propounded long lists of our "goal values." Without necessarily going into refinements and complexities of psychological categories, speakers should have in mind the general wants of man which may serve as a guide to the selection of materials. These "wants of man," from the pen of Thomas Robert Malthus, are typical:

1. RECOGNITION: This is the motive for prestige that is highlighted by the Vance Packard best seller, *The Status Seekers;* but it is also the desire to feel a sense of achievement, of accomplishment, not just from others' regard for the external signs of success but from the achievements themselves.

2. RESPONSE: The human being wants the kind of love and interest that grows out of sensitivity to an understanding of feelings that one person may have for another.

3. NEW EXPERIENCE: From infancy, the human being is curious to explore. He wants to see new things, feel new sensations, hear a different kind of music or speech, experiment with tastes and smells, learn about far-off places and new ideas.

4. SECURITY: Every man and woman wants to reach a position where he or she can feel assured that all of these wants will be reasonably met, that physical and psychical needs will be satisfied.

We are not, each of us, motivated to the same extent by each of these wants. Indeed, they are often in conflict. And because of many fundamental psychological experiences we vary in the degree to which we will allow ourselves even to recognize or express these wants. A conservative and careful business executive may, for instance, be more motivated by his need for security than by his desire for new experience. On the other hand, drives for new experience and perhaps recognition, in spite of insecurities, have given us our Galileos, Columbuses, and astronauts.

Try these definitions of human wants on yourself. What are your goals in present and future life? And how might your motivations be classified in these terms? You may think of other sources of appeal. Remember them and use them in your persuasive speaking. Select those validating materials which will appeal to these needs: not just to one but to several. If you would have a listener admire or join a fraternity, you will want evidences of friendships and sympathy (response), of opportunities to achieve academically and in student activities (recognition), of excitement and creative activities (new experience), and of the stability of a home and encouragement to study (security).

As in the case of the reasoning processes, it is important to fortify the appeal processes by accumulating many validating materials. As we have said, it is these supporting materials that accomplish the communication; that lead, through both reasoning and appeal processes, to the desired listener response.

The Image of the Speaker

In discussing the "major factors influencing effects" in communication, Carl I. Hovland summarized a number of experimental studies by saying, "*Who* says something is usually as important as *what* is said in the determination of the impact of a communication." One study, for instance, presented a recorded speech on compulsory health insurance to groups of college students. Some heard the speaker introduced as the Surgeon-General of the United States; others heard the same speaker introduced as a Communist; still others heard him as a college sophomore. Listeners who heard "Surgeon-General" approved of the ideas in the speech and, of course, those who heard "Communist" tended to reject the ideas.[3]

It is seldom that a listener separates, in his mind, a speaker from his ideas. In other words, he is using response processes that begin

[3] Franklyn S. Haiman, "An Experimental Study of the Effects of Ethos in Public Speaking," *Speech Monographs,* 1949, pp. 190–202. This and other studies on the influences of the communicator himself are cited by Carl I. Hovland, "Effects of the Mass Media of Communication," in Gardner Lindzey, editor, *Handbook of Social Psychology.* Reading, Mass.: Addison-Wesley, 1954, Vol. II, pp. 1071–1080.

with the speaker, himself, as well as those that begin with the speaker's validating materials. Further, he is not really responding to the flesh-and-blood speaker before him. The listener is in the position of the blind man examining an elephant. He is responding only to what he knows and learns about the speaker both prior to the speaking event and during it. Thus, the listener is responding to the speaker *as he exists in the nervous system of the listener* or as he is perceived by the listener. He is responding to his own image of the speaker.

Such classical writers as Aristotle and Quintilian recognized the importance of this personal element in speaking. It has been known through the ages that the honest man is believed in the same situations in which the dishonest man is looked upon with distrust.

Response to the logic of the image takes place when the listener reasons that the idea makes sense because the speaker said it; that the idea is logically acceptable because the speaker is known to have integrity or authority or special experience. "You may not like to hear me say this," a speaker might declare, "but I tell you from my own experience . . ." If the image of the speaker is one of trustworthiness, the logical response is acceptance of his idea.

This is why Quintilian insisted that an effective speaker is first of all "a good man" and, secondly, one who "speaks well." More, and often far more, than his validating materials, the speaker who is known for his incorruptibility has that image "going for him"; he is persuading through the channels of the reasoning processes which begin with the speaker himself as premise. And the very fact of the abundant use of validating materials contributes to his image of authority and experience. We may jest with the Chinese philosopher who said, "He who earns a reputation as an early riser can afford to sleep all day." But speaker images are neither so shallowly nor so permanently installed. Our idols fall when we discover their feet of clay. Remember the TV quiz-show scandals. The speaker who destroys in his listener some important aspect of his image reduces the probability, sometimes to the vanishing point, that he may again be effective.

The thing to remember, both as speaker and listener, is that a most potent force for good and for effectiveness lies in the natural tendency of listeners to reason from the image of the speaker to his ideas or conclusions.

There is another channel of response that has parallel signifi-cance: a channel of *response to the appeal of the speaker*. Some analysts of the presidential campaigns of 1952 and 1956 have described a reasoned response of listeners to their image of Eisenhower's sincerity. Others have said that his appeal to his listeners was as a "father image." Both response patterns were probably operating. The important thing to recognize is that listeners may arrive at an idea or conclusion from a speaker's premise just because he said it. Many psychological phenomena contribute to this kind of appeal. We like those who remind us in one way or another of others whom we like, or we distrust others on the same, sometimes flimsy basis. This has an effect upon how their ideas appeal to us. It is important to understand complex human psychology as much as we can and thus to become more aware of the sources of image appeals.

Three specific speaker characteristics can be noted as making some contribution to this channel of response: interest in listeners, personal involvement, and appearance.

INTEREST IN LISTENERS. If the listener's image of a speaker includes the information that the speaker is interested in the welfare and happiness of the listener, a favorable response to the speaker's conclusion can follow. But if the image is like that of the professor who said that a university would be a wonderful place if it weren't for the students, neither listening nor appeal are likely to follow. If you consider your classroom speaking as a routine recitation without adapting it or yourself to the interests and experiences of your classmates, your image, too, will block the responses you are seeking. This is another function of audience analysis. Your questions communicate your interest and make your interest a part of that image which your listeners have of you. A lecturer we know frequently sits among the members of an audience for a long time before it is his turn on a program, to observe their behavior, interests, worries, and reactions. He then talks about his observations, relating them to his subject, and immediately earns the image of a person interested in the members of the group.

In interpersonal relations of any kind, on a street corner or as a moderator of *I've Got a Secret* on television, the speaker who elicits response is the one who is obviously interested in the listener or listeners.

PERSONAL INVOLVEMENT AND ENTHUSIASM. You have heard speakers who have impressed you with their basic inner attitudes toward the problems they are discussing; you have, in consequence, had your own inner responses heightened. Yet in class you may hear students discuss great issues of life and death, war and peace, justice and injustice, without revealing any evidence of real concern for the joy and sorrow, violence and nobility, disappointment and triumph that they describe, simply because they are not themselves personally involved. If an abiding interest in the listener is one source of speaker-image appeal, certainly interest in the subject is another. This is why you have been urged to choose topics for speaking in which you have or can develop a sincere and live interest.

The speaker who is apparently "all wrapped up" in his subject, and who is perceived as being so, will create an image of great appeal to his listener. His own enthusiasm will be infectious, and so induce a similar reaction. It is a truism that a salesman can sell better if he himself is sold on his product.

APPEARANCE. The third source of image appeal is the appearance of the speaker: his dress, his posture, his movements, all of which add to listener perception of sincerity, directness, enthusiasm, and confidence. The speaker's appearance and bearing will often affect, also, the image of interest and involvement. The speaker who makes no effort to dress appropriately or to address listeners directly will at least seem disinterested in them and the subject; while the speaker who is tastefully attired and animated is indicating by his attitude that there is importance in the occasion, listeners, and topic. Then appearance also can and will contribute to the appeal of the speaker's image as the listener responds to other aspects of both the speaker and his ideas.

○ **PERSUASION AND THE VALIDATING FORMS AND METHODS**

It should be clear from the foregoing discussion of the reasoning and appeal channels of response that careful and abundant selection of validating forms and methods, as discussed in Chapter 7, is essential to the persuasion process. It is by way of these materials, adapted to the audience, that listeners will move to the feeling, belief, or action sought, through one or more of the response processes described.

We have mentioned certain safeguards in the use of some of the forms of materials and some of the methods. It should be kept in mind, in addition to these admonitions, that the factors of attention and interest should not be overlooked in the effort to build an airtight case.

Select also those materials which give promise of fascinating, captivating, or otherwise holding your listeners' interest, concern, and comfort.

○ PERSUASION AND LANGUAGE

We know that different words and phrases carry different shades of meaning and feeling; that the very sound of certain words affects our states of mind and dispositions. Certain words cause us to feel enlivened and aroused, whereas others do little to stimulate feeling. The language of a speaker will at times be quieting and at times invigorating. Words which call up past associations, reviving attitudes and former states of mind, become in themselves sources of feeling and believing responses. When words, phrases, and sentences are used to provide strong impact through appeal, and especially when they serve to construct images of one kind or another, we know that the speaker is succeeding not only in establishing his ideas but, more important, in doing so vividly and with real intensity of feeling.

In persuasive speaking, especially in strengthening feeling or in that part of a talk to create new belief in which you strengthen the *common premise,* cultivate the use of the rhetorical question, emotion-charged words, alliteration, rhythm, and imagery.

Those are the principles that have contributed to speeches that have been particularly memorable. Winston Churchill elicited from half a world great gratitude when he paid tribute to the Royal Air Force with the words, "Never in the field of human conflict was so much owed by so many to so few." The conclusion of Lincoln's second inaugural address is a fine example of phrasing with high appeal: "With malice toward none; with charity for all; with firmness in the right, as God gives us to see the right, let us strive on to finish the work we are in; to bind up the nation's wounds; to care for him who shall have borne the battle, and for his widow and his orphan—to do all which may achieve and cherish a just and lasting peace among ourselves, and with all nations."

Such expressions are not vague platitudes and meaningless utterances; they are phrases which have inspired in men the highest zeal and on occasion have even reversed the course of history. When Churchill during World War II said that he had nothing to offer the people of England but "blood, sweat, and tears," he lifted the British to the highest pinnacle of sacrifice and effort. And when President Kennedy said, "Ask not what your country can do for you, but, rather, what you can do for your country," the administration was inundated by sincere requests to know what could be done for our nation.

Similarly the speech student, interested in sharing ideas and in directing the attitudes and conduct of his fellow students, has an opportunity to develop the use of language for obtaining more than "Ho-hum" responses, for generating genuine and forceful feeling and belief.

○ ORGANIZING AND DEVELOPING FOR PERSUASION

We have earlier described listener processes for moving from a premise to a conclusion by response to the logic of the speaker's ideas or his image, and by response to the appeal of the speaker's ideas or his image. When we think of organizing ideas and materials for persuasion we may think even more broadly of the premise-to-conclusion process. In other words, persuasion must begin with a listener belief or attitude or feeling—that particular belief or attitude or feeling which can serve as a premise to lead by logic and appeal to the conclusion or the proposition or central idea of the speaker. This will be of particular importance in speaking to create a belief, or to evoke action based on a new belief.

If you set out to persuade your classmates that merely "getting out the vote" is a questionable policy, you would probably begin with the belief that both you and the class share that each voter should be an informed voter. Further, you would stimulate, strengthen, reinforce this common premise in your listeners to the point where they agree with you quite strongly that the informed voter, rather than chance, should determine the outcomes of elections and referendums. This, then, becomes the starting point—the common premise—for listener processes of logic and appeal leading to the conclusion that to urge to the polls those who have neither interest nor an ability to discriminate between candidates or issues may not be an appropriate policy or activity. Similarly, existing beliefs in man's right to privacy may be bolstered as a common premise leading by logic and appeal to a belief that wire-tapping should be outlawed. Or an audience may agree that the ultimate happiness and security of a child when he becomes an adult is more important than the avoidance of unpleasant childhood behavior, and be led in their thinking from this common premise, reinforced, to the acceptance of a moderate policy of "permissiveness" at home and in the schools.

There are certain special methods of developing the talk for persuasion which are designed, in essence, to identify and bolster in listeners the common premise and to lead them to the speaker's conclusion. Although it may be said that argument is not only occasionally inevitable in, and sometimes essential to, decision-making, frequently more is gained by the avoidance of argument with the listener, in which case the speaker achieves the needed responses by the principle of agreement. These special methods, then, are of value because they stress and, in one way or another focus on, the common premise, and increase the necessary listener agreement at each step in the persuasive process.

Problem-Solving Method

One procedure in speaking for persuasion is the problem-solving method, in which the listeners have a sense of inquiring into a problem with the speaker, instead of having a solution to the problem thrust upon them. For a full understanding of the application and organization of development for persuasion, you will need to note the steps of inquiry, since these steps can provide a skeleton for your outlining in preparation for use of the problem-solving method. Briefly noted, those steps are: Analysis of the problem, its background, history, and causes; examination of the stakes of those involved; establishment of criteria for judging solutions; examining all possible solutions; matching solutions against criteria; arriving at the best solution. Chapter 15 discusses these steps in detail.

Although not applicable in all cases of persuasion or even in all cases where the desired response is a new belief, this method has many advantages that will enhance effectiveness whenever speaker and listeners alike are deeply concerned about a problem which affects them and to which there are many possible solutions.

These advantages may be stated as:

1. The speaker who invites his listeners to confront the problem with him in order that they may cooperate to reach the best possible decision creates an image of concern for the general welfare instead of defending a vested interest.

2. The speaker who has himself arrived at his solution to the

problem through inquiry, which he is now going to share with his listeners, is most likely to be sure that he is right, confident that his listeners have much to gain, and convinced that he has found the best solution. He stimulates an image of authority and involvement.

3. If inquiry has convinced the speaker more forcefully than any other analysis of the question or its solutions could have, it is likely that this experience will be the most effective available for the listeners, too.

4. The problem-solving method of organization provides the combined advantages of most of the other special methods in persuasion: (a) *common ground* stems from speaker involvement, at the outset, not in a particular proposal or solution but in the common problem; (b) *indirect development* takes place as listeners are asked first to examine the evidence of a present difficulty, of its causes, and of personal involvement before coming to conclusions about them; (c) the *yes-response* occurs as the solution which will be accepted by the listeners is shown to meet each of the accepted criteria which have been established to judge all solutions; and (d) the *this-or-nothing* method applies to the latter part of the persuasion, in which it is seen that the one solution, more effectively than any of the others which were posed, satisfies those criteria.

As you face the need to engage in persuasive speaking, keep these special methods in mind, select from them or adapt them to the special requirements of each particular situation. Above all, keep in mind the concept of the *common premise,* which must be an attitude or belief shared with the listeners from which they may move through logical and appeal processes to the response which you seek. If you cannot find that common premise, keep looking until you do. If there is no common premise in a given situation, persuasion will be almost or entirely impossible.

Common Ground

The Common-Ground Method is based on the assumption that the common cause overrides audience differences, that a solution is far more important than continued bickering, and that danger and defeat can be met only by joint effort and general recognition that common welfare is dependent upon cooperative thinking, feeling, and acting. In such a method the speaker reveals that he is free of personal, selfish, and ulterior motives, emphasizes points of agreement instead of conflict between himself and the audience and among the members of the audience, and places uppermost the importance of high, unified purpose. This method is not to be conceived as a trick of the trade but rather as a point of view that must be employed in the solution of human problems of an interpersonal nature. It is the method of the minister with his people when he faces an issue of conflict which might split his church into opposing camps. Just as truly, it is the method of any speaker or leader working for a unified program of action for civic changes, school improvements, or political reforms. Use of the common-ground method obliges the speaker to reveal his own goodwill, at the same time as it enables him to plead for mutual understanding, to emphasize that minor differences must be subordinated to a greater good, and, it is hoped, to silence persistent animosities which undermine the ability of all concerned to see the problem in its true light.

Abraham Lincoln used this method in his second inaugural address. As he analyzed the conflict that brought on the Civil War he presented the common ground in the mutual responsibilities of the people in the crisis, four years after it had started:

Neither party expected for the war the magnitude or the duration which it has already attained. Neither anticipated that the cause of the conflict might cease with, or even before, the conflict itself should cease. Each looked for an easier triumph, and a result less fundamental and astounding. Both read the same Bible, and prayed to the same God; and each invokes His aid against the other.

It may seem strange that any men should dare to ask a just God's assistance in wringing their bread from the sweat of other men's faces; but let us judge not, that we be not judged. The prayers of both could not be answered—that of neither has been answered fully.

You may see that use of the common ground method provides a *common premise* which includes potent response to the speaker, himself, for his image is that of a man who is "in the same boat" with his listeners. Think, therefore, of the possibilities as you use the method of common ground for the avoidance of conflicting attitudes and for engendering the spirit of community interest in the solution of the problems you present to your audience.

Indirect Development

When a speaker declares to his listeners, "I am going to convince you," "I shall persuade you," or "I am here to impress you," the image he calls up is likely to evoke the response: "I dare you." Further, if the central or main ideas of his talk are stated at the outset and if they are unacceptable assertions to the listeners, the validating materials, however excellent, may never really be responded to. Thus, instead of making obvious frontal attacks, a speaker may offer supporting materials first. If these meet the tests for validating forms and methods discussed in Chapter 7, they are acceptable to the listeners, for they provide a whole series of mutual premises, and they do lead the listeners more probably to acceptance of the main ideas and from there to acceptance of the central idea. Note, then, that while your outline will have main ideas with their support following, if the nature of your talk demands that you apply indirect development, you will be reversing the order of ideas and their validating materials in your speaking.

Examples of this method are legion in the history of public address, for its effectiveness has long been evident. One example of its use is that of Clarence Darrow in his famous defense speech in behalf of Richard Loeb and Nathan Leopold, Jr., when, in the midst of his appeal to save their lives, he stated:

> To believe that any boy is responsible for himself or his early training is an absurdity that no lawyer or judge should be guilty of today. . . . None of us are bred perfect and pure, and the color of our hair, the color of our eyes, our stature, the weight and fineness of our brain, and everything about us could, with full knowledge, be traced with absolute certainty to somewhere; if we had the pedigree it could be traced just the same in a boy as it could in a dog, a horse or cow.

The implication was clear that these boys could not be held responsible for their acts.

Use of the method of indirect development is certainly not to be interpreted as meaning that a speaker is never to make direct or concrete proposals for action. Indeed, in many speeches he does state explicitly, especially in his closing appeals, what specific steps he would like his hearers to take and act upon. Usually, a candidate running for office will give concrete reasons why votes should be cast for him; similarly, a speaker pleading for money to carry out an enterprise will ask that people give liberally. The indirect method of motivation has to be carried out by suggestions that touch off the inner impulses of the listeners.

Direct Development

The method of direct development, in which ideas are stated *before* their supporting materials, is best used for occasions on which the listeners are in basic agreement with the speaker—or at least they are not strongly opposed. The speaker's attitude, of course, is not one of "Now I am going to convince you." Rather he makes it clear that he has some strong personal positions or beliefs that he thinks the audience will accept, he states them, and he proceeds to build his case as effectively as possible.

This method of development will apply frequently in situations where the desired response is one of strengthened feeling and in which validating materials have been selected predominantly for their *appeal*.

But it will often apply equally well, where opposition is not strong, in speaking to create a new belief in which validating materials have been selected for response to the *logic* of the ideas. In this case, however, it is all the more important that the attitude of the speaker contribute to an image of authority, of conviction, and of genuine concern for the welfare of the listeners. Further, early, forceful reinforcement of the common premise is essential to move listeners to consider ideas which may, at first hearing, seem unacceptable.

In applying the direct-development method, the speaker outlines his contentions and then presents the arguments and appeals that support those contentions.

The Yes-Response

The method of yes-response is also one of indirection and the avoidance of conflict. The speaker will use this method because he knows it is often necessary to build up a series of favorable responses or approvals before he can gain assent for his proposal. In other words, it is an awareness on the part of the speaker that his proposal, which may require money and sacrifice, will not be accepted unless he prepares his listeners for what he is asking of them. For example, if the speaker wants to increase the amount of money available for public education, he cannot abruptly tell overburdened taxpayers that they must dig deeper into their pockets to build additional schools and to raise the salaries of teachers. Such a demand probably would be countered by many objections. But he knows that parents want the best for their children, and he can count on their saying "yes" to his declaration that education is vital in our highly competitive society. He can also appeal to the pride and concern of the listeners that the local schools must not be inferior to those in surrounding towns, lest their children be placed at a disadvantage. He may therefore employ such a rhetorical question as "Can we not provide as good an opportunity for our children as the other towns of the county provide?" To an equal extent, the speaker can count on a yes-response to his remarks that the increased school population has naturally increased demands on the facilities of the schools and to his demonstration that many of the facilities are inadequate, unsanitary, or even dangerous. On such grounds he is very likely to win a response of "Yes, these conditions must be remedied at once."

Thus, step by step, the persuasive speaker strengthens not just *one* common premise but a series of them, which lead logically and with some appeal to a final "yes" from his listeners to his major plea. In brief, the use of the yes-response method indicates an awareness on the part of the speaker that his listeners cannot be motivated until they have responded favorably to a number of primary considerations or premises which are basic to the larger one being stressed. Actually, the method can be looked upon as positive rather than negative, a method whereby agreement is stressed rather than the points of conflict, so that the speaker and audience become cooperators rather than antagonists.

The This-or-Nothing Method

Very often a speaker is confronted with the obligation of showing that his proposition must be accepted in preference to any other that might be offered. In many persuasive speeches it is inevitable that alternative solutions be compared and contrasted. Sometimes there are more than two solutions under consideration; seldom is there only one. Thus, the speaker advocating his own plan has two obligations: on the one hand, he must demonstrate the inadequacies of all other solutions, or proposals for serving the common need, and, on the other, he must prove that his recommendation is the only sure and safe one to follow. By use of the this-or-nothing method to eliminate all other means of meeting or solving the issue, the speaker becomes positive about what he wants done.

In brief, the procedure to be followed by the speaker using the this-or-nothing method is to eliminate, in order, all solutions but the one which he is advocating as the inevitably right one. For example, speakers may advocate military preparedness because other methods, such as concessions and appeasements, have inevitably drawn the threat of war nearer. In World War I, Woodrow Wilson used this method when he proved that all alternatives, such as armed neutrality, were impossible and said, "We will not choose the path of submission and suffer the most sacred rights of our nation and our people to be ignored or violated." This was his way of saying that the only solution was to go to war because "The world must be made safe for democracy. Its peace must be planted upon the trusted foundations of political liberty."

The Tried-and-Proved Method

A second method of showing that acceptance of your idea is necessary lies in demonstrating that it has indeed already been accepted and approved elsewhere in a form or forms similar to that which the speaker is presenting. If a large number of people have found the method the most desirable, then it follows that others will find themselves increasingly favorable toward it. By bringing a given audience to see that the solution presented is not radical or unwarranted but one already accepted on a large scale, the speaker can be genuinely positive in saying that this is the course we must pursue. As an example of this method, President Franklin D. Roosevelt, early in his first administration, advocated controlled production in agriculture as a sound solution because it had long been a practice in industry:

> You and I have heard big manufacturers talk about control of production by the farmer as an indefensible "economy of scarcity." And yet these same manufacturers never hesitate to shut down their own huge plants, throw men out of work, and cut down on the pur-

chasing power of whole communities whenever they think they must adjust their production to an oversupply of the goods they make. When it is their baby who has the measles, they call it not "an economy of scarcity," but "sound business."

In contrast to the yes-response method which provides for the listener a series of common premises, the this-or-nothing method offers listeners consideration of a series of conclusions, only one of which is most appropriate in following logically and by appeal from the common premise or problem.

○ OUTLINING FOR PERSUASION

The basic patterns of organizing and outlining the persuasive speech have been discussed in Chapter 6 and should be emphasized again. Certainly, when to stimulate feeling and change of conduct are the goal of all your efforts in choosing your subject and in planning its presentation, great care should be exercised in the step-by-step arrangement of what is to be said. To help you to achieve fully your goal of genuine persuasion, let us consider some principles which contribute to the effective and desirable arrangement of the ideas and materials you may want to use.

The Introduction

Although no two introductions are ever precisely alike and although the plan for the introduction should never be mechanical and stilted, certain general guides can be kept in mind.

Your opening remarks should capture the interest and attention of the audience. This applies with particular force when the object is persuasive.

You should strive to establish as soon as possible a common-ground relationship between yourself and the audience and among the members of the audience. This is especially necessary in the speeches to convince and to actuate, inasmuch as you know that the listeners often hold different, even diametrically opposed, points of view; as a consequence, it is vital that you do all that is possible early in the speech to allay these differences and animosities so that clear and unprejudiced thinking may prevail for the consideration of the problem you will be discussing.

You should emphasize the significance of the problem or the common premise. Arouse your listeners' vital interest and concern in it, and make evident its relation to the economic, social, and moral well-being of all who are gathered together with you.

Be sure you give all definitions and explanations necessary for the clear understanding of the subsequent materials of the speech. If you are speaking on federal aid to education, for example, be sure to make clear what you mean by federal aid.

You should, as in informative speaking, indicate the direction the speech will take by eliminating points of view which are irrelevant or outside the scope of your specific plans, so that the basic or important points of the speech can be kept in the center of attention.

Sometimes you may give a brief summary of the main points which you will discuss in the body of the speech, although the method of indirect development is often preferable. When clarity is the chief aim, a prior summary is especially desirable. The summary may, however, create or polarize antagonism if you state too directly or dogmatically the points you intend to prove. Thus, when the problem is to avoid emphasis upon audience disagreement with the speaker, such a forecast of the arguments of the speech should be avoided. Suggestion and greater use of the indirect method of implying the points may prove more effective. Remember that how you outline the introduction will be determined to some extent by the method of organization which you choose. In some cases the common premise is developed and reinforced here. In others it is developed and strengthened throughout the talk.

Be sure to develop an effective transition to enable you to move from the introduction to the body of the speech.

The Body

Quite naturally the major consideration in organizing the body of the speech is the orderly arrangement of the points, contentions, and ideas that you will present. You will also be concerned with the materials you intend to use in the over-all task of persuasion. In addition, keep in mind such other considerations as being genial and good-natured, occasionally using humor to lighten tensions and to create a friendly attitude among your hearers, interpolating several internal summaries to keep the main ideas before the audience, and carefully planning transitions from one point to the next throughout the body of the speech.

In every persuasive speech the speaker must make a fundamental decision regarding the chief method he should employ in so organizing his speaking as to achieve the results he desires. In the body of the speech it is essential that the over-all development be appropriate to the occasion and the purpose of the speaking, since different subjects, audiences, and speakers require different methods of organization. To that end, remember two things:

1. You will choose or create an organization of the main ideas so that they follow from the common premise both logically and through appeal. Remember also that the main ideas must focus on the central idea—supporting it and making it more believable or more intense to the listener.

2. You will order your ideas with their validating ideas following in your outline, but you may speak about the validating ideas first in organizing them by one method or another (except in direct development). Remember that outlining affords you experience in *analyzing* and *confirming* the support relationships of your ideas and materials. It may frequently be found most effective to reverse their order in speaking.

The Conclusion

The chief purpose of the conclusion is to achieve a final and cumulative impression that will contribute to acceptance of your proposal by the listeners. Each situation will require careful thought regarding the most appropriate method of concluding, but certain general recommendations should be helpful.

Summarize your major contentions for purposes of clarity and to make evident the unity of your presentation.

Make specifically designed appeal for the kind of response you desire. In so doing, make the proposal or course of action that you advocate stand out favorably in contrast to the alternatives of taking no action or taking an action that you believe to be inadvisable or ineffective. In speaking to convince, your task is to win agreement and intellectual acceptance of your ideas and points of view. In the speech to stimulate, your concern is to lift your audience out of a complacent and apathetic state of mind to one of renewed enthusiasm and revitalized ideals.

In the speech to actuate, the appeal should be for action, either immediate or deferred. This appeal, as we have insisted earlier, must be specifically designed to move listeners to the action. Merely to ask for generalized action is not enough. If an immediate and sacrificial contribution of money is needed, you will not only make your most potent appeal in the conclusion, but you will have arranged for envelopes, receipt books, blank checks. If a pledge is required, you will have pledge cards already distributed to be filled out as you conclude with your strongest statements. If congressional letter-writing is to be elicited, your conclusion will convince your listeners that such writing is effective and you may have data sheets to guide your listeners' writing (although you should admonish them to write clearly individual letters). The conclusion not only makes the action most attractive to the listeners but makes it as easy as possible for them to take that action.

To accomplish the above goals, select appeals that have both universal and personal applications. Frequently such methods as the telling of stories of heroism and sacrifice serve admirably to motivate. Inspirational quotations which are of particular significance to your theme and problem may well serve to motivate your hearers.

Your own personal sincerity and honesty of purpose must be evident. You may draw upon your own feelings of concern for the problem and make clear that the conviction you seek to stimulate in your audience is one which you yourself believe. Ordinarily this should be made evident by your materials and manner of speech rather than by a direct statement.

Select for the very closing or final statement the strongest and most highly significant remarks you can make. The very end of the speech should be the most emphatic and memorable.

○ CONCLUSION

Persuasion is an essential part of daily, democratic living. We will make "freedom of speech" work for us only if we are willing to listen to persuasion and to learn as much as we can about it. Persuasive purposes are to strengthen feeling, create belief, or induce listener action based upon such feeling or belief. In stimulating appropriate action, speakers must plan specific appeals for making that action attractive to and relatively easy for the listeners. Persuasion has been discussed in its relationships with gaining understanding and enjoyment.

Stress has been placed on learning to understand listener motives for ideation—for formation and acceptance of ideas—and the listener processes which operate in moving from a premise to a conclusion:

1. by response to the logic of the speaker's ideas,
2. by response to the appeal of the speaker's ideas, and
3. by response to the image of the speaker.

Organizing for persuasion offers a choice of methods which may be adapted to particular circumstances. Important specifics on outlining have been emphasized with the reminder that basic and indispensable as it is, the order in which you itemize evidence in the outline may not necessarily provide the most effective sequence in speaking.

EXERCISES

Questions for Discussion

1. What are your attitudes toward persuasion? Toward controversy? Do you have one standard for political speakers and another for advertisers?

2. How many times have you been involved in persuasion as speaker or listener in the past twenty-four hours?

3. What can be gained from "listening to the other side"? Even if your mind is made up?

4. Is it right for people to try to influence the attitudes, feelings, or beliefs of others?

5. Why is it necessary to plan specifically to induce action? Shouldn't the strengthened feeling or new belief be enough to spark action?

6. How can you tell the difference between persuasive and informative speaking by your classmates? Does the speaker always know his purpose?

7. Why is the study of inquiry so important to persuasion?

8. Do you think that "emotional" appeals by speakers are fair? Or do you consider them unethical?

9. Is there any "subliminal" persuasion in the speaker-listener situation?

10. Why can't induction deal with certainties instead of probabilities? Do any of the logical processes mentioned deal with certainties? Why?

11. Why is it a mistake to assume that when one event follows another there is causality involved?

12. Does the image of President Kennedy instilled in your nervous system appeal to you? Does that appeal help or hinder him in his communication with you? How about Dwight Eisenhower? Barry Goldwater? Gary Moore?

13. Do you believe that you can develop an ability to use stimulating, vivid, colorful language in persuasion? Why?

14. How is the problem-solving method of organization related to the other methods?

15. When might you organize persuasive speaking by direct development?

16. Do you talk about ideas in the same order as they appear in your outline? Why would you not follow that order?

17. What is meant by the *common premise*?

Projects for Speaking and Writing

1. Listen to a televised speech that is designed to persuade the American public or some segment of it. Analyze the speaker's purpose, his method of persuasion, his common premise, the listener processes of reasoning and appeal that were planned for, the effect of the speech upon you, and the effect of the speech on its intended audience.

2. Plan a series of two classroom talks to persuade, which would culminate in a new listener belief. The first is to be designed to strengthen the attitude, feeling or belief which becomes the common premise for the second.

3. For your next assignment, plan your speaking as it might be done according to at least three different methods and then select the one which you think will be most effective.

4. List ten topics suitable for persuasive speaking, and phrase a specific purpose and central idea for each. Indicate clearly which topics would be developed in order to strengthen feeling, create new belief, or induce action.

5. List five recent decisions which you have made. Try to determine what processes of reasoning and what processes of appeal led to each decision.

6. Plan with another member of your speech class to talk on a controversial issue in such a way that you will be, sincerely, on different sides of the issue. Have listeners ballot on how they feel about the issue before and after both of you speak. With the help of the listeners, try to analyze what made the difference, if there is a difference.

Chapter 14

Entertaining

THE ABILITY TO BE AN ENTERTAINING CONVERSATIONALIST is highly prized. If you have envied such an individual, or if you happen to be one yourself, you may be interested in finding what qualities make a person entertaining. In all probability, you will have noted that such a conversationalist talks easily and without any apparent strain or hardship. If his talk is self-conscious, it is not because of any feeling of insecurity but is rather a pleasant manner of self-dramatization. He probably has a deep strain of good humor and of genuine liking for people. His talk may not be exceptionally witty, but it will have a pervasive quality of lightness and optimistic gaiety or of racy excitement. When he talks of serious topics, he highlights their unusual aspects with an imaginative appreciation for suspense and vivid imagery. If he tells stories, he does so with such spontaneity and naturalness that you never worry about whether the point may get lost or "fall flat." His range of interests is doubtless unusually broad, and he is likely to be exceptional in his ability to see unusual aspects of even commonplace situations.

To learn to be entertaining is no easy task. It is notable that the many books written on the meaning and methods of the comic tend to be dull—and that even the best of them (for example, Max Eastman's *The Enjoyment of Laughter* and Albert Rapp's *The Origins of Wit and Humor*) cannot claim to educate people to be humorists. Neither is it easy to attain the ability to relate dramatic or unusual narratives with a pitch of excitement rising inevitably toward the climax. It is thoroughly unsound to believe that speakers are born and not made; nevertheless, the ability to be entertaining *seems* to be an innate, rather than an acquired skill. Even so, there are ways of improving one's skill in entertaining speaking, and there are at least three major reasons why you should undertake to gain increased proficiency in it.

○ WHY STUDY ENTERTAINING SPEECH?

The primary reason for cultivating the ability to entertain is that all people benefit by the catharsis of tension-breaking narratives or laughter and gaiety. Much of life is a serious struggle: to learn, to mature, to excel, to earn a living, to accumulate property, to exercise influence, to solve problems, and to improve living conditions. Many of the conditions of life create tension and nervous strain; unless there are opportunities for genuine enjoyable relaxation, the mind becomes taut and even neurotic. Moreover, modern living is a complex of personal competition—an inevitable breeding ground of jealousy, envy, and ill will; good comradeship and mutual understanding would gradually become more and more difficult to maintain were it not for opportunities for people to meet together with no other purpose than simple enjoyment. The ability to be entertaining should be cultivated as a debt owed to one's fellows, as well as to oneself. The individual without such a quality leads a difficult life and can be a source of strain among his associates. Perhaps you may know such a person, who has every competence except the saving sense of humor. If so, the opinion which is generally held concerning him ought to be a serious warning of the need to develop geniality in yourself.

The second reason for trying to improve your own ability as an entertaining speaker is that such speaking is highly regarded. Chairmen of program committees for many kinds of clubs (from the Bible Society of the local church to the Society for the Advancement of Management) know that for special meetings—especially for annual banquets to which the members' wives are invited—the participants want to avoid serious discussions and hear a relaxing speech of entertainment. A speaker who is genuinely entertaining is always in demand. On your own campus this fact is doubtless very apparent—when fraternities and sororities hold open house meetings for returning graduates, when honor societies hold their annual initiation meetings for new members, when faculty-student dinners are held. Women's clubs, businessmen's luncheon clubs, fraternal orders, and labor unions like to hold occasional fellowship meetings when serious business is forgotten and entertainment is the order of the day. Genial toastmasters, speakers skilled in presenting suspenseful stories and humorous after-dinner speakers are not easy to find. So long as people enjoy good-humored association, the entertaining speaker will always be sought out, appreciated, and rewarded with gratitude and admiration.

The third reason for seeking to develop skill in entertaining speech will apply directly to you even if you are convinced that the role of entertainer is not one that you either can or wish to enact. This reason is that entertainment should be an incidental but valuable part of even serious speaking. Every idea should be as interesting as possible. The need for humorous relief in serious speaking is explained by the need for contrast and variety. Minds bombarded with argument, facts, pathos, and challenging statements tend to become dulled or satiated so that the effect the speaker seeks to achieve is weakened. An entertaining interlude is restful and relaxing; moreover, by contrast it makes the succeeding serious point more impressive. An absorbing narrative, or reference to striking facts (such as, "One tenth of the people who have ever lived on earth are alive today") can serve the same purpose.

○ CHARACTERISTICS OF ENTERTAINING SPEECH

The widely held notion that entertainment is identical with humor is—like the premature report of Mark Twain's death—greatly exaggerated. Humor is indeed a major wellspring of entertaining speech. It is a gushing, effervescent source of enjoyment, as welcome as a cool stream of water in a dry land. Laughter is one of mankind's best medicines. When a person who is known as a good storyteller gets a sparkle in his eyes and a crinkle of humor around his lips as he breaks a pause in the conversation with, "Did you hear the one about the fellow who . . . ?" his listeners lean forward with eager anticipation. Laughter draws people together and safeguards individuals from frustrated unhappiness. When it is announced that an entertaining speaker is scheduled for a meeting, the audience gathers in eager anticipation of enjoying some hearty laughs. Nevertheless, despite the importance of humor, experience reminds us that not all entertainment is confined to the humorous.

When you pick up a detective story to read, or watch Perry Mason or go to hear a talk by an explorer just back from the wilds of the Amazon Valley you do not expect to laugh, but you do expect to be entertained. What you are seeking is akin to humor in its function, although not in its nature: you want to find relaxation through avoidance of the humdrum or demanding realities of everyday life. What the book reviewers call "escape literature" is entertainment of this type. It may be serious in the sense of dealing with the issues of life and death—indeed, much of it is highly melodramatic—but it is far removed from the serious business of living. This is so because it is marked by a high degree of unfamiliarity and remoteness from your own individual or community concerns.

GOOD HUMOR. Whether comic or not, entertaining speech is marked by good humor and geniality. The tension of conflict and personalized competition is strained out. Good fellowship and the enjoyment of other people's company are emphasized, rather than the struggle to excel or succeed. If this seems not to be the case in recitals of crime, which are often marked by unusual brutality, the fact is that such narratives are remote and unreal; they happen, but not to such people as you—and certainly not to you yourself. In many entertaining speeches even depictions of violence are burlesqued with a touch of ridicule or through unrealistic exaggeration, which is introduced as a deliberate notice to the audience not to take the struggle seriously. But note that belittling comments, satire, sarcasm, ill-natured irony, or acrimonious jests are not entertaining but weapons of attack. In all speaking that is really entertaining, "nobody is mad at nobody"; good humor is the first rule.

UNREALITY AND EXAGGERATION. The quality of unreality which has already been noted deserves to stand among the basic characteristics of entertaining speech. Whether the speaking is humorous or not, the audience should clearly be led to understand that the speaker is not trying to depict life as it truly is, to deal with serious problems that really exist. An entertaining speech about a foreign land deals with the quaint and interesting customs of the people visited, not with their problems or achievements. A ludicrously exaggerated discussion of how to park your car in the busy downtown business district might be entertaining, but an earnest analysis of traffic control would not be. Reality is a pressing business requiring serious thought; unreality is an escape mechanism as necessary as the escape valve on a steam boiler and as welcome as the unexpected dismissal of classes to permit celebration of a football victory. This kind of entertainment is illustrated by the movie, "Along Came Jones," in which Gary Cooper was advised, "Shoot 'em in the right eye first. It spoils their aim."

THE UNUSUAL. Any description of unknown facts, or narrative of unusual experiences, will be entertaining if presented with zest for the purpose of enjoyment, rather than with the aim to inform or persuade. The spirit of the presentation is as important in effecting the result as is the nature of the material itself. A speaker may discuss the "golden horde" of bees, giving a great deal of explicit information on how they live. If his purpose is to entertain, he will present the information with heightened drama, or with playful good humor. He will emphasize those aspects of the facts which are most interesting— not necessarily the most significant. And the conclusion toward which his presentation leads may be fanciful, such as, "Bees are much like people, only less quarrelsome"; or, "The hive is like a home, with one mother, no father, some lazy brothers, and a lot of hard-working sisters." The accent is upon the unusual for its own sake, not for what it might teach.

COMEDY. The causes of laughter have never been satisfactorily explained, although many attempts have been made; but everyone agrees that laughter is both a manifestation and a cause of pure enjoyment. Comedy covers a wide range of communication, from sharp and sometimes caustic wit to slapstick and broad jesting, and includes jokes, which are brief anecdotes marked by good humor and having an unexpected and enjoyable climax. Some specialists in humor have defined the joke as a story with an ending that disappoints the expectation but that is actually more enjoyable than the one that was anticipated. Both good humor and unreality are indispensable to the joke— as in the familiar story of Pat, who stepped into an elevator shaft, fell ten stories, then came running back up to warn his friend Mike, "Watch out for that first step. It's a humdinger!"

SYMPATHY. The characters in an entertaining speech may endure all manner of strange mishaps, but they don't get hurt. In the preceding anecdote, the humor depends on the fact that after his ten-story fall Pat was still able to run back upstairs without pain and with no thought except for his friend. The thin line separating pathos and humor lies at precisely this point: in pathetic stories the hero suffers pain; in humorous stories he suffers no more than a shock of harmless surprise or a momentary loss of dignity. Master entertainers, such as Mark Twain and Charlie Chaplin, are greatly admired for their ability to shift back and forth between tears and laughter—but their skill depends upon their knowing that this line exists and on which side of the line their antics fall.

WIT. Irony, whimsey, paradox, puns, burlesque, and all forms of verbal play (even including baby talk and mimicry of drunken speech or of dialects) comprise forms of wit which have always been part of the stock in trade of skilled humorists. Shakespeare's Falstaff and the melancholy Jacques are well-known examples. Oscar Wilde's distortion of accepted proverbs so as to display the modicum of truth in their opposites is another familiar example. Wit is one of the highest forms of humor—and for that reason is often confined to speakers who are experienced and unusually capable humorists.

IRRELEVANCE. Incongruity, or the pretense of finding logical relationships where obviously none exist, is another characteristic of entertaining speech. This quality was utilized by the speaker who said: "My reason for going to college is that I'm overweight, my father has cross-eyes, and my mother won't let us buy a blue automobile. Now those reasons may not seem very convincing to you, but they're better than my roommate's claim that he came here because he'd rather hear professors lecture than not have real maple syrup on his pancakes at home. Now just stick with me and I'll explain why these reasons are more realistic than the explanation half the students on the campus may have to offer for wanting to get a college education. In the first place, being overweight and dumb gets you nowhere except to be the laughing stock of your home town. But when you get a college education, you can really begin to throw your weight around. . . ." Thus the speech proceeds, making no real sense, but in a spirit of nonsense that never deviates into logic but always threatens that it may—perhaps, in the next sentence.

IRREVERENCE. Serious sacrilege or rebellion against authority is frowned upon and punished with disapproval or discipline. As a result, individuals feel so penned in by social conventions, regulations, and laws that permissible flouting of authority or of established codes is a frequent source of entertainment. Because of this, off-color stories and jokes about the minister or the absent-minded professor are common. Pomposity is always a subject for wit. Mother-in-law jokes also arise from this same enjoyment of the acceptably irreverent. Privates in the Army like to jest about the presumed awkwardness or dumbness of sergeants. When irreverence breaks out of the bounds of the permissible, however, listeners wince at the speaker's bad taste. But so long as basic respect for law, morals, and authority is not affronted, jests at their expense are generally appreciated.

○ DELIVERY

The chief requirements for the delivery of entertaining speeches are that the speaker be poised, confident, and in full mastery of the situation and that he exude an unmistakable spirit of good will toward his subject and his audience. Tension, uncertainty, and lack of command are barriers through which entertainment cannot penetrate. The speaker should never have to struggle either for thoughts or words. His physical bearing should advertise unmistakably to his audience that he knows precisely what he will do or say next, and his words should pour out effortlessly as though from an inexhaustible stream. If the audience feels that the speaker is struggling to remember what he intended to say next, that he is unsure of his ability to carry it off, or that he is worried about his own lack of poise, they will empathically suffer with him and be unable to enjoy his speech. Ease and confidence of bearing and manner are the first requirements for the effective delivery of the entertaining speech.

The delivery of entertaining speeches should also be marked by the speaker's clear acceptance and conveyance of the speech purpose: to entertain. The speaker must make it plain to the audience that he is not striving to wrestle with their judgments, to inform their intellects, or to change their attitudes. His sole purpose is to help them have a good time.

If the speaker has peculiarities of voice, diction, dress, or manner —if, for example, he is wearing odd clothing as an incident to initiation into a fraternity, or if he speaks with a marked dialect, or if he has unruly hair that simply will not obey a comb—these very characteristics can be adapted to the entertaining speech as positive aids. They can be utilized as a comedian utilizes props in a comedy program. This may be done by exaggerating the peculiarities and relating them to the entertaining content of the speech.

Finally, in speaking for entertainment, adaptation to and rapport

Good will is contagious . . .

The storyteller, the quipster, the speaker who would give his listeners enjoyment, exudes confidence and good will. He speaks in a ready and free manner—adapted to the nature of the occasion, the mood of the audience, and the character of his subject.

with the audience are absolute necessities. The speaker must leave no doubt that his subject and his manner are precisely suited to the occasion. His speech should be adapted to the nature of the occasion, the mood of the audience, and the character of his subject. No speaker should violate good taste. A jest which shocks the audience has no entertainment value; instead it creates a barrier to any further effective communication with his hearers.

One of the reasons for assigning speeches of entertainment even to students who object that entertainment is not in their line, is to afford practice in the delivery of other kinds of speaking that especially demand qualities of ready and free delivery. For the qualities of delivery that are indispensable for speeches of entertainment are also, with very little change, admirable in most other speeches. This is especially true of ease of bearing, mastery of the situation, and the maintenance of close rapport with the listeners.

Problems in Producing Humor

When first confronted with the necessity of giving a humorous speech, students are likely to raise such questions as the following:

1. *Should I deliver humor "dead-pan," or should I show evident enjoyment of my own jesting?*

There is no generalized answer. Undoubtedly very few people have the ability to deliver humorous speeches effectively with a dead-pan expression. If you are one of those who can do so, this method should probably be used. Mark Twain, in his serious essay "How to Tell a Story" demands that this method be used—and he himself was an adroit master of it. Bob Hope, George Burns, and Jack Paar use the dead-pan method for "breaking" a jest, but after an interval Hope joins in the audience's laughter. You will have to discover your own special type of ability through trial and error and learn to deliver your entertaining speeches by whichever method best suits your own talents.

2. *If I do not use the dead-pan technique, to what extent should I participate in audience laughter at my own humor?*

This question can be answered more positively than the foregoing one. By all means join in the general laughter (unless you use the dead-pan method); but never lead the laugh; never laugh harder and louder, than the audience; and never continue to laugh after your listeners' enjoyment of the humor has begun to taper off. As the speaker, you should be among the last to start laughing and among the first to stop. Otherwise, your speech may get out of control, and the audience may end by laughing at rather than with you.

3. *Where can I find good jokes?*

Many magazines and newspapers publish occasional jokes as "fillers" or even have regular humor columns. Bennett Cerf, among others, has published several books of jokes which are readily available. Few days pass without your having heard a joke or two, for people love to tell them. If you follow the advice offered in Chapter 5 to keep a permanent record of the good jokes you read or hear, you will not be without one when the need arises.

4. *Should I tell humorous anecdotes that my listeners may have heard before?*

You should certainly resist the temptation to tell that sidesplitting joke that you heard on last night's television comedy hour or read in the last issue of the *Reader's Digest,* for listeners are usually not going to be sent into gales of laughter by hearing an echo of a joke that so recently entertained them. Even less recent jokes are often generally familiar—you know how often friends have tried to tell you humorous anecdotes that you have already heard several times. Two ways to avoid filling your entertaining speech with hackneyed jokes are suggested in the answers to the following two questions.

5. *How can I give my humor a really individual twist?*

Comedians (or their writers) seldom invent new comic situations. What the humorists do is to change the locale and the characters of stock anecdotes. One method of individualizing your humor is to revise an anecdote to fit your local community and to people it with individuals well known to the audience—or perhaps even present in it. The caution to be observed is not to relate personalized situations of a biting or ridiculing character—for this destroys the essential characteristics of good humor and sympathy, discussed above. Many a speaker has avoided the risk of hurting others' feelings by making himself the butt of the jest.

6. *Is there a better way to be humorous than by telling jokes?*

Indeed there is! The best humor is generally evolved from the extended depiction of an imaginary experience or situation—as in the earlier example of the young man's explanation of why he came to college. The stringing together of a series of jokes is such a precarious way of constructing an entertaining speech that you should be wary of it—although if you are another Bob Hope it may prove to be effective. If, however, you do build your speech around a string of jokes, they should all be related in subject matter (about libraries and reading, for example) and should be closely related to the local scene. The light-hearted, jesting, exaggerated description of a real or imagined experience—such as, "My Troubles in Rearing a Family of Goldfish"—is normally a much sounder body for a speech of entertainment than is even a superior collection of jokes.

7. *What do I do if I just can't be funny?*

You can learn to be, if you will follow the principles set forth in this section. But if you are still doubtful, read the following section and be comforted.

○ NON-HUMOROUS SPEECHES OF ENTERTAINMENT

We have already made it clear that humor is not the only ingredient of entertaining speeches—although, when a speech is billed as entertaining, it is humor that the audience normally expects. What is basically required is that the speech must help the audience to escape from reality. This principle of the entertaining speech permits subject matter of a wide variety. Principal sources include the following.

ADVENTURE. Adventure may be characterized as an experience that has no special purpose except excitement. When a famed mountaineer was asked why he wanted to climb Mount Everest, he replied, "Because it's there." A man who goes into the wilderness to look for gold is an entrepreneur; one who goes for the sheer pleasure of pitting his wit and strength against the elemental forces of nature is an adventurer. Similarly, in relating stories of daring, the speaker's whole point —if entertainment is his aim—is not to show how some social or individual gain was achieved but to re-create for his listeners a sense of the thrill of the experience. Few college students (or few people in general, except as a consequence of war) have ever had any great adventures, in this sense. It is entirely permissible, however, to tell an audience about an adventure of which you have read, provided only that you give proper credit to the source and find an appropriate reason for recounting this specific adventure to this specific audience.

PERSONAL EXPERIENCES. Actually, autobiography is the chief resource of any writer or speaker. The late Lee Emerson Bassett once said in the introduction to a talk, "Forgive me if I seem to speak about my own experiences, but after all, they are the only ones I've ever had." For humorous speeches, you can recall and recount—with the embroidery of rhetorical exaggeration—embarassing or ridiculous predicaments into which you have fallen in the past. For a non-humorous speech of entertainment, you may be tempted to tell of a pleasurable fishing trip which you once made into the Canadian lake country or of an automobile trip to some national parks. This kind of experience is seldom a fruitful source of entertainment (unless you can show colored slides of the scenery), for most of your original enjoyment arose from emotional reactions to beautiful scenes or from the sheer pleasure of novelty, both of which are difficult to re-create in a speech. However, you doubtless have had some experience which can be related in the spirit of an "escape" narrative: a frightening experience with a stranger who gave you a lift while you were hitch-hiking, a night spent alone in the woods, an attempt to earn money as a door-to-door salesman, an encounter with a dangerous dog, an evening alone at home when you thought you heard thieves in the basement. If your experiences seem to you to have been insufficiently exciting to serve as entertaining narratives, perhaps you can recall some of your dreams which better fit the requirements. Or you might invite your listeners to join you in an imaginary excursion you would like to take if you could.

READING. Doubtless you recall some books you have read which were especially thrilling or stimulating, not because of their message but because of the excitement of the narrative. To attempt to compress a three-hundred-page book into a five-minute speech would scarcely prove successful, but such a book may well have contained an incident or a character which you could describe to your audience in an attempt to create for them as vivid and pleasurable an impression as the book itself made upon you.

DRAMATIC FACTS. Besides humor and dramatic narrative, you may be able to draw upon the large category of startling and unusual facts. If you have been an amateur student of astronomy, for example, you will have stored up in your mind some truly fascinating facts about the infinite expanse of the universe. Similarly, the world of insects (the life of an ant colony, for example) abounds in amazing features. So does the collecting of stamps or coins. So does the structure of the human brain—or the anatomy and functioning of the stomach of a cow—or the behavior of electricity under varying conditions. The customs of a primitive African tribe and the code of behavior among pickpockets provide interesting details. In a sense, speeches on such subjects may be considered informative; but if your purpose in discussing them is primarily not to instruct but to entertain, your listeners can readily be induced to relax and simply enjoy listening to what you have to say.

○ AFTER-DINNER SPEAKING

After-dinner speeches are widely, although somewhat inaccurately, considered to be lightly entertaining. As a matter of fact, dinner meetings have become very popular as occasions for seriously purposive addresses. Political parties hold $100-a-plate fund-raising dinners, at which partisan leaders make talks extolling the party virtues and castigating the rival party. Business concerns hold dinners at which the employees are addressed by management representatives on company policies. Many clubs hold weekly luncheon meetings at which speeches of varied purposes are heard. The dinner table has become almost as popular as the auditorium as a setting for speeches to inform and to persuade, as well as to entertain.

Various reasons explain the rapid growth in the popularity of the dinner meeting as a locale for serious speeches. One obvious reason is to intrigue the interest of the guests, who might fail to attend a regular meeting but are more likely to attend a dinner. This reason is well illustrated by the frequency of fund-raising dinners organized by philanthropic organizations and by college alumni secretaries. Another and more basic reason was stated almost two centuries ago by Dr. Samuel Johnson when he told Boswell, "Sir, a good dinner lubricates business."

Companionable dining helps put listeners into an agreeable frame of mind and thus makes them more receptive to the ideas to be presented. This sound reason explains why executives like to assemble their employees around a dinner table when they wish to outline for them the policies by which their work will be directed. It also explains why salesmen so frequently treat prospective customers to dinner before undertaking to make a sale.

Still another reason for the increased number of dinner meetings is that people always enjoy gathering under pleasant circumstances, and especially when they can eat together. Good food, like laughter, promotes the unity, as opposed to the disunity, of mankind. Many a businessman who does not enjoy listening to speeches is nevertheless willing to sit through one every Thursday noon because he so much enjoys the fellowship of the club luncheon.

Any speaker who is invited to make an after-dinner speech should bear in mind several considerations of importance.

GOOD HUMOR. Whether or not his speech is primarily entertaining, it almost certainly should be good-humored, especially in the introduction. As has been emphasized, the distinctive feature of a dinner meeting is its conviviality and good-fellowship. In such a setting, vituperation and attack are seldom appropriate. On occasion political speakers use the dinner meeting as a locale for a biting attack upon their party's opponents; but in such cases the listeners are typically so in sympathy with the speaker's views that to them the speech does not sound controversial. It has rather the spirit of a "pep talk" at a football rally and is, after all, what they came expecting to hear.

COMPREHENSIBILITY. Precisely because it is delivered immediately after a meal, the after-dinner speech should be relatively easy to understand. It is a simple physiological fact that digestion slows down mental processes. So long as the stomachs of the listeners are filled, their brains cannot be loaded with intricate problems of reasoning. Perhaps all after-dinner speakers should imagine their auditors' holding up a large placard proclaiming, *"We have had it!"*

BREVITY. Normally an after-dinner speech should be relatively brief. The evening lecture hall may provide a band of listeners ready and eager to hear an hour-long address by an expert on international affairs. But they have come to the hall just prior to the start of his speech, whereas the dinner audience has already been seated for an hour or more before the speaker is introduced. No matter how interesting he may be, the muscles of the diners cannot help becoming tired and cramped. In order to obviate this difficulty to some extent, before the speaking program begins the toastmaster should ask the audience to rise, to adjust their chairs so as to face the speaker, and perhaps to remain standing long enough to sing one or two songs.

○ ORGANIZING ENTERTAINING SPEECHES

As is true of all other types of speaking, the speech to entertain is organized around a dominant and unifying specific purpose. For one speech it might be: "I want my audience to experience the thrill of hunting lions on the African veld." For another it might be: "I want my audience to enjoy a humorous burlesque about why athletes take cold showers." For another it might be: "I want my audience to be pleasantly amazed at the social customs of honey bees." The first step in the preparation is always to arrive at a clear and precise statement of the specific purpose. For the second step, you should strictly discipline yourself to select main ideas and supporting materials which will focus the attention of the listeners on a dominant theme or central idea. It is difficult to establish a definite pattern of organization for the entertaining speech because of the wide variety of possibilities, but we shall now suggest some of the possible patterns of organization.

Introduction

The chief purpose of an introduction to any speech is to prepare the audience for what will follow. Since entertainment is to be the purpose of this type of speaking, the introduction must signal your intention to your listeners clearly and unmistakably. In part this will be accomplished by what you say: by the humorous or exaggerated or unreal or striking formulation of your subject. In even greater part, however, your intent to entertain has to be indicated by the quality of your voice and by your whole bearing and manner. Everyone enjoys being entertained, but it is difficult to be entertained "unawares." Listeners need to prepare themselves to take what is to be said lightly and in a spirit of nonchalant abandon. Thus, above all in the introduction to your speech of entertainment, be sure to speak and act with an easy unconcern which will make it very evident that what is to follow will not be momentous but will be presented in a spirit of enjoyment.

Body

Naturally the organization of the body of the speech will vary greatly, depending upon whether your objective is to entertain with a humorously exaggerated description of a situation, with a dramatic narrative of adventure, or with a selection of strikingly unusual facts.

For the last-named type, the *topical order* usually serves best. For the narrative speech, the *chronological order* may be preferable, although you will certainly want to arrange your materials carefully to build up to the climax. For the humorous speech, since irrelevance is often one of its characteristics, it might even be feasible and desirable to link your main ideas together in a deliberately illogical sequence. However, in some cases, for example if you are giving a humorous explanation of how your cousin Susie unknowingly frightens away all her potential beaux, it may be essential to develop your materials according to a strictly logical organization. In general, the body of your speech to entertain will adhere to the same principles of organization as do your other speeches.

Conclusion

For a speech based on a dramatic narrative, the conclusion is the climactic ending of the story—normally containing an element of surprise. If your speech comprises a series of unusual facts, you may conclude by demonstrating that the most unusual fact of all is the combination or over-all view of the preceding details. For example, one speaker entertained a group of engineering students with striking evidence that characters from outer space may be masquerading among us as human beings. He concluded with this parody:

> Just see the clever Martian;
> He has all the fun.
> I wish I were a Martian. . . .
> Look out! I may be one.

The conclusion to a humorous speech may be simply an especially good final anecdote. Or you may conclude in a semi-serious vein by pointing out that there is something to be learned even from the accumulation of jests. Although conclusions of speeches to entertain vary in accordance with the form of the speech, as do the conclusions of the other types of speeches, their chief function is always to reinforce the central idea and hence the specific purpose of the speaker.

○ CONCLUSION

Learning to deliver an effective speech of entertainment has great value both for and of itself and for its contribution to mastery of other kinds of speeches. Typical characteristics are good humor, unreality, the unusual, comedy, sympathy, irrelevance, and irreverence. The delivery of this type of speech needs especially to be characterized by qualities of self-control, poise, mastery of the situation, and good rapport with the audience. Many inexperienced speakers are doubtful of their ability to be genuinely entertaining, because they believe that they cannot give effective humorous speeches. However, not all entertaining speeches must be humorous, and sources of non-humorous entertainment may be found in adventure, personal experiences, reading, and dramatic facts.

After-dinner speaking has been given special attention—even though no longer as exclusively a showcase for the display of wit—both because it has become so widespread a practice and because it is still popularly associated with entertaining speaking. Because of the nature of the occasion, as we have said, after-dinner speeches should usually be good-humored, relatively easy to understand, and comparatively brief.

The organization of the speech to entertain does not differ markedly from that of other speeches, though it may seem looser in form. However, the speaker must take especial care that his introductory remarks and his whole manner of speaking will quickly and clearly indicate to his listeners that what is intended is their enjoyment, nothing more. And this is precisely the spirit that should animate the entire speech, for entertainment will only result in creating an atmosphere of enjoyment.

EXERCISES

Questions for Discussion

1. Discuss entertainment as "escape from reality." How does this principle apply to humorous speaking? To other types of entertaining speech?

2. Define: humor, pathos, entertainment, joke, climax, irreverence, irrelevance, wit, satire, whimsey, paradox, sarcasm, ridicule.

3. What are the values of attaining skill in entertainment?

4. Discuss the six characteristics of entertaining speech; illustrate as many as you can by reference to speeches you have heard or to radio and television comedy or adventure programs.

5. Join in a class discussion of the characteristics of several noted contemporary radio, television, or motion-picture comedians. What do they have in common? How do they differ? What can you learn from them that will help you in learning to give public speeches of entertainment?

6. Discuss each of the special problems in entertaining speaking—including the considerations especially applicable to delivery and organization.

7. Referring back to Chapter 8, consider the special problems of style as they are related to entertaining speeches.

8. What particular common ground do you find in this chapter and Chapter 9?

9. To what extent and in what way should entertainment be used in speeches to inform and speeches to persuade?

Projects for Speaking and Writing

1. Analyze yourself from the point of view of ability to entertain. Are your abilities—actual or potential—greater in the field of humor or in relating adventurous narratives and unusual facts? Do you feel a special need for developing the entertaining aspects of your personality? What suggestions can you make for your own improvement in this regard?

2. Outline briefly both a humorous and non-humorous speech of entertainment. Practice each one, preferably before a friend, and decide which one to develop more fully for presentation in class.

3. If you have not already done so (after reading Chapter 5) start an orderly collection of humorous anecdotes. Even as you record them, practice rephrasing them in fresh terms of references to your own localized situation.

4. Read a humorous narrative—such as Mark Twain's "The Invalid's Story," or "Jim Baker's Blue-Jay Yarn," or James Thurber's "The Day the Dam Broke," or any other of your own choice. Then try your hand at relating (either in writing or in speech) a humorous incident based on your own experience, observation, or imagination.

5. Read or listen to a humorous speech and write a serious analysis—or present such an analysis as an informative speech—indicating what made it entertaining. What changes would you recommend?

6. Review some of your recent speeches, and indicate in what ways you might have improved them by the insertion of brief entertaining touches. How could you have made the over-all development of your ideas more entertaining while, at the same time, making them also more effective in accomplishing your serious purpose?

Chapter 15

Discussion and
Parliamentary Law

BY FAR THE MOST FREQUENT USE of your abilities as a communicator is in discussion situations. For every speech you make, you will probably participate in a great many more discussions. This is also the most important medium in which to utilize your total communicative ability, for you are both speaker and listener, with constant exchange between these roles. Discussion affords you the greatest opportunities for adaptation of speech principles to different people and subjects and the greatest need for flexibility and resourcefulness.

Most discussion is informal and without specific preparation, in the form of conversation, "bull sessions," and casual contacts with others. Here you call upon all the principles of good speaking and listening almost without giving conscious thought to them, and the larger your storehouse the better discussant you will be. There are other discussion situations of a more formal nature for which you will prepare more carefully. One of these may occur in an approaching fraternity meeting where a certain subject is due to be discussed and there is much controversy over it. You read up on the subject so that you can help supply some facts and information, and you shape your thinking in relation to what your findings say. Or if a more formal situation lies ahead, such as a panel in front of an audience, you will prepare in other ways.

347

This chapter deals with the principles and techniques for planning, participating in, and leading discussions. Many of these are adaptations of speech principles we have already discussed. Others are special principles peculiar to the discussion process. But we have frequently pointed out that we do not have a new and separate set of speech principles for every situation; we learn *adaptation* and *flexibility of application.*

Our first principle of discussion, then, is to review and apply all the speech principles you have already learned. See how you make use of them in preparing for discussions in your speech course and in the countless situations you are in daily. If you make a list of these in any typical day, you may be amazed at the number and variety of times you are in some need of talking things over with others.

○ THE NATURE OF DISCUSSION

There are many ways to define discussion, but the important aspect to remember is that it is the *exchange of ideas* among two or more persons, *in a cooperative spirit.* In informal social conversation we have no particular goal except that of having a cordial and pleasant time. In a business conference or the meeting of a club the goal is to arrive at a specific decision. In a public panel the goal may be to try to solve a problem but not necessarily to reach a decision. The purpose of discussion, then, may be to solve a problem, gather information, learn, make a decision, or simply to enjoy each other's remarks.

In this chapter we are concerned chiefly with problem-solving discussion.[1] This is, in essence, the application of scientific method or inquiry to the group solution of human problems. No scientist confronted with a problem, such as finding an appropriate metal for acid-carrying pipes or arriving at a hypothesis of a quantum theory, jumps to a solution. Yet, in areas of human affairs, we are all prone to do this. Mention the parking problem and a solution immediately comes to mind. The same is true for problems involving farm surpluses, highway safety, or college grading.

When we limit ourselves to the acceptance or rejection of a so-

[1] For a fuller treatment of the problem-solving method consult any textbook on group discussion, such as H. E. Gulley, *Discussion, Conference, and Group Process.* New York: Holt, Rinehart and Winston, 1960.

lution, we curtail our ability to solve problems. We have only two courses open to us. When, on the other hand, we ask, "How can we solve this problem?" we are in a position to consider all possible solutions and, like the scientist, establish standards by which to evaluate each of them to arrive at what is truly the best or at a combination of solutions which is far superior to any single one.

Group discussion for problem-solving requires, then, an attitude of inquiry, a willingness to investigate and learn even at the expense of exploding a pet theory. It also requires that the participants agree on the guiding principles of discussion. This does not mean that they agree, at the outset, on how the problem should be solved; but they do agree that their opinions are flexible, based upon honest, open-minded, scientific inquiry. Further, the participants agree that their own individual preparation, their own investigation and study of the problem, is essential to assure maximum information on which to base decisions.

○ THE PATTERN OF DISCUSSION

The pattern of inquiry is similar for scientist and for discussant:

1. Determine the nature and importance of the problem.
2. Analyze the history, background and causes of the problem.
3. Determine who is involved and what they stand to gain or lose in the solution of the problem.
4. Establish criteria for evaluating solutions.
5. Offer all possible solutions.
6. Evaluate solutions.
7. Arrive at the best available solution or combinations of solutions.

At the outset, when the problem or question is put before the group, it is important that the participants agree on what, specifically, is really the nature and extent of the problem. Too often the possibility is overlooked that there may not be any problem or that it is not as important as it was first felt to be. If a group in discussion finds that there is no serious difficulty, in spite of the strong beliefs that have prevailed that one or another solution should be applied, then that group has had a successful discussion.

It is in the next step, that most discussion encounters difficulty, the tendency being to give superficial attention to the analysis of the history, background, and causes of the problem. This may lead to giving serious consideration, later on, to a solution that has been tried already and failed. Most persons in a discussion are too anxious to offer solutions. This can be a drawback if action is taken before the problem is thoroughly analyzed. The analysis should include the answers to questions like these: What was the origin of this situation or problem? Who was responsible? When did it start? How did it start? What's been done about it?

No solutions should be introduced during this phase of the discussion. Both leader and participants have an obligation to be sure that the problem is first fully explored. Suppose you are discussing the question, "What can be done to improve the parking situation in this community (or on this campus)?" Many in the group probably have specific suggestions to make. But you first need to know certain facts, such as: the present available parking facilities, the number of cars to be served, the peak hours of need, the present regulations and fees, the growth-rate that has contributed to the problem, the apparent inadequacies and inequities, and other possible causes and contributing factors.

Frequently the leader is at fault in giving a brief resumé of the problem and assuming that he has supplied all the necessary information for solving it. His first question too often is, "What do you folks think we should do about this?" Such a question is very much out of order at this stage, for it is solution-centered rather than problem-centered, and the group is not ready for it yet. He should exhaust all available knowledge from the group first. If he does not, then it is the responsibility of members to insist that attention be centered on problem analysis.

In the solution to any problem under discussion, there are *people* involved. Ideally, in a discussion, all groups who have a stake in the problem should be represented, but frequently they are not. So participants need to be aware of just who is involved, to what extent, and what they stand to gain or lose when the problem is solved. Without this information to build on, it is impossible to create a complete set of criteria for evaluating the solutions. And without as complete a set of standards as possible, no judgment of any of the solutions can be made that will be realistic and applicable to the real situation.

A proposed solution to a public problem that meets everybody's criteria but the taxpayers' is not likely to be accepted.

In listing criteria, then, any which the group understands to stem from the involvement of some individual or group are accepted. The finally derived best solution may not meet all criteria, but you hope that it will. After all, if a solution meets all of your own standards, you probably will have no objection if it is also designed to meet those of anyone else who may be involved.

The next major step, that of offering possible solutions, should be started with a clear understanding that here, too, contributions by members of the group are to be as clearly *understood* as possible, *not* debated. A major hazard of this step is the tendency to start evaluating suggested solutions too soon. As a speaker, be sure that you achieve your informative goal, that your listeners understand just how the plan or proposal would work. As a listener, be sure that your communicative goal is to see clearly how the solution would work; it must not be, at this point, to evaluate.

If a group goes too directly into evaluation, it may fail to have put before it some solutions that might be better than the one adopted. In the parking problem, adding new fields might seem to be a solution until the group considers the possible alternatives of allowing fewer cars on campus or providing a shuttle bus service from distant fields to the campus. In other words, during this period, the group should avoid argument and be receptive toward all possible solutions.

The practice of "brainstorming," wherein the prime rule is that no critical or evaluative comment can be made on suggestions, is sometimes appropriate to the interchange of possible solutions. While of limited value in most practical discussions, the spirit of this method is helpful: that of searching for creative solutions and postponing critical evaluation in the interim.

It is in the next stage of discussion that evaluation takes place. If the criteria and the solutions suggested are clearly understood by all, it will be easy for the group to see, solution by solution, which criteria are met and which are violated. Such matching of solutions and criteria is the procedure for arriving at the best solution. There may be some argument and opinion, but we should always keep an open mind and show a willingness to listen to the thinking of others in the group. Our listening should be sympathetic and sensitive to the views of others. This is the essence of good discussion, remembering that we are engaged in deliberative thinking—which includes an appreciation of the facts and of views of others.

In reaching decisions and determining a course of action, most discussions follow the principle of *consensus,* in which the group comes to feel that it is in substantial agreement.[2] No vote is taken, particularly in public discussions such as a panel or symposium, or in a forum following one of these programs or following a lecture. If a vote is to be taken, parliamentary procedure—as discussed later in this chapter—is usually employed. Consensus does not imply unanimous agreement or that everyone in the group actually expresses his view.

The form of discussion may determine to what extent the group wishes to arrive at a specific decision or course of action. Discussion situations may be *public,* including the panel, symposium, debate, and forum or group; and *private,* including the conference, the interview, and conversation.

The *panel* is a commonly used form in which four or five persons sit in front of a larger audience and engage in problem-solving discussion. After they have finished, the group as a whole enters into the discussion in a *forum.* The *symposium* similarly involves several persons who discuss the topic in a prearranged order, with each person making a talk on a particular phase of the question, usually standing and facing the larger group. After they have spoken, there is a forum period. The *debate* is more formal and presents two or more persons who speak on opposite sides of a clearly defined proposition or issue. The debate is not typical discussion, in that it deals only with one solution (pro and con), and the speakers express their own opinions without yielding to the views of their "opponents."

Private discussion takes place chiefly in the conference, committee, interview, or social conversation. The chief distinguishing feature is that there is no audience, and everyone is an equal participant.

In most situations where a panel, symposium, or even the whole

[2] For a fuller treatment of the values and limitations of reaching agreement by consensus, cf. Harold P. Zelko, *Successful Conference and Discussion Techniques.* New York: McGraw-Hill, 1957. The various forms of public and private discussion and use of many specific methods are also discussed in detail in this book.

group is interested in discussing a problem or situation in the form of a question, it is not necessary to move through all the stages of the discussion process or to arrive at a decision. Usually such programs have a time limit, and it is important to keep within this. If the problem analysis requires more time than anticipated, this step should nevertheless be completed, even if it means that the group will not have sufficient opportunity to evaluate all the possible solutions. The leader and the group should use their best judgment in this respect.

Public discussions frequently take the form of a program in which it is important to select and word the topic carefully.

Stating the Topic

The individual, frequently the discussion leader, who has the responsibility for planning a discussion should give careful attention to the selection of a good topic. Sometimes the reason for the meeting itself provides the discussion topic. Once a general subject has been determined, it is important that it be carefully stated. A few specific rules implement this principle:

1. State the topic in question form.
2. Keep the question narrow enough so that it can be adequately discussed in the time available.
3. Phrase the question clearly.
4. Avoid an either-or question, unless a debate is being planned.
5. The topic should be problem-centered, not solution-centered.

Discussion topics should usually be phrased in a way that allows for a variety of solutions. A statement such as "How should we handle the problem of student drinking?" is better than "Should we forbid student drinking?" If we consider the time available, the topic "How should labor unions be regulated?" would be more difficult to discuss adequately than "What should be done about picketing?" A *debate* topic poses a specific plan or solution which requires that the debaters take one side or the other. Note the difference between the discussion topic and the debate topic in the following examples:

Discussion: "How can we best develop our trade with foreign countries?" or "What is the best solution to the foreign-trade problem?"

Debate: "Resolved: That we should follow a policy of high protective tariffs" or "Resolved: That we should follow a policy of free trade with foreign countries."

Outlining a Discussion

Most discussion meetings follow a pattern of organization similar to the problem-solving sequence. The leader bears the primary responsibility for keeping the discussion organized, but each member of the group should also make an analysis of the discussion topic and determine what should be said in each phase of the discussion. The outline is usually in question form. Whereas the public-speech outline expresses declaratively the points of the speaker, the discussion outline raises questions to be answered by the group. A guide for making a discussion outline form is shown below.[3]

Discussion Outline

Introduction
1. How can attention best be directed to the problem?
   a. What is its immediate relation to the group?
   b. How can it be defined?
2. How may the discussion participants best be introduced to the larger group?

The Problem
1. What is the problem?
2. How serious is the problem today?
3. What are its present manifestations?
4. When, and why, did it start?
5. What has been done about it?
6. Whom does it affect? By what standards will they judge solutions?

Possible Solutions
1. What relevant solutions can members of the group propose?
2. Are the solutions phrased tentatively, permitting wide latitude for combining, eliminating, or revising them in terms of standards of evaluation the group will apply?

[3] For a fuller treatment and examples of discussion outlines, *cf.* Henry Lee Ewbank and J. Jeffrey Auer, *Discussion and Debate,* Rev. New York: Appleton-Century-Crofts, 1951.

Evaluate and Choose Best Solution
1. Will this solution remedy the problem?
   a. Will it eliminate the causes of the problem?
   b. Is it merely a temporary expedient?
2. Are we sure this is the best solution?
   a. What advantages does it have over other solutions?
   b. Will it bring new disadvantages?
   c. Is it practical? Will it work?
   d. What evidence supports it?

Action
1. How can we put this solution into operation?
2. What definite plan of action should be adopted?

○ PARTICIPATION

All the principles of good speaking apply to discussion and conference. Careful analysis of the occasion and subject, determination of the purpose, coherent organization of the main points and questions to be covered, logical and interesting use of supporting materials, and all the other factors that contribute to effective delivery are parts of the discussion process. In addition, there are some special qualities of a good discussion speaker which should be singled out for special attention. These have to do chiefly with the fact that he is one of several participants, and they involve his mental approach as well as his manner of speaking: attitude, conciliation, brevity, directness, and listening.

Attitude

You should approach any situation in which you are to converse, discuss, or confer with others with an attitude of respect for their information, opinions, and feelings. Open-mindedness and a sense of humor are most important features. A dogmatically stated point made by one speaker may conflict with an equally dogmatic opinion held by another, and friction often results from such a clash of equally unbending points of view.

If new information is presented which shows your position to be wrong, be ready to change it, and let your sense of humor operate freely. If you continue to believe that you are right, however, do all

Teamwork . . .

Valuable and valued discussion participants are intent upon achieving the group's goals. Success depends upon maximum teamwork and thus upon each member's meeting his speaking and listening responsibilities including the responsibility for preparation. Depending on the leader, alone, for preparation and ideas is like sending a quarterback out to face the opposing team—alone.

you honestly can to maintain your position in the face of refutation and argument. But in your preparation and your participation, try to analyze the subject or problem clearly and anticipate that others will think differently. The effective member of a discussion or conference group maintains a happy balance of open-mindedness, patience, tolerance, and sense of humor.

Conciliation

Conciliation involves adapting your remarks to the opinions of others and sometimes conceding opposing points of view. It involves accepting some of the points of view of others in order to integrate them with your own and with the over-all conclusions of the whole group. It involves the principle of common ground—the attempt to arrive at common thinking, common feeling, common agreement with other people. When you are taking up a point of another speaker with whom you do not agree, it is well to keep in mind these specific principles of refutation and adaptation.

1. *Take issue with the other person objectively and conservatively.* Such expressions as "I disagree thoroughly," "I don't agree with a thing you say," or "You are entirely wrong" do not constitute the approach of the conciliatory speaker. Give your opponent some credit, find some area of agreement, and you will more likely gain his adherence to your point of view.

2. *Take issue with the point, not with the person who makes it.* Such statements as "Your position shows ignorance of the subject," "If you'd read the newspapers once in a while," and "There isn't an ounce of truth in what you say" will serve to antagonize both the person you are refuting and other members of the group.

3. *Restate the other person's point clearly and accurately.* Do not be vague or abstract regarding which of his points you are referring to. Do not overstate or exaggerate what has been said. Do not put words in your opponent's mouth. Adapt your remarks clearly and precisely to what he has said, not to your feelings about what he said.

4. *Your own position should be so stated as to relate to that of the other person.* If you are refuting something he has said, give whatever credit you can to his position and refer to points of agreement before you state your own position: "There is probably a great deal of value in our knowing the facts Mr. X has presented, and I agree

that the more we know the better we can plan; but it is my belief that. . . ."

5. *Strengthen your position or present your information with as much factual and interesting material as you can.* It is in refutation that you should make all possible use of evidence and supporting material in developing your point.

6. *Do not extend your discussion once your point is clearly understood by the audience.* Conclude your remarks by clearly re-stating your position and summarizing what has been said, especially if the point has taken several minutes or may be somewhat obscure, but always observe the principle of brevity and stay with your point in a discussion of any sort.

7. *Be tactful.* The tone of the group is greatly affected by an attitude that goes out of its way to offend and insult or one that makes an active effort to be pleasant. Tact involves sensing the mood and atmosphere of the group; using judgment in the frequency and length of one's remarks; maintaining an air of modesty rather than boastfulness; and practicing all the other virtues of refinement and culture.

Brevity

In conversation, interviews, group discussion, conferences, or any situation in which there are other participants, make your individual contributions brief and to the point. Normally, make only one point each time you contribute. In the average group, perhaps one to two minutes should be the maximum limit for each individual contribution. The long-winded bumbler who rambles on and on while someone else is waiting to speak is resented by his associates.

Directness

Good speech delivery in the group situation requires speaking that can be heard and understood by all present. Look at different people from time to time, but *always look at people*. The ceiling- or rug-gazer gets little respect from others. In a larger group, do not make the mistake of speaking only to the chairman or to your immediate neighbors. In a panel, look briefly at the colleague to whose point you are referring, but look more frequently at your audience.

Attentiveness

Good listeners are hard to find. Most of us have to train ourselves to appreciate the value of keeping silent, just as we have to train ourselves to be better speakers. The importance of listening in discussion is related to the principle of guarding against too much talking. Listening well has two values: conveyance to the speaker of a sense of your own interest in wanting to hear him; and the opportunity it provides you to analyze the views of others in the group. Taking advantage of this opportunity involves attentive listening, observing, and discerning the merits of the views advanced.

○ LEADERSHIP

The role of the leader in discussion involves a great deal more than merely sitting at the head of the table and allowing the participants to speak.[4] If the topic is interesting and stimulating, if the discussion is well organized, if the participants offer meaningful contributions, the leader should probably receive more credit than he often does. For good discussion is rarely accidental. Although each participant has many responsibilities, as has already been pointed out, the leader usually has more to do than anyone else. His responsibilities may be considered under the two headings of planning and leading.

Planning

The leader must carefully plan for whichever type of meeting he is to lead. Although his role is basically the same in all forms of discussion, it takes on different aspects for a panel-forum, a large public meeting, a committee meeting, or a staff conference. The leader should therefore plan in accordance with the type of meeting and program chosen. If, in addition, he is responsible for the choice of topic, he should give careful consideration to discharging this responsibility. In a public panel or symposium for which he is helping to organize the program and therefore to select panel members, he

---

[4] A comprehensive discussion of leadership, with specific application to the discussion process, is found in Franklyn S. Haiman, *Group Leadership and Democratic Action*. Boston: Houghton Mifflin, 1951.

From each his best . . .

The discussion leader should be selected for his knowledge of discussion principles and his ability to draw from each participant his best and most useful contributions. Effective leadership is not "showing off" or "running things"; it is stimulating, reminding, structuring, and guiding.

should try to invite people who are informed and whose points of view on the subject differ. One of the most common and most serious failures at this stage of planning for a public forum is the failure of the chairman to arrive at a proper understanding with each participant as to the point of view he will maintain, his relations with other speakers, and even the length of his speech or the total length of the program.

Planning also includes arranging for the meeting or conference facilities. This appears simple, but a chairman who has not planned properly may find himself at the last minute trying to fix the lights, locate chairs, blackboard, chalk, pointer, or extension cord, and arranging many other details which, as members of the audience, we usually take for granted. The room should be properly arranged, with the best possible visibility for the entire group, good hearing range, good lighting, and effective arrangement of the speakers and all physical details.

In a public discussion meeting, such as the panel or symposium, the participants should be in view of the group, preferably on a raised platform, and seated in a semicircle with the leader in the center. In a small conference or committee discussion, it is best to seat all the participants around a table facing one another.

Planning includes preparing a discussion outline which shows the major areas of the discussion topic, leading questions, and names of speakers in relation to the various phases of the topic. It is sometimes well, especially in a panel, to give all participants copies of the discussion outline and go over this prior to the discussion.

Leading

It is difficult here to consider all the problems of leading a discussion as they may arise in the many different types of meetings. The committee chairman may be a very informal leader; the staff-conference leader may sit back and let the members around the table do most of the talking while he exercises little control; the public-forum leader may be more formal in introducing members of the symposium and very alert in guiding discussion; the leader of a business meeting has to be concerned with parliamentary procedure in addition to all the other principles of discussion. But fundamentally every good discussion leader has to assume these functions:

1. Establish a pleasant relationship between himself and the group and maintain the same among members of the group.
2. Introduce the subject, topic, or problem.
3. Introduce members or participants.
4. Start and stimulate discussion.
5. Guide the discussion.
6. Encourage all members to participate.
7. Control the discussion.
8. Conciliate and resolve tension.
9. Use the blackboard, charts, or other visual aids (when appropriate).
10. Make transitions and summaries.

The leader's opening remarks should be brief and thought-provoking. He may explain the timeliness, importance, and purpose of the meeting, perhaps with a little humor to establish a pleasant mood. In a public discussion, the members of the panel should be introduced to the larger group. The discussion should be started by posing a question to a panel member or to the conference group or by introducing the first speaker in a symposium.

Stimulating, guiding, spreading, and controlling discussion are the truly challenging responsibilities of the discussion leader. He uses questions and leading statements to provoke thought and solicit contributions. He encourages everyone to participate, especially the person who is shy and retiring. He controls the few who want to speak all the time so that others are allowed to speak. He carefully guides the trend of the discussion through its most appropriate logical sequence. He does not allow too much time to be spent on any one phase of the subject. He makes transitions and summaries from time to time for the benefit of the group, so that the trend of the discussion is always clear. He intercedes in an argument between two people and resolves its resulting tension. Reduction of tension may be achieved by according both participants some credit for their points of view, by adroitly turning to another speaker, another phase of the subject, or by tactful humor.

○ PARLIAMENTARY PROCEDURE

When a group engages in problem-solving discussion and arrives at a best solution, the next step is that of putting the solution

Core of the democratic process . . .

First inquiry, then discussion, then parliamentary debate is the sequence
that lies at the core of the democratic process. A knowledge of the
technique and the *philosophy* of parliamentary procedure is necessary in
our professional and fraternal groups, our corporations, our legislatures,
our clubs, and even in our homes.

into practice. In our form of democracy, this is accomplished by persuasion, based on the findings of the group, and frequently in some kind of parliamentary body. A Senate committee engages in inquiry into problems like foreign aid, law enforcement, or educational needs, and then proposes legislation appropriate to those problems. A labor union committee inquires into the need for educating its members on grievance procedures and proposes a program. A committee of your student government tackles the problem of housing and reports its proposal. A fraternity group considers what to do about study hours. The members, convinced through their experiences in inquiry, now become advocates for a proposed solution; they are ready to debate, in a parliamentary situation, for or against a proposal or solution. Frequently, they may try to recreate that experience in the minds of their listeners and will be applying the problem-solving method of development in persuasion.

This relationship of discussion and parliamentary debate is the core of democratic procedures as we know and live them. Inquiry followed by discussion or debate are the fundamental tools with which people direct their own affairs.

It is therefore important to understand something about parliamentary procedures and, most of all, to understand the philosophy of parliamentary law. That philosophy may be stated thus: It is not the rules which are important, but the process of finding, quickly and fairly, the *intent* of the group. You will find that a working knowledge of the rules will help you cooperate with others to achieve group intent.

In the first place, parliamentary procedure provides a regular and fixed order for taking up the business of a meeting. It next provides rules which help the group to make decisions with regard to any item of business which comes before it. The purpose of parliamentary procedure, then, may be summarized as the provision of an orderly method for taking up business one issue at a time and in proper sequence, expediting the will of the majority, protecting the majority and the minority, and according equal rights to each member of the group.

The presiding officer of a business meeting is a combination of discussion leader, chairman of an assembly, and parliamentarian. He must be alert both to rules of procedure and to good discussion methods. A group which has been informally discussing a problem and its solution can crystallize its opinion and adopt a course of action by proposing the solution as a motion and taking action on it.

Forming a Permanent Organization

Most permanently organized groups conduct their meetings according to established parliamentary procedure. If a group of people decide to form a permament organization, they should proceed in the following order:

1. Call a preliminary meeting of interested persons.
2. Ask one member to preside and call the meeting to order.
3. Elect a temporary chairman and a temporary secretary.
4. Appoint a committee to draw up a constitution.
5. Call a later meeting at which the constitution committee submits a proposed constitution.
6. Adopt the constitution by considering it paragraph by paragraph, amending and discussing each section and article, but not voting on the acceptance of the various parts until the whole document has been considered and amended.
7. Elect permanent officers and hold meetings as provided in the constitution.

Order of Business

The proper sequence for conducting the business of the meeting is as follows:

1. Calling the meeting to order.
2. Reading of the minutes.
3. Reports of officers and standing committees.
4. Reports of special committees.
5. Unfinished business.
6. New business.
7. Adjournment.

Some Common Terms

There are some widely used terms of parliamentary procedure which should be remembered.

MEETING: A meeting is one convening of the group.

SESSION: A session is a series of meetings.

VOTING: Voting involves the indication by members of a position for or against the matter on the floor. Voting is usually oral, or *viva voce*. If this method is impractical, votes may be cast by show of hands or by standing. If the group wishes, voting may be by written ballot.

DIVISION: The term division is used when a voice vote is not clear and a show of hands is taken. Any member of the assembly may call for a division.

MAJORITY AND PLURALITY: A majority is more than half of the votes cast; a plurality is a vote in excess of that for any other one candidate or issue but less than half of the total (occurring most frequently in elections of officers). For example, in a body of 50 members, one candidate may receive 22 votes, the second 18, and the third 10—in which case there is no majority; another vote may then be taken on the two top candidates. Some motions require a two-thirds vote—that is, two-thirds of the members voting.

QUORUM: A quorum is the number of members necessary to transact business. This is usually determined by the constitution. If not specifically stated, a majority of the members constitutes a quorum.

GENERAL CONSENT: Many times the chairman will make a proposal, or a member will suggest a course of action, on which no vote is taken but the group's assent is assumed. The chair usually says, "If there is no objection . . .," and in the absence of objection he assumes general consent of the group. This practice often facilitates business.

Motions

Parliamentary procedure is a system of motions. The main business is placed before the group by a main motion, and it is out of the discussion, amendment, adoption, rejection, or postponement of this motion that other motions grow. In addition to the main motion, the various kinds of motions are classified as *subsidiary, privileged,* and *incidental;* and *renewal motions.*

It is well to remember that a knowledge of ways to use the various kinds of motions is often as vital to the members of the group as it is to the chairman. A common misconception about procedure is that the average member need not be concerned with it so long as the chairman knows what to do. But this is the very reason why many members of a group are not active participants but sit back wanting to contribute but not knowing just how. It is of course difficult to keep in one's head all the rules about motions, but everyone can remember the basic principles and then familiarize himself with a handbook on procedure in order to be able to consult it as a ready reference.[5] We cannot provide a complete discussion of all the motions here, but we shall look briefly at the various classifications of motions and then present a composite table.

It is well to be able to answer the following questions about each type of motion:

1. What is its purpose? What is the use of the motion? What will it accomplish? Most of the subsidiary and privileged motions affect the main motion by enhancing, retarding, or preventing its passage.

2. What is its precedence or rank? This has to do with the relation of the motion to other motions which may be on the floor or which may be made after it. Which motion has higher rank, or precedence? In the composite table, the motions are shown in order of rank, which means, for example, that the motion to refer to a committee would be acted upon before a motion to amend, even though the latter had been on the floor first.

3. Is a second required? Most motions require a second.

4. Is it debatable? In other words, can the motion be discussed, or must it be voted on as soon as proposed?

5. Is it amendable? May amendments be made to it, or must it be voted on in the form submitted?

6. What vote is required for passage? Does it require a majority or a two-thirds vote to be passed?

The main motion is the core around which most parliamentary

---

[5] Among the many handbooks available, the following are recommended: Joseph F. O'Brien, *Parliamentary Law for the Layman.* New York: Harper, 1952, for an interesting, clear, and complete treatment; O. G. Jones, *Senior Manual for Group Leadership—An Instant Guide to Parliamentary Procedure* New York: Appleton-Century-Crofts, 1934, for a good flash system showing all the motions for quick reference; and Henry M. Robert, *Rules of Order, Revised* Chicago: Scott, Foresman, 1950, for a generally accepted authoritative treatment.

procedure operates. It is made after a member has been recognized by the chair, when no prior business is on the floor. He may say, "Mr. Chairman, I move that we hold a dance." The wording should be clear and brief and should contain one central idea. Most of the business of a group centers around the discussion of main motions.

When parliamentary law is applied strictly, no discussion is permitted until after a main motion has been made and seconded, and then the discussion must deal directly with the motion before the group. However, this rule is often not observed, and members frequently find it advantageous to explain a situation or a point of view before making a motion setting forth some definite proposal. Even in formal groups, it is sometimes advisable to provide for a period of free discussion in which all conflicting points of view may be discussed and a general basis of agreement reached before any specific motion is presented. The proper procedure then is to move that the assembly resolve itself into a "committee of the whole." This motion has to be seconded and may then be adopted by a majority vote. While the committee of the whole is convened, parliamentary rules are suspended and only main motions and amendments to them, appeals from the decision of the chair, parliamentary inquiries, and questions of personal privilege are in order.

Among the *subsidiary motions* are the two which, with the main motion, are the most important to understand, the *motion to amend* and the *motion to commit* (refer to a committee). Joseph F. O'Brien wrote, in *Parliamentary Law for the Layman,* that in groups "of fairly small size and closely knit memberships, the only motions wherein actual proficiency is imperative are the main motion, the motion to amend, and the motion to commit."

The *motion to amend* is the means whereby a main motion is perfected by the group before it comes to a vote. It requires a second and is discussed and voted upon before further consideration is given to the main motion. If the motion is "that our organization petition the University administration to establish a University bookstore," it may be amended by adding something or deleting something or striking out any of the words and substituting another in its place. For example, a member might address the chair and move to amend the motion by striking out "University administration" and substituting "Board of Trustees." After the motion to amend has been debated and voted upon, if it is passed, the amended motion is up for consideration; if it is rejected, the original motion is up for further consideration. A motion to amend may, in turn, be amended by the same process, but no more than one primary and one secondary (i.e., amendment to the primary) amendment may be pending at the same time.

The *motion to commit* could very well apply to the example of the University bookstore. A member may perceive that the problem is not clear or that there may be a better solution. He might address the chair and move that the motion be referred to a committee for investigation, study, and recommendations. It is wise to specify *what* committee, and, if it is to be a special committee, how many shall serve on it and how the members are to be selected. The motion to commit usually includes instruction on when the committee is to report. The form might be: "Mr. Chairman, I move that this motion be referred to a committee of three, appointed by the chair, with instructions to report at our next meeting."

Other subsidiary motions consist of actions that may be taken on the main motion other than a direct vote for its acceptance or rejection. In the table that follows they are listed as: to postpone indefinitely (which is an indirect way of defeating the main motion and sometimes may win the votes of some who would not vote against it directly); to amend (as previously discussed); to refer to committee (as previously discussed); to postpone to a specifically stated time (when it will come up again as a main item, taking precedence over other questions); to limit or extend the time allowed for debate; to proceed to a vote on the main question (for which purpose the procedure is to "move the previous question"); and to table the motion under consideration (which cannot then be taken up until another motion is made to take it from the table).

As the name implies, subsidiary motions are attached to the main motion and therefore may be introduced while the main motion is under discussion. They take precedence over it and must be disposed of by a vote before any further discussion of the main motion is permitted. If a subsidiary motion is defeated, the main motion is again before the house; if a subsidiary motion is adopted, the main motion is handled in accordance with the intent of the subsidiary motion.

Privileged motions consist of all points by which the welfare of individuals or of the group is protected. For this reason, a member

Chart of Parliamentary Motions

The motions are listed in order of rank or precedence, with the highest motion on the list having highest rank down to the main motion. Incidental motions have no order of precedence among themselves but are considered when made, with precedence over the motion they relate to.

Motion	Debatable?	Amendable?	Vote required?	Second required?	Interrupt speaker?
PRIVILEGED					
Fix time to which to adjourn (when other business pending)	No	Yes	Majority	Yes	No
Adjourn (when unqualified and time for next meeting is set)	No	No	Majority	Yes	No
Take a recess (when other business is pending)	No	Yes	Majority	Yes	No
Raise question of privilege	No	No	Chair decides	No	Yes
Call for orders of the day	No	No	Chair decides	No	Yes
SUBSIDIARY					
Lay on the table	No	No	Majority	Yes	No
Previous question (end debate)	No	No	Two thirds	Yes	No
Limit or extend debate	No	Yes	Two thirds	Yes	No
Postpone to definite time	Yes	Yes	Majority	Yes	No
Commit or refer to committee	Yes	Yes	Majority	Yes	No
Amend	Yes	Yes	Majority	Yes	No
Postpone indefinitely	Yes	No	Majority	Yes	No
MAIN MOTION	Yes	Yes	Majority	Yes	No
INCIDENTAL					
Appeal	Yes	No	Majority	Yes	Yes
Division of assembly	No	No	Chair decides	No	No
Division of question	No	Yes	Majority	No	No
Withdraw a motion	No	No	Majority	No	No
Point of order	No	No	Chair decides	No	Yes
Suspend rules	No	No	Two thirds	Yes	No
Object to consideration	No	No	Two thirds	No	Yes
Parliamentary inquiry	No	No	Chair decides	No	Yes
RENEWAL					
Take from the table	No	No	Majority	Yes	No
Reconsider	Yes	No	Majority	Yes	Yes
Rescind, repeal	Yes	Yes	Two thirds	Yes	No

may secure the floor at any time by addressing the chair and asking permission to "raise a question of privilege." If a member feels that the time has come for consideration of a motion that has been postponed to a definite time, he "calls for the orders of the day." The secretary then examines the record to see whether the time has come when a postponed question must be taken up.

Motions to take a recess or to adjourn are privileged motions and may be made whenever another member is not speaking. A question of personal privilege may be made at any time, even though a member interrupts a speaker to make it. Such a question would be raised if one member were insulted by a speaker, or if the public-address system failed to work so that the speaker could not be heard, or for any other similar reason requiring immediate decision.

Incidental motions cover a number of miscellaneous items concerning which the chairman may give a ruling or may call for a vote by the group. Included among them is a request for a secret ballot (instead of a vote by a show of hands); the division of a motion into two parts for separate voting on each; an appeal from a decision rendered by the chairman; objection to consideration of a question; an inquiry concerning parliamentary procedure; a request for further information on a matter being discussed, or a request for permission to withdraw or modify a motion which the speaker himself has submitted.

Renewal motions are those to reconsider a motion that has been acted upon or to rescind a motion that has been adopted, or to take from the table a motion that has been "tabled."

○ CONCLUSION

This chapter has pointed out the close relation between discussion principles and the general principles of effective speech. Although all principles of good speaking apply with certain adaptations to discussion, there are some, such as proper attitude, conciliation, brevity, directness, and listening which should be especially developed for discussion purposes. We have emphasized the application of all these principles to problem-solving in a cooperative group effort. The need for an attitude of inquiry and open-mindedness is essential.

When you serve as discussion chairman, you will be concerned with proper selection and wording of the topic as a question, and the planning and development of the discussion outline as a guide for leading the group, and your leadership responsibilities include those of stimulating, spreading, and guiding the participation of the group members. As a participant, your responsibility is to help the leader accomplish these objectives and be a cooperative and enthusiastic member.

When business is conducted and decisions are reached under the rules of parliamentary procedure, the members as well as the person in the chair need to be familiar with the basic rules and the philosophy behind them.

EXERCISES

Questions for Discussion

1. In what ways are the general principles of effective speech communication applicable to discussion?

2. Do you think that the classification of discussion as *public* and *private* is a logical one? What are the bases of this classification and the distinguishing characteristics of each form?

3. What are the forms of public discussion? Distinguish among them. In which one would it be easiest for you to participate? Why?

4. In selecting a discussion topic, what principles are applicable that are different from those applicable to selecting a topic for a speech? How should the discussion topic be worded?

5. Do you think that leadership or participation is the more important for you to learn? Consider this from the standpoint of your abilities and your future use of the discussion process.

6. What are the basic requirements of problem-solving discussion?

Projects for Speaking and Writing

1. Bring to class prepared statements of five discussion topics which you think would be appropriate for class discussion projects.

2. Prepare a discussion outline for one discussion topic showing the sequence to be followed and key questions you might use as a leader. Plan to make a two-minute introductory statement which would be appropriate in starting the discussion of the topic.

3. With the instructor's aid, select a topic and choose four members of the class to participate in a panel discussion of which you will be the chairman. Meet with the group, and determine which panel members will

respond to certain questions and discuss major areas of the subject. Be prepared to lead the discussion for about twenty minutes, then open the topic to the entire class for a forum and group-discussion period.

4. Plan a program similar to that described in the preceding exercise, but as a symposium in which each participant will make a four-minute talk on some phase of the topic. Make a discussion outline, then meet with the members of your group and decide the sequence of speaking, who will handle each phase of the subject, and how the speeches will fit together into an over-all discussion of the entire subject. Each speaker will prepare an outline of his own talk, showing as his specific purpose the point of view he will maintain and also showing how he plans to adapt to preceding speakers in his introduction as well as throughout his talk.

5. Make an analysis of the ways in which a discussion leader handled a program which you attended, showing his assets and weaknesses.

6. Analyze a discussion program you have heard, either personally or on radio or television, covering its organization, topic, speaker participation and adaptation, and leadership.

7. Organize the class into a business meeting run under rules of parliamentary procedure. Bring to class several ideas which you will present as main motions. Practice addressing the chair and making main motions. Let the chairman practice proper restatement of the motion to the group.

8. Hold a practice session in which members of the group offer various kinds of amendments to main motions. Keep the discussion of the amendments to a minimum so that the greater part of the practice can be on the proper phrasing of and action on amendments.

9. Plan a session of the class in which a controversial subject is up for discussion and opposite points of view are expressed. In answering a point of another speaker with whom you disagree, practice the principles of conciliation as discussed in this chapter. A formal debate, with two persons upholding each side of the proposition, might be the basis for this practice session.

Chapter 16

Special Applications

THE PURPOSE OF THIS BOOK has been to help you prepare yourself for a lifetime of speaking activities. As Chapter 17 indicates, there is much more to learn and many specialized areas of speech yet to be studied. In this chapter the suggestions made are to help you in some of the more common speech activities which you encounter as a student, as citizen, and as a worker in the community. The basic principles which you have been studying are adaptable to any kind of speaking situation you may encounter. Our aim here is simply to indicate what kinds of adaptation may be made (1) when you are asked to preside over a public meeting or to introduce a speaker; (2) in your everyday conversation; (3) in the job-interviews you will shortly be engaged in, and in other interviews; (4) in the kinds of conferences you will take part in on the job; and (5) when you have occasion to write and to read a speech or report.

○ THE JOB OF THE CHAIRMAN

You may be elected president of your fraternity, the PTA, or the Kiwanis Club, or even your town council; or you may be asked to preside over a meeting of your church, or of parents who wish to discuss scouting, or little league baseball or plans for a community swimming pool.[1] Sociologists tell us that in any sizable community

[1] For detailed treatment of the duties of a presiding officer, *cf.* Harry Simmons, *How to Run a Club.* New York: Harper, 1955; and Frank Snell, *How to Hold a Better Meeting.* Harper, 1958.

there are more groups than there are individuals. Many of these groups are wholly informal (family, friends, bridge clubs, etc.); but many of them require a presiding officer. Whether or not a meeting is productive depends initially upon the skill of the chairman. This is just as true of the small discussion group that meets in a private home once a month as it is of the annual stockholders' meeting of a large corporation. The three major responsibilities of any chairman are planning, presiding, and introducing speakers.

Planning

Preliminary arrangements for most meetings need not be elaborate; but if they are neglected confusion results and both the neglect and the confusion are depressing to speakers and discouraging to listeners. The chairman should manifest an air of calm assurance—and he can do this only if he actually is efficient in having the necessary details properly arranged.

1. *The meeting place.* Ideally, it should be just large enough—neither too large nor too small—for the size of the group. A bit of crowding is preferable to many empty seats. If twenty people are seated in a room that just holds twenty, there is a general feeling that the meeting is well attended; but if those same twenty people are scattered in an auditorium that seats 150, the atmosphere suggests lack of interest. Besides, it is far easier for a speaker to talk with his audience when it is seated close together and close to him. Unless cleanliness, orderliness, and proper heating, lighting, and ventilation may be taken for granted, the chairman should insure them by preliminary arrangements. A disordered, dark, and stuffy (or cold) meeting place gets any gathering off to a very bad start.

2. *Facilities.* If a speaker's rostrum, or blackboard, or easel chart, or slide projector is needed, the chairman should make sure it is on hand. If there are to be several speakers for a large gathering, the chairs should be arranged on the stage, where a pitcher of water and glasses alongside the lectern will often be welcome.

3. *Public address system.* If the audience numbers more than 200, a public address system may be required. Since loudspeakers and microphones need to be in perfect adjustment, they should be checked in advance of the meeting. If the speech is to be recorded, the recorder should be in place, perhaps on a table in front of the stage, and with

an experienced operator in charge. The microphone should be multi-directional and sufficiently sensitive so the speaker will not need to handcuff himself to it. If a lapel microphone is available, this will give the speaker maximum freedom of movement. If the speaker is unfamiliar with microphones, the chairman should reassure him that he may speak normally, perhaps with some special care to articulate carefully.

4. *Placement of speakers.* If there are several speakers, for a large meeting, the chairman should seat himself in the middle, but leave available to them the space behind the rostrum. Order of speaking may depend on the topics of the speakers; but the most important speaker is always the *last* on the program.

5. *Preliminary arrangements with speakers.* When speakers are invited, they should be told the nature of the audience and of the occasion, the expected size of the audience, the purpose the talk is to serve, and how long it should be. If there are to be several brief talks, to be followed by a longer one, the preliminary speakers should be informed politely but firmly how much time each is to have, and requested to conform strictly to the time limit. Speakers should be met by the chairman at the door as they arrive and treated with the courteous attention appropriate to honored guests.

Presiding

Whether the meeting is large or small, formal or informal, much of its success depends upon how well the chairman presides. The job is not too difficult, but it needs to be done with firm assurance and efficiency. Many meetings fail because of the bumbling inefficiency and self-consciousness of unskilled presiding officers. The sequence of duties is as follows:

1. *Start the meeting on time*—either precisely at the time announced, or within five or ten minutes. If there is need for a delay, an explanation should be made to the audience. If an adjournment time has been announced, try to adjourn the meeting on time.

2. *Establish an appropriate atmosphere with your opening remarks.* Once again, a calm assurance—a signal to the audience that the situation is being well handled by a chairman who knows his job—is the basic requirement. The audience should be greeted with warm friendliness. Reference to the reason for the meeting may be appro-

priate. The chairman is expected to establish the tone for the meeting, whether it is to be one of deep seriousness, of informal good fellowship, or of gay and relaxed enjoyment.

3. *Serve the essential needs of both speakers and listeners.* The speakers may appreciate a prearranged system of signaling to them when their allotted time is about to expire. The audience is entitled to protection from speakers who blatantly ignore time-limitations. Sometimes the chairman is obliged to interrupt a speaker to tell him pleasantly but firmly that his time is up. This may be embarrassing, but need not be if prior to the meeting the chairman has warned the speakers that each will be held strictly to the agreed-upon time limitations.

4. *Plan appropriate remarks between speeches.* These should normally take the form of a complimentary remark on the speech just ended, with a transitional sentence introducing the next speaker. At a banquet, when the chairman is serving as toastmaster, brief humorous stories often make appropriate interludes, provided they fit the occasion, relate to the speeches, and are well told.

Introducing Speakers

Speeches of introduction are often so ludicrously ineffective that experienced public speakers (and audiences) will be deeply grateful for simple efficiency in this role. Actually, the mistakes that are commonly made ought to be easily avoided. What needs to be done is as follows:

1. *Remember that the speech belongs to the speaker, not to the chairman.* The introduction should be brief (seldom more than two minutes) and should *not* summarize the chairman's views on the topic the speaker is to discuss. Your job is to present the speaker to his audience, briefly, directly, and with a respectful cordiality that will help make them eager to hear him and his message.

2. *Be prepared to say what needs to be said.* It is disconcerting to a speaker to be asked, a few moments before his speech, "What do you want me to say about you?" The chairman should take care to have well in advance, from the speaker, from his associates, or perhaps from his secretary, the kind of information which establishes the speaker's authority to speak on the subject. This may include his education, travel, and experience with the problem to be discussed. If he

has written a number of books, it is appropriate to refer to him as a "distinguished author," and to cite the titles of such of his books as are appropriate to the subject. The timeliness and importance of the topic may be mentioned—but, again, carefully avoiding expression of opinion on the subject, for this is the job of the speaker, not of the chairman.

3. *Avoid saying what ought not to be said.* The chief thing to avoid is describing the speaker as a "good speaker," or declaring that he is entertaining, or a master of platform arts. If he speaks well, the audience will soon discover the fact. To announce in advance that he is a skilled performer centers attention on his performance and interferes with his communication of ideas. Neither should the introduction outline the points he will make—nor be an admonitory lecture on what he ought to say. There should never be an apology for the smallness of the audience; however, if circumstances such as a blizzard have reduced the number well below expectations, it might be appropriate to explain that many wished to hear the speaker, but have been prevented from coming.

4. *Close the meeting appropriately.* What is often most appropriate is a brief but sincere statement of appreciation. If the speaker has presented one side of a controversial issue, it might be appropriate to thank him for expressing his views and to announce that in a subsequent meeting the other side of the question will be discussed. If a question-forum period is to follow the talk, the chairman's duty is to insure that a first question is secured quickly and readily. If no one immediately rises with a question, the chairman should turn to the speaker and ask a question himself. If the gathering is small, the chairman then retires to his seat and the speaker receives and deals with subsequent questions directly. If the audience is large, it is more courteous for the chairman to receive the questions as they are offered, to restate them clearly enough so everyone will hear, then turn the question over to the speaker.

As will readily be seen from the foregoing pages, the varied responsibilities of a chairman are in reality simple and natural. There would seem to be no need to review them—except that everyday observation demonstrates how badly the job of presiding and introducing speakers is often bungled. Anyone with reasonable poise and clear-mindedness should be able to preside over meetings with unobtrusive effectiveness. You can do so if you will observe the simple but essential directions which have been presented.

○ **CONVERSATION**

In the preceding chapters, you have been reminded from time to time that all the principles of good speech apply with proper adaptation to social conversation. Conversation is so varied that it is difficult to lay down any set prescriptions for it. It may consist of two friends chatting briefly on a street or bus, or of a dozen people gathered in relative formality to talk seriously about a new book or a current political campaign. It could be between two lovers exchanging ideas on plans for their future life together, or two businessmen arguing a matter of business ethics. It could be in the form of "kicking ideas around" or of analytical or persuasive discussion of them. In other words, the situations, the purposes, and the content of conversations vary widely. But there is almost as wide a variation in public speaking —which may range from a score of alumni hearing a humorous recital of their collegiate escapades at a reunion dinner, to an hour-long lecture to 5,000 people on conditions in Soviet Russia or a nationwide televised debate between rival candidates for the presidency.

What we have been concerned with in this book is to help you to attain skill in analyzing what you plan to talk about, to determine what is true about it and what your convictions concerning it may be; in analyzing the occasion and the listeners who will hear your talk, so that you may properly develop the means of making your ideas effective; and of organizing, illustrating, and supporting what you have to say so that it will be clearly understood, interesting, and attractive or appealing to those whom you seek to influence. All these skills are essential not only in public speaking and in formalized group discussions but also in social conversation.[2]

As a brief guide, we suggest the following cautions:

1. *A good conversationalist pays careful attention to all his listeners.* He tries to observe their reactions to what he is saying. If he meets strong opposition, he tries quickly to analyze the reasons, which

---

[2] For a detailed study of conversation, *cf. Conversation: The Development and Expression of Personality,* by Robert T. Oliver. Springfield, Ill.: Charles C Thomas, 1961.

quite probably relate less to what he says than to his manner of saying it. He should be quick to modify his manner and to approach topics with respectful consideration for the sincerity of the views of others who are present.

2. *A good conversationalist is sensitive to the desires of the group.* It may be that the topic he introduces is obviously of no interest to the others. In this case, he will either drop it, and find what the group does wish to talk about; or, if the topic is one he feels ought to be discussed, he will try to make it interesting by linking it to subjects in which they do feel a present interest. Similarly, if the others are in a mood for frivolity, he will not introduce a serious or argumentative note—at least not without successfully maneuvering a transition of mood to the one his topic calls for.

3. *A good conversationalist yields the floor readily to others.* There is always a danger that exuberance of mood or determined intensity of feeling about a topic may lead one conversationalist to seize the floor and to pour forth what he has to say with little awareness that others present also wish to express themselves. An extreme egotist is seldom a good conversationalist. He may be a good entertainer at such times as he can dominate a group, but this kind of entertainment is not true conversation—which always requires give and take and the exchange of ideas. Sensitivity to the feelings of others is essential. The chapter on Listening should be reviewed if you have any suspicion that you may talk longer or more often than you should.

4. *A good conversationalist will try to abide by the principle that the purpose of conversation is to engage the full participation of all present.* On occasion, even lengthy monologues are appropriate, as when someone has had a genuinely interesting experience the others are eager to hear about. But even in such instances, it is wise to be brief, and to suggest a ready willingness to cut off your remarks quickly. If the others really do want you to keep on talking, they will see that you do by asking questions. The chances are very great that your best course of action is to lead as quickly as you can from your experience to that of others. For example, if you are telling about an evening you had in a Paris nightclub, try to get to the point quickly, then add that this reminds you of the local night spot, thus inviting others to relate some of their own homebound experiences. If they are eager to know more of Paris, they will ask you; there is no need for you to force the issue.

Conversation is talk, and talk has been the subject of this entire book. There is no principle of communicative speech that does not apply when you gather for social chit-chat. The relaxed and informal character of conversation encourages you to speak freely and without tension; but it also permits you to engage in many violations of clarity and even of simple good taste. A good conversationalist is always so highly regarded that it is worth a great deal of concentrated attention to try to master the art. And it is well to remember that the foundation of success in it is to be deeply and broadly interested in other people, not immersed in your own feelings and ideas. As we have said in other connections, the chief general requirements are self-respect and respect for others. Out of this combination, healthful social relations are built.

◯ INTERVIEWS

An interview is a purposive conversation between two people, sometimes with a third (perhaps a secretary) present largely to record the proceedings. Examples are interviews between a lawyer and his client, or a doctor and his patient. You may have had an interview with your professor, to seek his counsel about your course of study, or with the Dean, perhaps to discuss your academic record, or with an athletic coach, perhaps to determine whether you should try out for the team. A significant interview that most college students have during the spring term of their senior year is with a prospective employer. In fact, typically, seniors may have interviews with several different employers in the process of deciding on a proper job.

The job-seeking interview is so important that special consideration must be given to its requirements. For it, as for all interviews, it is necessary to make careful preparation. You should have clearly in mind the precise purpose you wish to accomplish. You should think carefully about the other person, to decide what he will want to achieve by the interview, and how he will probably want to handle it. Preview what you will need to know, so that you have both the facts and your ideas about them readily in mind. You should dress appropriately, be at the appointed place on time, and demonstrate poise, ease, confidence, and respect for the other person as you talk.

In a job interview, it is probable that the prospective employer will want to take the lead in introducing topics for discussion. You

Not hit or miss . . .

In an interview—as in any other speaking—you have a communicative goal: a specific desired response from the interviewer. As with public speaking, appropriate forethought and careful preparation will increase your confidence and probability of success.

should be prepared to answer his questions concisely and directly, and should watch for cues in his manner as to whether your answers are either too brief or too lengthy. It may be that he wants to determine how well you think on your own, without too much guidance, in which case he may ask extremely "open-end" questions—such as, "What are you most interested in?" It is wise in preparing for a job interview to have some ideas about what your life-goals are, what kinds of work you most want to do. In this kind of statement it is appropriate to refer with due modesty to your being prepared to undertake particular kinds of responsibility.

In general, however, it is worthy of emphasis that you should not talk specifically about your qualifications—except in direct answer to questions. The presumption is that the interviewer will already have a summary of your general training and will have, or will secure, statements from teachers or others about your abilities. What is most important is to demonstrate that you are interested in the company he represents—that you know something about it, that you appreciate its possibilities, opportunities, and requirements. It is proper for you to ask him questions that will both reveal your understanding of the company and will elicit particularized information you have been unable to locate in your research on it.

You should not go into any interview "to find out what will happen." If you are summoned by the Dean to discuss your college record, you know whether it is good or bad, and whether you are to be praised or reprimanded. In the latter case, it is well to have in mind remedial measures which you plan to put into effect. If you are to interview your academic adviser about your course of study, you should identify in advance the problems that need to be solved, and distinguish between the decisions you will have to make yourself and those on which you will need his counsel or perhaps his decision. In a job interview, it is folly to fail in advance to find out all you can about the company and about specific areas of its work in which you would like to engage. So many people appear at interviews poorly prepared that you will surely make an excellent impression if you simply adhere to the simple but essential principles which we have briefly indicated.

The final consideration is when and how to terminate the interview. This will be done on the initiative of the person by whom you are being interviewed. In most cases he will give a small but definite cue that he thinks the time has come for it to end. You will do well to watch for a tendency on his part to alter his posture, lean forward slightly, and seem to be about to rise, or to listen meaningfully to his words, which may hint that in his view the purpose of the interview has been accomplished. In either case, it is your cue to rise promptly, thank him for his interest, and leave.

○ CONFERENCES

As soon as you enter upon a job, whether teaching school or in business, you will very likely be asked to participate in conferences. A conference differs from public discussion, as described in Chapter 15, in several significant ways.[3] First, it is private—not intended to influence an audience but to deal with problems of concern to the conferees. Second, it is often not devoted to a single problem but may cover several. Third, the use of the process will vary with the nature of the decision to be reached and the methods favored by the leader. The supervisor who calls it may present alternative solutions and seek the counsel of the group on which should be put in effect. At other times a conference may be called to determine the cause of some difficulty—a slowdown in production, or a spirit of dissatisfaction on the part of some employees, or a slackening of consumer demand for a product. Fourth, in a typical conference the leader frequently is in a position of authority over the others and is seeking their advice, rather than engaging as an equal in consideration of the problem before the group.

What you should expect when you attend a conference is that before it is called you will have been informed of its purpose and perhaps specifically of the part you are to play in it. You may be advised that you will be asked for a report on your work, or on some aspect of it. Even if not so advised, you had best have your state of affairs clearly in mind, so that if the question of what you are doing comes up you will be well prepared to account for the area of your responsibility.

Many conferences are called primarily for the purpose of disseminating information that the conferees should have. It is well to listen carefully and to ask questions if clarification is needed. Other conferences may be in the form of committee meetings of co-equal

[3] For details, cf. *Successful Conference and Discussion Techniques,* by Harold P. Zelko. New York: McGraw-Hill, 1957.

Conference groups may be small or large. The small group above has no leader, but its purposes are clear in the minds of each member because it is meeting as a committee of a larger conference. The small size of the group permits easy and rapid interaction among its members. In the larger group below, both the atmosphere and the proceedings are somewhat more formal, and as a result interaction is necessarily slower. The chairman has succeeded, however, in making the participants feel both relaxed and attentive.

participants, in which problems are discussed and recommendations for their solution are to be sought. Here the requirements are very much the same as in a small group discussion.

In the conference, as in all speaker-listener situations, rapport and circularity of response are essential. Your attitude should be one of interest in what others have to present and of a willing acceptance of responsibility to make your own contributions. Often it is necessary to exercise special care to suggest what you have in mind and yet show regard for the feelings of others who are present. Because a conference usually involves people who are working at parallel tasks, there are likely to be some competitive feelings and personal sensitivity. Interpersonal conflicts may be avoided by such an approach as indicating that what you have to say is based solely on your own observation, or perhaps upon a body of facts you have carefully gathered and evaluated. In any event, a conference is no place in which to suggest by word or manner a criticism of the competency or motives of others who are present. What is needed is teamwork and cooperation.

○ THE MANUSCRIPT SPEECH

The emphasis throughout this book has been upon extemporaneous speaking: that is, careful preparation of the ideas and their organization, using the language that reflects the immediacy of the speaking situation. This is the kind of speaking which is vastly to be preferred as a vehicle for learning the varied skills and insights needed in communicative speech. It is also the kind of speaking that is almost always done on the various community occasions when you may be asked to speak.

Nevertheless, in twentieth-century America the manuscript speech has an important place. You may be asked to present a written report to your class or to your professional fraternity. If you are to give a talk over the radio, almost certainly you will write and then read it. On television, you may well be obliged to write out your talk, whether you then read it (perhaps from a teleprompter) or extemporize with the written text in mind as a guide. If you enter a profession or do research in a natural science, you may be invited to present a "paper" (actually a written speech) at a convention. On formal occasions of some types—typically in a eulogy at a memorial service, at a club meeting commemorating a deceased member, or even when awards are being presented—it is common for the talks to be written and read.

Many lawyers write out extensive briefs, in effect summarized speeches, which insure that the facts and the law are properly explored and interpreted, and in some courtroom speaking, especially before a judge, they may follow these briefs rather closely in their extemporaneous speaking. Many ministers write out their sermons, some to read them, some to extemporize from the written text before them. Finally, executives in prominent positions often use written speech texts, partly to insure that they do not speak unwisely on crucial issues, partly to assist the press in quoting them accurately, and sometimes to have the complete text available for publication.

These are some of the reasons why skill in composing and reading of manuscript speeches is likely to be useful to many who expect to enter the professions or who may play increasingly important roles in corporate and community life. There is still another reason which applies to all of us. Extemporaneous speaking has above all the virtue of immediate adaptability to a live audience situation; its chief demerit is that it does not help greatly (and may actually hamper) the development of stylistic excellence. The development of compelling paragraphs, the skillful transition from one idea to another, the sweeping progression of an idea through successive stages to a culminating climax, and the choice of exactly the right words and phrases are all qualities of style that are best developed at the writing desk, where time is available for careful thinking and for second thoughts on better ways of phrasing.

Every writer has a full wastepaper basket, reflecting the number of times he has to rewrite in order to achieve a final composition that shows marks of naturalness and the inevitability of precisely the right words in the right order. Speakers seldom have this kind of opportunity *as speakers*—though nothing prevents them from parallel development as writers. But speaking itself, with all its extemporaneous liveliness and seeming spontaneity, can profit from experience in stating and restating ideas until they finally are cast into the most effective form.

Even speeches which are to be presented in a genuinely extemporaneous manner may, on occasion, properly be written out in advance. In this case, the writer of the speech develops with far greater care than he could by any other means precision of structure, a parallelism and vividness of imagery, and a cogency of concise statement.

He has time to meditate upon turns of phrasing, upon metaphors and similes, upon witticisms and fresh ways of restating common ideas. When he then rises to deliver his talk, not by reading it, and not from memory, his mind is nonetheless prepared to utilize qualities of communicative speech which otherwise would be unattainable. Much of the objection to memorized speeches derives from the fact that they cannot possibly be immediately shaped to the atmosphere and events of the precise situation in which they are presented. Aside from this, many other objections arise from their being poorly written and poorly presented. If it is complained about a speech that it sounds "like an essay trying to stand on its hind legs," the complaint is not due alone to its having been written and memorized, but in part also to the fact that it was not written with the directness and spontaneous style of good talk. Once again, for students of speech, whose primary business is to acquire qualities of communicative speaking, our advice very strongly is to avoid written speeches and to follow strictly the extemporaneous methods of preparation that have been developed in the preceding chapters. Nevertheless, there are occasions when a speech should be written, and some occasions when it also should be read. To help you to prepare for such occasions, the following counsel is suggested.

Writing the Manuscript

The principles of good organization and the methods of achieving clarity, purposiveness, and interest that have been discussed in connection with extemporaneous speaking also apply directly to the writing of a manuscript speech. It is highly advisable to cultivate the ability to "talk your ideas" onto paper. Many people find their thinking processes inhibited when they sit at a typewriter or take up a pen. The important consideration is to know clearly what you want to communicate, then (with your knowledge, your purpose, and your expected readers in mind) say it. Theoretically, there is no reason why writing should be any harder than speaking. If it is more difficult, it is because when you put words on paper, they stare back at you; you can see what you have just said. If it is confused, or inexact, weak, or incomplete, falling far short of what you intended, these factors naturally concern you and may arouse a positive fear of putting down other words to follow them. The problem, however, is not that writing is difficult. The problem is that you have found yourself out. You know, now, that your ideas are not as clear, or precise, or well-founded as you had fondly thought them to be. If, on the other hand, the ideas you write down do make good sequential sense, the ability to look at them should be a positive help in moving forward with the further development of your thinking. Nothing and nobody can put ideas into your head except yourself—through your own reading, observing, listening, and thinking. But after you do have materials worthy of development, the following suggestions may help:

1. *Start with an outline.* Chapter 6 is just as pertinent a guide to writing a speech as to extemporaneous speaking. You have to know what you intend to do, and how you are to accomplish it, before you can do it. Without a plan you are as helpless as would be a ship's captain setting out to cross the ocean with neither a chart nor a compass.

2. *Develop your plan to accord with your purpose, your audience, and the length of the speech.* For a twenty-minute talk to be given to your local club on the occasion of your election to the presidency, you will have to consider carefully what must or should be included, and how much time (or space) can be allotted to each portion of it. Then you can block out your materials to serve as a guide in the writing.

3. *Try to write with an oral style.* This is difficult, for the tendency is to be more formal in writing than in speaking. It may help to imagine you are writing the speech as a letter to a close friend. It may help to think of yourself as conversing with a friend, and putting down on paper the words and phrases you would speak. Here a review of the section on style in Chapter 8 will be useful.

4. *Plan to rewrite your draft, perhaps several times.* The best of professional writers do a great deal of rewriting; it is highly presumptuous for an amateur to think he himself need not do so. President Franklin D. Roosevelt, who was famous for the warmly intimate and personal style of his "fireside chats," and who (despite his corps of speech-writers) did a great deal of work himself on the polishing of his speeches, often revised a particular speech six or eight times— always in the effort to make it sound more spontaneous and conversationally direct. It is helpful to read your speech manuscript aloud, trying to use the natural rhythms of spoken sentences; wherever it is difficult to do this, the passage should be revised.

○ SPEAKING FROM MANUSCRIPT

Reading a speech that you have written requires all the qualities of good extemporaneous speaking style, plus the ability to "pick up" from the page what is written there. The manuscript stands between you and the listeners and can be a substantial barrier to communication. On the other hand, you will recall that in Chapter 1 we discussed various ways of converting barriers into bonds. The fact that you have gone to the trouble of writing out your speech is a guarantee to the audience that you have taken the speaking occasion seriously and that your intention is to give them your best. You should not permit the use of the manuscript further to suggest that, perhaps, you are afraid to trust yourself to speak extemporaneously. You will profit from the good effects and avoid the bad ones if you are so familiar with your manuscript that you can read from it with great ease and not remain bound to the text. Often it is wise to insert an extemporaneous addition from time to time, particularly as a method of bringing the present audience situation directly into your speech. The following specific suggestions may help you:

1. *Think of your written manuscript as a sequential development of ideas.* In other words, do not think of it as pages of words. Be idea-conscious, not word-conscious.

2. *Be thoroughly familiar with your manuscript.* Actual memorization of it may be impractical—and even if you do memorize it, you should still follow the mode of reading from it. It is not difficult, however, to become so closely familiar with the speech as written that you know where on a page a new idea begins, where transitions are located, where important points of emphasis appear. The speech should be typed up in such a manner that each new page starts with a new paragraph.

3. *Underlining or marginal marks may be used to help you note what you intend to emphasize.*

4. *Keep in mind that your function is to communicate.* Most faults in the presentation of manuscript speeches result from the style of reading them—as though the speaker were reading to himself. Your mind, and therefore your voice and manner, should propel your words out toward the audience, to reach them and bring them into the communicative process. Your voice and manner should reflect the urgency to communicate your ideas. What sometimes happens is that the de-

sire to communicate your message has been substantially satisfied in the writing of it; then, when you come to read it, the communicative fire has burned out. As a matter of fact, whatever work you have done up to this point, nothing constructive happens to the audience except as it is carried to them by your presentation. If you stand with your eyes glued to the pages and your voice droning on in the monotone that signals you are talking to yourself not to them, your audience will turn its attention elsewhere. You perhaps can recall occasions when you have drowsed through the dull reading of a lacklustre speech. If you are lucky, you may also have heard some manuscript speeches presented with such lively communicativeness that you may never have realized they were not extemporaneous.

○ SPECIAL OCCASIONS

Sometimes you may find yourself invited to give a speech to mark a specific occasion. This could be at a Mother-and-Daughter banquet, or on the Fourth of July, or on Veterans' Day, or at a high school commencement, or to your class at reunion. Other such occasions would be the award of some kind of trophy, or the acceptance of such an honor, or the arrival or departure of a visiting official, or at an inauguration, or the organization meeting of a club. On all such occasions, the subject matter to a degree and the purpose very largely are predetermined by the nature of the event. Sometimes these talks are called "speeches of courtesy," for they serve largely a ceremonial need. The speaker is expected primarily to say what all feel in common, though for this reason there is not less but more of a need to develop some elements of originality.

Commonly such talks are brief. Often they are rather formal in tone. Even so, they should always be marked by a depth and sincerity of feeling which gives them genuine warmth. The natural content of such talks is likely to be emotional, but care should be taken to prevent sentimental "sloppiness." It is desirable to have a thread of sound ideas, perhaps a relatively new interpretation of the meaning of the occasion—although this should not go counter to the understanding the audience has of the event. This is no time for crusading or the persuasive support of new ideas; the speaker is in a sense the spokesman for the public.

Brief, appropriate, fresh . . .

The ceremonial speech on special occasions draws its content from the nature of the event. Listeners appreciate and prefer remarks to oratory; they expect to join the speaker in feelings of enthusiasm or warmth for whatever is being commemorated; they anticipate a striking, humorous, or fresh view of the event or of their involvement in it.

The content of the speech may be drawn chiefly from the history and purpose of the day or the organization. Often it is anecdotal, and it may derive freshness from references to current developments. In general, you should draw upon all you have learned concerning preparation, organization, and presentation, with special emphasis upon your responsibility to speak for the thinking and feelings of your listeners.

○ CONCLUSION

This chapter has drawn together varied types of speaking in which all of us do or may engage: some constantly, in conversation; and some possibly, in the manuscript speech. The point we think most worthy of emphasis is that *all* speaking is "speech on a special occasion." Whatever kind of speaking you may do should profit from your study of the principles set forth in the preceding chapters. Whenever you confront any kind of challenge to use speech with communicative effectiveness, you should have derived from this study the basic means of dealing with it. However, since speaking is an enormously complex activity, and since so much of importance often depends on its being done well, we invite your serious attention to the following chapter, which is designed to introduce you to fields of further study as well as to invite you to formulate personal plans for individual study and continued self-improvement.

EXERCISES

Questions for Discussion

1. What are the duties of the chairman, and how should he perform them?

2. What elements of good speaking should be manifest in conversation?

3. How may you plan for an interview? How should you comport yourself in an interview?

4. What responsibilities may you expect to have in a conference? How should you fulfill them?

5. Discuss the similarities and differences between preparation and presentation of the manuscript speech and the extemporaneous speech. What are the advantages to be sought through practice in writing speeches?

6. What would you identify as the particular characteristics of the speech for special occasions?

Projects for Speaking and Writing

1. Have half the class assume a role as speaker with a specific subject in mind and representing a specific well-known figure in public life. Have the other half of the class serve as chairman-introducers, each introducer in turn introducing one of the speakers.

2. Bring in the text of a speech from a recent newspaper and practice reading parts of it to the class.

3. For one of your extemporaneous speeches in class write out the development of one of the main points in full.

4. Analyze several conversational situations in which you participated on a given day, some with two, some with more than two participants. With regard to each, record the purpose of the conversation and the general subject or subjects. What part did you play in the discussion? How often did you speak? When did you supply information? When were you expressing opinion? Who was the most talkative in the group? The most argumentative?

5. Plan to hold a conversation with a friend in front of the class, as though you met casually on the street. Initiate the discussion as you would in such circumstances. Exchange ideas for several minutes, and then ask the class to analyze the manner and remarks of both you and your friend.

6. Prepare to participate in an interview in which you have a specific persuasive purpose to accomplish, such as selling something or getting the other person to agree to a plan or proposal. Make the following written preparation: a one-page analysis of the other person; an outline of the sequence of the interview in which you give the setting and the exact statement of purpose on the title page, followed by an analysis of what you will do in each of the steps. Your analysis should show the major points you intend to stress, the major objections you expect to be raised, and the supporting evidence you will use. The interview will be conducted before the class, but as though you did not have an audience. Both participants should talk as they would in an actual interview situation, the person being persuaded interrupting frequently with questions and objections.

PART IV

LOOKING
AHEAD

Chapter 17

Responsibility for
Further Growth

YOUR FIRST COURSE IN SPEECH is ending, but your responsibility for the further development of your own abilities in oral communication remains. Some of you will enroll in more advanced courses in speech. All will find your need for competence in speech increasing as you proceed with your advanced college work, prepare for job interviews at graduation time, and then take your places as active citizens in the community and as productive workers in your chosen vocations. It is relevant to recall here the testimony of the renowned masterspeaker, Chauncey Depew: "There are few assets which can so quickly help a young man to success in life as the ability to speak reasonably well." In this course you have doubtless made considerable progress, but further progress lies ahead.

◯ SOCIAL RESPONSIBILITY

College graduates should be outstanding for their ability to bring to bear all their available knowledge and convictions upon the solution of personal, civic, and vocational problems as they arise. The right to speak freely is counterbalanced by the duty to speak up with helpful comments when difficulties must be faced. Research workers in many fields are continuously amassing vast new bodies of facts; people with the ability to think clearly and speak effectively must lead their communities in applying these facts to the solution of the complex problems of modern living.

Integrity

The social responsibility of speakers was never more important than in our time, when television and radio make it possible for a single speaker to influence the thinking of millions. Fortunately, the advantage which such mass media of communication give to demagogues is at least partially counteracted by universal education, by the widespread availability of information and contrary opinions in newspapers, and by the large number of conflicting points of view which may be heard on all significant issues of the day. The increasing frequency of discussion panels and question-and-answer periods following public lectures evidences the demand by audiences to have a fair opportunity to examine contrasting points of view. The all-too-frequent emphasis upon salesmanship without due regard for the merit of what is being sold has given a dangerous popularity to the idea that students need aim little higher than to learn how to "sell themselves."

Every section of this book has stressed the fact that effective speaking grows out of sound character—that effective speech depends upon the thoughtful and informed relationship of what you say to truth and to the needs of your fellowmen. From the ancient time when Plato denounced the Sophists as speakers skilled in "making the worse appear the better reason," thoughtful men have warned against speech used to mislead rather than inform or uplift. Professor Carl Dahlstrom has wisely warned that, "Society does not need more individuals who have ways and means of selling themselves, of taking advantage of the ignorant and the sentimental, of putting something over on gullible people, of vainly seeking even a noble end *via* stinkingly corrupt means; but society is sadly in need of men and women who can become proficient and known in their professions without loss of personal integrity or sacrifice of self-respect."[1]

Despite the dangers of sophistic demagoguery, it is still true that mankind has benefited so greatly from effective oral communication that the great German novelist Thomas Mann was moved to declare,

[1] Carl Dahlstrom: A Proposed Preface to a Text on Public Speaking," *Quarterly Journal of Speech,* Vol. 24 (October, 1938), pp. 418–424.

"Speech is civilization," to which the French novelist Camus further added that we live in "a civilization of dialogue."

As people confront the problems of living together in a highly competitive society, either they can seek cooperative understanding through discussion or they must—as an alternative—struggle to achieve victory or ensure survival by other means. The achievement of understanding and agreement through speech is still far from a universal attainment. But the effort to arrive at understanding by negotiation lies at the heart of what we know as modern civilization. Speech properly used is among the highest of civilizing agencies.

Unethical speaking may arise from an individual's cynical belief that he can best advance his own interests by clever deceit. More often, however, unethical effects result not from deliberate intent but from carelessness or laziness. The misstatement of facts and the consequent influencing of audiences to wrong conclusions may generally be avoided by observing the following rules.

1. *Investigate a subject fully before communicating opinions about it.* Because you should speak only from a sound background, you have the obligation to be silent if you do not understand what you are called upon to discuss. "I don't know" is a valuable and too rarely used phrase. When you do speak, you have an obligation to be *morally thoughtful*—to know what you are talking about before you try to influence the thinking of your associates.

2. *Recognize that what you say will have influence.* Do not yield to the feeling that you yourself and what you say will not exercise any important influence and that therefore the hard labor of preparation is really unnecessary. Actually, you may exercise far more influence than you believe you do. Especially if you are known as a person of good will and general common sense, most listeners who hear you speak on a topic concerning which they know little will tend to accept even your lightly uttered, casual opinions as probably true.

3. *Be personally responsible for your statements.* Do not comfort yourself with the feeling that if you do make errors of fact or judgment someone else can and will correct them, for such an attitude makes you an impediment, rather than a help, to progress. William James, the famous psychologist, once said that people with a sense of religious responsibility can be identified by their tendency to avoid saying, "Someone must do it; but why should I?" and to say instead, "Someone must do it; why not I?"

Balanced Judgment

Experience unfortunately demonstrates that even good and thoughtful speakers have to be warned always to keep in mind the necessity for balanced judgment. It is easy while addressing an audience to become intoxicated with your own eloquence. When you strive to make a point emphatically, you may have a natural tendency to exaggerate it. Your desire to accumulate such incontrovertible evidence that no one can refute your conclusions may lead you to overstate your point of view and so to ignore or gloss over the arguments against it. This is both immoral and persuasively ineffective. You should not hold convictions—much less try to impose them upon an audience—unless a careful analysis of *all* the available facts will support them. Further, since listeners wish to exercise their own critical judgments in evaluating a point of view, it is generally persuasively effective for a speaker to show them that in his own thinking he has carefully considered alternative points of view before rejecting them. All of us know speakers who notably have "the gift of gab"—and for this reason are sometimes considered to be good speakers—but who really exercise very little influence because their listeners unconsciously sense that their tongues are more active than their brains. Exaggeration is a form of verbomania to which many public speakers are susceptible.

No student should complete a course in speech without a serious re-examination of the responsibilities as well as the values of communicative speech. Meanwhile, he should look ahead to the question of how he will continue to develop his own growing skills.

○ PERSONAL RESPONSIBILITY

What, then, is the responsibility you owe to yourself for further growth as a speaker? This is the inevitable question you must answer as you prepare to close the pages of this book and conclude your speech course. A basic and fundamental drive in all of us is self-improvement, by which we achieve personal satisfaction, advancement, and recognition within our social and economic environment. It is significant that in this chapter your responsibility to society is discussed before your responsibility to self. For we must realize that none of us lives in a social vacuum, or on Robinson Crusoe's island.

Everything we do and plan must be in relation to others; and there is no part of you, as a person, that is more vital in this respect than your speaking and listening.

Regardless of how much we have enjoyed a course or how much we believe we have learned, we experience a natural feeling of relief when it is ended. This is manifested in many ways, perhaps by a forceful slamming of the book and at least a momentary impulse to throw it away. But can you throw your speech book away? Can you, for more than a brief, fleeting moment, say that your interest in speech training and speech development has ended? Even as you go out the door of your classroom from your final meeting, you are using speech to discuss your thoughts with your friends. And as you stride down the hall to your other classes, as you go on to your graduation, to your first job, and through each successive step in your growth as a person, you will be using your speaking and listening to help you move ahead. At least as a symbol of its future importance to you and as a constant reminder of your need for continuing speech development, you will perhaps wish to keep this book on your shelf.

The standards you set at the beginning of the course for your own development as a speaker should now be examined carefully in terms of what you think you have accomplished in your speech training. Go back now and quickly leaf through the pages of Chapter 2. Have you reached the standards you set? Do you now feel that they were realistic, or do they need revision? Even if you have not yet reached them, should they remain as you set them, perhaps high but nevertheless representing the speaking goals you truly want to achieve? The quite natural feeling that a student has after he has completed any course in self-improvement is one of doubt whether he has really achieved the goals he set at the beginning of the course. Most of us are not too disappointed when we recognize that we have not. For we understand that we have achieved as much as we could have expected in the time spent—and perhaps more. To be satisfied with our achievements to date but to regard them as only a beginning upon which future achievements must be built constitutes a realistic concluding attitude.

Let us recall that in the early chapters we stressed the importance to the student of a sound foundation of knowledge of speech principles and systematic practices. You are now ready to consider how you will continue to build your ability upon this base. You should not be disappointed, therefore, that you have not yet developed your full capacities. It is well to recall that good speakers spend a lifetime of effort in striving toward their ideal. What lies ahead for you as a speaker; and what further steps will you pursue to prepare yourself?

○ FUTURE SPEECH DEMANDS

What course will your life take? Will your vocational place be that of a lawyer, doctor, salesman, banker, homemaker, engineer, supervisor in industry, teacher, or scientist? Whichever of these careers you follow, you will be confronted with many demands for good speech ability. It is unnecessary to enumerate these demands here, for they have been stressed throughout the pages of this book, but it might be interesting to note briefly the stress laid upon speech training by several business and professional organizations.

In regard to seeking employment, you should note that the National Industrial Conference Board concluded after a major survey that the factor considered most important by personnel directors is the way in which a job applicant speaks and handles himself. This factor was found to be predominant over such others as education, extracurricular activities, grades, job experience, and letters of recommendation.

An obvious indication of the importance of good speech in the various professions and business occupations noted above is the emphasis they place on speech training. Organizations in all fields sponsor in-service training courses to improve the speaking of their members. In the legal profession, the American Law Institute includes a course in public speaking in its annual and regional institute programs. The American Medical Association and the various state medical associations have sponsored speech-training clinics for doctors as part of their convention programs. The American Institute of Banking has a continuing program of training in "Effective Speaking" as part of its broad educational program for bank employees. The Engineers' Council for Professional Development has made studies of the communication problems and responsibilities of engineers and has issued several training documents in the field of speech improvement.

In industry and business, there are unnumbered instances of such training programs. The American Management Association, one of the foremost societies for the improvement of industrial management, sponsors a program of training in "Executive Action," in which executives are given training in speech and conference leadership, among other communication skills. The National Association of Manufacturers includes "Effective Speaking" as an integral part of its Industry Leaders Program, whose purpose is the development of industrial management personnel. Within the in-service training programs of industries and government, there is increasing evidence of training in speech and communications. Such well-known companies as Standard Oil, General Motors, Goodyear Tire and Rubber, United States Steel, International Harvester, American Telephone and Telegraph Company, Aluminum Company of America, du Pont, and others, large and small, offer speech training to their supervisors, salesmen, and other employees. Labor unions emphasize training in speech and in leadership of meetings in their locals as well as in their national or regional educational institutes and in workshops held in conjunction with universities and colleges.

Many universities are cooperating with industrial management and labor unions in the training and development of their employees as better speakers, by conducting training courses within the organizations and by holding conferences and workshops for industrial and union personnel who are interested in improving their speech and communications.

For the general public, the businessman, the housewife, and the worker, there is further evidence of the interest and desire for improvement through speech training. The adult-education programs of many communities sponsor speech-training courses. Many individuals enthusiastically affiliate with clubs and meetings for the sole purpose of assembling and practicing public speaking. The Toastmaster's Clubs program is an example of this movement. Organizations such as the PTA and the Future Farmers of America invariably include a training unit in effective speaking as part of their regional and national conventions. In virtually all walks of life we may observe evidence of the fact that success, personal satisfaction, and speaking ability go hand in hand.

○ THE FIELD OF SPEECH

The first chapter discusses communicative speech problems and opportunities as they apply to the twentieth-century student who has the opportunity to study speech under circumstances far different from those of college students of previous generations. It is an interesting revelation to compare the catalogue offerings of institutions at the turn of the century with those of the present day.

Fifty years ago or less, most speech courses were listed in departments of English under such titles as Elocution, Expression, or perhaps Oral English and were confined almost wholly to drills in voice and gesture according to mechanical precepts. Such concepts as "communicativeness," "conversational mode," "social responsibilities of the speaker," or "the success of a speech depends in the first instance on its contents" would hardly have been encountered. The field of speech as we know it today is scarcely a half-century old, and the contemporary speech curriculums, taught by the more than six thousand members of the Speech Association of America in American colleges and universities, as well as in high schools and elementary institutions, offer a thrilling story of a part of modern American education.[2]

Some Historic Developments

A frequent experience of speech teachers is to hear a student say after his first course that it proved much more rewarding than he had expected and then to be asked for recommendations for additional speech courses. Sometimes, too, a student discovers through his speech courses, or perhaps his extracurricular speech activities, that he has a great interest in the field, would like to major in it, and perhaps plans graduate study and a career in the field of speech. In such a situation, the instructor discusses the demands of the field on the lives and talents of people who enter it; evaluates the specific assets and limitations of the student; points out which areas of the field require specialized training and which offer choice opportunities for service; and, finally, may review for the student certain historic landmarks in the development of the profession. The Speech Association of America is composed of professionally trained people who have entered the field through academic work and practical speech activities and who have

---

[2] For a review of significant developments in many areas of speech, *cf. Re-Establishing the Speech Profession: The First Fifty Years,* edited by Robert T. Oliver and Marvin Bauer, containing historical and evaluative surveys by twenty scholars in the field. Obtainable from Burton H. Byers, Executive Secretary of the Speech Association of the Eastern States, Queens College, Flushing 67, N. Y. [$1.50]

come to appreciate its historic developments. To know about some of these developments may be valuable to you, for sometimes we can best look ahead by looking backward.

AN EVENT OF 1914.   Early speech courses were offered, for the most part, in departments of English. Soon after the turn of the century, several progressive young men who were teaching in these departments came increasingly to believe that fundamentally speech courses belong in an independent department. More important, speech training, as they conceived it, should not consist of rules and techniques of the elocutionists. These men were familiar with earlier great writings in the field, such as Aristotle's *Rhetoric* and Quintilian's *Institutes of Oratory,* and were students of the world's greatest public speakers. When they could not obtain sympathetic understanding of their desire to broaden the field of speech, they initiated a bold move and organized what they called the National Association of Academic Teachers of Public Speaking; in 1917 the name of the organization was changed to the National Association of Teachers of Speech; and in 1945, the name was changed again to the Speech Association of America. When the first association was formed, its founders launched an official publication, the *Quarterly Journal of Public Speaking.* In time, also, the name of the journal was changed, first to the *Quarterly Journal of Speech Education* and subsequently to the *Quarterly Journal of Speech.*

SUBSEQUENT DEVELOPMENTS.   The founders of the new organization, concerned about the future academic status of their organization, were determined to create separate departments in their respective institutions, which would be free from the dominance of other departments and perhaps later offer graduate work.

Moreover, before long the term *public speaking* seemed too restricted. For public-speaking teachers were soon joined by teachers of oral reading, by specialists in dramatics, by professional persons who were searching for the causes and cures of speech disorders, by others interested in voice science, and by phoneticians, whose interest lies in the problems of pronunciation, voice, and diction. In short, the word *speech* was soon adopted as more accurate than *public speaking.* This accounts for the changes that were made in the name of the national organization and its official publication, as well as for changes in the philosophy and principles of speech therapy and in general speech teaching.

During this period, speech training was advancing in institutions of higher learning as well as in public schools. Not only did under-graduate speech courses increase in number, so that students were able to major in the field, but graduate work was developed, so that by the 1920's the M.A. degree in speech was offered in a large number of institutions and by the 1930's the Ph.D. degree in speech was firmly established.

RECENT DEVELOPMENTS. The phenomenal development of the field of speech during and since the 1920's has led to additional changes and innovations. The changes in the names of the official organization and journal are indicative of the growth of the field. Other develop-ments also deserve recording for their historic significance and for the student who wishes to know the profession as it has come to be today.

Sponsorship of two additional official national publications in speech is one recent development. The growing significance of grad-uate research in speech caused leaders in the field to feel the need of a research publication that would be devoted entirely to reporting, often in lengthy monographs, on the research projects in progress. This need led to the founding in 1934 of *Speech Monographs,* which includes, in addition to articles of a research nature, an annual cumu-lative index to the M.A. theses and doctoral dissertations from all institutions offering graduate degrees in speech. Still another journal was initiated in 1952, called *The Speech Teacher,* which contains articles on methods and problems of teaching speech.

The establishment of the following regional associations and their official journals has been a concomitant development: Speech Asso-ciation of the Eastern States, *Today's Speech;* The Southern Speech Association, *Southern Speech Journal;* The Western Speech Associa-tion, *Western Speech;* The Central States Speech Association, *Central States Speech Journal.*

Two related national organizations and their journals deserve also to be mentioned in the story of twentieth-century speech develop-ments. They are the American Speech and Hearing Association, which publishes the *Journal of Speech and Hearing Disorders* and the *Journal of Speech and Hearing Research,* and The American Educational Theater Association, which publishes the *American Educational Theater Journal.*

Other associations, with their journals, that are of particular interest to students of speech include: The National Society for the Study of

Communication, with its *Journal of Communication;* The International Society for General Semantics, publisher of *Etc.: A Review of General Semantics;* The National Association of Educational Broadcasters, with its *NAEB Journal;* and the many state speech associations, most of which publish annual or quarterly bulletins, newsletters, or special reports and monographs. Also of direct interest to students of speech are the journals in sociology, social psychology, and other closely related fields.

Hence, the interested student may look ahead to a lifetime of stimulating affiliations in the field of speech, which in its twentieth-century history has built traditions, has produced scholars and teachers, has charted educational patterns, and has helped to shape the lives and destinies of untold numbers of people within the classrooms and without.

The Modern Speech Curriculum

If you decide to take additional speech courses, or to major in speech, the total offerings of your department should be studied for information and guidance. Especially if you should aspire to a speech major or to graduate work in speech, you should inquire whether the types and kinds of courses offered are ones you could enter upon with enthusiasm and genuine interest. Moreover, since graduate degrees are essential to the student who plans to teach speech, the prospective teacher should study the curriculum with careful attention to the most advanced offerings and the areas of the field that are most adequately covered.

In its growth over the past twenty-five years, the speech field has come to encompass certain rather distinct areas of study, and the trained personnel of departments have become experts in one or another of them. The areas of speech may be designated as follows: *rhetoric and public address,* including courses in public speaking, oral communication, business speaking, parliamentary law, argumentation and debate, discussion, exposition, general semantics, persuasion, history of oratory, rhetorical theory and criticism; *oral interpretation; dramatic art; speech science,* including the psychology of speech, voice science and phonetics; *speech therapy,* including speech correction, pathology, and audiology; and *radio and television.*

○ YOUR PLAN FOR FURTHER GROWTH

What, then, should be your plan for further growth as a speaker? Perhaps it will include further formal training, such as enrollment in other speech courses, both during your undergraduate years and after you have established yourself in a professional or business career. If you do not contemplate further formal training, however, you must yourself establish and carry through a plan for your continual development. This should not be haphazard, but should be planned to include at least the following elements.

1. *Continue to read about and study speech principles.* As already indicated, you should not feel satisfied that you have completely mastered the principles, even merely as methods and tools to be borne in mind. Continue to read in the field of speech—in other speech books, in periodicals, and elsewhere. And pick up your textbook occasionally to reread and review what you have already learned, in order to incorporate the principles more firmly into your attitudes, your habits of thought, and your active practice.

2. *Take advantage of your speaking opportunities.* In your social and business contacts, in meetings and organizations, and in all other social relations, speak up when the opportunity arises and when you have something worthwhile to say. This does not mean that you must develop the reputation of always wanting to talk. It does mean that you should be sufficiently moved by the importance of your own convictions to want to accept speaking assignments or engagements when they are offered to you. It also means that you should participate fully in the discussions of business and social meetings and that you should make your influence felt in the life of your community.

3. *Be a critical listener.* One of the best (and easiest) ways to develop as a speaker is to continue to make yourself a better listener. As you evaluate and make critical analyses of the speeches of others, your own understanding of speech principles will become more acute. You should therefore make it a habit, as part of your plan for further growth, to attend and listen to good speeches whenever you can. Make such listening a part of your free-time program of recreation and continuing self-education.

4. *Continue to evaluate yourself and your standards.* As you develop ever increasing ability, you will grow more confident and more at ease in speaking. You will also be pleased with your own

personal growth and progress. It is therefore well to review your standards and your attainments and to note the specific areas in which you need improvement. In this way you can concentrate on one item at a time and reach in it the standard of achievement you deem necessary. Bear in mind that you are not striving to be the perfect speaker—your aim is rather to discharge your speaking responsibilities fully and to your own satisfaction as well as to that of your listeners.

5. *Take additional, specialized courses in speech.* During this course you have just completed, you have learned much that you need to know—but it takes time and guided practice to establish lastingly the skills, habits, and attitudes needed for effective oral communication. Besides, you will find urgent need for such abilities as persuasive speaking, discussion, oral reading, parliamentary law, and use of radio and television facilities—each field is covered in an advanced course. Other specialties, such as speech science, rhetoric, the history of public address, the psychology of speech, and speech therapy, are available for students who develop a professional interest in the field.

○ **CONCLUSION**

This chapter has been intended to help you determine your final attitudes and answer your final questions as you conclude this introductory course. Speech competence carries with it a heavy and continuous social responsibility: to use your new skills for the benefit of your fellows as well as of yourself. Whether or not you plan to take additional courses in speech, you will certainly be confronted with increasing demands on your speaking and listening competence, and you should continuously go forward to make yourself a better speaker —and listener.

EXERCISES

Questions for Discussion

1. The class may discuss the various demands upon responsible speakers in our society and the needs for good speaking which will be increased after graduation from college.
2. What has been happening in the past fifty years to effect sub-

stantial changes in the field of speech? How do these changes relate to what you know about developments in other fields of knowledge?

3. What specific areas of speech might you profitably study in further courses? What would be the advantages, and the disadvantages, of majoring in speech? What qualities should a speech major possess? Toward what goals might he aim?

4. What changes would you like to see in the course offerings in speech at your own college?

Projects for Speaking and Writing

1. Draw up a systematic plan to guide your own continuing development in speech.

2. What can and should you do in other courses and through independent study to help you meet needs you know will be urgent and to improve aspects of your speaking which you know are in need of improvement?

3. Why should the conclusion of a course, like graduation, be a "commencement"?

Index

Accuracy as a stylistic quality, 187
Actuating, 72–76, 283–284, 291, 295–296, 326–327
Adamic, Louis, quoted, 231–232
Adams, John Quincy, 9
Adventure as source for entertaining, 339
After-dinner speaking, 341–342
Allport, Gordon, quoted, 18
Aluminum Company of America, 403
American Educational Theater Association, 406
American Educational Theater Journal, 406
American Institute of Banking, 402
American Law Institute, 402
American Management Association, 402
American Medical Association, 402
American Speech and Hearing Association, 406
American Telephone and Telegraph Company, 403
Analogy
  as a validating method, 154, 160, 163–164, 285, 306–307
  in visual aids, 251–252
Analysis of ideas, 52, 115, 144–153, 284
  by classification, 150–151
  by definition, 126, 147
  by description, 147–148
  by discrimination, 148–149
  by limitation, 146–147
  main, *see* Main ideas
  preliminary, 144–145
  by qualification, 149–150
  by redefinition, 151–153
Anderson, Virgil, 215n.
Anecdotes
  in the conclusion, 127
  for validation, 159–160
Appeal
  of speaker's ideas, 307–310
  of speaker image, 310–313
Appeals
  special, 308–309
  vital, 309–310
Arabian Nights, quoted, 164
Aristotle, 7, 9, 30, 37, 300, 311, 405
Articulation, 194, 211–216, 218–220, 286
  defined, 218
  diagnosing and correcting differences in, 213–215
Artistic speaking, 36–38
Attention, 120–121, 125, 169–177, 252
Attitude
  in discussion, 355–357
  in listening, 238–239, 242

Audience adaptation, 37–38, 41, 61–62, 63, 103, 126, 129, 176, 206, 236–237, 239, 273, 278, 287, 308–309, 312, 335–337
  in conversation, 380–381
  in discussion, 357–358
Audience analysis, 58–59, 63–66, 81, 125, 308–309, 312
Audio-visual aids, 264–266
Auditory code, 194–195, 211–224
Auer, Jeffrey, 302n., 354n.

Baccus, J. H., 166n.
Bacon, Francis, quoted, 87, 98, 109
Baird, A. Craig, 8n., 36n.
Baldwin, Charles Sears, 9n.
Barbara, Dominick A., 11n., 233n., 240n.
Barriers
  to communication, 13–21, 193, 218, 228–230, 252, 262, 275, 278, 337, 390
  to listening, 233–242
Barzun, Jacques, 107n.
Bassett, Lee Emerson, quoted, 339–340
Battiscombe, G. Gunn, 7n.
Bauer, Marvin, 404n.
Beecher, Henry Ward, quoted, 174–175
Berlo, David, 5n., 56n.
Blackboard, use of, 253–257
Body of speech, 119–124, 176–177
  in entertaining, 343–344
  in informing, 281–283
  in persuading, 324–325
Bois, J. Samuel, 42n.
Borah, William E., 244
Borden, Richard C., 120–121
Brainstorming, 351
Brevity
  in after-dinner speaking, 342
  in discussion, 358
  in speech of introduction, 377
Brief, 129–138
Broadcasts as aid, 97
Bronstein, Arthur J., 221n.
Browning, Robert, quoted, 43
Bryan, William Jennings, 30, 53, 188; quoted, 189
Bryson, Lyman, 5n.
Buffon, Georges Louis Leclerc de, quoted, 184
Burke, Edmund, 40
Burns, George, 337
Burns, Robert, 212
Byers, Burton, 404n.

Camus, Albert, quoted, 399
Cardozo, Benjamin, quoted, 112
Carter, Elton S., 153n.

411

Cartoons as visual aids, 250, 251, 253
Castiglione, Baldassare, 9
Causal method of organization, 122, 282
Causality, 305–306
Central idea, 37, 59, 69, 72–73, 81–88, 146–147
    related to specific response, 82–85
Central States Speech Association, 406
Central States Speech Journal, 406
Ceremonial speaking, 391–393
Cerf, Bennett, 338
Chairman
    duties of, in discussion, 350, 353, 354, 359–362, 371–372
    duties of, in parliamentary procedure, 364–365, 366–367
    as presiding officer, 374–379
Chaplin, Charlie, 334
Charts as visual aids, 253, 257–260, 262–263
Chronological method of organization, 122, 281–282, 344
Chumbley, Thomas W., quoted, 180–181
Churchill, Winston, quoted, 314
Cicero, 8, 30
Circular response, 23, 24, 92, 203–204, 207–208, 232–233, 386
Clarification
    in informative speaking, 285–286
    as a stylistic quality, 187
Clinical problems in speech, 214–215
Code
    auditory, 194–195, 211–224
    linguistic, 194–195
    visual, 196–211
Colloquial style, 185, 189
Comedy in entertaining speaking, 333
Committee
    referral to, 369
    use of discussion in, 352
    of the whole, 368
Common ground
    in discussion, 357
    establishing, 126, 280, 323–324
    method in persuasion, 317–318
Common premise in persuasion, 314, 315–321, 324, 325
Communication
    barriers to, 13–21, 193, 218, 228–230, 252, 262, 275, 278, 337, 390
    defined, 11
    discursive versus presentational, 251
    and expression, 10–13, 26, 208, 249
Comparing and contrasting as validating method, 154, 160, 163–164, 285, 306–307
Complete-sentence outline, 129–138
Comprehensibility in after-dinner speaking, 342
Conciliation in discussion, 357–358, 362
Conclusion, 37, 59, 81, 119–121, 127–128, 208
    of talk to entertain, 344
    of talk to inform, 283–284, 298–299
    of talk to persuade, 325–326
Concreteness as factor of interest, 178–180

Conference, 258–259, 262, 286, 287, 352, 358, 362, 374, 384–386
    differentiated from public discussion, 384
    planning a, 375–376
Confidence, 55–58
    and pitch of voice, 216
    and voice quality, 218
Conflict as factor of interest, 178, 182
Consensus in group discussion, 352
Consent, general, 366
Conversation, 37, 83, 96, 112, 155, 162, 185, 202, 203–204, 206–207, 209, 236, 286, 287, 329, 352, 358, 374, 379–381
Conversational mode, 203–204
Convincing, 71, 73–75, 291, 294–296
Coolidge, Calvin, 231
Correctness of style, 184–185
Criteria for judging solutions, 349, 350–351
Criticism of speaking, 232, 244, 406
Crocker, Lionel, 34*n.*, 166*n.*
Crowell, Merle, quoted, 230
Cumulating as validating method, 160–162, 285, 301

Dahlstrom, Carl, quoted, 398
Darrow, Clarence, quoted, 319
Debate, 352, 364
    limitation of, 369
Decision-making
    and listening, 232
    through persuasion, 290–291, 316
Deduction, 302–303
Definition as analysis, 126
de Gaulle, Charles, 188; quoted, 189
Delivery, 192–224
    auditory aspects of, 194–195, 211–224
    in discussion, 355–362
    of entertaining speech, 335–337
    of manuscript speech, 390–391
    misconceptions about, 192–194
    principles of, 202–211
Demosthenes, 30, 40; quoted, 202
Depew, Chauncey, quoted, 9, 395
Developing ideas, 59, 143–167
    in informative speaking, 284–286
    in persuasive speaking, 313–323
Dewey, John, 120–123
Diagnosis of speech needs, 43
Dialects, regional, 221
Direct development in persuasion, 320
Discursive and presentational communication, 251
Discussion, 347–364
    adaptation of speech principles in, 347–348, 355
    conciliation in, 357–348, 362
    defined, 348
    leadership, 350, 353, 354, 359–362
    outline, 354–355
    participation in, 355–359
    pattern of, 349–352
    problems, stating, 353
    public, 352, 359–361, 384
    purposes of, 348

Discussion—(*Continued*)
  related to parliamentary procedure, 362–365
Division of assembly, defined, 366
Douglas, Stephen A., 182
Dow, Clyde W., 153*n*.
Dramatic art, 405
  as area of speech, 407
Dramatic facts as sources for entertaining, 340–341
Drawings as visual aids, 253–260, 262–264
du Pont de Nemours and Company, E. I., 403

Easel pad as visual aid, 253, 257–260
Eastman, Max, 329
Economy as stylistic quality, 187
Educational Film Guide, 264*n*.
Educators' Guide to Free Films, 264*n*.
Effects norm for judging speaking, 38–42
Egerer, Herbert, quoted, 162
Eisenhower, Dwight D., 231, 290, 312
Eliot, Charles W., quoted, 9, 159–160
Eliot, George, quoted, 10
Ellis, William T., 166*n*.
Emerson, Ralph Waldo, 108; quoted, 80, 98
Emotional proof, 300, *see also,* Appeal
Empathy, 198–202, 203, 211, 232, 254, 335
  defined, 198
Engineers' Council for Professional Development, 402
Entertaining speech, 75–76, 123–124, 127–128, 166, 329–346
  after-dinner, 341–342
  exaggeration in, 332–333
  nonhumorous, 123–124, 329–335, 339–341
  related to informing, 273–277, 331
  related to persuading, 299–300, 331
Esthetic speaking, 36–38
Etc.: A Review of General Semantics, 407
Ethical speaking, 8, 34–36, 79–80, 101–102, 105–106, 154, 187, 311, 396–398
Etiquette in speaking, 206–208
Evaluation of speaking, 232, 244, 408
Ewbank, H. L., 302*n*., 354*n*.
Exaggeration in entertaining speaking, 332–333
Examples
  of analysis, 116–118
  hypothetical, 158–159
  of outlining, 130–138
  as a validating form, 154, 158–159
Exposition, *see* Informing
Expression and communication, 10–13, 26, 204, 208, 249
Extemporaneous speaking, 205–206
  related to manuscript speaking, 386–391

Fairbanks, Grant, 215*n*.
Familiarity as factor of interest, 178, 180–181

Fearnside, W. Ward, 304*n*.
Feedback, 22–25, 92, 207–208, 232–233, 287
  in conferences, 386
  in conversation, 203–204
Fife, Iline, 153*n*.
Films as visual aids, 253, 262–266
Filmstrips as visual aids, 253, 262–266
Flannel board as visual aid, 260–262
Force as stylistic quality, 189
Formality of style, 185–186
Forms of support, *see* Validation of ideas
Forum, 352, 359
Foster, William T., 129*n*.
Funk, Walter, quoted, 164
Future Farmers of America, 403
Future speech demands, 402–403, 408–409

General consent, 366
General Motors, 403
General response desired, 69–76
  action, 72–76, 283–284, 291, 295–296, 326–327
  consent, parliamentary, 366
  entertainment, 75–76, 123–124, 127–128, 166, 329–346
  new belief, 71, 73–75, 291, 294–296
  strengthened feeling, 71, 73–75, 291–293, 296
  understanding, 71–73, 122, 127, 271–289
Gesture, 195, 197–198, 203, 207–210, 212, 253
Ghiselin, Brewster, 60*n*.
Goffman, Erving, 18*n*.
Goldin, Judah, 231
Good humor in entertaining speaking, 332, 338, 342
Goodyear Tire and Rubber Co., 403
Graduate work in speech, 406, 407
Grady, Henry, 183
Graff, Henry F., 107*n*.
Graphs as visual aids, 253, 257–260, 262–264
Gray, Giles Wilkeson, 7*n*.
Group discussion, 286, 287
Group thinking, 52
Guided tours as visual aids, 253
Gulley, H. E., 348*n*.

Hahn, Elise, 215*n*.
Haiman, Franklyn S., 310*n*., 359*n*.
Hall, Edward T., 192*n*.
Handouts as visual aids, 253, 262
Harding, Harold, 8*n*.
Hargis, Donald E., 215*n*.
Henry, Patrick, 30
Historical perspective as validating form, 154–155, 284
Hitler, Adolf, quoted, 24–25, 164
Hoijer, Harry, 21*n*.
Hollingworth, H. L., 63*n*.
Holther, William B., 304*n*.
Holtzman, Paul D., 240*n*.
Hoogenboom, Ari, 305
Hope, Bob, 337, 339

Hovland, Carl I., 113n.; quoted, 310
Huff, Darrell, 156n.
Humor
    in entertaining speaking, 123–124, 329–335, 337–339
    as factor of interest, 178, 182–183
    in the introduction, 175

"Iceberg technique," 93, 139, 162, 278, 301, 303–304
Ideas, see Analysis of ideas
Illustration, 166–167, see also Validation of ideas
Image of the speaker
    defined, 311
    effects of, 38, 80, 92, 101–103, 200–202, 207, 211–212, 237, 244, 252–253, 292, 309, 310–313, 320, 359, 378, 383, 400
Imagery as stylistic quality, 188–189
Impromptu speaking, 206, 286
Indirect development, 182, 243
    in persuasion, 317, 319
Induction, 303–305
Informing, 71–73, 122, 127, 271–289
    in discussion, 351
    related to entertaining, 273–277, 331
    related to persuading, 273–277, 296–299, 331
    with visual aids, 251, 264
Initial summary, 281, 283, 324
Inquiry, 104–106, 120–123, 144–147, 294, 297, 316–317
    by groups, 348–354
    pattern of, 349–352
    related to persuasion, 294, 297, 316–317, 364
Interest, 169–170, 177–183, 252
    factors of, 178–183
    personality and, 177–178
    subject matter and, 178
International Harvester, 403
International Society for General Semantics, 407
Interview, 286, 287, 352, 358, 374, 381–384
Introduction, 37, 59, 119–121, 124–126, 174–176, 207
    of a discussion, 354, 362
    to entertaining speech, 343
    to informative speech, 280–281, 298
    to persuasive speech, 323–324
    speech of, 374, 377–379
Irrelevance in entertaining speaking, 334
Isocrates, 7

James, William, quoted, 181, 397
Jebb, Richard, 9n.
Jesus, 159–160
Johnson, Eric W., quoted, 9–10
Johnson, Samuel, quoted, 87, 228, 341
Johnson, Wendell, quoted, 11, 242n.
Jones, O. G., 367n.
Journal of Communication, 407
Journal of Speech and Hearing Disorders, 406

Journal of Speech and Hearing Research, 406

Kagemni, 5
Keltner, John W., 144n.
Kennedy, John F., 38n., 223, 231; quoted, 188, 315
Kenyon, John S., 221n.
Key-word outline, 138
Knott, Thomas A., 221n.
Knower, Franklin H., 286n.

Langer, Susanne, 251n.
Language, 20–22, 37, 59, 84, 198, 202, 278, 285–286
    as barrier to listening, 239–240
    functions, 151–153, 194–195
    and persuasion, 314–315
    Sapir-Whorf hypothesis, 21
    spoken versus written, 186–187
    and style, 183–190
Leadership, 52–53, 74, 204–205, 258–259, 262, 293, 374–379
    in conferences, 384
    in discussion, 350, 353, 354, 356, 359–362, 371–372
    and listening, 230–231
    in parliamentary groups, 364–365, 366–367
Learning, 42–44, 60, 81, 86–87, 104–105, 109–110, 198, 306, 349
    new skills, 32–33, 43
    visual, 248–250
Lee, Irving J., 42n.
Limb, Ben C., 271n.
Lincoln, Abraham, 12, 70–71, 92, 159, 160, 182, 187, 236; quoted, 314, 318
Lindesmith, Alfred R., 63n.
Lindzey, Gardner, 310n.
Listener attitudes, reinforcing, 71, 73–75, 291–293, 296, 320, 325–326
Listener motives for ideation, 300–313
    appeal, 307–310
    appeal of speaker image, 311–313
    logic, 300–307
    logic of speaker image, 311
Listener–speaker
    barriers, 13–21, 193, 218, 228–230, 233, 242, 262, 390
    bonds, 13–21, 390
    common ground, 15–17, 126, 280, 323–324
    function, 19–20
    role, 18–19
    status, 17–18
Listening, 81, 113–114, 203–204, 212–214, 226–247, 272, 286, 287
    barriers to, 233–241
    in conferences, 386
    in discussion, 351–352, 359
    improving, 242–245
    preparation for, 242
    rate of, 236
    responsibility for, 227–230, 290–291, 307, 396–397, 406
    for speech materials, 96–98, 105
    values of, 230–233

Logic, 235, 300–307
Lomas, Charles W., 215n.

McBurney, James H., 31n.
McGrath, Earl James, 42n.
Magnetic board as a visual aid, 260–262
Main ideas, 115–119, 129–134, 165
    principles guiding selection of, 118–119
Majority, defined, 360
Malthus, Thomas Robert, 309
Mann, Thomas, quoted, 396–397
Manuscript speech, 206, 374, 386–391
Maps as visual aids, 248–250, 253
Marshall, George C., 231
Materials, speech
    authenticity of, 101–106
    choosing, 58–59, 81, 90–111, 179
    recording, 106–109
    sources of, 62–63, 93–101, 106–110
    testing, 96
    using, 37, 60–61, 101–106
Maturity, 51–53
Meaning, 240
    visual code, 194–202, 208, 210–211
Meeting, defined, 366
    planning a, 375–376
Metaphor, 164
Milton, John, 43
Models as visual aids, 253, 260–262
Molière, quoted, 3
Monroe, Alan H., 120–121
Morse, Wayne, 99
Motion pictures as visual aids, 253, 264–266
Motions, parliamentary
    to adjourn, 371
    to amend, 368–369
    chart of, 370
    to commit, 369
    incidental, 366, 371
    main, 366–368
    to postpone action, 369
    privileged, 366, 369–371
    renewal, 366, 371
    subsidiary, 366, 368–369
Motivation to understand, 273–275, 278, 281

Narrative
    in the conclusion, 127–128
    in entertaining speaking, 123–124, 329–335, 339–341
    in the introduction, 125
    as a validating form, 154, 159–160
National Association of Educational Broadcasters, 407
NAEB Journal, 407
National Association of Manufacturers, 403
National Industrial Conference Board, 402
National Society for the Study of Communication, 406–407
Nelson, Harold E., quoted, 250
Nichols, Alan, 302n.

Nichols, Ralph G., 227n.
Nonhumorous entertainment, 123–124, 329–335, 339–341
Novelty as factor of interest, 178, 181

Objectivity in informative speaking, 278–280
Objects as visual aids, 253, 260–262
O'Brien, Joseph F., 367n., quoted, 368
Occasions for speaking, 63–67, 126
    to actuate, 295–296
    to create new belief, 73–75, 294
    to entertain, 75, 330–331, 341–342
    to gain understanding, 71–73, 272, 286–287
    from manuscript, 386–388
    special, 391–393
    to strengthen feelings, 73–75, 293
Oliver, Robert T., 31n., 34n., 121n., 379n., 404n.
1001 and 1 (Educational Screen Magazine), 264n.
Oral interpretation of literature, 405
    as area of speech, 407
Order of business in parliamentary group, 365
Organization, 37, 43, 58–59, 112–140, 206
    causal method of, 122, 285
    chronological method of, 122, 281–282, 344
    for entertaining, 342–344
    indirect development of, 182
    for informing, 280–284
    of the manuscript speech, 389
    pattern of, 119–128, 281–283
    for persuading, 315–326
    spatial method of, 122, 282
Outlining, 58–59, 128–138
    complete sentence, 129–138
    for entertaining, 342–344
    for informing, 280–284
    key-word, 138
    for manuscript speech, 389
    for persuading, 315–326
    rules for, 132–134
    topical, 129–134

Paar, Jack, 337
Packard, Vance, 309
Panel discussion, 347, 348, 352, 359–361, 362
Parables for validation, 159–160
Parallelism as a stylistic quality, 188
Parent-Teachers Association (PTA), 403
Parliamentary procedure, 352, 361, 362–373
    for forming an organization, 365
    leadership in, 366–367
    participating in, 366–367
    philosophy of, 363–364, 372
    related to discussion, 362–365
Perception, 102, 109, 152, 170, 180, 198, 212–213, 220, 232, 233, 235, 238, 239–241, 279–280, 311, 313
Personal experiences as sources for entertaining, 339–340

Personal proof, *see* Speaker image
Personality and speech, 4, 11*n.*, 18, 169–170, 177–178, 183–184, 194, 202, 209
Personalization, 180, 280, 308–309
  of style, 184, 186–187
Persuading, 71, 73–75, 106, 122–124, 127, 166, 290–328
  common premise in, 314, 315–321, 324, 325
  defined, 291
  in parliamentary groups, 364
  related to entertaining, 299–300, 331
  related to informing, 273–277, 296–299, 331
  related to inquiry, 294, 297, 316–317, 364
Phifer, Gregg, 153*n.*
Philip of Macedonia, 40
Phonetics, 220–222, 405, 407
Photographs as visual aids, 253, 262–263
Planning meetings, 375–376
Plato, 7–8; quoted, 398
Plot, technical, 130–131, 134–138
Plurality, defined, 366
Practice, 3, 45–46, 59, 96, 138–140, 193, 222
Preparation for listening, 242
Preparation for speaking, 45, 51–191
  in conferences, 384–386
  in discussion, 349–351, 354–356, 357
  ethically, 397
  in the future, 408–409
  in interviews, 381–384
  to introduce a speaker, 377–379
  in leading discussion, 359–361
  from a manuscript, 386–391
  mental attitude in, 54–58
  need for, 52–54
  starting early in, 56, 59, 95
  steps in, 58–59
Presentational and discursive communication, 251
Problem-solution, 120–123
  discussion, 348–362
  method in persuasion, 123, 316–317, 364
Projectors as visual aids, 262–266
Pronunciation, 185, 211–212, 220–223
Proofs, *see* Listener motives for ideation
Ptah-Hotep, 7, 17

Quarterly Journal of Speech, 405
Questioning
  direct, 162
  hypothetical, 163
  leading, 163
  rhetorical, 125, 163
  of speakers, 378
  as a validating method, 43, 154, 160, 162–163, 285
Quintilian, 8, 9, 30, 202, 311, 405
Quorum, defined, 366
Quotations, 37, 108–109
  in the conclusion, 127
  as a validating form, 155–156

Radio and television as speech area, 407
Rankin, Paul, T., 227*n.*

Rapp, Albert, 329
Rapport between speaker and listeners, 335–337, 386
Rate of listening, 236
Rate of speech, 217, 235–236
Reading as source for entertaining, 340
"Ready-made speeches," 59–60, 67, 104
Reasoning, 235
Recording
  speech materials, 106–109
  speeches, 375–376
  voice and articulation, 212–215
Reinforcing listener attitudes, 71, 73–75, 291–293, 296, 320, 325–326
Response
  circular, *see* Circular response
  general, *see* General response
Responsibility as a listener, 227–230, 290–291, 307, 398–399, 408
Responsibility as a speaker
  ethical, *see* Ethical speaking
  personal, 400–402
  social, 397–400
Restating as a validating method, 154, 160–161, 285
Rhetoric and public address as speech area, 407
Rhythm as stylistic quality, 188
Robert, Henry M., 367*n.*
Role-playing, 18–19
Roosevelt, Franklin D., 20, 21, 244; quoted, 185–186, 322–323, 389
Roosevelt, Theodore, 30–31, 231
Rules of good listening, 245

St. Augustine, 9
Sandburg, Carl, 71*n.*
Sapir, Edward, 21
Sattler, William M., 153*n.*
Schwab, Charles, 230
Session, defined, 366
Shakespeare, William, 108, 334; quoted, 61, 85, 188
Shannon, William V., quoted, 41
Simile, 164
Simmons, Harry, 374*n.*
Slides as visual aids, 253, 262–266
Smith, Alfred E., quoted, 167
Smith, Bromley, 8*n.*
Southern Speech Association, 406
Southern Speech Journal, 406
Spatial method of organization, 122, 282
Speaker image
  defined, 311
  effects of the, 38, 80, 92, 101–103, 200–202, 207, 211–212, 237, 244, 252–253, 292, 309, 310–313, 320, 359, 378, 383, 400
Speaker–listener
  barriers, 13–21, 193, 218, 228–230, 233, 242, 262, 390
  bonds, 13–21, 390
  common ground, 15–17, 126, 280, 323–324
  function, 19–20
  role, 18–19
  status, 17–18

Speaker responsibility, *see* Responsibility as a speaker
Speaking
  artistic, 36–38
  ceremonial, 390–391
  good humor in, 332, 338, 342
  from manuscript, 390–391
  occasions for, *see* Occasions for speaking
Special applications of speech principles, 374–394
  as chairman, 374–379
  in conferences, 384–386
  in conversation, 379–381
  in interviews, 381–384
  in manuscript speaking, 386–391
  on special occasions, 391–393
Specific response desired, 76–81
  related to central idea, 82–85
Specificity as factor of interest, 178, 180
Speech and hearing therapy, 405
  as speech area, 407
Speech Association of America, 404–405
Speech Association of the Eastern States, 404*n.*, 406
Speech, body of, *see* Body of speech
Speech demands, future, 402–403, 408–409
Speech education
  attitudes toward, 3
  in business and industry, 402–403
  contributions to general education, 42–44, 60
  future, 408–409
  history of, 403–407
  purposes of, 9–10, 104
Speech, field of, 403–407
Speech file
  building, 106–109, 338
  methods in recording for, 106–107
  suggested categories for, 107–109
Speech in democracy, 32, 74, 197, 238, 290–291, 307, 326
Speech mechanisms, 216–218
Speech Monographs, 406
Speech principles, *see* Special applications
Speech purposes, 19–20, 38–42, 58–59, 61, 69–81
Speech science, 405
  as an area of speech, 407
Speech Teacher, The, 406
Stage fright, 4, 5, 26, 70, 71, 203, 208
  and preparation, 55–58, 70
  and purposiveness, 80
  and visual aids, 252
Standard Oil Company, 403
Standards
  of effective speech, 28–48, 211, 401, 408–409
  for judging central ideas, 85–88
  for judging problem solutions, 349, 350–351
  of style, 184–187
Statistics
  meaningful presentation of, 103, 156–157
  as a validating form, 156–158
Stevens, Leonard A., 227*n.*

Stevenson, Adlai, 41, 109
Stimulating, talking to, *see* Listener attitudes
Stock issues, 123
Stories
  in the conclusion, 127
  in entertaining speaking, 123–124
  in the introduction, 125
  for validation, 159–160
Strauss, Anselm, 63*n.*
Style, 36–38, 59, 64, 169–170, 183–190
  correctness of, 184–185
  economy as quality of, 187
  force as a quality of, 189
  formality of, 185–186
  imagery as a quality of, 188–189
  in informative speaking, 285–286
  in the manuscript speech, 387–391
  parallelism as a quality of, 188
  in persuasion, 314–315
  spoken versus written, 186–187
Subliminal communication, 197, 200–202
Sublimity of style, 186
Summary, initial, 281, 283, 324
Support, *see* Validation of ideas
Suspense as factor of interest, 178, 182
Sympathy
  and empathy, 198–200
  in entertaining speaking, 333–334
Symposium, 352, 359–361, 362

Testimony, 37, 108–109
  in the conclusion, 127
  as a validating form, 155–156
This-or-nothing method in persuasion, 317, 321–323
Thomas, Charles K., 221*n.*
Thonssen, Lester, 8*n.*, 36*n.*
Titles for speeches, 172–174
Toastmaster's Clubs, 403
Today's Speech, 406
Topical method of organization, 122, 282
Topical outline, 129–134, 344
Topics
  choosing, 42–44, 58–63, 77–78, 81, 83, 97, 313
  for discussion, 353
  listing, 107
  narrowing, 116–118
  significance of, 42–43, 80
Transition, 37, 124, 126, 163, 174, 187, 283, 285, 286, 324–325
  in conversation, 380
  in group discussion, 362
  in manuscript speaking, 387, 390
  between speakers, 377
Tried-and-proved method in persuasion, 322–323
Truman, Harry S, 161
Twain, Mark, 334, 337

Understanding, gaining of, 71–73, 122, 127, 271–289
  in discussion, 351
  related to persuading, 273–277
  with visual aids, 251, 264
United States Steel, 403
Unusual in entertaining speaking, 333

Validation of ideas, 35, 107–109, 153–167, 249, 281
    cumulating as method of, 160–162, 285, 301
    forms, 154–160, 284
    in informative speaking, 284–286
    methods, 160–166, 285
    parables for, 159–160
    in persuasion, 300–307, 313–314
VanderMeer, Abram W., quoted, 250
Vandragen, Daniel, 215n.
Variety
    as factor of interest, 178, 181–182
    of style, 184
Visual aids, 59, 195, 248–267
    drawings as, 253–260, 262–264
    films as, 253, 262–266
    graphs as, 253, 257, 260, 262–264
    in group discussion, 362
    handouts as, 253, 262
    maps as, 248–250, 253
    photographs as, 253, 262–263
    slides as, 253, 262–266
    as a validating method, 154, 165–166
Visual code, 196–211
Vital appeals, 181, 309–310
Vitality as factor of interest, 178, 181
Vividness
    as factor of interest, 178, 180
    of style, 184–185

Voice, 22, 194, 211–218, 286
    diagnosing and correcting, 213–215
    loudness, 216–217
    pitch, 216
    quality, 217–218
Voting, types of, 366

Wallace, Karl, 34n.
Webster, Daniel, 30
Western Speech, 406
Western Speech Association, 406
White, Eugene E., 31n.
Whorf, Benjamin Lee, 21
Wilde, Oscar, 334
Williams, George, quoted, 90
Wilson, John, 9
Wilson, Woodrow, quoted, 56, 322
Winans, James Albert, quoted, 171–172, 388
Wit in entertaining speaking, 334
Wrage, Ernest J., 31n.
Wright, Frances, quoted, 9

Yes-response method in persuasion, 317, 320–321
Yirak, Linda, quoted, 188–189

Zelko, Harold P., 352n., 384n.
Zelko, Marjorie E., 134n.; quoted, 134–138